FREE Test Taking Tips Video/DVD Offer

To better serve you, we created videos covering test taking tips that we want to give you for FREE. **These videos cover world-class tips that will help you succeed on your test.**

We just ask that you send us feedback about this product. Please let us know what you thought about it—whether good, bad, or indifferent.

To get your **FREE videos**, you can use the QR code below or email freevideos@studyguideteam.com with "Free Videos" in the subject line and the following information in the body of the email:

a. The title of your product

b. Your product rating on a scale of 1-5, with 5 being the highest

c. Your feedback about the product

If you have any questions or concerns, please don't hesitate to contact us at info@studyguideteam.com.

Thank you!

NASM CPT Study Guide 2024-2025

3 Practice Tests and NASM Personal Training Prep Book [4th Edition]

Lydia Morrison

Written and edited by TPB Publishing.

ISBN 13: 9781637756751

Table of Contents

Welcome

Dear Reader,

Welcome to your new Test Prep Books study guide! We are pleased that you chose us to help you prepare for your exam. There are many study options to choose from, and we appreciate you choosing us. Studying can be a daunting task, but we have designed a smart, effective study guide to help prepare you for what lies ahead.

Whether you're a parent helping your child learn and grow, a high school student working hard to get into your dream college, or a nursing student studying for a complex exam, we want to help give you the tools you need to succeed. We hope this study guide gives you the skills and the confidence to thrive, and we can't thank you enough for allowing us to be part of your journey.

In an effort to continue to improve our products, we welcome feedback from our customers. We look forward to hearing from you. Suggestions, success stories, and criticisms can all be communicated by emailing us at info@studyguideteam.com.

Sincerely,
Test Prep Books Team

FREE Videos/DVD OFFER

Doing well on your exam requires both knowing the test content and understanding how to use that knowledge to do well on the test. We offer completely FREE test taking tip videos. **These videos cover world-class tips that you can use to succeed on your test.**

To get your **FREE videos**, you can use the QR code below or email freevideos@studyguideteam.com with "Free Videos" in the subject line and the following information in the body of the email:

a. The title of your product
b. Your product rating on a scale of 1-5, with 5 being the highest
c. Your feedback about the product

If you have any questions or concerns, please don't hesitate to contact us at info@studyguideteam.com.

Quick Overview

As you draw closer to taking your exam, effective preparation becomes more and more important. Thankfully, you have this study guide to help you get ready. Use this guide to help keep your studying on track and refer to it often.

This study guide contains several key sections that will help you be successful on your exam. The guide contains tips for what you should do the night before and the day of the test. Also included are test-taking tips. Knowing the right information is not always enough. Many well-prepared test takers struggle with exams. These tips will help equip you to accurately read, assess, and answer test questions.

A large part of the guide is devoted to showing you what content to expect on the exam and to helping you better understand that content. In this guide are practice test questions so that you can see how well you have grasped the content. Then, answer explanations are provided so that you can understand why you missed certain questions.

Don't try to cram the night before you take your exam. This is not a wise strategy for a few reasons. First, your retention of the information will be low. Your time would be better used by reviewing information you already know rather than trying to learn a lot of new information. Second, you will likely become stressed as you try to gain a large amount of knowledge in a short amount of time. Third, you will be depriving yourself of sleep. So be sure to go to bed at a reasonable time the night before. Being well-rested helps you focus and remain calm.

Be sure to eat a substantial breakfast the morning of the exam. If you are taking the exam in the afternoon, be sure to have a good lunch as well. Being hungry is distracting and can make it difficult to focus. You have hopefully spent lots of time preparing for the exam. Don't let an empty stomach get in the way of success!

When travelling to the testing center, leave earlier than needed. That way, you have a buffer in case you experience any delays. This will help you remain calm and will keep you from missing your appointment time at the testing center.

Be sure to pace yourself during the exam. Don't try to rush through the exam. There is no need to risk performing poorly on the exam just so you can leave the testing center early. Allow yourself to use all of the allotted time if needed.

Remain positive while taking the exam even if you feel like you are performing poorly. Thinking about the content you should have mastered will not help you perform better on the exam.

Once the exam is complete, take some time to relax. Even if you feel that you need to take the exam again, you will be well served by some down time before you begin studying again. It's often easier to convince yourself to study if you know that it will come with a reward!

Test-Taking Strategies

1. Predicting the Answer

When you feel confident in your preparation for a multiple-choice test, try predicting the answer before reading the answer choices. This is especially useful on questions that test objective factual knowledge. By predicting the answer before reading the available choices, you eliminate the possibility that you will be distracted or led astray by an incorrect answer choice. You will feel more confident in your selection if you read the question, predict the answer, and then find your prediction among the answer choices. After using this strategy, be sure to still read all of the answer choices carefully and completely. If you feel unprepared, you should not attempt to predict the answers. This would be a waste of time and an opportunity for your mind to wander in the wrong direction.

2. Reading the Whole Question

Too often, test takers scan a multiple-choice question, recognize a few familiar words, and immediately jump to the answer choices. Test authors are aware of this common impatience, and they will sometimes prey upon it. For instance, a test author might subtly turn the question into a negative, or he or she might redirect the focus of the question right at the end. The only way to avoid falling into these traps is to read the entirety of the question carefully before reading the answer choices.

3. Looking for Wrong Answers

Long and complicated multiple-choice questions can be intimidating. One way to simplify a difficult multiple-choice question is to eliminate all of the answer choices that are clearly wrong. In most sets of answers, there will be at least one selection that can be dismissed right away. If the test is administered on paper, the test taker could draw a line through it to indicate that it may be ignored; otherwise, the test taker will have to perform this operation mentally or on scratch paper. In either case, once the obviously incorrect answers have been eliminated, the remaining choices may be considered. Sometimes identifying the clearly wrong answers will give the test taker some information about the correct answer. For instance, if one of the remaining answer choices is a direct opposite of one of the eliminated answer choices, it may well be the correct answer. The opposite of obviously wrong is obviously right! Of course, this is not always the case. Some answers are obviously incorrect simply because they are irrelevant to the question being asked. Still, identifying and eliminating some incorrect answer choices is a good way to simplify a multiple-choice question.

4. Don't Overanalyze

Anxious test takers often overanalyze questions. When you are nervous, your brain will often run wild, causing you to make associations and discover clues that don't actually exist. If you feel that this may be a problem for you, do whatever you can to slow down during the test. Try taking a deep breath or counting to ten. As you read and consider the question, restrict yourself to the particular words used by the author. Avoid thought tangents about what the author *really* meant, or what he or she was *trying* to say. The only things that matter on a multiple-choice test are the words that are actually in the question. You must avoid reading too much into a multiple-choice question, or supposing that the writer meant something other than what he or she wrote.

5. No Need for Panic

It is wise to learn as many strategies as possible before taking a multiple-choice test, but it is likely that you will come across a few questions for which you simply don't know the answer. In this situation, avoid panicking. Because most multiple-choice tests include dozens of questions, the relative value of a single wrong answer is small. As much as possible, you should compartmentalize each question on a multiple-choice test. In other words, you should not allow your feelings about one question to affect your success on the others. When you find a question that you either don't understand or don't know how to answer, just take a deep breath and do your best. Read the entire question slowly and carefully. Try rephrasing the question a couple of different ways. Then, read all of the answer choices carefully. After eliminating obviously wrong answers, make a selection and move on to the next question.

6. Confusing Answer Choices

When working on a difficult multiple-choice question, there may be a tendency to focus on the answer choices that are the easiest to understand. Many people, whether consciously or not, gravitate to the answer choices that require the least concentration, knowledge, and memory. This is a mistake. When you come across an answer choice that is confusing, you should give it extra attention. A question might be confusing because you do not know the subject matter to which it refers. If this is the case, don't eliminate the answer before you have affirmatively settled on another. When you come across an answer choice of this type, set it aside as you look at the remaining choices. If you can confidently assert that one of the other choices is correct, you can leave the confusing answer aside. Otherwise, you will need to take a moment to try to better understand the confusing answer choice. Rephrasing is one way to tease out the sense of a confusing answer choice.

7. Your First Instinct

Many people struggle with multiple-choice tests because they overthink the questions. If you have studied sufficiently for the test, you should be prepared to trust your first instinct once you have carefully and completely read the question and all of the answer choices. There is a great deal of research suggesting that the mind can come to the correct conclusion very quickly once it has obtained all of the relevant information. At times, it may seem to you as if your intuition is working faster even than your reasoning mind. This may in fact be true. The knowledge you obtain while studying may be retrieved from your subconscious before you have a chance to work out the associations that support it. Verify your instinct by working out the reasons that it should be trusted.

8. Key Words

Many test takers struggle with multiple-choice questions because they have poor reading comprehension skills. Quickly reading and understanding a multiple-choice question requires a mixture of skill and experience. To help with this, try jotting down a few key words and phrases on a piece of

scrap paper. Doing this concentrates the process of reading and forces the mind to weigh the relative importance of the question's parts. In selecting words and phrases to write down, the test taker thinks about the question more deeply and carefully. This is especially true for multiple-choice questions that are preceded by a long prompt.

9. Subtle Negatives

One of the oldest tricks in the multiple-choice test writer's book is to subtly reverse the meaning of a question with a word like *not* or *except*. If you are not paying attention to each word in the question, you can easily be led astray by this trick. For instance, a common question format is, "Which of the following is...?" Obviously, if the question instead is, "Which of the following is not...?," then the answer will be quite different. Even worse, the test makers are aware of the potential for this mistake and will include one answer choice that would be correct if the question were not negated or reversed. A test taker who misses the reversal will find what he or she believes to be a correct answer and will be so confident that he or she will fail to reread the question and discover the original error. The only way to avoid this is to practice a wide variety of multiple-choice questions and to pay close attention to each and every word.

10. Reading Every Answer Choice

It may seem obvious, but you should always read every one of the answer choices! Too many test takers fall into the habit of scanning the question and assuming that they understand the question because they recognize a few key words. From there, they pick the first answer choice that answers the question they believe they have read. Test takers who read all of the answer choices might discover that one of the latter answer choices is actually *more* correct. Moreover, reading all of the answer choices can remind you of facts related to the question that can help you arrive at the correct answer. Sometimes, a misstatement or incorrect detail in one of the latter answer choices will trigger your memory of the subject and will enable you to find the right answer. Failing to read all of the answer choices is like not reading all of the items on a restaurant menu: you might miss out on the perfect choice.

11. Spot the Hedges

One of the keys to success on multiple-choice tests is paying close attention to every word. This is never truer than with words like *almost*, *most*, *some*, and *sometimes*. These words are called "hedges" because they indicate that a statement is not totally true or not true in every place and time. An absolute statement will contain no hedges, but in many subjects, the answers are not always straightforward or absolute. There are always exceptions to the rules in these subjects. For this reason, you should favor those multiple-choice questions that contain hedging language. The presence of qualifying words indicates that the author is taking special care with his or her words, which is certainly important when composing the right answer. After all, there are many ways to be wrong, but there is only one way to be right! For this reason, it is wise to avoid answers that are absolute when taking a multiple-choice test. An absolute answer is one that says things are either all one way or all another. They often include words like *every*, *always*, *best*, and *never*. If you are taking a multiple-choice test in a subject that doesn't lend itself to absolute answers, be on your guard if you see any of these words.

12. Long Answers

In many subject areas, the answers are not simple. As already mentioned, the right answer often requires hedges. Another common feature of the answers to a complex or subjective question are qualifying clauses, which are groups of words that subtly modify the meaning of the sentence. If the question or answer choice describes a rule to which there are exceptions or the subject matter is complicated, ambiguous, or confusing, the correct answer will require many words in order to be expressed clearly and accurately. In essence, you should not be deterred by answer choices that seem excessively long. Oftentimes, the author of the text will not be able to write the correct answer without offering some qualifications and modifications. Your job is to read the answer choices thoroughly and completely and to select the one that most accurately and precisely answers the question.

13. Restating to Understand

Sometimes, a question on a multiple-choice test is difficult not because of what it asks but because of how it is written. If this is the case, restate the question or answer choice in different words. This process serves a couple of important purposes. First, it forces you to concentrate on the core of the question. In order to rephrase the question accurately, you have to understand it well. Rephrasing the question will concentrate your mind on the key words and ideas. Second, it will present the information to your mind in a fresh way. This process may trigger your memory and render some useful scrap of information picked up while studying.

14. True Statements

Sometimes an answer choice will be true in itself, but it does not answer the question. This is one of the main reasons why it is essential to read the question carefully and completely before proceeding to the answer choices. Too often, test takers skip ahead to the answer choices and look for true statements. Having found one of these, they are content to select it without reference to the question above. The savvy test taker will always read the entire question before turning to the answer choices. Then, having settled on a correct answer choice, he or she will refer to the original question and ensure that the selected answer is relevant. The mistake of choosing a correct-but-irrelevant answer choice is especially common on questions related to specific pieces of objective knowledge.

15. No Patterns

One of the more dangerous ideas that circulates about multiple-choice tests is that the correct answers tend to fall into patterns. These erroneous ideas range from a belief that B and C are the most common right answers, to the idea that an unprepared test-taker should answer "A-B-A-C-A-D-A-B-A." It cannot be emphasized enough that pattern-seeking of this type is exactly the WRONG way to approach a multiple-choice test. To begin with, it is highly unlikely that the test maker will plot the correct answers according to some predetermined pattern. The questions are scrambled and delivered in a random order. Furthermore, even if the test maker was following a pattern in the assignation of correct answers, there is no reason why the test taker would know which pattern he or she was using. Any attempt to discern a pattern in the answer choices is a waste of time and a distraction from the real work of taking the test. A test taker would be much better served by extra preparation before the test than by reliance on a pattern in the answers.

Bonus Content & Audiobook

We host multiple bonus items online, including all 3 practice tests in digital format and the audiobook version of this study guide. Scan the QR code or go to this link to access this content:

testprepbooks.com/bonus/nasm

The first time you access the tests, you will need to register as a "new user" and verify your email address.

If you have any issues, please email support@testprepbooks.com.

Introduction to the NASM

Function of the Test

A passing score on the National Academy of Sports Medicine (NASM) Certified Personal Trainer (CPT) exam is required in order to obtain a NASM personal trainer certification. The test is typically taken by individuals seeking jobs or careers as personal trainers in gyms, health clubs, medical fitness facilities, or other related businesses. The exam assesses the necessary knowledge and skills of aspiring personal trainers including concepts of biomechanics, anatomy and physiology, nutrition, fitness assessments, exercise programming and technique, coaching clients, behavior modification, and professional responsibilities.

NASM offers several exam preparation programs. Candidates may register for the "Exam Only" option, which, as the name suggests, is only the exam. NASM recommends that this option should be reserved for those candidates with significant formal education and experience with exercise science and fitness training. NASM also offers two types of money back guarantees: the Exam Pass Guarantee and the Job Guarantee. The Exam Pass Guarantee is offered exclusively as part of NASM's Guided-Study Program, which is an exam preparation program that candidates can register for and participate in to optimize their chances of success on the exam. The fee for this program will be refunded to candidates who have met all of the program requirements yet fail to pass the exam on the first attempt. The Job Guarantee, offered exclusively as part of NASM's CPT Development Program, also will refund the preparation program fees to test takers who fail to land a job in the industry within 90 days of obtaining certification, as long as they meet a variety of job-seeking and program requirements. Details regarding these programs and their restrictions are available on the NASM website.

Test Administration

The NASM Certified Personal Trainer exam is offered in hundreds of locations across the United States and Canada, as well as some international locations. In the United States and Canada, the test is offered at PSI testing centers. International candidates must call NASM to register and should allow at least 4-6 weeks for scheduling. While not required, NASM recommends registering at least 60 days prior to the desired test date to allow sufficient preparation time. Note that a valid government-issue ID is required for admittance into the PSI testing center.

To qualify to take the test, registrants must have earned or be within 90 days of earning a high school diploma or the equivalent, and must hold current adult CPR and AED certificates (with live skills checks, not purely online). Proof of CPR/AED certification is required upon arrival to the testing center, prior to admittance. Although not a verifiable requirement, NASM does state that one requirement of candidates is a passion for helping clients reach their fitness goals. Candidates may request eligibility exceptions, which will be reviewed by NASM's Disciplinary & Appeals Committee. Test Takers who fail to pass the exam on the first attempt may retake the exam after a one-week waiting period. If the candidate is still unsuccessful after the second attempt, he or she must wait at least thirty days before a retake is permitted. Candidates must wait a full year before attempting to take the exam again for each repeated failure after the third attempt.

NASM will provide testing accommodations for candidates with documented disabilities in accordance with the Americans with Disabilities Act. Examples of accommodations included extended testing time, a

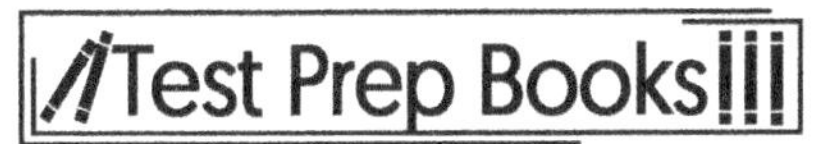

sign language interpreter, a test reader, seating modifications, or other accessibility aids. Candidates should submit their accommodation requests in writing on the designated accommodations form (available on NASM's website) at least thirty days prior to their desired test date to allow sufficient time for processing and approval. Candidates will receive NASM's accommodations decision in writing.

Test Format

Specific test conditions vary from test location to test location, but the test is always conducted on a computer in one two-hour session. The exam is comprised of 120 multiple-choice questions broken into six domains, as follows:

Domain	% of Exam
Basic and Applied Sciences and Nutritional Concepts	15%
Client Relations and Behavioral Coaching	15%
Assessment	16%
Program Design	20%
Exercise Technique and Training Instruction	24%
Professional Development and Responsibility	10%

Test takers may not bring any reference materials, phones, calculators, or other materials into the testing room. Twenty of the questions serve as "pretest" questions and are used as part of NASM's continual process of exam development. These questions do not affect a test taker's score, although he or she will not be alerted as to which exam questions serve as these unscored, pretest questions. They are randomly spaced throughout the exam.

Scoring

The test is scored by converting the number of correct answers to a scaled score from 0 to 100 points, with the passing score set at 70. The purpose of the scaled score is to allow for comparison between different versions and administrations of the exam. There is no penalty for guessing, as only the total number of correct answers matters. Scores and passing status are reported immediately upon completion of the test, although final scores are released roughly two weeks after test administration, once NASM verifies the score. A certificate will also be mailed to candidates who successfully pass the exam. It should be noted that candidates who achieve the scaled score of 70 (the passing cutoff) will only be notified of their passing status and not provided with their actual score, while candidates who do not pass will be provided with their score in addition to their non-passing status.

Recent/Future Developments

NASM continually updates and assesses the validity and content of the exam. New questions and new topics are rotated into the NASM Certified Personal Trainer exam on an annual basis, with the goal of keeping the test up-to-date with the latest developments in the field.

Study Prep Plan for the NASM

1 **Schedule -** Use one of our study schedules below or come up with one of your own.

2 **Relax -** Test anxiety can hurt even the best students. There are many ways to reduce stress. Find the one that works best for you.

3 **Execute -** Once you have a good plan in place, be sure to stick to it.

One Week Study Schedule

Day 1	Basic and Applied Sciences and Nutritional Concepts
Day 2	Nutrition
Day 3	Assessment
Day 4	Program Design
Day 5	Exercise Technique and Training Instruction
Day 6	Practice Test #1
Day 7	Take Your Exam!

Two Week Study Schedule

Day 1	Basic and Applied Sciences and Nutritional Concepts	Day 8	Program Design
Day 2	Skeletal System Structure and Function	Day 9	Reactive Training
Day 3	Principles of Human Movement Science	Day 10	Exercise Technique and Training Instruction
Day 4	Nutrition	Day 11	Resistance Training Technique
Day 5	Client Relations and Behavioral Coaching	Day 12	Professional Development and Responsibility
Day 6	Assessment	Day 13	Practice Test #1
Day 7	Static Postural Assessment	Day 14	Take Your Exam!

One Month Study Schedule

Day 1	Basic and Applied Sciences and Nutritional Concepts	Day 11	Food and Supplement Label Reading	Day 21	Rest and Recovery
Day 2	Muscular System Structure and Function	Day 12	Client Relations and Behavioral Coaching	Day 22	Exercise Technique and Training Instruction
Day 3	Skeletal System Structure and Function	Day 13	Behavioral Coaching Methods	Day 23	Reactive Exercise Technique
Day 4	Circulatory System Structure and Function	Day 14	Barriers to Behavior Change	Day 24	Training Modification Based on Physical Signs and Symptoms
Day 5	Digestive System Structure and Function	Day 15	Assessment	Day 25	Professional Development and Responsibility
Day 6	Principles of Human Movement Science	Day 16	Static Postural Assessment	Day 26	Sales Concepts and Techniques
Day 7	Force-Couple Relationships	Day 17	Program Design	Day 27	Practice Test #1
Day 8	Nutrition	Day 18	General Adaptation Syndrome	Day 28	Practice Test #2
Day 9	Exercise Post-Oxygen Consumption (EPOC)	Day 19	Resistance Training Modalities	Day 29	Practice Test #3
Day 10	Portion Sizes, Meal Timing, and Meal Frequency	Day 20	Reactive Training	Day 30	Take Your Exam!

Build your own prep plan by visiting:
testprepbooks.com/prep

Basic and Applied Sciences and Nutritional Concepts

Anatomy

Anatomy is the structural makeup of an organism. The study of anatomy may be divided into microscopic/fine anatomy and macroscopic/gross anatomy. Fine anatomy concerns itself with viewing the features of the body with the aid of a microscope, while gross anatomy concerns itself with viewing the features of the body with the naked eye. Physiology refers to the functions of an organism, and it examines the chemical or physical functions that help the body function appropriately. Successful personal trainers must have a foundational understanding of anatomy and physiology in order to deliver safe, effective treatments to clients.

Terms of Direction

- *Medial* refers to a structure being closer to the midline of the body. For example, the nose is medial to the eyes.
- *Lateral* refers to a structure being farther from the midline of the body, and it is the opposite of *medial*. For example, the eyes are lateral to the nose.
- *Proximal* refers to a structure or body part located near an attachment point. For example, the elbow is proximal to the wrist.
- *Distal* refers to a structure or body part located far from an attachment point, and it is the opposite of *proximal*. For example, the wrist is distal to the elbow.
- *Anterior* means toward the front in humans. For example, the lips are anterior to the teeth. The term *ventral* can be used in place of *anterior*.
- *Posterior* means toward the back in humans, and it is the opposite of *anterior*. For example, the teeth are posterior to the lips. The term *dorsal* can be used in place of *posterior*.
- *Superior* means above and refers to a structure closer to the head. For example, the head is superior to the neck. The terms *cephalic* or *cranial* may be used in place of *superior*.
- *Inferior* means below and refers to a structure farther from the head, and it is the opposite of *superior*. For example, the neck is inferior to the head. The term *caudal* may be used in place of *inferior* and refers to a structure near the tail or posterior of the body.
- *Superficial* refers to a structure closer to the surface. For example, the muscles are superficial because they are just beneath the surface of the skin.
- *Deep* refers to a structure farther from the surface, and it is the opposite of *superficial*. For example, the femur is a deep structure lying beneath the muscles.

Body Regions

Terms for general locations on the body include:

- Cervical: relating to the neck (can also refer to the cervix, as in cervical cancer)
- Clavicular: relating to the clavicle, or collarbone
- Ocular: relating to the eyes
- Acromial: relating to the shoulder
- Cubital: relating to the elbow
- Brachial: relating to the arm
- Carpal: relating to the wrist
- Thoracic: relating to the chest
- Abdominal: relating to the abdomen
- Pubic: relating to the groin
- Pelvic: relating to the pelvis, or bones of the hip
- Femoral: relating to the femur, or thigh bone
- Geniculate: relating to the knee
- Pedal: relating to the foot
- Palmar: relating to the palm of the hand
- Plantar: relating to the sole of the foot

Abdominopelvic Regions and Quadrants

The abdominopelvic region may be defined as the combination of the abdominal and the pelvic cavities. The region's upper border is the breasts and its lower border is the groin region.

The region is divided into the following nine sections:

- Right hypochondriac: region below the cartilage of the ribs
- Epigastric: region above the stomach between the hypochondriac regions
- Left hypochondriac: region below the cartilage of the ribs
- Right lumbar: region of the waist
- Umbilical: region between the lumbar regions where the umbilicus, or belly button (navel), is located
- Left lumbar: region of the waist
- Right inguinal: region of the groin
- Hypogastric: region below the stomach between the inguinal regions
- Left inguinal: region of the groin

A simpler way to describe the abdominopelvic area is to divide it into the following quadrants:

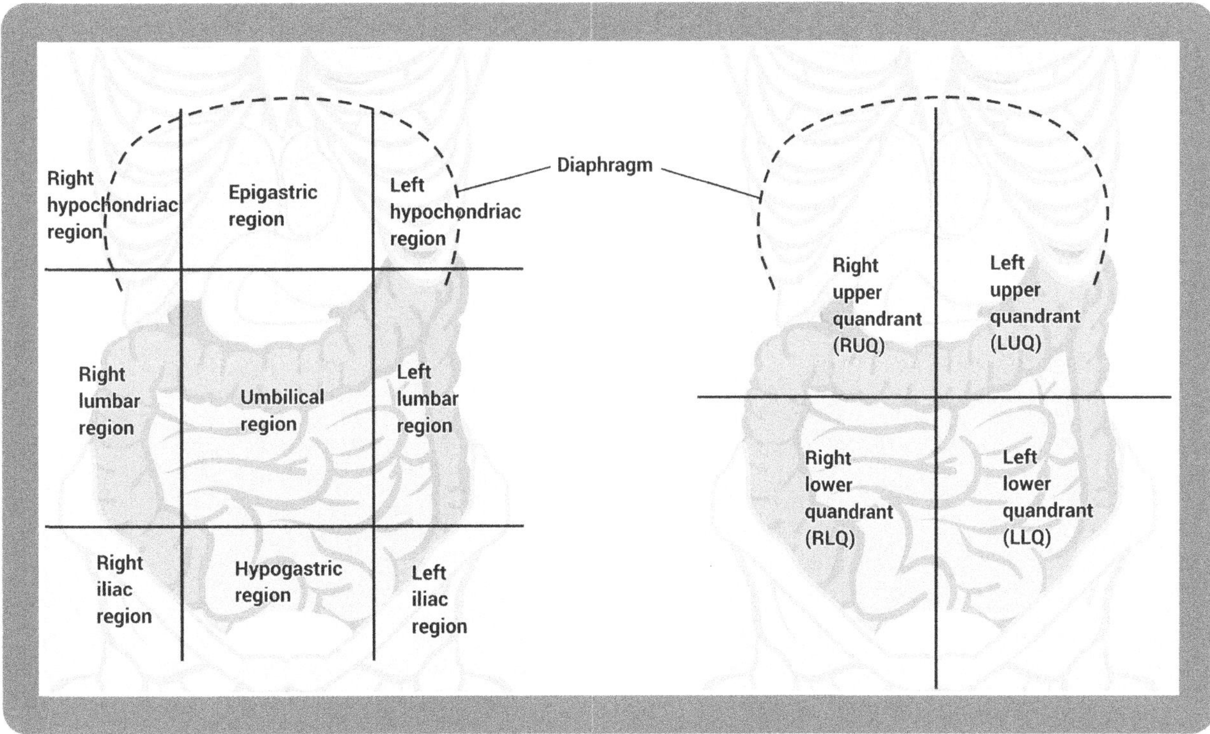

- Right upper quadrant (RUQ): Encompasses the right hypochondriac, right lumbar, epigastric, and umbilical regions.
- Right lower quadrant (RLQ): Encompasses the right lumbar, right inguinal, hypogastric, and umbilical regions.
- Left upper quadrant (LUQ): Encompasses the left hypochondriac, left lumbar, epigastric, and umbilical regions.
- Left lower quadrant (LLQ): Encompasses the left lumbar, left inguinal, hypogastric, and umbilical regions.

Nervous System Structure and Function

The human nervous system coordinates the body's response to stimuli from inside and outside the body. There are two major types of nervous system cells: neurons and neuroglia. Neurons are the workhorses of the nervous system and form a complex communication network that transmits electrical impulses termed action potentials, while neuroglia connect and support the neurons.

Although some neurons monitor the senses, some control muscles, and some connect the brain to other neurons, all neurons have four common characteristics:

- Dendrites: These receive electrical signals from other neurons across small gaps called *synapses*.
- Nerve cell body: This is the hub of processing and protein manufacture for the neuron.
- Axon: This transmits the signal from the cell body to other neurons.

- Terminals: These bridge the neuron to dendrites of other neurons and deliver the signal via chemical messengers called neurotransmitters.

Here is an illustration of a neuron:

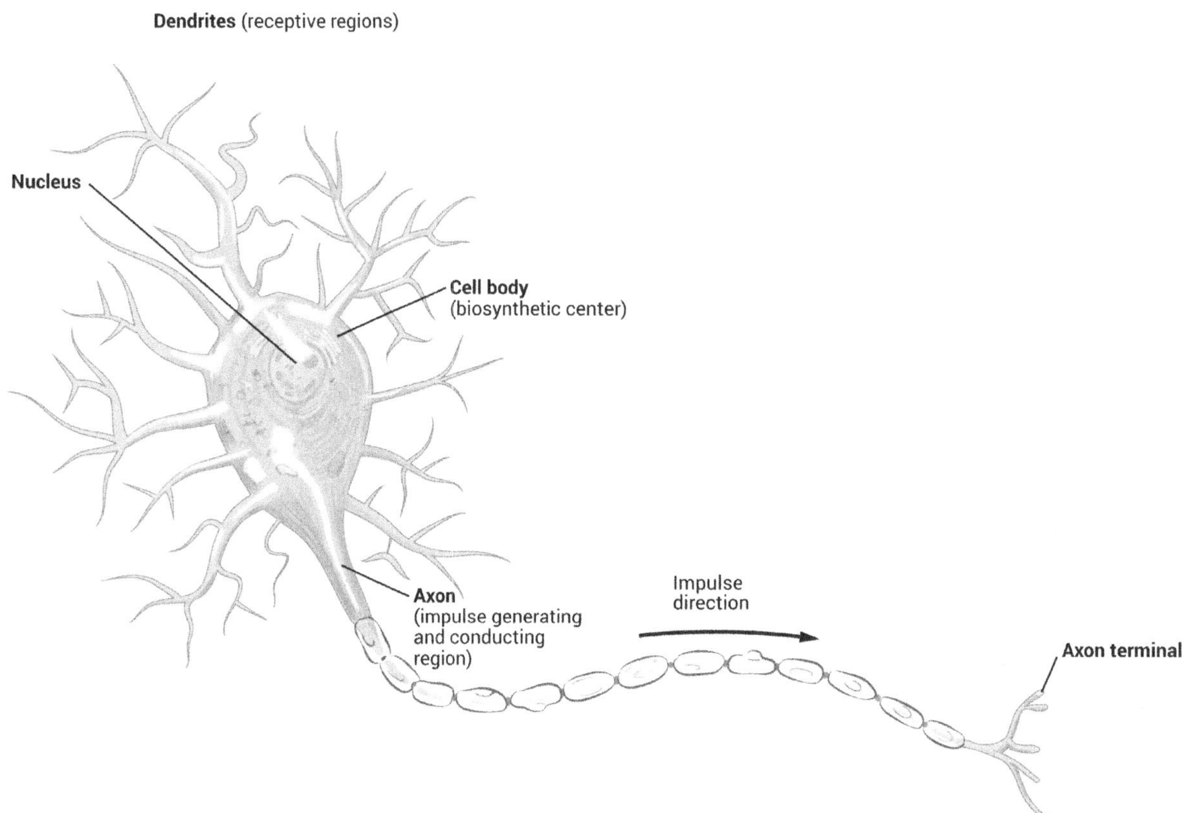

There are two major divisions of the nervous system: central and peripheral.

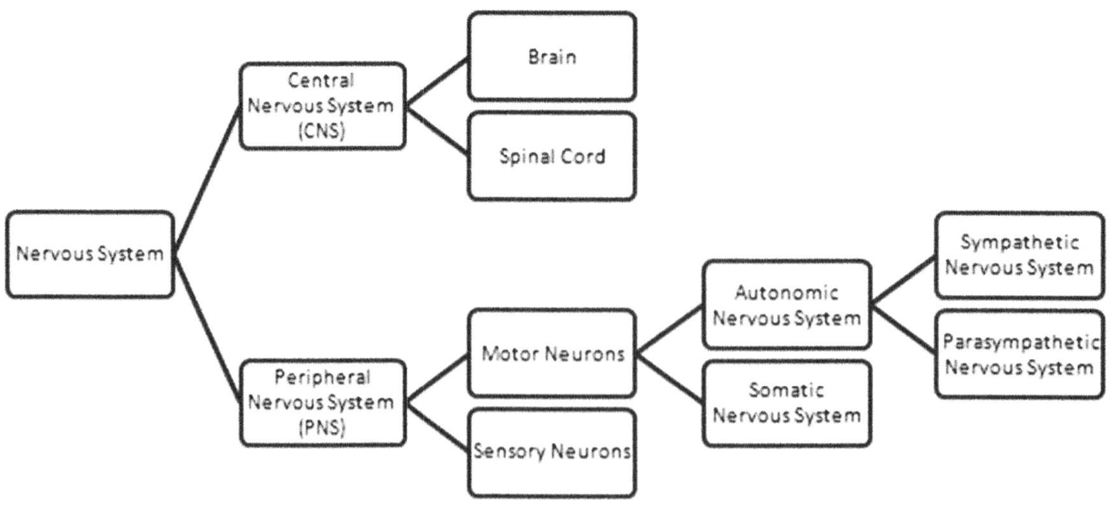

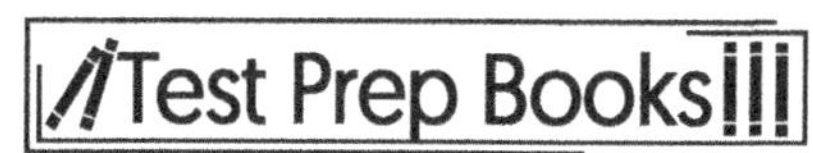

Central Nervous System

The central nervous system (CNS) consists of the brain and spinal cord. Three layers of membranes called the meninges cover and separate the CNS from the rest of the body.

The major divisions of the brain are the forebrain, the midbrain, and the hindbrain.

Forebrain

The *forebrain* consists of the cerebrum, the thalamus and hypothalamus, and the rest of the limbic system. The *cerebrum* is the largest part of the brain, and its most well-researched part is the outer cerebral cortex. The cerebrum is divided into right and left hemispheres, and each cerebral cortex hemisphere has four discrete areas, or lobes: frontal, temporal, parietal, and occipital. The frontal lobe governs duties such as voluntary movement, judgment, problem solving, and planning, while the other lobes are more sensory. The temporal lobe integrates hearing and language comprehension, the parietal lobe processes sensory input from the skin, and the occipital lobe processes visual input from the eyes. For completeness, the other two senses, smell and taste, are processed via the olfactory bulbs. The thalamus helps organize and coordinate all of this sensory input in a meaningful way for the brain to interpret.

The hypothalamus controls the endocrine system and all of the hormones that govern long-term effects on the body. Each hemisphere of the limbic system includes a hippocampus (which plays a vital role in memory), an amygdala (which is involved with emotional responses like fear and anger), and other small bodies and nuclei associated with memory and pleasure.

The midbrain is in charge of alertness, sleep/wake cycles, and temperature regulation, and it includes the substantia nigra which produces melatonin to regulate sleep patterns. The notable components of the hindbrain include the medulla oblongata and cerebellum. The **medulla oblongata** is located just above the spinal cord and is responsible for crucial involuntary functions such as breathing, swallowing, and regulating heart rate and blood pressure. Together with other parts of the hindbrain, the midbrain and medulla oblongata form the brain stem; the brain stem is the most basic and ancient part of the brain that would have been developed through evolution, and it connects the spinal cord to the rest of the brain. To the rear of the brain stem sits the cerebellum, which plays key roles in posture, balance, and muscular coordination. The spinal cord itself, which is encapsulated by the protective bony spinal column, carries sensory information to the brain and motor information to the body.

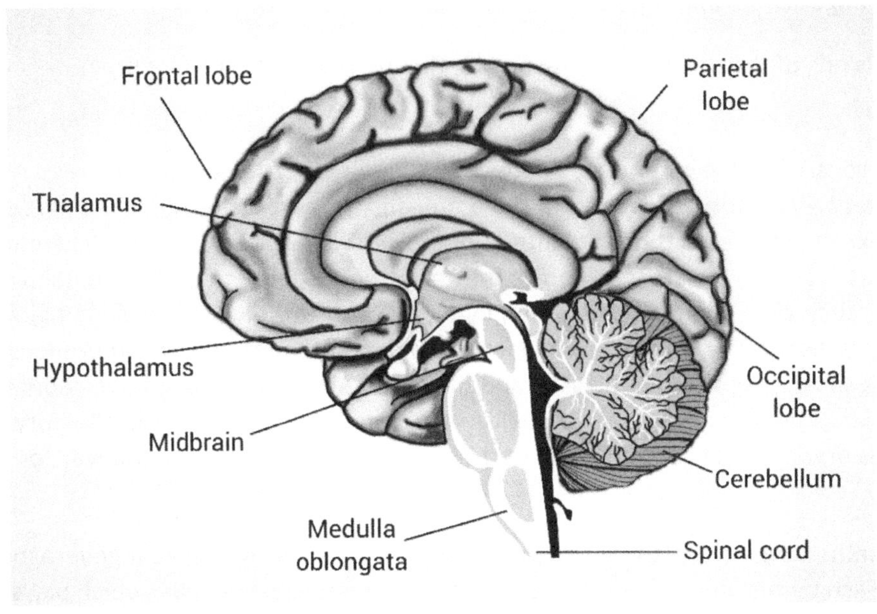

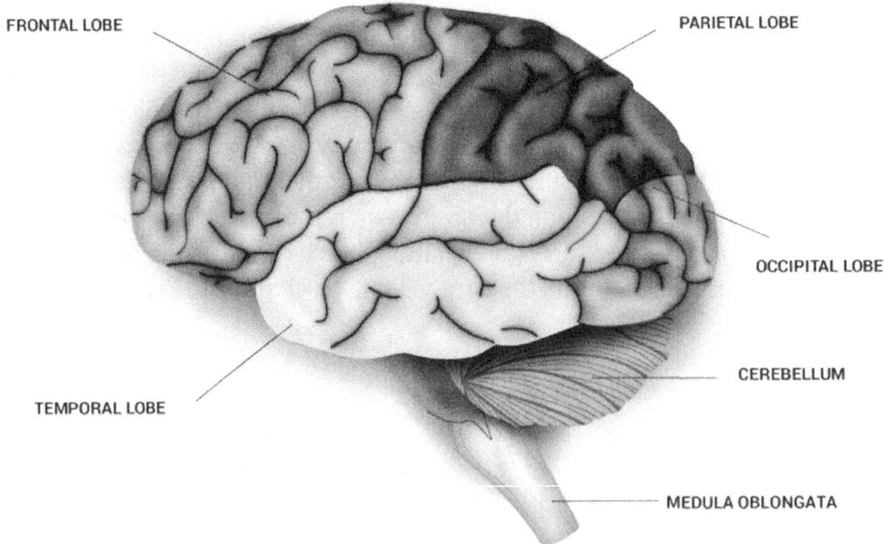

Peripheral Nervous System

The peripheral nervous system (PNS) includes all nervous tissue besides the brain and spinal cord. The PNS consists of the sets of cranial and spinal nerves and relays information between the CNS and the rest of the body. The PNS has two divisions: the autonomic nervous system and the somatic nervous system.

Autonomic Nervous System

The autonomic nervous system (ANS) governs involuntary, or reflexive, body functions. Ultimately, the autonomic nervous system controls functions such as breathing, heart rate, digestion, body temperature, and blood pressure.

The ANS is split between parasympathetic nerves and sympathetic nerves. These two nerve types are antagonistic and have opposite effects on the body. Parasympathetic nerves predominate resting conditions, and decrease heart rate, decrease breathing rate, prepare digestion, and allow urination and excretion. Sympathetic nerves, on the other hand, become active when a person is under stress or excited, and they increase heart rate, increase breathing rates, and inhibit digestion, urination, and excretion.

Somatic Nervous System and the Reflex Arc

The somatic nervous system (SNS) governs the conscious, or voluntary, control of skeletal muscles and their corresponding body movements. The SNS contains afferent and efferent neurons. Afferent neurons carry sensory messages from the skeletal muscles, skin, or sensory organs to the CNS. Efferent neurons relay motor messages from the CNS to skeletal muscles, skin, or sensory organs.

The SNS also has a role in involuntary movements called reflexes. A reflex is defined as an involuntary response to a stimulus. They are transmitted via what is termed a reflex arc, where a stimulus is sensed by a receptor and its afferent neuron, interpreted and rerouted by an interneuron, and delivered to effector muscles by an efferent neuron where they respond to the initial stimulus. A reflex is able to bypass the brain by being rerouted through the spinal cord; the interneuron decides the proper course of action rather than the brain. The reflex arc results in an instantaneous, involuntary response. For example, a physician tapping on the knee produces an involuntary knee jerk referred to as the patellar tendon reflex.

Muscular System Structure and Function

The muscular system of the human body is responsible for all movement that occurs and is the principle system that personal trainers should familiarize themselves with. There are approximately 700 muscles in the body that are attached to the bones of the skeletal system and that make up half of the body's weight. Muscles are attached to the bones through tendons. Tendons are made up of dense bands of connective tissue and have collagen fibers that firmly attach to the bone on one side and the muscle on the other. Their fibers are actually woven into the coverings of the bone and muscle so they can withstand the large forces that are put on them when muscles are moving.

There are three types of muscle tissue in the body: Skeletal muscle tissue pulls on the bones of the skeleton and causes body movement; cardiac muscle tissue helps pump blood through veins and arteries; and smooth muscle tissue helps move fluids and solids along the digestive tract and contributes to movement in other body systems. All of these muscle tissues have four important properties in common: They are excitable, meaning they respond to stimuli; contractile, meaning they can shorten and pull on connective tissue; extensible, meaning they can be stretched repeatedly, but maintain the ability to contract; and elastic, meaning they rebound to their original length after a contraction.

Muscles begin at an origin and end at an insertion. Generally, the origin is proximal to the insertion and the origin remains stationary while the insertion moves. For example, when bending the elbow and moving the hand up toward the head, the part of the forearm that is closest to the wrist moves and the part closer to the elbow is stationary. Therefore, the muscle in the forearm has an origin at the elbow and an insertion at the wrist.

Body movements occur by muscle contraction. Each contraction causes a specific action. Muscles can be classified into one of four muscle groups based on the action they perform. Primary movers, or agonists, produce a specific movement, such as flexion of the elbow. Synergists are in charge of helping the primary movers complete their specific movements. They can help stabilize the point of origin or provide extra pull near the insertion. Some synergists can aid an agonist in preventing movement at a joint. Stabilizers are the muscles that keep the body stable when the agonists and synergists are doing their jobs. Antagonists are muscles whose actions are the opposite of that of the agonist. If an agonist is contracting during a specific movement, the antagonist is stretched. During flexion of the elbow, the biceps' brachii muscle contracts and acts as an agonist, while the triceps' brachii muscle on the opposite side of the upper arm acts as an antagonist and stretches.

Skeletal muscle tissue has several important functions. It causes movement of the skeleton by pulling on tendons and moving the bones. It maintains body posture through the contraction of specific muscles responsible for the stability of the skeleton. Skeletal muscles help support the weight of internal organs and protect these organs from external injury. They also help to regulate body temperature within a normal range. Muscle contractions require energy and produce heat, which heats the body when cold.

Muscle Anatomy

Orientation/Directional/Regional Anatomical Terms

The following anatomical terms are commonly used in the description of muscle origins, insertions, and actions:

Superior (cranial): Near or toward the upper part of the body, i.e., toward the head. The clavicle is superior to the iliac crest.

Inferior (caudal): Toward the lower part of a structure or the body and away from the head. The talus is inferior to the patella.

Anterior (ventral): At or near the front of the body. The sternum is anterior to the spine.

Posterior (dorsal): At or near the back of the body. The spine is posterior to the sternum.

Medial: Near or at the body's midline. The nose is medial to the ears.

Lateral: Away from the body's midline. The ears are lateral to the nose.

Bilateral: On either side of a central axis or midline. The body has many bilateral (paired) structures including the legs, eyes, lungs, etc.

Ipsilateral: On or affecting the same side of the body. Ipsilateral appendages (e.g., hands and feet) are located on the same side of the body.

Contralateral: On or affecting the opposite sides of the body. A stroke that occurs on the right side of the brain may affect the function of the left arm.

Intermediate: Located between two structures—one that is medial and one that is lateral or one that is superior and one that is inferior. The knee is intermediate to the ankle and hip.

Proximal: Location of the origin or point of attachment of the body part towards the trunk and away from the appendages. The thigh is proximal to the ankle.

Distal: Location of the origin or point of attachment being away from the body. The ankle is distal to the knee.

Superficial (external): Near the outside or surface of an object or body.

Deep (internal): Inside, away from the surface of an object or body.

Axial: Associated with the center of the body. When considering the skeleton, the body's head, neck, and trunk make up the axial skeleton.

Appendicular: Refers to the body's appendages, such as the legs and arms.

Abduct: A movement away from the body's midline. When doing jumping jacks, the first phase of the arm movement abducts away from the side of the body en route to its position above the head.

Adduct: A movement toward the body's midline. The second phase of the arm movement during jumping jacks (returning them back in line with the trunk) demonstrates adduction.

Specific Muscle Names

One of the easiest ways to remember specific muscle names is to group the muscles by body regions. The following table of muscles, grouped by region, provides the name and action of the muscle as well as the origin (the anchoring end of the skeletal muscle, typically on a bone) and insertion (the end of the skeletal muscle that attaches to the bone or tissue that moves during the contraction). Muscles that are of primary relevance (e.g., muscles critical for sport/activity movements and muscles that aid respiration) to the personal trainer are included in this list. Examples of resistance exercises that target specific muscles are also provided. Please bear in mind that this is not an exhaustive list, but rather covers the most relevant muscles for trainers.

Muscle	**Origin (immovable end of muscle)**	**Insertion (movable end of muscle)**	**Action**	**Resistance Exercise(s)**
Erector spinae: iliocostalis (most lateral), longissimus (intermediate), spinalis (most medial)	Varies for each column	Varies for each column	Prime mover of back extension; each side consists of three columns (iliocostalis, longissimus, and spinalis muscles).	Seated rows Dumbbell rows Power jerk Stiff-leg dead lift Dead lifts Back extensions Lumbar extensions

Muscle	Origin (immovable end of muscle)	Insertion (movable end of muscle)	Action	Resistance Exercise(s)
Trapezius	Occipital bone, ligamentum nuchae, and spines of C7 and all thoracic vertebrae	A continuous insertion along acromion and spine of scapula and lateral third of clavicle	Stabilizes, raises, and rotates scapula; middle fibers retract (adduct) scapula; superior fibers elevate scapula (i.e., shrugging shoulders); inferior fibers depress scapula (and shoulder).	Back presses Bent-over lateral raises Arnold presses Lateral dumbbell raises Chin-ups Seated cable rows Dumbbell rows Dead lifts Power clean Power snatch Power jerk Lateral pull-downs Machine shoulder press Dumbbell prone posterior raise
Rhomboid major	Spinous processes of T2–T5	Medial (i.e., vertebral) border of scapula	Retracts, elevates, and rotates scapula	Dead lift Bent-over lateral raises Alternate front arm raises Dumbbell pull-overs Chin-ups Dumbbell one-arm row Seated cable rows Lateral pull-downs
Rhomboid minor	Spinous processes of C7–T1	Medial border of scapula	Retracts and elevates scapula	Dead lift Bent-over lateral raises Alternate front arm raises Dumbbell pull-overs Chin-ups Dumbbell one-arm row Lateral pull-downs Seated cable rows
Levator scapulae	Transverse processes of C1–C4	Medial border of scapula	Elevates scapula; flexes neck to same side	Dead lifts

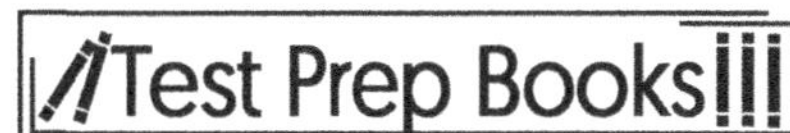

Muscle	Origin (immovable end of muscle)	Insertion (movable end of muscle)	Action	Resistance Exercise(s)
Serratus anterior	Series of muscle slips from ribs	Entire anterior (ventral) surface of vertebral border of scapula	Pulls scapula anteriorly and downward; abducts scapula	Back presses Arnold presses Alternate front arm raises Incline dumbbell press Dumbbell pull-overs Bench press, dumbbell Dumbbell fly Machine shoulder press
Pectoralis minor	Anterior surfaces of ribs three through five	Coracoid process of scapula	Abducts scapula, pulling it forward and downward; draws rib cage superiorly (raises ribs)	Incline dumbbell press Dumbbell pull-overs Bench press, dumbbell Bench press, barbell Incline press, dumbbell Dumbbell fly
Pectoralis major	Medial 1/2 of clavicle, sternum, and costal cartilages of ribs one through six	Greater tubercle of humerus	Prime mover of arm flexion; rotates arm medially, adducts humerus; pulls arm across chest	Triceps dips Arnold presses Alternate front arm raises Push-ups Barbell pull-overs Bench press, dumbbell Dumbbell fly
Teres major	Posterior surface of scapula at inferior angle	Intertubercular groove of humerus	Posteromedially extends, medially rotates, and adducts humerus; synergist of latissimus dorsi	Dumbbell pull-overs Barbell pull-overs Chin-ups Lateral pull-downs Dead lifts Dumbbell one-arm row Lateral pull-downs Seated cable rows

Muscle	Origin (immovable end of muscle)	Insertion (movable end of muscle)	Action	Resistance Exercise(s)
Latissimus dorsi	Spines of lower six thoracic vertebrae, lumbar vertebrae, lower three to four ribs, and iliac crest	Intertubercular groove of humerus	Prime mover of arm extension; arm adductor; medially rotates humerus at shoulder	Dumbbell pull-overs Barbell pull-overs Chin-ups Lateral pull-downs Seated rows Dead lifts Dumbbell one-arm row Seated cable rows
Deltoid	Spine of scapula, acromion, and lateral 1/3 of clavicle	Deltoid tuberosity of humerus	Prime mover of arm abduction (at shoulder); extends and flexes arm	Dead lift Triceps dips (anterior deltoid) Back presses Bent-over lateral raises Lateral dumbbell raises Alternate front arm raises Push-ups Seated cable rows Dumbbell rows Power clean Power snatch Power jerk Bench press, dumbbell Dumbbell fly Dumbbell one-arm row Lateral pull-downs Machine shoulder press Dumbbell prone posterior raise

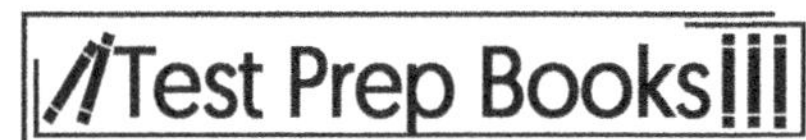

Muscle	Origin (immovable end of muscle)	Insertion (movable end of muscle)	Action	Resistance Exercise(s)
Rotator cuff: supraspinatus, infraspinatus, teres minor, subscapularis	Varies for each muscle	Varies for each muscle	Medially or laterally rotates arm at shoulder; supraspinatus assists abduction; stabilizes shoulder joint, helping to prevent downward dislocation of humerus	Back presses Bent-over lateral raises Dumbbell rows Dumbbell prone posterior raise
Biceps brachii	Short head: coracoid process of scapula; long head: tubercle above glenoid cavity of scapula	Radial tuberosity of radius	Flexes elbow joint and supinates forearm and hand	Dumbbell curl Hammer curl Barbell curls Chin-ups Lateral pull-downs Dumbbell one-arm row Seated cable rows
Brachialis	Anterior, distal 1/2 of humerus	Coronoid process of ulna	Flexes elbow	Dumbbell curl Hammer curls Barbell curls Chin-ups Lateral pull-downs Dumbbell one-arm row Seated cable rows
Brachioradialis	Lateral supracondylar ridge at distal end of humerus	Base of styloid process of radius	Flexes forearm at elbow	Hammer curls Dumbbell curls Barbell curls Chin-ups Seated rows Dumbbell one-arm row Lateral pull-downs Seated cable rows

Muscle	Origin (immovable end of muscle)	Insertion (movable end of muscle)	Action	Resistance Exercise(s)
Triceps brachii	Long head: infraglenoid tubercle of scapula; lateral head: posterior humerus above radial groove; medial head: posterior humerus below radial groove	All three heads: olecranon process of ulna	Extends forearm at elbow	Push-downs Reverse push-downs Lying dumbbell triceps extensions Triceps kickbacks Seated dumbbell triceps extensions Triceps dips Back presses Arnold presses Push-ups Dumbbell pull-overs Power snatch Bench press, dumbbell Machine shoulder press
External oblique	Outer surfaces of lower eight ribs	Outer lip of iliac crest and linea alba	Tenses abdominal wall and compresses abdominal contents	Dead lifts Sit-ups Leg raises Dumbbell side bends Abdominal crunch
Internal oblique	Lumbar fascia, iliac crest, and inguinal ligament	Cartilages of lower ribs, linea alba, and crest of pubis	Tenses abdominal wall and compresses abdominal contents	Dumbbell side bends
Transverse abdominis	Inguinal ligament, lumbar fascia, cartilages of last six ribs, iliac crest	Linea alba and crest of pubis	Compresses abdominal components	Pelvic floor exercises Planks
Rectus abdominis	Crest of pubis and symphysis pubis	Xiphoid process and costal cartilages of ribs five through seven	Flexes and rotates lumbar region of vertebral column; fixes and depresses ribs, stabilizes pelvis when walking; tenses abdominal wall, increases intra-abdominal pressure	Dead lifts Sit-ups Leg raises Dumbbell side bends Abdominal crunch

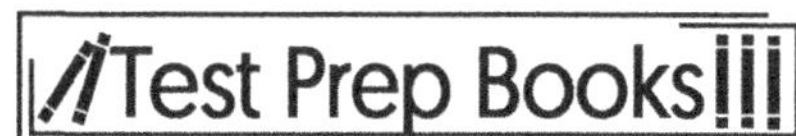

Muscle	Origin (immovable end of muscle)	Insertion (movable end of muscle)	Action	Resistance Exercise(s)
Psoas major (iliopsoas)	Lumbar intervertebral discs; bodies and transverse processes of lumbar vertebrae	Lesser trochanter of femur via iliopsoas tendon	Flexes thigh; also affects lateral flexion of vertebral column; important postural muscle	Leg raises Barbell lunge
Iliacus (iliopsoas)	Iliac fossa and crest, lateral sacrum	Femur on and immediately below lesser trochanter of femur via iliopsoas tendon	Prime mover for flexing thigh or for flexing trunk on thigh during a bow	Leg raises Barbell lunge
Gluteus maximus	Sacrum, coccyx, and posterior surface of ilium	Posterior surface of femur and fascia of thigh	Major extensor of thigh; generally inactive during standing and walking; laterally rotates and abducts thigh	Dead lifts Power clean Power snatch Power jerk Back squat Front squat Barbell lunge Stiff-leg dead lift Leg press Back extensions
Piriformis	Anterior surface of sacrum	Superior border of greater trochanter of femur	Abducts and rotates thigh laterally; stabilizes hip joint	Dead lifts
Hamstring group: biceps femoris, semitendinosus, semimembranosus	Ischial tuberosity (specifics vary on muscle)	Varies on muscle	Extends thigh and flexes knee; laterally or medially rotates leg, especially when knee is flexed	Dead lifts Standing leg curls Seated leg curls Power clean Power snatch Power jerk Back squat Front squat Barbell lunge Stiff-leg dead lift Leg press Leg curl Back extensions

Muscle	Origin (immovable end of muscle)	Insertion (movable end of muscle)	Action	Resistance Exercise(s)
Quadriceps group: vastus lateralis, medialis and intermedius, rectus femoris	Varies on specific muscle	Patellar ligament to tibial tuberosity	Extends and stabilizes knee	Dead lifts Leg extensions Power clean Power snatch Power jerk Back squat Front squat Barbell lunge Leg press
Gastrocnemius	Lateral and medial condyles of femur	Posterior surface of calcaneus	Plantar flexion of foot; flexes knee	Standing leg curls Seated leg curls Standing calf raises Power clean Power snatch Power jerk Barbell lunge Standing heel raise
Soleus	Head and shaft of fibula and posterior surface of tibia	Posterior surface of calcaneus	Plantar flexion of foot	Standing calf raises Power clean Power snatch Power jerk Barbell lunge

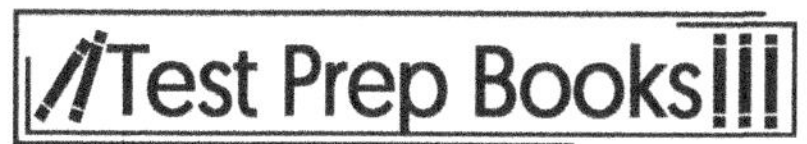

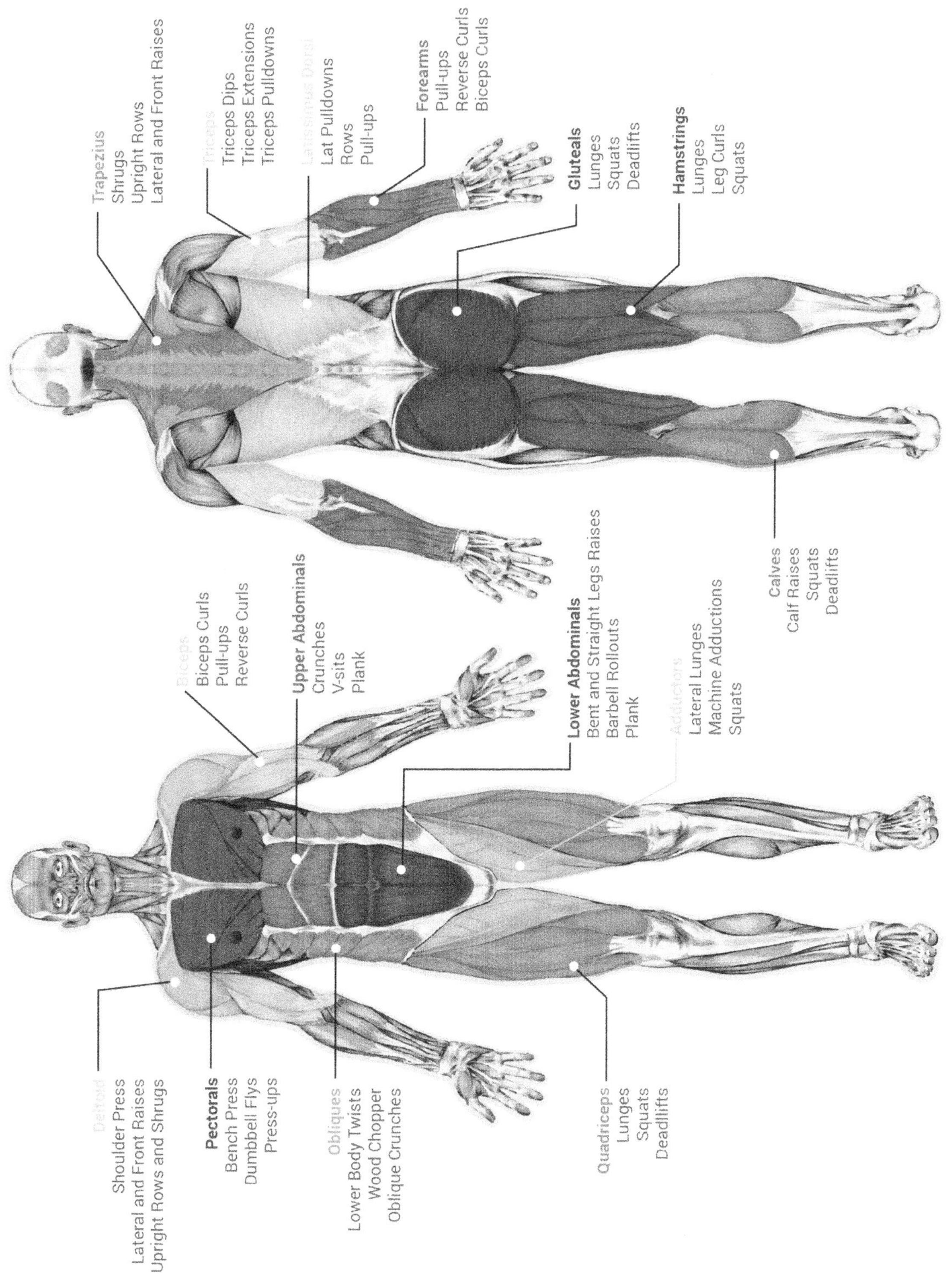

Deltoid
Shoulder Press
Lateral and Front Raises
Upright Rows and Shrugs

Pectorals
Bench Press
Dumbbell Flys
Press-ups

Obliques
Lower Body Twists
Wood Chopper
Oblique Crunches

Quadriceps
Lunges
Squats
Deadlifts

Biceps
Biceps Curls
Pull-ups
Reverse Curls

Upper Abdominals
Crunches
V-sits
Plank

Lower Abdominals
Bent and Straight Legs Raises
Barbell Rollouts
Plank

Adductors
Lateral Lunges
Machine Adductions
Squats

Calves
Calf Raises
Squats
Deadlifts

Trapezius
Shrugs
Upright Rows
Lateral and Front Raises

Triceps
Triceps Dips
Triceps Extensions
Triceps Pulldowns

Latissimus Dorsi
Lat Pulldowns
Rows
Pull-ups

Forearms
Pull-ups
Reverse Curls
Biceps Curls

Gluteals
Lunges
Squats
Deadlifts

Hamstrings
Lunges
Leg Curls
Squats

Muscle Belly Anatomy

Muscle fibers: Also called muscle cells or myocytes, muscle fibers are long, striated, cylindrical cells approximately the diameter of a human hair (50–100 micrometers). Many nuclei are dispersed throughout the cell, which is covered by a fibrous membrane called the sarcolemma. Up to 150 muscle fibers can be bundled together into parallel fasciculi, with each fasciculus covered by perimysium (i.e., connective tissue) and each muscle fiber covered by endomysium, another type of connective tissue.

Sarcolemma: The sarcolemma is a thin elastic membrane, surrounding each muscle fiber, that consists of a phospholipid bilayer (like eukaryotic cell membranes) and an outer membrane with collagen and other structural elements.

Sarcoplasm: Sarcoplasm is the special term for the cytoplasm of a muscle fiber. Sarcoplasm is filled with myofibrils and contains the components required for muscular contraction, including various proteins, protein filaments, mitochondria, the sarcoplasmic reticulum, stored glycogen, enzymes, and ions.

Sarcoplasmic reticulum: The sarcoplasmic reticulum is a network of tubular channels (i.e., transverse [T] tubule system) and vesicles, which together provide structural integrity to the muscle fiber. The sarcoplasmic reticulum also acts as a calcium ion (Ca^{2+}) pump, moving Ca^{2+} ions from the sarcoplasm into the muscle fiber. Influx of Ca^{2+} ions from the sarcoplasm into the muscle fiber results from an action potential in the sarcomere, causing the depolarization that initiates muscle movement.

Myofibril: Myofibrils consist of long, thin (approximately 1/1000 millimeter) chain proteins, such as actin, myosin, and titan. Bunches of myofibrils and nuclei together make a muscle fiber.

Myofilament: Myofilaments primarily consist of protein chains containing actin and myosin and are the smaller components of the myofibrils within striated muscle fibers. A sarcomere is composed of myofilaments.

Sarcomere: The smallest functional unit of a muscle fiber, a sarcomere contains the actin and myosin proteins responsible for the mechanical process of muscle contractions. Located between two Z-lines, actin and myosin filaments are configured in parallel, end to end, along the entire length of the myofibril. The varying arrangement of actin and myosin segments within the sarcomere causes the alternating light and dark pattern of skeletal muscle seen histologically. The sarcomere has four defined segments: A-band, H-zone, I-band, and Z-line. Each sarcomere is composed of a basic repeating unit between the Z-line located at each end of the sarcomere. The A-band contains both actin and myosin. The H-zone, a region located in the center of the sarcomere within the A-band, contains only myosin filaments. The I-band contains only actin filaments and consists of two connected sarcomeres on either side of the Z-line.

Transverse tubular system: The T-tubular system is perpendicular to the myofibril and two sarcoplasmic channels. The lateral end of each tubule channel terminates as a Ca^{2} storing vesicle. Each Z-line region contains two vesicles and a T-tubule. T-tubules pass through the muscle cell, open externally from the inside of the cell, and touch the sarcolemma on the surface of the cell. The vesicles and T-tubules spread the action potential (i.e., wave of depolarization) from the surface of the cell's outer membrane to all inner regions of the cell. Depolarization releases Ca^{2+} from vesicles, initiating contractile motion.

Myosin: The interaction between myosin, the thick filament, and actin, the thin filament, causes the sarcomere to shorten as the muscle contracts. Myosin is often described as resembling a bunch of golf clubs, with the heads forming the attachment site along the actin myofilaments, which resemble a string of beads. Myosin is also responsible for splitting adenosine triphosphate (ATP). The phosphate released from ATP hydrolysis provides the energy required for myosin to produce the power stroke, causing the myosin head to grab onto the actin and pull the filaments closer together as muscle contraction occurs.

Actin: This is the protein that forms the thinner myofilament. The myofilament consists of two strands of actin in a double helix configuration. As mentioned, the sarcomere contracts when actin and myosin (the thick filament) bind together and complete a power stroke.

Troponin: Troponin, a protein located at regular intervals along the actin filament, binds with the Ca^{2+} released from the sarcoplasmic reticulum. This causes a conformational change in tropomyosin, exposing the binding site on the actin filaments for the myosin heads to form cross-bridges.

Tropomyosin: Tropomyosin is a protein in the I-band located along the actin filament in a groove formed by the double helix configuration of the two actin strands. The conformational change of troponin moves the tropomyosin deeper into the groove, allowing the actin and myosin cross-bridge to rapidly attach, pulling the toward the center of the sarcomere in a contractile action. When troponin is not affecting tropomyosin (i.e., no Ca^{2+} release), it inhibits actin and myosin bonding, which prevents a constant state of muscle contraction.

Acetylcholine (ACh): Vesicles located at the terminal end of motor neurons release the neurotransmitter ACh when an action potential arrives at the terminal end of a motor neuron. ACh diffuses across the synaptic space of the neuromuscular junction, and this excites the sarcolemma, initiating muscle contraction.

Muscular Dynamics Involved During Movement Patterns

Sliding Filament Theory

The sliding filament theory states that muscle shortening and lengthening is due to the movement of actin and myosin sliding past each other and reducing the distance between the Z-lines of the sarcomere because the overlap of the filaments increases. As the myosin cross-bridges attach and detach from actin filaments, the muscle fiber shortens due to the contractile action. Because minimal calcium is in the myofibril under resting conditions (during *resting phase*), very few myosin cross-bridges are bound with actin (i.e., actomyosin protein complex) because the binding sites are blocked. During the *excitation-contraction coupling phase*, the muscle releases an electrical discharge, and this starts a series of chemical events on the surface of the muscle cell, causing the release of calcium inside the muscle cell from the sarcoplasmic reticulum. The Ca^{2+} binds with troponin, resulting in tropomyosin moving farther into the double helix groove, allowing rapid binding of actin and myosin filaments and the power stroke that pulls the actin toward the center of the sarcomere.

During the contraction phase, the enzyme myosin adenosine triphosphatase (ATPase) breaks down ATP into adenosine diphosphate (ADP). The ADP on the myosin cross-bridge globular head is replaced with ATP so that the myosin head has energy to detach from the actin and then re-cock and grab on to the next binding spot on the actin filament, helping to "slide" down and create the sarcomere shortening needed for muscular contraction. If ATP and Ca^{2+} are still available, the entire contraction process (i.e., Ca^{2+} binds to troponin, myosin cross-bridge binds with actin, power stroke causes sarcomere contraction, actin and myosin uncouple, myosin head position is reset) is repeated in the muscle fiber during the *recharge phase*. Relaxation occurs when Ca^{2+}, ATP, ADP, or ATPase is no longer available. The *relaxation phase* also occurs when motor neurons stop releasing ACh, the Ca^{2+} levels in the sarcoplasmic reticulum return to baseline, and myosin and actin uncouple.

All-or-None Principle

This principle states that when an action potential in a motor neuron reaches the sarcolemma, the action potential will either elicit activation of all the muscle fibers connected to the motor neuron or no activation of any of the muscle fibers will occur. Partial activation of just some fibers will not occur.

Neuromuscular Anatomy

Motor unit: This is the functional unit of the neuromotor system. It consists of the motor neuron and all of the muscle fibers it innervates. Motor unit function depends on the morphological and physiological characteristics of the muscle fibers innervated by the motor neuron.

Motor neuron (nerve cell): The motor neuron consists of an alpha motor neuron (cell body), axon, and dendrites. It transmits nerve impulses from the spinal cord to the muscle fiber. A myelin sheath surrounds the axon, with nodes interrupting the myelin every 1–2 millimeters. The alternation of myelin and nodes allows an electrical current (i.e., nerve impulse) to quickly move down the axon with impulses "jumping" from node to node. The terminal branches end at the neuromuscular junction.

Neuromuscular junction (AKA motor end plate): This is the functional connection (chemical synapse) between the end of the myelinated motor neuron and the muscle fiber. It transmits the nerve impulse from the motor neuron to the muscle fiber, initiating the stimulation of the nerve fiber by chemical transmission. The action potential reaches the terminal branches, and ACh is released across the synaptic space, stimulating the sarcolemma. When enough ACh is released, an action potential is generated and travels the length of the muscle fiber, causing it to contract.

Muscle spindles: Muscle spindles are proprioceptors that sense the rate and magnitude of increases in muscle tension as the muscle lengthens with an eccentric muscle contraction. The spindles contain *intrafusal fibers* (modified muscle fibers) contained in a sheath of connective tissue that runs parallel to the normal *extrafusal muscle fibers*. As a muscle lengthens, the muscle spindles are stretched, activating a sensory neuron in the spindle that sends an impulse to the spinal cord. In the spinal cord, the signal coming from the sensory neuron synapses with a motor neuron, which travels back to innervate the extrafusal muscle fibers. Motor neurons activate the muscle, causing a reflexive muscle action called the stretch reflex. This causes muscle contraction, the spindles shorten, and the sensory impulses stop. Increasing loads cause the spindles to stretch more. The muscle force (F_M) and power are potentiated by this reflexive contraction.

Somatic nervous system: The somatic nervous system innervates skeletal muscles and is responsible for conscious control of voluntary movements.

Autonomic nervous system (ANS): The ANS innervates smooth and cardiac muscles as well as glands. It is also responsible for visceral motor actions (e.g., pumping the heart, food movement through

the digestive tract). The ANS, sometimes called the involuntary nervous system, is not under conscious control. It has two subdivisions: the sympathetic and parasympathetic nervous systems.

- Sympathetic nervous system (SNS): The SNS prepares the body for action and is sometimes called the fight-or-flight system. During exercise, the SNS is responsible for directing blood away from the digestive tract and skin and toward the skeletal muscles, heart, and brain. Physiological responses associated with the SNS include increased blood pressure (BP), heart rate, and blood glucose levels; sweating; and dilation of the pupils and lung bronchioles.

- Parasympathetic nervous system (PNS): The PNS is considered the "resting and digestion system" because its primary function is conserving body energy by maintaining body activities at baseline levels. The PNS is responsible for digestive tract motility, smooth muscle activity associated with urination and defecation, pupil constriction, and gland secretion.

Types of Muscle

Smooth Muscle has spindle-shaped fibers that are shorter and narrower than skeletal muscle fibers. Smooth muscle fibers only contain one nucleus and do not have striations. Sheets of these muscle fibers form the walls of blood vessels and the hollow organs of the urinary, digestive, respiratory, and reproductive tracts. The contraction and relaxation of smooth muscle is responsible for peristalsis, which moves substances through the digestive tract

Cardiac Muscle is only located in the wall of the heart. The contraction of this muscle pumps blood.

Skeletal Muscle is primarily used in the movement of bones at joints and for maintaining posture.

Muscle Fiber Types

Type I muscle fibers: Also known as slow-twitch muscle fibers (slow-oxidative fibers), metabolically, these fibers have a large capacity for aerobic energy supply and are relatively resistant to fatigue. Type I fibers have a limited ability to rapidly generate force because of their low anaerobic capacity and low myosin ATPase activity. Compared to type II fibers, type I muscle fibers have slower calcium-handling abilities, contract more slowly, have reduced glycolytic capacity, and they have numerous and relatively large mitochondria. Type I muscle fibers play an important role in endurance sports that rely on a sustained energy supply, such as long-distance running (e.g., 5,000 meters, marathon), soccer, cross-country skiing, and distance cycling and swimming.

Type IIa muscle fibers: Also known as fast-twitch muscle fibers, these fibers are energy inefficient, easily fatigable, and have low aerobic power. Type IIa fibers have a moderate capacity for both anaerobic and aerobic energy production. These fibers can be classified as fast-oxidative/glycolytic fibers, and they can rapidly generate force due to high myosin ATPase activity and anaerobic power. Type IIa fibers are surrounded by a greater number of capillaries than type IIx fibers, allowing for greater aerobic metabolism.

Type IIx muscle fibers: Also a type of fast-twitch muscle fiber (sometimes called type IIb fibers), type IIx fibers have less capacity for aerobic energy production, making them more fatigable than type IIa fibers. Type IIx fibers, considered to be fast-glycolytic (FG) fibers, have the greatest capacity for anaerobic energy production and the fastest shortening velocity, so they can generate significant force.

Note that many sports (e.g., rowing, tennis, boxing, wrestling, soccer) require both type I and type II muscle fibers.

Types of Musculature Structures

Skeletal muscles vary in shape and function because of the various arrangements of the muscle fascicles. The table below provides the name of the fascicular arrangements, the structure of the fascicles, and an example of a muscle having each fascicular arrangement.

Name of Fascicular Arrangement	Structure of Fascicular Arrangement	Muscle Example
Circular	Fascicles are arranged in a concentric ring	Obicularis oris (muscles surrounding mouth)
Convergent (sometimes called radiate)	Muscle has a broad origin and is fan- or triangular-shaped	Pectoralis major; gluteus medius
Parallel/longitudinal	Long axis of fascicles is parallel to long axis of muscle.	Rectus abdominis
Unipennate	Short fascicles insert obliquely into only one side of tendon	Extensor digitorum longus; tibialis posterior
Bipennate	Fascicles insert into opposite sides of one central tendon	Rectus femoris
Multipennate	Tendon branches within the muscle	Deltoid
Fusiform	Spindle-shaped muscles	Biceps brachii

Here's an illustration of this:

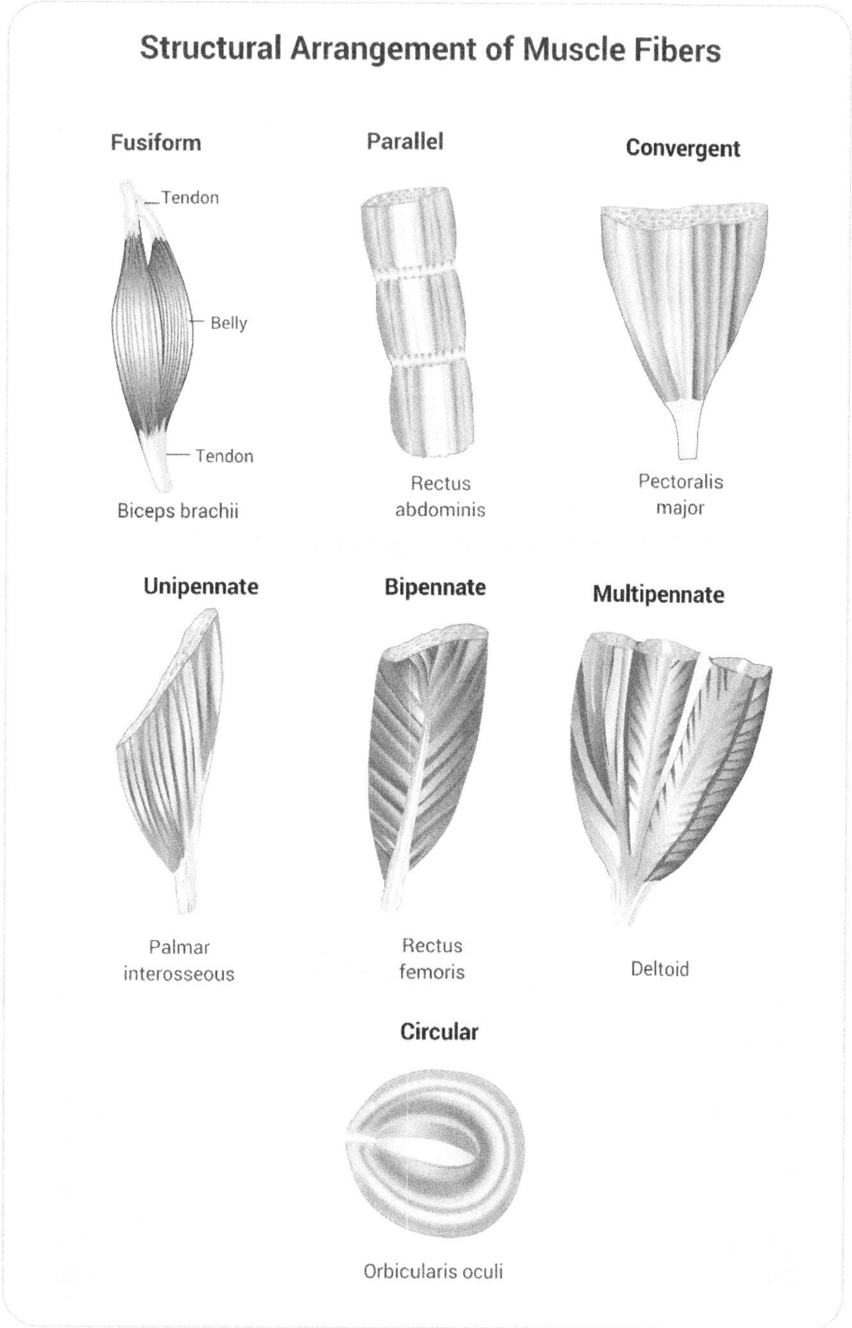

Structural Arrangement of Muscle Fibers

Fusiform
Tendon
Belly
Tendon
Biceps brachii

Parallel
Rectus abdominis

Convergent
Pectoralis major

Unipennate
Palmar interosseous

Bipennate
Rectus femoris

Multipennate
Deltoid

Circular
Orbicularis oculi

Neuromuscular Responses to Exercise

Motor Unit Recruitment Patterns

Motor units contain only one type of muscle fiber (i.e., type I, type IIa, type IIx). The ability to produce force is a requirement in all sport activities. There are two ways that motor units modulate force production: summation and size principle.

Summation

Summation is dependent upon how frequently motor units are activated. A single activation will cause a minimal muscle twitch with little force production, but if that motor unit continues to be activated at a greater frequency, there can be a summative effect of these twitches, resulting in greater force production.

Size Principle

The second method used to modulate force production is dependent upon how many motor units are activated. If greater force is needed for an activity, more motor units will be recruited. This phenomenon, called the *size principle*, describes the interrelationship between force, motor unit recruitment thresholds, and firing rates. The smallest motor units are recruited first, and as more force is needed, larger motor units (that innervate more muscle fibers) are activated. Ascending recruitment of smaller to larger motor units allows the continuum of low- to high-force production and smooth muscle movements when force changes, while conserving energy.

Selective Recruitment

This is an exception to the size principle. Under some circumstances, trained clients can inhibit the activation of small motor units. This allows larger motor units to be activated immediately when rapid force production (e.g., vertical jump) is needed.

Nerve Conduction

When the electrical nerve impulse from the motor neuron arrives at the motor junction, ACh is released, converting the impulse into a chemical stimulus. This generates an action potential—a wave of depolarization—that travels the length of the muscle fiber through the T-tubules, causing the release of Ca^{2+}, which initiates the series of events leading to the contractile movement of the actin and myosin filaments.

Electromyography (EMG)

Surface and intramuscular EMG is used to assess the quality and quantity of the electrical activity within skeletal muscles resulting from neural activation by motor units. Greater neural activation is implicated when there is an increase in EMG signal.

Skeletal System Structure and Function

The skeletal system consists of the 206 bones that make up the skeleton, as well as the cartilage, ligaments, and other connective tissues that stabilize them. Bone is made of collagen fibers and calcium inorganic minerals, mostly in the form of hydroxyapatite, calcium carbonate, and phosphate salts. The inorganic minerals are strong but brittle, and the collagen fibers are weak but flexible, so the combination makes bone resistant to shattering. There are two types of bone: compact and spongy. Compact bone has a basic functional unit, called the Haversian system. Osteocytes, or bone cells, are arranged in concentric circles around a central canal, called the Haversian canal, which contains blood vessels. While Haversian canals run parallel to the surface of the bone, perforating canals, also known as the canals of Volkmann, run perpendicularly between the central canal and the surface of the bone. The concentric circles of bone tissue that surround the central canal within the Haversian system are called lamellae.

The spaces that are found between the lamellae are called lacunae. The Haversian system is a reservoir for calcium and phosphorus for blood. Spongy bone, in contrast to compact bone, is lightweight and porous. It has a branching network of parallel lamellae, called trabeculae. Although spongy bone forms an open framework inside the compact bone, it is still quite strong. Different bones have different ratios of compact-to-spongy bone, depending on their functions. The outside of the bone is covered by a periosteum, which has four major functions. It isolates and protects bones from the surrounding tissue; provides a place for attachment of the circulatory and nervous system structures; participates in growth and repair of the bone; and attaches the bone to the deep fascia. An endosteum is found inside the bone, covers the trabeculae of the spongy bone and lines the inner surfaces of the central canals.

One major function of the skeletal system is to provide structural support for the entire body. It provides a framework for the soft tissues and organs to attach to. The skeletal system also provides a reserve of important nutrients, such as calcium and lipids. Normal concentrations of calcium and phosphate in body fluids are partly maintained by the calcium salts stored in bone. Lipids that are stored in yellow bone marrow can be used as a source of energy. Yellow bone marrow also produces some white blood cells. Red bone marrow produces red blood cells, most white blood cells, and platelets that circulate in the blood. Certain groups of bones form protective barriers around delicate organs. The ribs, for example, protect the heart and lungs, the skull encloses the brain, and the vertebrae cover the spinal cord.

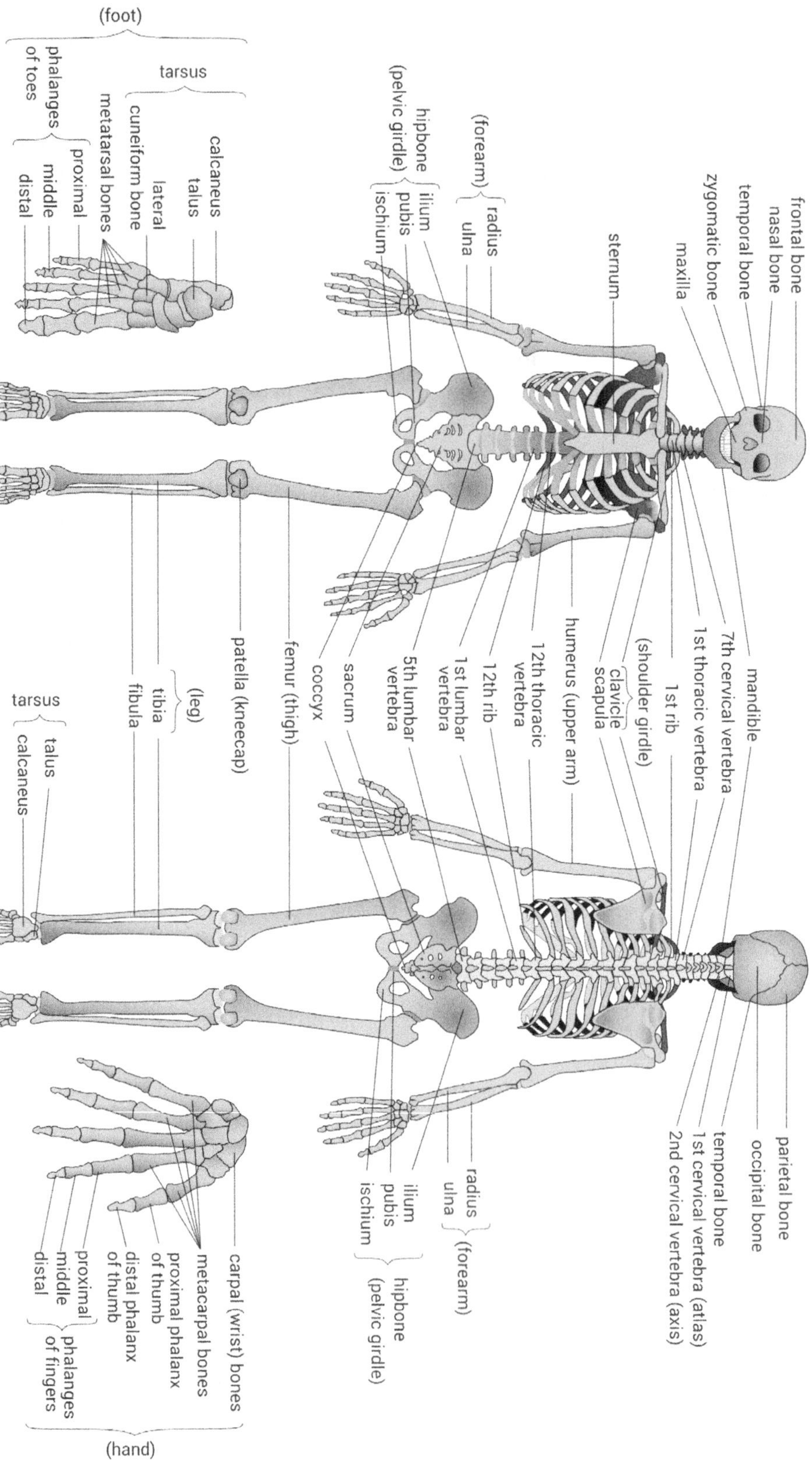

frontal bone
nasal bone
temporal bone
zygomatic bone
maxilla
sternum
(forearm) radius
ulna
hipbone (pelvic girdle) ilium
pubis
ischium
(foot)
tarsus
calcaneus
talus
lateral
cuneiform bone
metatarsal bones
phalanges of toes
proximal
middle
distal
mandible
7th cervical vertebra
1st thoracic vertebra
1st rib
(shoulder girdle) clavicle
scapula
humerus (upper arm)
12th thoracic vertebra
12th rib
1st lumbar vertebra
5th lumbar vertebra
sacrum
coccyx
femur (thigh)
patella (kneecap)
(leg) tibia
fibula
tarsus
talus
calcaneus
parietal bone
occipital bone
temporal bone
1st cervical vertebra (atlas)
2nd cervical vertebra (axis)
radius
ulna
(forearm)
ilium
pubis
ischium
hipbone (pelvic girdle)
carpal (wrist) bones
metacarpal bones
proximal phalanx of thumb
distal phalanx of thumb
proximal
middle
distal
phalanges of fingers
(hand)

Bone and Connective Tissue Anatomy

Bones

The human skeleton has approximately 206 bones and these bones provide protection and support for the body. Bones can be divided into the *axial* (skull, vertebral column, sternum, and ribs) and *appendicular* (the right and left clavicle and scapula and the left and right bones of the arm, forearm, and hand; the left and right coaxial and the left and right bones of the leg and foot) *skeletons.* Bones consist of varying amounts of spongy (*trabecular*) and compact (*cortical*) bone. A shell of dense cortical bone surrounds interlocking columns of trabecular bone called osteons. Bone marrow – composed of adipose tissue, vasculature, and the manufacturing site of blood vessels – occupies the space between the trabeculae and blood vessels and extends from the marrow cavity to cortical bone. *Bone periosteum*, connective tissue that covers all bones, is attached to tendons.

Collagen

Collagen is the primary structural component of all connective tissue. Bones, ligaments, and tendons are Type I collagen, and cartilage is composed of Type 2 collagen. Both types of collagen are formed from procollagen molecules, which consist of three protein strands in a triple helix formation. An enzyme produces active collagen, which aligns with other collagen molecules to form long filaments that are the components of microfibrils that form bundles as bone grows. The strength and durability of collagen stems from strong cross-linking bonds, formed between adjacent collagen bundles. The longitudinal grouping of these bundles together forms ligaments and tendons. The bundles can also be arranged in layered sheets of varying directions, as found in fascia, bone, and cartilage.

Tendons and Ligaments

Tendons are fibrous connective tissue connecting muscle to the periosteum of bone. Muscle contractions pull the tendon, causing the attached bone to move. Ligaments are fibrous connective tissue connecting bone to bone. Ligaments contain elastin, a type of elastic protein that provides the stretch needed for normal joint movement. Tendons and ligaments contain relatively few cells that require little oxygen and nutrients for metabolic activity. Because of the limited vasculature and circulation in tendons, regeneration after injury takes a significant amount of time and is sometimes not possible without surgical intervention.

Bone and Connective Tissue Responses to Exercise and Training

Bone

Anaerobic Training

Minimal essential strain (MES) is the stimulus threshold required to initiate new bone growth. Anaerobic training can stimulate bone growth and should utilize specificity of loading and progressive overload to do so. Specificity of loading requires the use of specific movement patterns and exercises that directly load the targeted growth region of the client's skeleton. Exercises should involve multiple joints and apply increasingly heavier external loads. The anaerobic exercise components of mechanical load that stimulate bone growth are the intensity of the load, the speed of loading, the direction of the force, and the volume of the loading. Bone deposition follows Wolff's Law, which states that bone remodels according to the forces placed upon it; if forces are sufficient in intensity and frequency, bones become stronger, building additional matrix and mineralization. The inverse is also true that if there is not enough strain and physical resistance to bones, they atrophy and thin with disuse.

Aerobic Training
Aerobic programs that stimulate bone growth must be high-intensity weight-bearing activities (e.g., running, aerobics). The intensity of activity has to increase progressively to ensure continual overload of the bone. Because bone responds to the intensity and rate of external loading, when it is no longer possible to increase activity intensity, increasing the rate of the limb movement is required. This can be achieved with high-intensity interval training (HIIT).

Connective Tissue

Anaerobic Training
High-intensity anaerobic training causes connective tissue growth and structural changes. Increased enzyme activity, due to anaerobic training, results in the formation of collagen that aligns with other collagen molecules to form long filaments. Specific changes within a tendon include an increase in collagen fibril diameter, number, and packing density. These adaptations increase the tensional forces that the tendon can withstand. Anaerobic training increases tendon stiffness, which is directly associated with muscular recoil and power production – an important component of performance in some sports.

Aerobic Training
Similar to bone, aerobic exercise intensity that exceeds the strain put on connective tissue during normal activities is required for connective tissue changes to occur.

Endocrine System Structure and Function

The endocrine system is made of the ductless tissues and glands that secrete hormones into the interstitial fluids of the body. Interstitial fluid is the solution that surrounds tissue cells within the body. This system works closely with the nervous system to regulate the physiological activities of the other systems of the body to maintain homeostasis. While the nervous system provides quick, short-term responses to stimuli, the endocrine system acts by releasing hormones into the bloodstream that get distributed to the whole body. The response is slow but long-lasting, ranging from a few hours to a few weeks.

Hormones are chemical substances that change the metabolic activity of tissues and organs. While regular metabolic reactions are controlled by enzymes, hormones can change the type, activity, or quantity of the enzymes involved in the reaction. They bind to specific cells and start a biochemical chain of events that changes the enzymatic activity. Hormones can regulate development and growth, digestive metabolism, mood, and body temperature, among other things. Often small amounts of hormone will lead to large changes in the body.

The endocrine system has the following major glands:

- Hypothalamus: A part of the brain, the hypothalamus connects the nervous system to the endocrine system via the pituitary gland. Although it is considered part of the nervous system, it plays a dual role in regulating endocrine organs.

- Pituitary Gland: A pea-sized gland found at the bottom of the hypothalamus. It has two lobes, called the anterior and posterior lobes. It plays an important role in regulating the function of other endocrine glands. The hormones released control growth, blood pressure, certain

functions of the sex organs, salt concentration of the kidneys, internal temperature regulation, and pain relief.

- Thyroid Gland: This gland releases hormones, such as thyroxine, that are important for metabolism, growth and development, temperature regulation, and brain development during infancy and childhood. Thyroid hormones also monitor the amount of circulating calcium in the body.
- Parathyroid Glands: These are four pea-sized glands located on the posterior surface of the thyroid. The main hormone secreted is called parathyroid hormone (PTH) and helps with the thyroid's regulation of calcium in the body.
- Thymus Gland: The thymus is located in the chest cavity, embedded in connective tissue. It produces several hormones important for development and maintenance of normal immunological defenses. One hormone promotes the development and maturation of lymphocytes, which strengthens the immune system.
- Adrenal Gland: One adrenal gland is attached to the top of each kidney. It produces adrenaline and is responsible for the "fight or flight" reactions in the face of danger or stress. The hormones epinephrine and norepinephrine cooperate to regulate states of arousal.
- Pancreas: The pancreas is an organ that has both endocrine and exocrine functions. The endocrine functions are controlled by the pancreatic islets of Langerhans, which are groups of beta cells scattered throughout the gland that secrete insulin to lower blood sugar levels in the body. Neighboring alpha cells secrete glucagon to raise blood sugar.
- Pineal Gland: The pineal gland secretes melatonin, a hormone derived from the neurotransmitter serotonin. Melatonin can slow the maturation of sperm, oocytes, and reproductive organs. It also regulates the body's circadian rhythm, which is the natural awake/asleep cycle. It also serves an important role in protecting the CNS tissues from neural toxins.
- Testes and Ovaries: These glands secrete testosterone and estrogen, respectively, and are responsible for secondary sex characteristics, as well as reproduction.

Neuroendocrine Physiology

The organs and glands of the *endocrine system* release hormones that regulate physiological processes and maintain homeostasis when the body is confronted with external stimuli or environmental stressors such as altitude or exercise. The endocrine system releases hormones that regulate blood glucose levels, metabolism, tissue growth, recovery, reproduction, and mood. *Neuroendocrine physiology* refers to the interaction between the nervous and endocrine systems whereby hormones are released from glands receiving direct neural stimulation.

Functions of Hormones

Hormones are chemical messengers or signaling molecules produced by endocrine glands and other specific cells, which are created, stored, and released into the blood to stimulate specific physiological responses. Hormones are classified into three categories. Fat-soluble *steroid hormones* (e.g., cortisol, testosterone) passively diffuse across cell membranes and are responsible for primary and secondary sex characteristics, and are involved in metabolic control, immunity, fluid balance, and inflammation. *Polypeptide hormones* (e.g., insulin, growth hormones) are made of chains of amino acids inside the nucleus of cells. Because they are not fat-soluble, they serve as secondary messengers, signaling other hormones and hormonal cascades. *Amine hormones* consist of the amino acids tyrosine (e.g., dopamine, norepinephrine, epinephrine) and tryptophan (e.g., serotonin). Amine hormones bind to membrane receptors and work via secondary messengers. Hormones can also be categorized into *anabolic* and *catabolic*, where anabolic hormones promote tissue building and catabolic ones break down cellular components.

How Hormones Work

The *lock and key principle* refers to a binding mechanism of hormones and enzymes where the hormone receptor site has a specific structure that allows a single hormone to bind to the site, similar to a key fitting one specific lock. This principle is a simplistic view of hormone binding that does not take into account cross-reactivity, allosteric binding sites, or the need for the aggregation of several linked hormones to produce the optimal signal. *Cross-reactivity* occurs when a hormone fits the receptor but needs to interact with other hormones to produce a response. Some receptors have *allosteric binding sites* where substances other than the specific hormone can increase or decrease the response to the primary hormone via feedback loops.

Anabolic Hormones

Testosterone, growth hormone, and insulin-like growth factors are the primary anabolic hormones involved in muscle remodeling and growth.

Testosterone: Testosterone is the primary androgen (male sex hormone) in human physiology. Both males and females are affected by testosterone, although males have significantly higher levels of testosterone. Testosterone increases protein synthesis and the rate of cellular metabolism and red blood cell production. Testosterone is produced by the testes in males and the ovaries and adrenal glands in females.

Growth Hormone: The anterior pituitary gland secretes growth hormone, which has a significant influence on metabolism and energy availability. It is responsible for increasing the uptake of amino acids into skeletal muscle, and for increasing protein synthesis, facilitating the growth of Type I and Type II muscle fibers. Growth hormone has numerous other roles including decreasing glucose utilization and glycogen synthesis, increasing the availability of glucose and amino acids, increasing collagen synthesis and cartilage growth, and enhancing immune cell function.

Insulin-Like Growth Factors (IGFs): The majority of the growth-promoting effects of growth hormone are indirectly controlled by IGFs. These growth-promoting proteins are produced by skeletal muscle, bone, the liver, and other tissues. IGFs stimulate the uptake of amino acids from the blood to be used for cellular proteins and the uptake of sulfur needed for the cartilage matrix.

Adrenal Hormones

Hormones produced by the adrenal gland play a critical role in the fight-or-flight response and are also responsive to exercise stress. Cortisol and catecholamines are the adrenal hormones that are most important in exercise training.

Cortisol: Cortisol, a glucocorticoid secreted by the adrenal cortex, is a catabolic hormone in skeletal muscle; however, its principle role is to ensure that energy is available. It is a primary signaling hormone for carbohydrate metabolism and is associated with the storage of glycogen in muscle tissue. Cortisol increases the production of glucose in the liver and glycogen production in skeletal muscles. Overtraining can cause chronically high levels of cortisol, which can result in loss of strength and lean muscle mass.

Catecholamines: Epinephrine, norepinephrine, and dopamine are secreted by the adrenal medulla and have a significant role in many physiological functions. In muscle, epinephrine and norepinephrine increase muscle blood flow due to vasodilation, elevate blood pressure (BP), increase the rate of muscle contraction, increase energy availability, enhance metabolic enzyme activity, and increase testosterone secretion rates.

Neuroendocrine Responses to Exercise and Training

Anaerobic Responses

During anaerobic training, hormones have a variety of regulatory roles that impact homeostatic mechanisms tasked with keeping functions of the body within normal ranges during exercise and rest. There are four primary endocrine responses to anaerobic training:

1. Acute anabolic hormone responses to anaerobic exercise are crucial for both exercise performance and the resultant training adaptations. For up to 30 minutes after anaerobic resistance training, testosterone, growth hormone, and cortisol concentrations are elevated. Such changes generally occur rapidly and are quickly stabilized as the body responds to the homeostatic challenges associated with acute and long-term exercise training. Hormone levels are elevated most with resistance exercises that utilize large muscle groups or with moderate- to high-volume and -intensity exercises are combined with short rest intervals. The demands of acute anaerobic exercise cause increases in the concentration of catecholamines. Increased catecholamine concentrations are associated with the regulation of force production, energy availability, the rate of muscle contraction, and increased concentrations of testosterone and other hormones.

2. Chronic changes in acute hormonal responses: When a client participates in a long-term resistance training program, changes in endocrine function correspond to the increased exercise stress that the body is capable of handling. It is thought that any chronic adaptations in hormonal response patterns to acute anaerobic exercise may enhance the client's ability to handle and maintain higher-resistance exercise intensities for longer time periods.

3. Chronic changes in resting hormone concentrations after anaerobic exercise have not consistently been found with growth hormone, testosterone, or insulin-like growth factor. Resting-state hormone concentrations likely reflect factors such as muscle tissue response to intensity or volume changes in the resistance training program. The elevated concentrations of hormones after resistance training are great enough to influence muscle tissue remodeling, so increased resting concentrations of hormones are not necessary to facilitate training adaptations. Chronically high levels of anabolic steroids can be detrimental, causing downregulation (i.e., decreased number of receptors on target cell surface) of hormone receptors. Clients using such performance enhancers try to combat this by cycling the drugs.

4. Hormone receptor changes have been shown to occur in response to resistance training. For example, androgen receptors seem to be upregulated within 48-72 hours after training. Changes in receptors mediate adaptations stimulated by hormonal responses.

Clients can use resistance training to manipulate the endocrine system response and enhance training adaptations. For example, increasing the number of muscle fibers recruited for a resistance exercise increases the potential remodeling of the entire muscle.

Additionally, acute increases in serum testosterone concentrations can be achieved by using the following methods individually or in combination:

- Perform exercises such as squats, dead lift, and power clean, which target large muscles.
- Use heavy resistance loads that are 85-95% of one-repetition maximum (1RM).
- Performing multiple exercises or multiple sets to achieve moderate- to high-volume.
- Utilize short rest intervals of 30-60 seconds.

Growth hormone concentration levels can be increased acutely using one or both following training methods:

- Perform three sets of each exercise at high intensity with short (i.e., 1-minute) rest periods.
- Consume carbohydrates and protein before and after resistance training sessions.

Optimization of adrenal hormone responses can be achieved by the following method:

- Perform high-volume resistance exercises that utilize large muscles combined with short rest periods. This causes the body to experience adrenergic stress. Note that adequate rest and a varied training protocol should be utilized to avoid this stress leading to nonfunctional overreaching or overtraining.

Aerobic Responses

High-intensity aerobic training enhances the secretion of hormones in response to maximal aerobic exercise. This response likely improves the client's ability to handle and maintain high aerobic exercise intensities over long periods of time.

Circulatory System Structure and Function

The circulatory system is a network of organs and tubes that transport blood, hormones, nutrients, oxygen, and other gases to cells and tissues throughout the body. It is also known as the cardiovascular system. The major components of the circulatory system are the blood vessels, blood, and heart.

Blood Vessels

In the circulatory system, blood vessels are responsible for transporting blood throughout the body. The three major types of blood vessels in the circulatory system are arteries, veins, and capillaries. Arteries carry blood from the heart to the rest of the body. Veins carry blood from the body back to the heart. Capillaries connect arteries to veins and form networks that exchange materials between the blood and the cells.

In general, arteries are stronger and thicker than veins, as they withstand high pressures exerted by the blood as the heart pumps it through the body. Arteries control blood flow through either

vasoconstriction (narrowing of the blood vessel's diameter) or vasodilation (widening of the blood vessel's diameter). The blood in veins is under much lower pressures, so veins have valves to prevent the backflow of blood.

Most of the exchange between the blood and tissues takes place through the capillaries. There are three types of capillaries: continuous, fenestrated, and sinusoidal.

Continuous capillaries are made up of epithelial cells tightly connected together. As a result, they limit the types of materials that pass into and out of the blood. Continuous capillaries are the most common type of capillary. Fenestrated capillaries have openings that allow materials to be freely exchanged between the blood and tissues. They are commonly found in the digestive, endocrine, and urinary systems. Sinusoidal capillaries have larger openings and allow proteins and blood cells through. They are found primarily in the liver, bone marrow, and spleen.

Blood

Blood is vital to the human body. It is a liquid connective tissue that serves as a transport system for supplying cells with nutrients and carrying away their wastes. The average adult human has five to six quarts of blood circulating through their body. Approximately 55% of blood is plasma (the fluid portion), and the remaining 45% is composed of solid cells and cell parts.

There are three major types of blood cells:

- Red blood cells, or erythrocytes, transport oxygen throughout the body. They contain a protein called hemoglobin that allows them to carry oxygen. The iron in the hemoglobin gives the cells and the blood their red colors.
- White blood cells, or leukocytes, are responsible for fighting infectious diseases and maintaining the immune system. There are five types of white blood cells: neutrophils, lymphocytes, eosinophils, monocytes, and basophils.
- Platelets are cell fragments that play a central role in the blood clotting process.

All blood cells in adults are produced in the bone marrow—red blood cells and most white blood cells are produced in the red marrow, and some white blood cells are produced in the yellow bone marrow.

Heart

The heart is a two-part, muscular pump that forcefully pushes blood throughout the human body. The human heart has four chambers—two upper atria and two lower ventricles separated by a partition called the septum. There is a pair on the left and a pair on the right. Anatomically, *left* and *right* correspond to the sides of the body that the patient themselves would refer to as left and right.

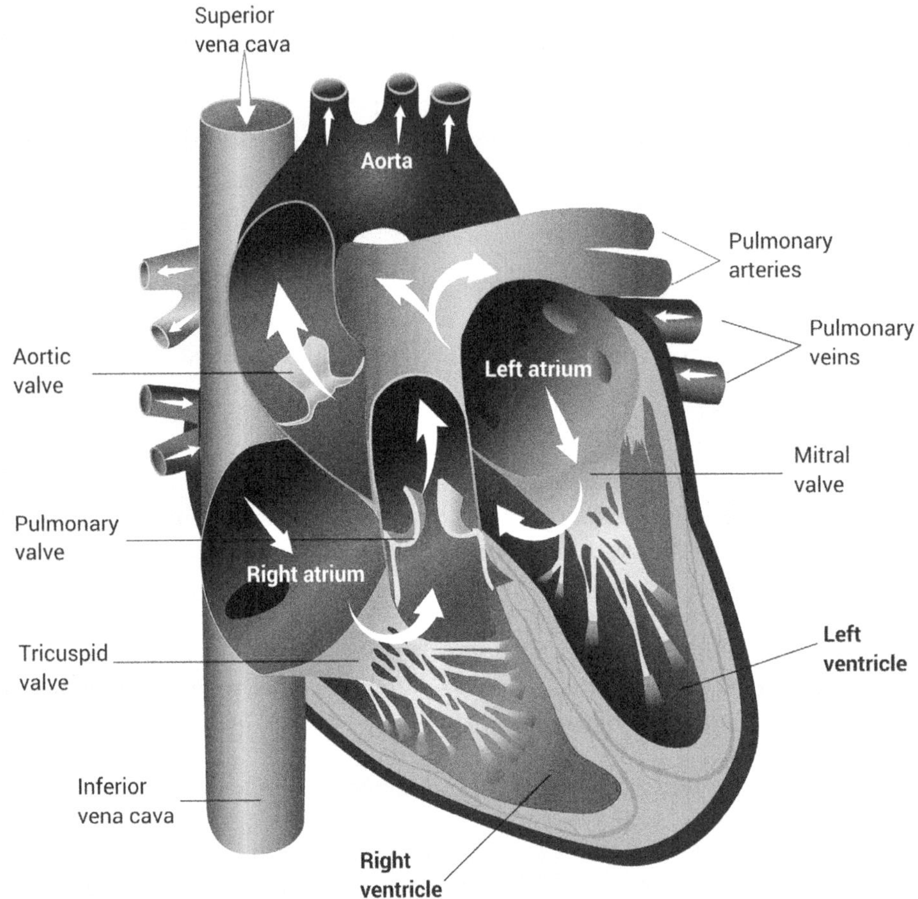

Four valves help to section off the chambers from one another. Between the right atrium and ventricle, the three flaps of the tricuspid valve keep blood from flowing backwards from the ventricle to the atrium, similar to how the two flaps of the mitral valve work between the left atrium and ventricle. As these two valves lie between an atrium and a ventricle, they are referred to as atrioventricular (AV) valves. The other two valves are semilunar (SL) and control blood flow into the two great arteries leaving the ventricles. The pulmonary valve connects the right ventricle to the pulmonary artery, while the aortic valve connects the left ventricle to the aorta.

Cardiac Cycle

A cardiac cycle is one complete sequence of cardiac activity. The cardiac cycle represents the relaxation and contraction of the heart and can be divided into two phases: diastole and systole.

Diastole is the phase during which the heart relaxes and fills with blood. It gives rise to the diastolic blood pressure (DBP), which is the bottom number of a blood pressure reading. Systole is the phase during which the heart contracts and discharges blood. It gives rise to the systolic blood pressure (SBP), which is the top number of a blood pressure reading. The heart's electrical conduction system coordinates the cardiac cycle.

Types of Circulation

Five major blood vessels manage blood flow to and from the heart: the superior vena cava and inferior vena cava, the aorta, the pulmonary artery, and the pulmonary vein.

The superior vena cava is a large vein that drains blood from the head and the upper body. The inferior vena cava is a large vein that drains blood from the lower body. The aorta is the largest artery in the human body and carries blood from the heart to body tissues. The pulmonary arteries carry blood from the heart to the lungs. The pulmonary veins transport blood from the lungs to the heart.

In the human body, there are two types of circulation: pulmonary circulation and systemic circulation. Pulmonary circulation supplies blood to the lungs. Deoxygenated blood enters the right atrium of the heart and is routed through the tricuspid valve into the right ventricle. Deoxygenated blood then travels from the right ventricle of the heart through the pulmonary valve and into the pulmonary arteries. The pulmonary arteries carry the deoxygenated blood to the lungs. In the lungs, oxygen is absorbed, and carbon dioxide is released. The pulmonary veins carry oxygenated blood to the left atrium of the heart.

Systemic circulation supplies blood to all other parts of the body, except the lungs. Oxygenated blood flows from the left atrium of the heart through the mitral, or bicuspid, valve into the left ventricle of the heart. Oxygenated blood is then routed from the left ventricle of the heart through the aortic valve and into the aorta. The aorta delivers blood to the systemic arteries, which supply the body tissues. In the tissues, oxygen and nutrients are exchanged for carbon dioxide and other wastes. The deoxygenated blood along with carbon dioxide and wastes enter the systemic veins, where they are returned to the right atrium of the heart via the superior and inferior vena cava.

Respiratory System Structure and Function

The respiratory system mediates the exchange of gas between the air and the blood, mainly through the act of breathing. This system is divided into the upper respiratory system and the lower respiratory system. The upper system comprises the nose, the nasal cavity and sinuses, and the pharynx. The lower respiratory system comprises the larynx (voice box), the trachea (windpipe), the small passageways leading to the lungs, and the lungs. The upper respiratory system is responsible for filtering, warming, and humidifying the air that gets passed to the lower respiratory system, protecting the lower respiratory system's more delicate tissue surfaces. The process of breathing in is referred to as *inspiration* while the process of breathing out is referred to as *expiration*.

The Lungs

Bronchi are tubes that lead from the trachea to each lung and are lined with cilia and mucus that collect dust and germs along the way. The bronchi, which carry air into the lungs, branch into bronchioles and continue to divide into smaller and smaller passageways, until they become alveoli, which are the smallest passages. Most of the gas exchange in the lungs occurs between the blood-filled pulmonary capillaries and the air-filled alveoli. Within the lungs, oxygen and carbon dioxide are exchanged between the air in the alveoli and the blood in the pulmonary capillaries. Oxygen-rich blood returns to the heart and is pumped through the systemic circuit. Carbon dioxide-rich air is exhaled from the body. Together, the lungs contain approximately 1,500 miles of airway passages, and this extremely high amount is due to the enormous amount of branching.

Breathing is possible due to the muscular diaphragm pulling on the lungs, increasing their volume and decreasing their pressure. Air flows from the external high-pressure system to the low-pressure system inside the lungs. When breathing out, the diaphragm releases its pressure difference, decreases the lung volume, and forces the stale air back out.

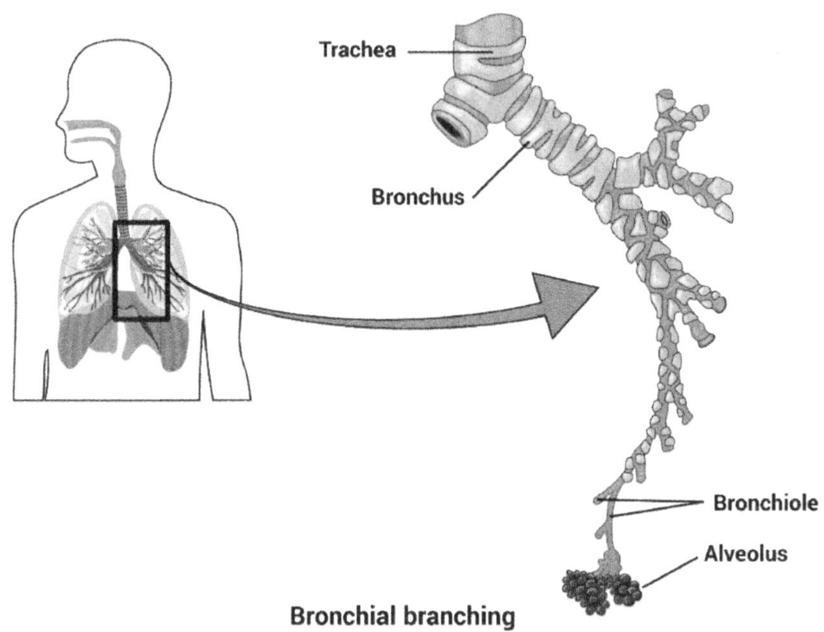

Bronchial branching

Functions of the Respiratory System

The respiratory system has many functions. Most importantly, it provides a large area for gas exchange between the air and the circulating blood. It protects the delicate respiratory surfaces from environmental variations and defends them against pathogens. It is responsible for producing the sounds that the body makes for speaking and singing, as well as for non-verbal communication. It also helps regulate blood volume and blood pressure by releasing vasopressin, and it is a regulator of blood pH due to its control over carbon dioxide release, as the aqueous form of carbon dioxide is the chief buffering agent in blood.

Digestive System Structure and Function

The human body relies completely on the digestive system to meet its nutritional needs. After food and drink are ingested, the digestive system breaks them down into their component nutrients and absorbs them so that the circulatory system can transport the nutrients to other cells to use for growth, energy, and cell repair. These nutrients may be classified as proteins, lipids, carbohydrates, vitamins, and minerals.

The digestive system is thought of chiefly in two parts: the digestive tract (also called the alimentary tract or gastrointestinal tract) and the accessory digestive organs. The digestive tract is the pathway in which food is ingested, digested, absorbed, and excreted. It is composed of the mouth, pharynx, esophagus, stomach, small and large intestines, rectum, and anus. *Peristalsis*, or wave-like contractions of smooth muscle, moves food and wastes through the digestive tract. The accessory digestive organs are the salivary glands, liver, gallbladder, and pancreas.

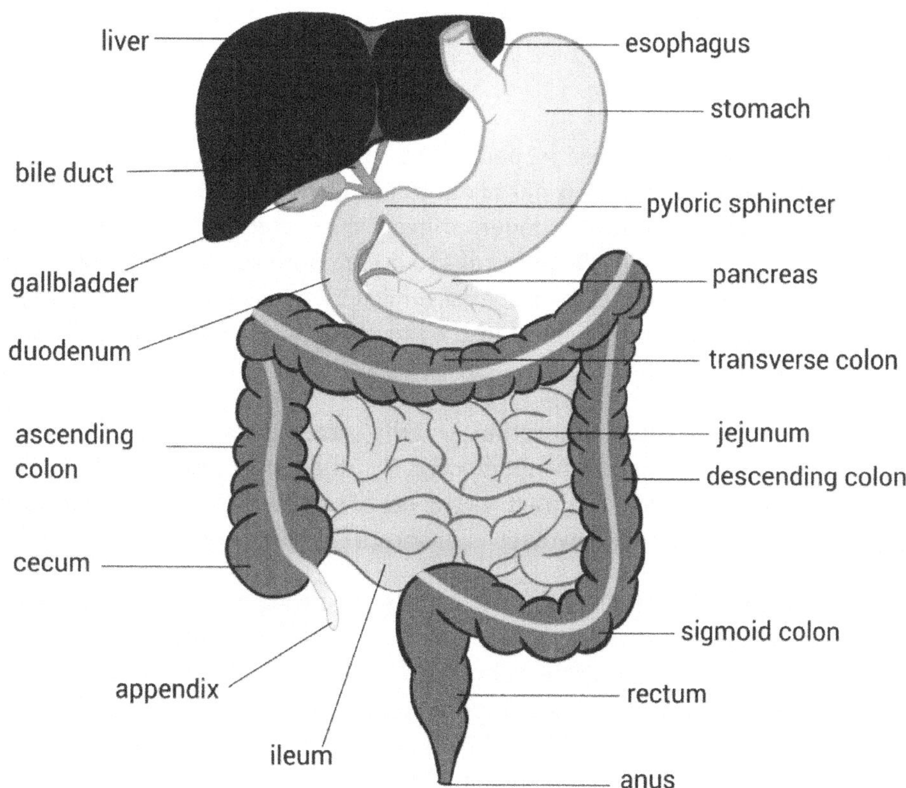

Mouth and Stomach

The mouth is the entrance to the digestive system. Here, the mechanical and chemical digestion of the food begins. The food is chewed mechanically by the teeth and shaped into a *bolus* by the tongue so that it can be more easily swallowed by the esophagus. The food also becomes more watery and pliable with the addition of saliva secreted from the salivary glands, the largest of which are the parotid glands. The glands also secrete amylase in the saliva, an enzyme which begins chemical digestion and breakdown of the carbohydrates and sugars in the food.

The food then moves through the pharynx and down the muscular esophagus to the stomach.

The stomach is a large, muscular sac-like organ at the distal end of the esophagus. Here, the bolus is subjected to more mechanical and chemical digestion. As it passes through the stomach, it is physically squeezed and crushed while additional secretions turn it into a watery nutrient-filled liquid that exits into the small intestine as *chyme*.

The stomach secretes many substances into the *lumen* of the digestive tract. Some cells produce gastrin, a hormone that prompts other cells in the stomach to secrete a gastric acid composed mostly of hydrochloric acid (HCl). The HCl is at such a high concentration and low pH that it denatures most proteins and degrades a lot of organic matter. The stomach also secretes mucous to form a protective film that keeps the corrosive acid from dissolving its own cells; gaps in this mucous layer can lead to peptic ulcers. Finally, the stomach also uses digestive enzymes like proteases and lipases to break down proteins and fats; although there are some gastric lipases here, the stomach mostly breaks down proteins.

Small Intestine

The chyme from the stomach enters the first part of the small intestine, the *duodenum*, through the *pyloric sphincter*, and its extreme acidity is partly neutralized by sodium bicarbonate secreted along with mucous. The presence of chyme in the duodenum triggers the secretion of the hormones secretin and cholecystokinin (CCK). Secretin acts on the pancreas to dump more sodium bicarbonate into the small intestine so that the pH is kept at a reasonable level, while CCK acts on the gallbladder to release the *bile* that it has been storing. Bile, a substance produced by the liver and stored in the gallbladder, helps to emulsify or dissolve fats and lipids.

Because of the bile, which aids in lipid absorption, and the secreted lipases, which break down fats, the duodenum is the chief site of fat digestion in the body. The duodenum also represents the last major site of chemical digestion in the digestive tract, as the other two sections of the small intestine (the *jejunum* and *ileum*) are instead heavily involved in absorption of nutrients.

The small intestine reaches 40 feet in length, and its cells are arranged in small finger-like projections called villi. This is due to its key role in the absorption of nearly all nutrients from the ingested and digested food, effectively transferring them from the lumen of the GI tract to the bloodstream, where they travel to the cells that need them. These nutrients include simple sugars like glucose from carbohydrates, amino acids from proteins, emulsified fats, electrolytes like sodium and potassium, minerals like iron and zinc, and vitamins like D and B12. Vitamin B12's absorption, though it takes place in the intestines, is actually aided by *intrinsic factor* that was released into the chyme back in the stomach.

Large Intestine

The leftover parts of food that remain unabsorbed or undigested in the lumen of the small intestine next travel through the large intestine, which is also referred to as the large bowel or colon. The large intestine is mainly responsible for water absorption. As the chyme at this stage no longer has any useful nutrients that can be absorbed by the body, it is now referred to as *waste*, and it is stored in the large intestine until it can be excreted from the body. Removing the liquid from the waste transforms it from liquid to solid stool, or feces.

This waste first passes from the small intestine to the cecum, a pouch that forms the first part of the large intestine. In herbivores, it provides a place for bacteria to digest cellulose, but in humans most of it is vestigial and is known as the appendix. The appendix has no known function other than arbitrarily becoming inflamed. From the cecum, waste next travels up the ascending colon, across the transverse colon, down the descending colon, and through the sigmoid colon to the rectum. The rectum is

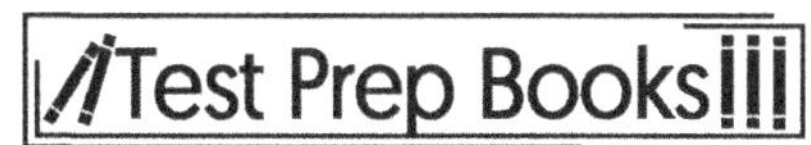

responsible for the final storage of waste before it is expelled through the anus. The anal canal is a small portion of the rectum leading through to the anus and the outside of the body.

Pancreas

The pancreas has endocrine and exocrine functions. The endocrine function works to regulate blood sugar levels. It involves releasing the hormone insulin, which decreases blood sugar (glucose) levels, or glucagon, which increases blood sugar (glucose) levels, directly into the bloodstream. Both hormones are produced in the islets of Langerhans, insulin in the beta cells and glucagon in the alpha cells.

The major part of the gland has an exocrine function, which consists of acinar cells secreting inactive digestive enzymes (zymogens) into the main pancreatic duct. The main pancreatic duct joins the common bile duct, which empties into the small intestine (specifically the duodenum). The digestive enzymes are then activated and take part in the digestion of carbohydrates, proteins, and fats within chyme (the mixture of partially digested food and digestive juices).

Characteristics of the Energy Systems

Bioenergetics

Bioenergetics refers to the flow of energy within a biological system and is primarily focused on how macronutrients, containing chemical energy, from food (i.e., carbohydrates, proteins, fats) are converted into biologically usable forms of energy to perform work.

Catabolism

Catabolism is the process of breaking large molecules into smaller molecules to make energy available to the organism. For example, carbohydrates are catabolized to provide fuel for exercise and normal physiological processes. Catabolism also can involve the breakdown of muscle tissue during periods of heavy training volume, low caloric intake, or high stress.

Anabolism

Anabolism is the process of restructuring or building larger compounds from catabolized materials, such as assembling amino acids into structural proteins, which are needed to maintain homeostasis and to generate new muscle tissue.

Exergonic Reaction

Exergonic reaction are chemical reactions that result in the release of energy from the system, which can then be used to perform work. These reactions are spontaneous and favorable.

Endergonic Reaction

A type of chemical reaction that requires the input of energy. In the body, this energy comes in the form of adenosine triphosphate (ATP). These reactions are not spontaneous and are typically involved with anabolic processes.

Metabolism

Metabolism is the sum total of all catabolic and anabolic reactions occurring in the human body. Essential physiological processes such as muscle growth and hormone balance rely on these reactions and continually occur so that the body can maintain homeostasis. It is possible to evaluate a client's energy expenditure (metabolic rate) and fitness level using direct or indirect calorimetry.

Adenosine Triphosphate (ATP)

ATP is a high-energy molecule used for muscle contractions, movement, and other life-sustaining metabolic processes. ATP is an intermediate molecule (consisting of three primary parts—an adenine, a ribose, and three phosphates in a chain) that allows energy to transfer from exergonic to endergonic and catabolic to anabolic reactions. ATP is generated and replenished in skeletal muscles by three energy systems: phosphagen, glycolytic, and oxidative.

ATP Hydrolysis

Hydrolysis is a general term for any chemical reaction that breaks a chemical bond via the addition of water. ATP hydrolysis splits the ATP molecule into adenosine diphosphate (ADP) and usable energy. The enzyme adenosine triphosphatase (ATPase) is the catalyst for the hydrolysis of ATP. The following equation shows the reactants (left of arrow), enzyme (middle), and products (right of arrow) for ATP hydrolysis:

$$\text{ATP} + \text{H}_2\text{O} \leftarrow \text{ATPASE} \rightarrow \text{ADP} + \text{P}_\text{i} + \text{H}^+ + \text{Energy}$$

Adenosine Diphosphate (ADP)

When ATP undergoes hydrolysis, ADP (containing two phosphate groups), an inorganic phosphate molecule, a hydrogen ion, and free energy are produced.

ATPase

ATPase is the enzyme responsible for catalyzing the breakdown of ATP to ADP. The dephosphorylation reaction results in the release of energy used to carry out other chemical reactions.

Myosin ATPase

Myosin ATPase catalyzes ATP hydrolysis, providing the energy for cross-bridge recycling.

Calcium ATPase

Calcium ATPase is the enzyme that provides the energy used to regulate calcium movement by pumping it into the sarcoplasmic reticulum.

Sodium-Potassium ATPase

This enzyme controls the sodium potassium concentration gradient in the sarcolemma after depolarization to maintain the cellular resting potential. For every two K^+ ions pumped into the cell, there are three NA^+ ions pumped out.

Adenosine Monophosphate (AMP)

AMP results from ADP hydrolysis, which cleaves the second phosphate group, leaving one.

Biological Energy Systems

There are several basic biological energy systems in muscle cells that replace ATP. The phosphagen and glycolytic systems occur in the sarcoplasm and are anaerobic mechanisms, which means that they do not require oxygen. The electron transport chain (ETC) and Krebs cycle are aerobic mechanisms that require oxygen and occur in the mitochondria. The cellular respiration systems act in concert, rather than individually, to provide all required energy during exercise or rest.

Principles of Human Movement Science

Functional Biomechanics

Levers

Levers are rigid or semi-rigid bodies that pivot on a fixed point, or fulcrum, and when F_M is applied (i.e., effort), the lever moves a load (i.e., resistive force [F_r]). Joints act as the body's fulcrums when bones and muscle interact. Muscle contraction provides the force required to move an object against a resistive force. The load consists of the bone, the tissue over the bone, and whatever load is being moved. The three types of levers differ based on the relative position of three elements: F_M, F_r, and the fulcrum. Levers are relevant to sport activities because they allow a specific amount of effort to move a heavier load or to move a load farther or faster than would otherwise be possible. Most muscles in the body operate as third-class levers.

Joints

Joints are the junctions between bones that control movement. *Fibrous joints*, such as those in the skull, allow almost no movement, whereas *cartilaginous joints*, such as intervertebral joints, allow a limited amount of movement. *Synovial joints*, such as the elbow, allow the greatest amount of movement and ROM. Sport and exercise movements primarily occur around synovial joints (see the table below for specific synovial joints) because of the ROM and reduced friction that they afford.

Synovial Joint Type	Movements	Examples
Ball-and-socket	Rotation and movement in all planes	Hip, shoulder
Condylar	No rotation; variety of movements in different planes	Joints between phalanges and metacarpals
Plane	Twisting or sliding	Joints between various bones of the ankle and wrist
Hinge	Flexion and extension	Elbow
Pivot	Rotation	Joint between the proximal ends of the ulna and radius
Saddle	Variety of movements; primarily in two planes	Joint between carpal and metacarpal of thumb

Joints can also be classified based on the type of movement they allow, specifically, the number of directions that joint rotation can occur. A uniaxial joint, such as the elbow, rotates around only one axis and operates as a hinge. The wrist and ankle are examples of biaxial joints, which allow movement around two perpendicular axes. Multiaxial joints, such as the shoulder and hip joint, allow movement around three axes (any direction in space).

Fulcrum: The fixed pivot point of a lever.

Muscle force (FM): The force generated by the contraction of a muscle.

Resistive force (FR): An external source of resistance (e.g., gravity, friction, weights, inertia) that counters the action of the F_M.

Torque: Also called moment, torque is the extent that a force tends to rotate an object around a specific fulcrum. Muscles pull on bones to create movement, maintain body position, and resist movement, and this force acts on the bones (levers) at the joints. Torque can be quantified as the magnitude of the force multiplied by the length of the moment arm and is measured in Newton meters (N·m).

Moment arm: Also called the lever arm, force arm, or torque arm, the moment arm is the perpendicular distance from the line of action (i.e., the long line that passes through the point where force is applied in the direction of the force exerted) of the force to the fulcrum.

Mechanical advantage: It is the trade-off of distance and force, because it is the ratio of the moment arm through which an applied force acts (i.e., F_M) through the F_r.

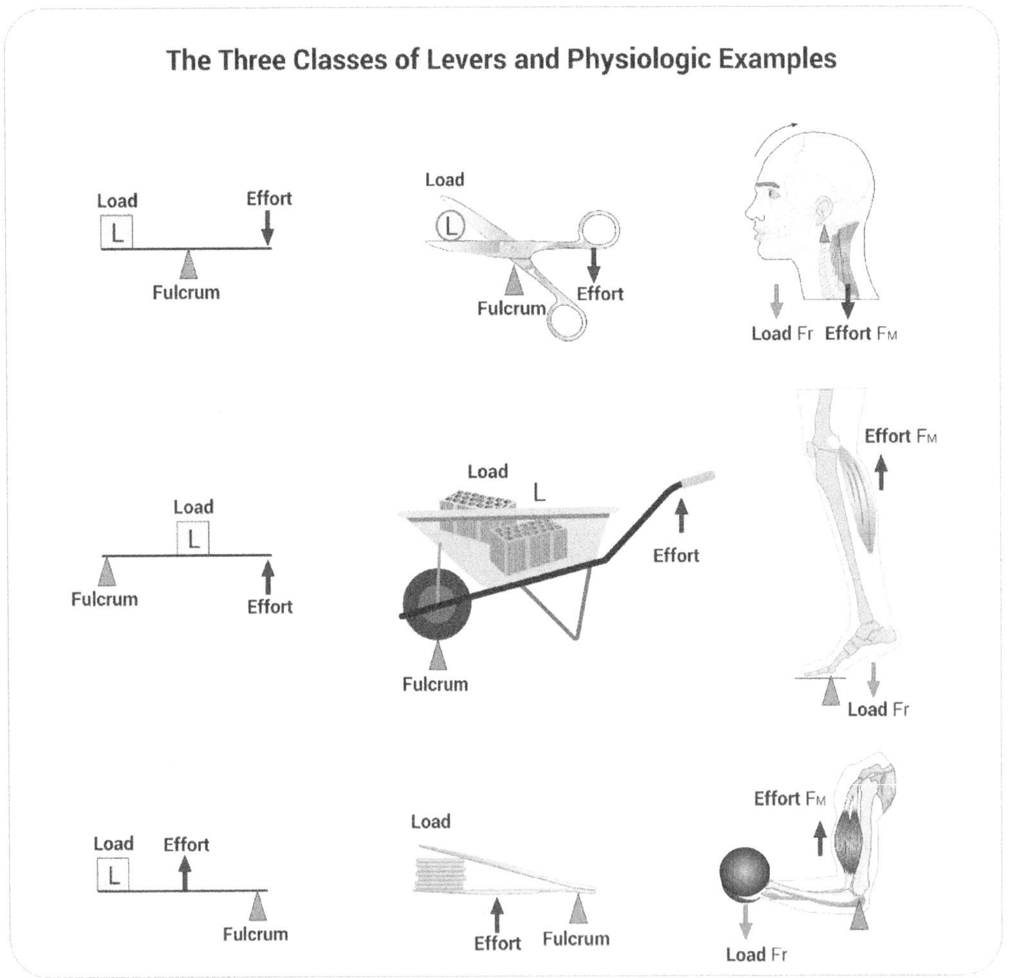

First-class lever: A first-class lever (e.g., a seesaw) has the F_M applied at one end of the lever; the F_r is at the other end, with the fulcrum located somewhere in the middle (i.e., $F_r \rightarrow$ fulcrum$\rightarrow$ F_M). The forearm can serve as a first-class lever during triceps extension exercises. The fulcrum is the elbow joint; F_M comes from the contraction of the triceps, and the F_r is the weight machine.

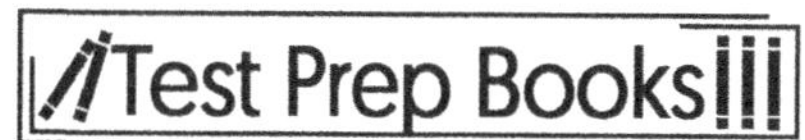

Second-class lever: Consists of a fulcrum at one end, the F_M is applied to the other end, and the F_r is between the ends (i.e., fulcrum→ F_r→ F_M). A wheelbarrow is a second-class lever. The wheel is the fulcrum, the F_r is the load in the wheelbarrow, and the F_M is applied to the handles. An example of a second-class lever in the body is standing on one's toes. The metatarsophalangeal joints act as the fulcrum, body weight is the load, and the calf muscle provides the effort as it pulls up on the heel.

Third-class lever: F_r is at one end of the lever, F_M is applied in the middle of the lever, and the fulcrum is at the other end (i.e., F_r → F_M →fulcrum). A biceps curl is an example of a third-class lever; the F_r is the barbell, F_M is the contraction of the biceps, and the fulcrum is the elbow joint.

Kinetic Laws and Principles of Movement

Velocity

Velocity is the rate of change of distance over time. Velocity and speed are often used interchangeably, but it is important for the personal trainer to separate the terms. Speed is the rate at which an object covers a distance, and velocity describes how fast and in what direction an object is moving. Velocity is calculated by dividing the distance traveled by the amount of time it took to cover that distance.

Force

Force is best visualized as a push or pull exerted on one object by a second object. It is the interaction of two physical objects that have both size (magnitude) and direction. Force is measured in Newtons (N) and can be calculated using the formula: $F = m(a + g)$; where F is force, m is the mass of a dumbbell or other object, a is instantaneous acceleration, and g is acceleration resulting from gravity (9.81 meters/second/second). The number of cross-bridges formed between actin and myosin filaments determines the amount of force produced at any moment in time.

Force-Velocity Curve

The force-velocity curve graphically represents the relationship between velocity (meters/second), plotted on the x-axis, and force (N), plotted on the y-axis. The curve shows the inverse relationship between force and velocity, such that as force increases, velocity decreases, and vice versa. The personal trainer must understand this relationship when planning a training program. For example, if a client is strong but not fast, more time should be spent training at a lower force intensity (e.g., back squats at 30% of one-repetition maximum [1RM] instead of at 90% of 1RM) and a faster velocity in order to improve speed.

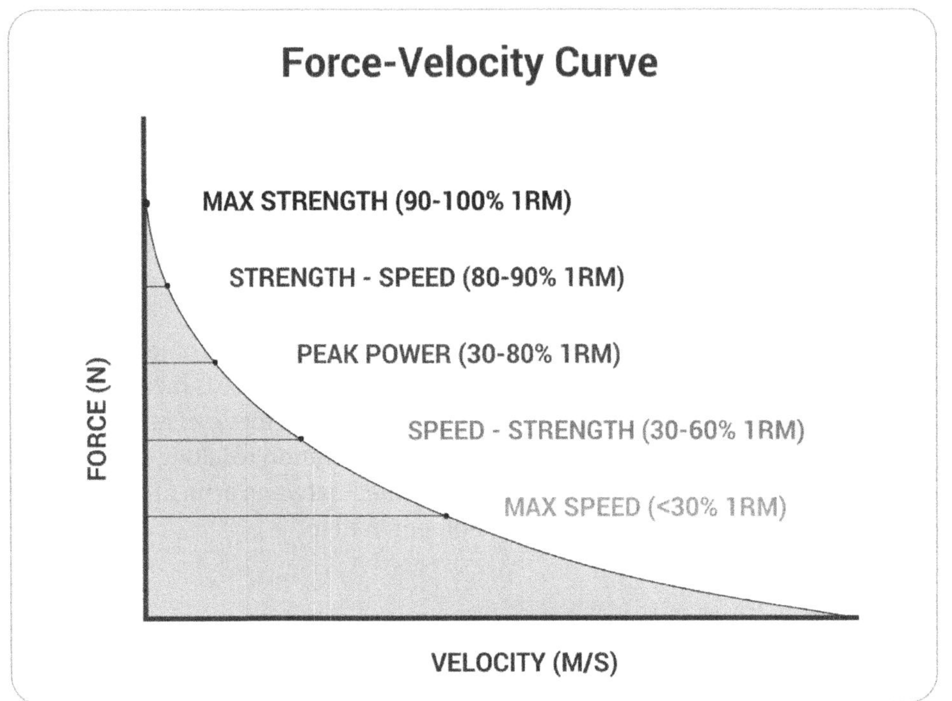

Force-Time Curve

The force-time curve graphically represents the relationship between time (milliseconds), plotted on the x-axis, and force, plotted on the y-axis.

Rate of force development (RFD): The RFD is the change in force divided by the change in time. It has significant relevance for sports where the timing of movements or explosiveness is critical. The generation of maximum force in minimum time is an index of explosive strength.

Momentum

Momentum is the amount of motion that an object has. It is calculated as the velocity multiplied by the object's mass, and like velocity, momentum is a vector quantity with a direction. Momentum is relevant to sports because it can be used for performance assessment. For example, a client having a mass of 125 kilograms and running at 10 meters/second will have more momentum than a client running at the same velocity who is 100 kilograms. Momentum can also play a role in injuries, particularly in collision sports (e.g., rugby, American football) because clients having a large mass can hit or tackle another client with more momentum than clients with less mass moving at the same speed.

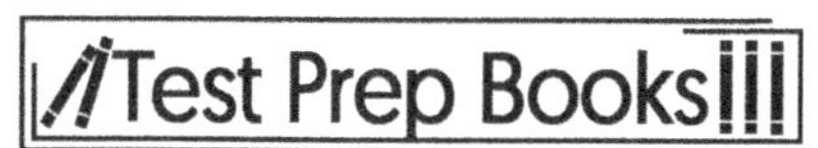

Impulse

Impulse is the product of the time required to generate a force and the amount of the force. This quantity is represented as the area under the force-time curve. Impulse increases by improving the RFD, with the magnitude of change in the momentum of an object being contingent upon impulse.

Work

Work, measured in Joules [J], is calculated as the applied force on an object multiplied by the distance that the object is displaced (in the direction the force is applied). Quantifying work is useful for strength programs because a client's training volume over the course of a training session, day, week, or the entire season can provide information about how well the client can handle varying amounts of training volume and intensity.

$$Work = Force \times Displacement$$

Power

Power is the rate that work is performed and it can be calculated as work divided by time. Power can also be calculated as the product of force applied to an object and velocity. Power is usually measured in watts (W), but it can also be measured in horsepower (hp). Power must be considered, in addition to work, when designing a fitness program. Training should consider the power associated with a client's sport or activity, and it should use various power outputs relevant to sport-specific movement velocities. Because power is the product of force and velocity, improving either of these components will improve the client's RFD and explosiveness.

$$Power = Work/Time$$

Center of Gravity (COG)

The balance point of an object when torque is equal on all sides is the COG. The COG is also the point where the planes of the body intersect. From a sports perspective, the lower a client's COG, the more stability he or she has. For example, hockey players skating with flexed knees low over the puck have increased stability, making it more difficult for opponents to get the player off of the puck.

Center of Pressure (COP)

COP refers to the point of application of ground reaction force, which is the force that is exerted by the supporting surface (e.g., ground) on the body. COP is relevant for postural control and gait and contributes to balance and stability. A tennis player may shift his or her COP medially and laterally as seen when the player moves from side to side before receiving a serve.

Planes of Motion

A plane is an imaginary flat surface. The three primary planes of the human body are frontal, sagittal, and transverse. The frontal, or coronal, plane is a vertical plane that divides the body or organ into front (anterior) and back (posterior) portions. The sagittal, or lateral, plane is a vertical plane divides the body or organ into right and left sides. The transverse plane is a horizontal plane that divides the body or organ into upper and lower portions.

The position where a person is standing with arms at the side and the palms of the hands facing forward is called the anatomical position. From this position, the body can be divided into three anatomical planes that cut the body into sections. These anatomical planes are important because they can be used to explain normal and athletic movements and the type of resistance exercises for training these movements.

Sagittal plane: This plane divides the body into right and left regions. Examples of body movements and related exercises that occur in the sagittal plane are provided below.

Body Movement	Example Sport/Activity That Utilizes the Movement	Related Exercise
Elbow extension	Shot put	Triceps push-down
Hip flexion	Football punter	Leg raises
Knee flexion	Diving (tuck dive)	Leg curl

Frontal plane: The frontal plane runs through the center of the body from side to side, dividing the body into front and back halves.

Body Movement	Example Sport/Activity That Utilizes the Movement	Related Exercise
Shoulder adduction	Swimming (breaststroke)	Wide-grip lateral pull-down
Ankle inversion	Resisted inversion	Soccer dribbling
Hip adduction	Standing adduction machine	Soccer side step

Transverse plane: The transverse plane is a horizontal plane that divides the body into upper and lower regions.

Body Movement	Example Sport/Activity That Utilizes the Movement	Related Exercise
Hip internal rotation	Basketball pivot movement	Resisted internal rotation
Lower back left rotation	Baseball batting	Medicine ball side toss
Lower back right rotation	Golf swing	Torso machine

Joint Angle

A joint angle is the angle, measured in degrees, between two body parts that are linked by a single joint. Body movements occur due to rotation around a joint or multiple joints with the force produced expressed as torque. Torque exerted varies by joint due to various characteristics of the joint (e.g., range of motion [ROM]; the relationship of muscle length versus force; leverage resulting from the use of joints as first-, second-, and third-class levers; and speed of contraction of muscles at the joint).

Muscle Action Spectrum

Concentric muscle action: This type of action occurs when the contraction force is greater than the resistive force (F_r), causing the muscle to shorten. The tension caused by the shortening of the muscle causes the joint to move. When a client is doing biceps curls, the elbow is initially extended. The concentric action of the biceps results in the shortening of the muscle, moving the elbow to a flexed position.

Eccentric muscle action: Eccentric muscle action occurs when the external resistance is greater than the muscle force (F_M). The muscle develops tension and lengthens During a biceps curl, the lowering of the weight when moving the arm from a flexed to extended position reflects the lengthening of the muscle, resulting from eccentric action.

Isometric muscle action: Isometric muscle action results when a muscle generates force and attempts to contract concentrically but is unable to because the resistive force is greater than that generated by the muscle. In this situation, the action does not cause movement or external work, but it does generate force. If a client is holding a fixed bar with elbows extended and attempts a concentric action to shorten the biceps, the biceps produce force, but movement does not occur (i.e., there is no change in the length of muscle fibers).

Isokinetic muscle action: Isokinetic muscle actions result in a dynamic movement performed at a constant velocity. These actions do not occur naturally. For the muscle movement to occur at a constant velocity, a machine such as a dynamometer (a device that allows constant velocity movement regardless of the amount of torque) must be used.

Force-Couple Relationships

Agonist

An agonist is a muscle or group of muscles that is most directly responsible for generating the force to produce a movement; it is also called a prime mover. When lowering the body in the downward phase of a squat, the agonists are the gluteus maximus and the quadriceps group.

Antagonist

Antagonists generate a motion or force that is the opposite of the agonist's motion. Sometimes an antagonist is a muscle, or muscle groups, that performs a protective action, such as decelerating a force acting on the body or helping stabilize working joints.

Synergist

A muscle that indirectly helps to generate force production during a movement or one that aids in stabilizing the agonist muscle as force is produced.

Neutralizer

Neutralizers prevent unwanted or extraneous movement by pulling against and canceling out the motion from the agonist. For example, when the elbow is flexed, supination is often undesirable, so the pronator teres counteracts the supination of the biceps so that only elbow flexion results.

Stabilizer

Also called a fixator, a muscle acting as a stabilizer muscle holds certain joints or body segments immobile, so that agonists can optimize movement and force production. For example, to do an abdominal exercise, the pelvis may be stabilized by the contraction of the muscles of the hip joint. It is often optimal to hold the insertion point or proximal joint stable, so that the working muscles have a more fixed end to pull from.

The muscles involved in the flexion of the forearm at the elbow joint and their roles in the movement are provided in the table below.

Muscle	Movement Role
Biceps brachii	Agonist (prime mover)
Triceps brachii	Antagonist
Deltoid	Stabilizer (fixator)
Brachioradialis	Neutralizer

Length-Tension Relationship

The length-tension relationship of muscle is such that a muscle's resting length indicates how much force a muscle can generate. A muscle at resting length achieves ideal overlap of actin and myosin filaments. The torque, or force, of a muscle may diminish as the muscle moves. While the actin and myosin filaments of a shortened muscle overlap too much, the actin and myosin filaments of a lengthened muscle do not overlap enough.

It is important to avoid false equivalencies between shortened muscles and overactive muscles, and likewise between lengthened muscles and underactive muscles. Lengthened muscles, or long muscles, often perform the primary role in a movement when the muscle that would perform the primary role, in normal circumstances, is engaged in another function. This is known as synergistic dominance. When this occurs, a lengthened muscle is best described as overactive rather than underactive.

A muscle's resting length provides a baseline for its possible force. Both long and short muscles may be weak compared with their strength at resting length.

Stretch-Shortening Cycle

Explosive activities, such as plyometrics, use the stretch-shortening cycle (the fast lengthening and shortening of a muscle) to create muscle contractions. The stretch-shortening cycle involves an eccentric phase, amortization phase, and concentric phase. A muscle shortens in the concentric phase and lengthens in the eccentric phase. The amortization phase is the transition between the eccentric and concentric phases. Muscle spindles are essential to the stretch-reflex response because they are the primary proprioceptive structures in the muscle. Muscle spindles respond to eccentric muscle action. When muscles experience eccentric contractions during plyometric exercises, the muscles and surrounding tendons stretch and store energy. This musculotendinous unit where elastic energy is stored is called the series elastic component (SEC). The SEC works like a spring that returns the lengthened muscle to its shortened state during a concentric contraction. As the muscle shortens, energy is released. A client can use this energy to generate enough force to complete the plyometric exercises.

Reciprocal Inhibition and Autogenic Inhibition

Golgi tendon organs (GTOs) are mechanoreceptors that lie parallel to extrafusal muscle fibers near the musculotendinous junction and detect tension changes in an active muscle, acting as feedback monitors. The increased tension caused by muscle shortening stimulates GTOs to relax the muscle via the inhibitory interneuron; this response is also called autogenic inhibition. Reciprocal inhibition occurs when a contracting muscle stimulates the GTOs, causing the opposing muscle to relax. The GTOs

respond to muscle tension by sending impulses to the spinal cord to elicit reflex inhibition. Importantly, GTOs protect the muscle and tendon from injury caused by an excessive load by prohibiting excessive tension to build up in a muscle. Stimulation of GTOs is graded based on the amount of tension a muscle develops. At low forces, the effect of GTOs is minimal. With increasing loads, the GTOs mediate more significant reflexive inhibition.

Joint Classifications and Actions

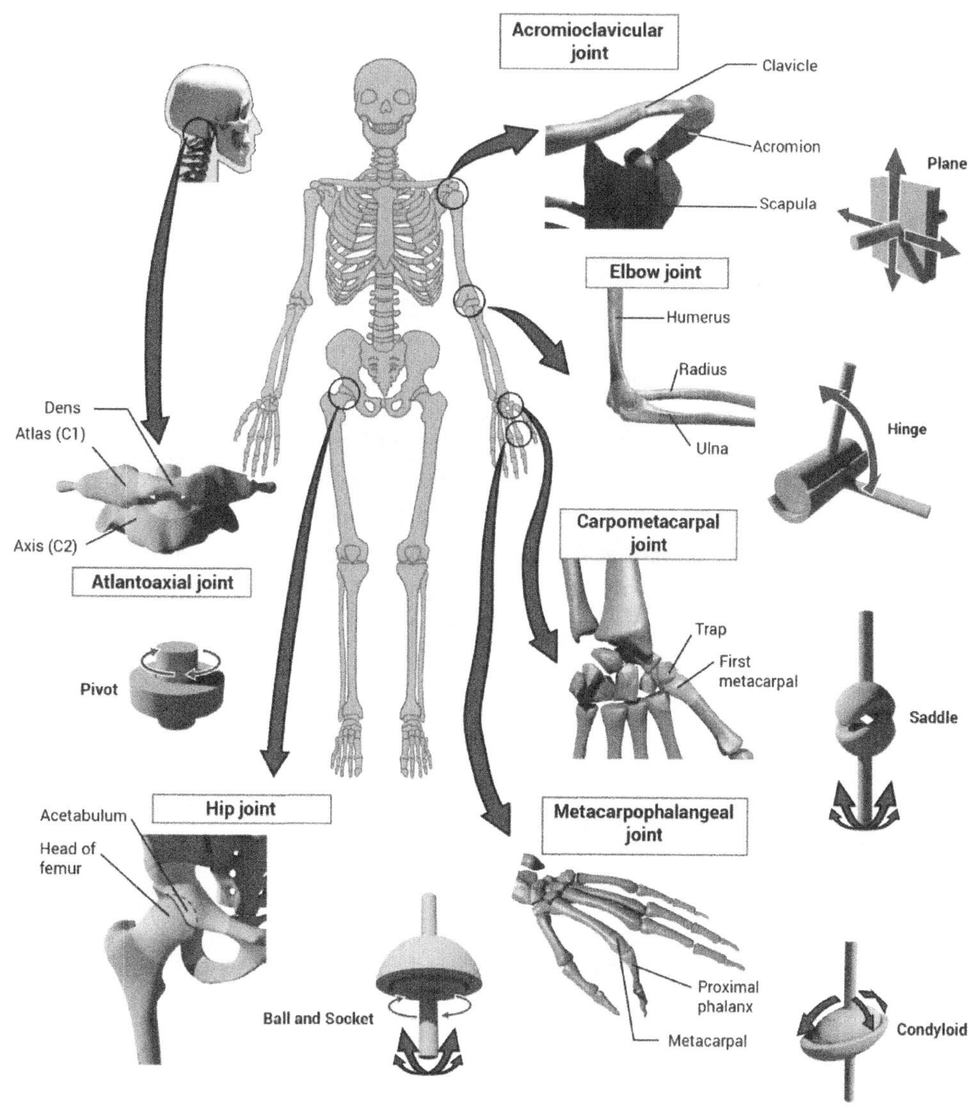

Joints can be classified based on structure of how the bones are connected:

- Fibrous joints: bones joined by fibrous tissue and that lack a joint cavity, e.g., sutures of the skull
- Cartilaginous joints: bones joined by cartilage and lack a joint cavity, e.g., the pubic symphysis

- Synovial joints: bones separated by a fluid-containing joint cavity with articular cartilage covering the ends of the bone and forming a capsule
- Plane joints: flat surfaces that allow gliding and transitional movements, e.g., intercarpal joints
- Hinge joints: cylindrical projection that nests in a trough-shaped structure, single plane of movement (e.g., the elbow)
- Pivot joints: rounded structure that sits into a ring-like shape, allowing uniaxial rotation of the bone around the long axis (e.g., radius head on ulna)
- Condyloid joints: oval articular surface that nests in a complementary depression, allowing all angular movements (e.g., the wrist)
- Saddle joints: articular surfaces that both have complementary concave and convex areas, allowing more movement than condyloid joints (e.g., the thumb)
- Ball-and-socket joints: spherical structure that fits in a cuplike structure, allowing multiaxial movements (e.g., the shoulder)

Each type of joint permits different movements, controlled by the shape of the joint and the muscles surrounding it. Personal trainers should be aware of these movements and the normal ROM to ensure that clients are performing exercises safely, are within a healthy range, and are utilizing a variety of motions to optimize health and muscular balance. Ball-and-socket joints, like the shoulder and hip, are the most mobile and allow flexion, extension, abduction, adduction, internal and external rotation, and circumduction. The elbow is a hinge joint and allows flexion and extension. Intervertebral joints are cartilaginous and allow flexion, extension, lateral flexion, and rotation. The ankle has a hinge joint (dorsiflexion, plantarflexion) and a gliding joint (inversion, eversion)

Here's a look at types of motion:

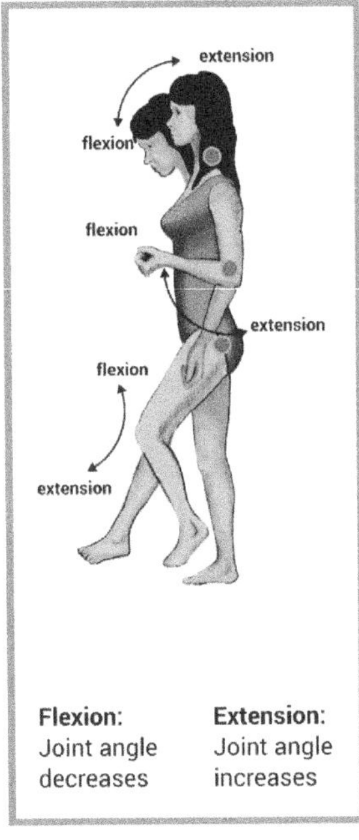

Flexion: Joint angle decreases

Extension: Joint angle increases

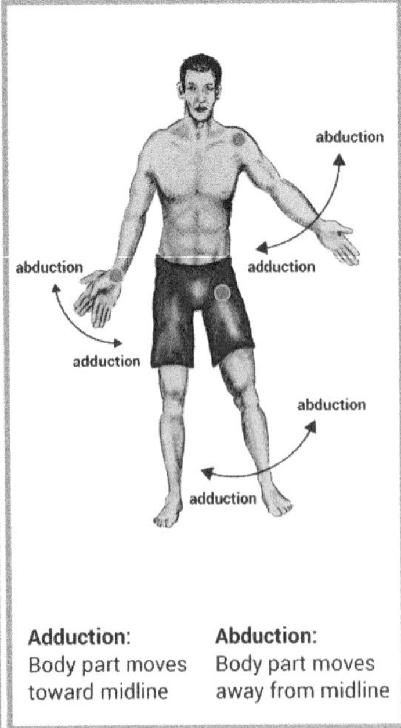

Adduction: Body part moves toward midline

Abduction: Body part moves away from midline

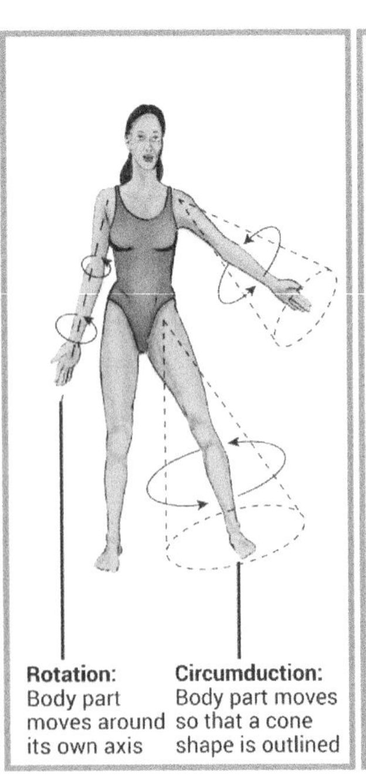

Rotation: Body part moves around its own axis

Circumduction: Body part moves so that a cone shape is outlined

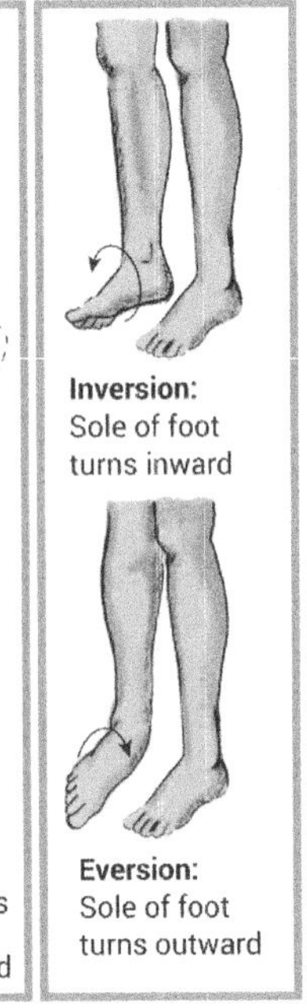

Inversion: Sole of foot turns inward

Eversion: Sole of foot turns outward

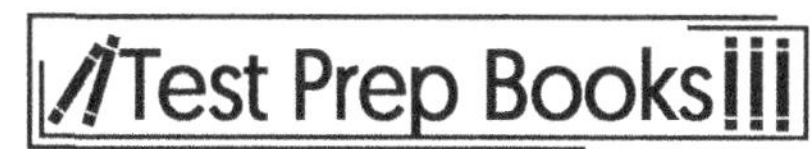

Integrated Muscle System

The global muscular system refers to four subsystems composed of larger muscles that work cooperatively to complete full body exercises. The local muscular system, also known as the stabilization system, refers to muscles that provide support and stability to the spine during joint movement.

The global muscular system is composed of the lateral, deep longitudinal, posterior oblique, and anterior oblique subsystems. The deep longitudinal subsystem mitigates stress when walking and running. It facilitates force between the torso and the ankle joint. Meanwhile, interactions between the deep longitudinal subsystem and the posterior oblique subsystem illustrate how the two subsystems work together. For example, these subsystems work together to complete specific rotational movements and exercises.

The posterior oblique subsystem includes many muscles in the back and buttocks. For example, interactions between the gluteus maximus and latissimus dorsi stabilize the sacroiliac (SI) joint. Conversely, the anterior oblique subsystem includes muscles in the same regions, just opposite those in the posterior oblique subsystem. Together, these two subsystems provide stability during rotational and swinging movements.

Principles of Motor Development

The cephalocaudal principle asserts that motor development proceeds from the top of the body. Neck muscles develop first because they must support the head. Muscle development continues through the shoulders, arms, torso, and legs. The proximal-distant principle asserts that muscle development proceeds from the central muscles of the body to the outward muscles, such as those in fingers and toes. Neither principle suggests a direct line of development. While muscles develop at regular intervals, they do not develop as a linear progression; development does not progress like a chain of falling dominoes.

The general-to-specific principle perhaps best illustrates the difference between interval development and linear development. The general-to-specific principle asserts that children develop more precise control of certain muscle groups over time. While a weak grip characterizes the beginning stages of muscle development in the fingers and hands, the strength of those specific muscles grows over time.

Many components of physical fitness, including agility and balance, depend on proper motor development. Fitness training helps clients and athletes develop agility, balance, speed, coordination, reaction time, and power. Both young and old clients benefit from improved motor control by completing fitness exercises. Motor control is defined by both deliberate and reflexive movements and actions. Balance depends on proper motor development and is improved through training. Initially, clients and athletes may wobble and need to reach out for support when they stand on one leg. As they develop better balance, they may wobble less and maintain steady posture.

Motor learning occurs naturally over time and is accelerated through exercise. Clients and athletes develop faster reaction time and hand-eye coordination through practice with reaction balls. This type of exercise may accelerate motor learning for young athletes, and it may help aging clients maintain current levels of personal fitness.

Nutrition

Macronutrients and Micronutrients

Carbohydrates and fats are the primary macronutrients used to fuel exercise. The breakdown of these substrates provides adenosine triphosphate (ATP) for the body to do work. Carbohydrates are the body's preferred energy source for most aerobic and anaerobic exercise, both during resistance and cardiovascular exercise. At very low levels of exertion, such as during walking, yoga, and gentle cycling, fats provide a greater proportion of the energy requirements. The body can only store a limited amount of carbohydrates in the form of muscle and liver glycogen (generally about 2000 kcal worth, depending on training status and body size), so as these stores deplete, reliance on fat and protein for energy increase. By ingesting some carbohydrates during extended endurance exercise, such as in marathon training or on long bike rides, the body can continue to have an ample supply of carbohydrates to prevent "hitting the wall" experiences that occur as energy levels drop when the body runs out of glycogen to feed into the Krebs Cycle and starts needing to use fat and protein more. These two substrates are slower burning fuels, so the intensity level permitted while burning these fuels is lower, resulting in decreased performance and speed.

Carbohydrates

Carbohydrates provide 4 kilocalories per gram and are a major source of fuel for the body during moderate- and high-intensity exercise, up to 2 hours in duration. Beyond approximately this duration, stores deplete and the body relies on fatty acid metabolism for sustained energy. Carbohydrates are used for energy immediately, if needed, but excess carbohydrates are converted to glycogen and stored in skeletal muscles and the liver or converted to fat if the body's glycogen stores are full. The amount of glycogen the body can store is influenced by a variety of factors including physical training status, basal metabolic rate, body size, and eating habits, but in general, the body can store about 15 grams per kilogram of body weight. In general, clients should consume about 6-10 grams of carbohydrate per kilogram of body weight daily, depending on the intensity, duration, and frequency of their training as well as their current health and physical goals.

Protein

Like carbohydrates, protein provides 4 kilocalories per gram. Protein, which consists of amino acids, is used to support the body in the development of tissues, enzymes, and hormones and to rebuild and repair muscles after exercise. In general, protein recommendations for clients fall in the range of 1.5-2.0 grams per kilogram of body weight daily, depending on the type, duration, and frequency of exercise. Excessive consumption of protein does not lead to increased muscle mass because protein in excess of physiologic needs is converted and stored as fat.

Fat

Fat provides 9 kilocalories per gram and contributes significantly to resting energy requirements as well as requirements during low-intensity and long-duration exercise. Fats can be divided into two basic categories: saturated and unsaturated. Saturated fats, which are primarily found in animal sources, include butyric, lauric, myristic, palmitic, and stearic acid, while unsaturated fats typically come from plant sources such as soybeans, nuts, seeds, olives, and avocados. Fats should comprise at least 15% of the total caloric intake; as much as 30%-40% can be acceptable, depending on the health, age, and needs of the individual. For clients, an intake of 30% fat (10% saturated, 10% polyunsaturated, and 10%

monounsaturated) aligns with dietary guidelines and should ensure an adequate – but not excessive – dietary intake.

The body's use of fat as an energy source during exercise depends on the length and intensity of the event and the client's fitness level. Generally speaking, two phenomena can describe a client's use of fat as an energy substrate during exercise: the crossover concept and the duration effect. The crossover concept refers to the fact that at lower intensities, the body is primarily using fat as a source of fuel, and as the intensity increases, the contribution of adenosine triphosphate (ATP) from carbohydrate metabolism increases. The duration effect is based on the principle that as the duration of the exercise bout increases, the body relies more heavily on fat, as carbohydrate stores deplete. Exactly how much of each fuel source is used also depends on the client's aerobic fitness; fitter clients typically can store more glycogen but also use fat at higher intensities of exercise. Lastly, there is some evidence to suggest that women derive a greater percentage of their energy needs from fat, compared to men, at a given exercise workload.

Vitamins and Minerals

Vitamin and mineral needs of clients may be increased, but typically can be met if a balanced, varied diet is consumed with foods such as lean meats/protein, fruits, vegetables, whole grains, and dairy. B vitamins such as thiamin, riboflavin, and niacin are required to support metabolic processes; vitamin D is required for calcium absorption; and vitamins C and E are required to mitigate stress oxidation in the body. Fat-soluble vitamins (A, D, E, and K) are stored in the body, so they should not be consumed in excessive quantities. If a client is not meeting their vitamins and minerals requirements through diet, a multivitamin-mineral supplement is needed. Such supplements will not directly improve athletic performance but will help to correct a nutrition deficiency if one is present, which may prevent illness or improve performance.

Sweating can lower electrolytes and minerals such as sodium, potassium, chloride, iron, calcium, phosphorus, and magnesium. Sodium and potassium help to regulate the body's water balance and also play a significant role in muscle contraction. Chloride also helps with fluid balance and nerve conductions. Iron plays an important role in the body's ability to transport and use oxygen, and calcium is critical for bone formation, nerve conduction, and muscle contraction. Phosphorus is involved in intramuscular oxidation processes, and magnesium helps support energy metabolism. Electrolytes (sodium, potassium, and chloride) and water need to be replaced during extended exercise, particularly in hot and humid environments, because they are lost in sweat.

Hydration

Hydration is important before, during, and after exercise not only for performance, but also for optimal health. A loss of 3 to 5% body weight in water may be tolerated without a corresponding loss of maximal strength, but moderate or severe dehydration (loss of greater than 5% body weight) can lead to decreased endurance capacity, decreased heat tolerance, and increased injury risk. Sweat rate can be estimated by weighing the body before and after exercise and subtracting any fluid consumed during exercise. While it is ideal to match fluid intake to body weight in ounces lost, clients should drink a minimum of one pint for each pound of lost weight to mitigate the effects of more substantial dehydration. Water is usually sufficient, but for prolonged activities over an hour or in particularly hot climates, sports drinks with electrolytes are a more appropriate choice.

Hydration and Electrolytes

The adult male body is about 60% water, while the female body is about 50–55% water. As a result, less than optimal hydration status can affect health and performance. Dehydration can cause headaches, sluggishness, mood changes, loss of cognitive functioning, and muscle cramping. Decreased physical performance can occur with just a 3% loss in body weight from dehydration. During exercise, perspiration helps mitigate the increase in body temperature. During strenuous activity, individuals can lose as much as 6–10% of their body weight via sweating, depending on the type and duration of the activity. It is important to maintain adequate hydration before, during, and after exercise; the recommendation is 8–12 cups of water per day plus replacement of fluid loss during exercise. Individual needs may vary, but during exercise, about 6–8 ounces of fluid are usually needed every 15–20 minutes of activity.

Within the context of adequate hydration, electrolyte balance must also be preserved. The five major electrolytes that are important to health are sodium, potassium, chloride, calcium, and magnesium. Sodium, which is needed to help maintain fluid balance, nerve function, muscle contractions, and acid-base balance, is the primary electrolyte lost in sweat and must be replaced. It is important to include sodium in fluids or food as part of the rehydration process after exercise so that overhydration, or hyponatremia, does not occur as a result of drinking water alone. Adding sodium to fluids also helps to improve the absorption of water and carbohydrates. Most commercial sports drinks are formulated to provide the optimal levels of sodium and carbohydrates in solution.

Children and seniors are particularly susceptible to dehydration during exercise. Children may be unaware of the need to replace fluids during activity and may need longer to acclimate to increased temperatures. When children are exercising in hot environments, they should be well hydrated before activity and drink plenty of fluid afterward. Aging leads to decreased lean body mass and, over time, decreased body water. Seniors may also be at risk for dehydration because of decreased sensitivity to thirst and diminished ability of the kidneys to concentrate urine in the absence of adequate hydration.

Guidelines for Caloric Intake and Expenditure

A daily calorie deficit of 500 to 1000 kcal is recommended for those looking to lose weight. This can be achieved through increased energy expenditure via activity and/or reduced caloric intake. Because each pound of fat has 3500 kcal, this should result in one to two pounds of weight per week. Faster rates are not recommended because they may result in loss of lean body mass and body water as well as fat mass. This can slow metabolism because muscle mass contributes to a higher metabolic rate than fat mass. A loss of one to two pounds per week preserves lean body mass and also improves adherence, since it typically is due to maintainable lifestyle changes rather than drastic starvation methods that are unhealthy and not sustainable, resulting in weight regain. Calorie restricting diets should emphasize healthy, nutrient-rich foods such as vegetables, fruits, legumes, lean proteins, and healthy fats as well as ample water for hydration.

It is not just calories—processed foods and empty calories such as chemically laden “diet foods” and sodas should be avoided, even if they appear to have lower calorie counts. Suggested rates of weight gain are similar and should also be achieved through healthy food choices, focusing on nutrient-dense foods such as nuts, seeds, vegetables, grains, fruits, and healthy fats. Calories expended during exercise need to be replaced. Clients may find that drinking calorie-rich beverages such as milk, almond milk, and pressed juices can be helpful.

Energy Systems

Phosphagen System (ATP-phosphocreatine [PC])

The phosphagen system utilizes ATP hydrolysis for high-intensity activities of short length (e.g., resistance training; short, intense sprints; other vigorous bouts up to about 10 seconds in duration) and is also active at the start of all types of exercise of varying intensities until the other systems have had time to start producing energy. This system relies on the breakdown of creatine phosphate (CP) for energy. Because ATP stores are quickly depleted and ATP is required for cellular functions other than muscle contractions, the phosphagen system uses CP stores to maintain ATP concentrations. This system is rapidly depleted after about 10 seconds of maximal intensity work, so the glycolytic system starts to engage and contribute energy after this point. It takes longer for glycolysis, and especially oxidative energy systems, to generate energy, which is why the phosphagen system is the initial source.

Creatine Phosphate (CP)

CP, also called phosphocreatine (PC), concentrations in muscles are four to six times greater than ATP muscle stores, with higher CP concentrations in Type II muscle fibers. The phosphagen system uses creatine kinase in the chemical reaction that combines a phosphate group from CP with ADP to replenish ATP. CP is stored in small amounts, limiting the phosphagen system to supplying energy for intense, short bouts of exercise.

$$\text{ADP} + \text{CP} \leftarrow \text{Creatine kinase} \rightarrow \text{ATP} + \text{Creatine}$$

Creatine Kinase

Creatine kinase is the enzyme required to catalyze the reaction that combines ADP and CP to form ATP and creatine. Elevated levels of creatine kinase in blood serum tests are an indicator of muscle damage (e.g., kidney failure, heart attack). In clients, too much work performed in a training session (single or aggregate sessions) can cause rhabdomyolysis, the rapid breakdown of muscles, elevating levels of creatine kinase in blood serum.

Adenylate Kinase

Also called myokinase, this enzyme catalyzes a reaction that replenishes ATP.

$$2\text{ADP} \leftarrow \text{adenylate kinase} \rightarrow \text{ATP} + \text{AMP}$$

Law of Mass Action/Mass Action Effect

This law states that the concentration of reactants, products, or both in solution will influence the direction of the reactions. These are often referred to as near-equilibrium reactions because they continue in the given direction based on the concentration of available reactants. This equilibrium is specific to the amount of ATP needed for the specific work being completed by the client. The reactions will continue until the exercise intensity is low enough for another energy system to take over or the exercise ends.

Glycolytic System

Glycolysis

Glycolysis is the breakdown of glucose to replenish ATP. Glucose either comes directly out of blood circulation or is broken down from glycogen stores in the muscles or liver, or is converted from other substrates. ATP replenished during glycolysis is slower than the replenishment provided by the single-step phosphagen system because glycolysis has ten steps and actually requires an investment of energy to drive some of the early steps in the energy pathway. The glycolytic system has an advantage, as it can produce significantly more ATP because of the relatively large supply of glucose and glycogen in the body versus the limited supply of CP.

Anaerobic Glycolysis (Fast Glycolysis)

ATP is produced by breaking down glucose without oxygen available during glycolysis. This process relies on converting pyruvate to lactate to replace ATP during short, high-intensity activity lasting 2 minutes or less. In the absence of oxygen, pyruvate does not get shuttled to the mitochondria for the Krebs Cycle. Instead, the lactate accumulates and must be broken down in the muscle or shuttled to the liver where it undergoes the Cori cycle.

Pyruvate

Pyruvate is the result of anaerobic glycolysis; one glucose molecule produces two pyruvate molecules. Pyruvate can either be converted to lactate in the sarcoplasm or be transported to the mitochondria for the Krebs cycle. Compared to pyruvate conversion to lactate, the Krebs cycle takes longer to replenish ATP because there are more steps required in the reaction series. However, the Krebs cycle can continue for a longer duration when exercise intensity is low. This process is aerobic glycolysis (also called slow glycolysis).

Pyruvate conversion to lactate: The enzyme *lactate dehydrogenase* catalyzes the reaction converting pyruvate to lactate. Lactate produced by anaerobic glycolysis can be cleared by oxidation within the muscle fiber, or it can be moved to the liver via the blood and converted into glucose. The process of the liver turning lactate to glucose is referred to as the *Cori cycle*.

The net reaction of glycolysis when pyruvate is converted to lactate:

$$\text{Glucose} + 2\text{P}_\text{i} + 2\text{ADP} \rightarrow 2\text{Lactate} + 2\text{ATP} + \text{H}_2\text{O}$$

Pyruvate transported to mitochondria for Krebs cycle: If oxygen is available, pyruvate and two molecules of nicotinamide adenine dinucleotide (NADH) will be transported to the mitochondria. Pyruvate is converted to acetyl-coenzyme A (acetyl-CoA) by pyruvate dehydrogenase, resulting in the loss of carbon (CO_2), and enters the Krebs cycle to resynthesize ATP. The Krebs cycle, a continuation of the substrate oxidation from glycolysis, is a series of reactions that results in the production of two ATP molecules.

The net reaction for glycolysis when pyruvate is transported to the mitochondria:

$$\text{Glucose} + 2\text{P}_\text{i} + 2\text{ADP} + 2\text{NAD}^+ \rightarrow 2\text{Pyruvate} + 2\text{ATP} + 2\text{NADH} + 2\text{H}_2\text{O}$$

Phosphorylation

Phosphorylation is addition of an inorganic phosphate to a molecule. Phosphorylation of ADP to ATP occurs by adding a phosphoryl (PO_3) group to ADP.

Substrate-Level Phosphorylation

Substrate-level phosphorylation is a single enzyme-generated reaction that uses ADP to directly resynthesize ATP. It occurs during anaerobic glycolysis (fast phosphorylation) and can occur during both anaerobic and aerobic activities.

Oxidative Phosphorylation

This is the process of ATP being resynthesized via the actions of the ETC. The oxidative system produces approximately thirty-eight ATP molecules when a molecule of glucose is processed all the way through glycolysis, the Krebs cycle, and the ETC. The oxidative system produces approximately 90% of the ATP yield while substrate-level phosphorylation accounts for approximately the remaining 10%.

Electron Transport Chain (ETC)

In addition to two pyruvate molecules produced by glycolysis, six molecules of NADH and two molecules of flavin adenine dinucleotide ($FADH_2$) are produced and used by the ETC. Hydrogen atoms, transported by NADH and $FADH_2$ to the ETC, are used to produce ATP from ADP. The hydrogen atoms form a proton concentration gradient down the ETC that produces energy required to synthesize ATP. NADH and $FADH_2$ molecules rephosphorylate ADP to ATP via the ETC with each NADH molecule producing three ATP molecules and each $FADH_2$ producing two ATP molecules.

Oxidative System

During low-intensity activity and while the body is at rest, ATP is primarily supplied by the oxidative system, which utilizes carbohydrates and fats as substrates. Fats, compared to carbohydrates and proteins, have the greatest capacity for ATP production through their metabolism. The gross energy production of a molecule of glucose is 40 ATP and this number climbs to 463 ATP molecules for one 18-carbon triglyceride molecule. Protein is not a primary substrate and is only used for energy during long-duration exercise (more than 90 minutes) or times of starvation. During rest, approximately 70% of the ATP is produced from fat metabolism, and approximately 30% comes from the breakdown of carbohydrates. With the initiation of high-intensity activity, nearly 100% of ATP comes from carbohydrates metabolism. During long bouts of submaximal exercise, carbohydrates are used initially (due to their faster metabolism), but there is a slow shift back to using fats as glycogen stores deplete.

Net ATP Production

The net ATP production from the oxidation of one glucose molecule can be determined by adding the number of ATP molecules produced during each process. During glycolysis, substrate-level phosphorylation and oxidative phosphorylation produce four and six ATP molecules, respectively. During the Krebs cycle, substrate-level phosphorylation produces two ATP molecules, oxidative phosphorylation of eight NADH produces twenty-four ATP molecules, and the two $FADH_2$ molecules produce four ATP. These processes combined yield a total of forty ATP molecules. Two ATP molecules are used by glycolysis, so the net ATP production is thirty-eight ATP molecules.

Exercise Post-Oxygen Consumption (EPOC)

Ventilation significantly increases during each resistance exercise set; however, ventilation is greatest during the first minute of recovery from a set. This increase in oxygen consumption via increased ventilation is termed excess post-oxygen consumption (EPOC). EPOC serves to help the body return to baseline after the work is performed and helps perfuse tissues to carry nutrients and remove waste, resynthesize hormones and metabolic intermediates, buffer lactate, etc.

Anaerobic training adaptations include increased tidal volume and breathing frequency with maximal resistance exercise, allowing for greater oxygen intake. Slower ventilation rates with increased tidal volume are seen with submaximal exercise.

Units of Energy Measurement

Often, units of energy measurement confuse those who are interested in nutrition and personal training. In science, *Calories* with a capital *C* and *calories* with a lowercase *c* indicate different units of measurement. A Calorie is equivalent to a kilocalorie, and one thousand calories are equal to one kilocalorie. A calorie—1/1000th of a Calorie—is too small a unit of measurement to measure the amount of energy that people consume in the food they eat or burn off during exercise. Therefore, nutritionists and trainers use the Calorie, which is equivalent to a kilocalorie, as their standard unit of measurement. This is a semantic difference, which indicates a different use of terms across disciplines. The important thing to know is that nutritionists and trainers do not refer to energy in terms of calories, even when they write the term using a lower-case *c*; instead, they measure energy in Calories/kilocalories.

Dietary Reference Intakes

Clients will often want to add supplements as part of their health and fitness plans. They may ask their fitness trainer to advise them on which supplements to take. For healthy clients, Dietary Reference Intakes, a series of publications that lists the values of nutrients that healthy people of different age groups need, will be the best source for determining which nutrients are needed and at what values. The values are given in four different ways, and each gives values for different age ranges and according to sex:

- RDA (Recommended daily allowance)—This intake level satisfies the daily nutrient needs for most healthy people.
- AI (Adequate intake)—When RDA isn't established, this level of daily intake provides an adequate amount of nutrition for healthy people.
- UL (Tolerable upper level intake)—The upper level is the maximum amount of a nutrient that should be consumed daily by most healthy people. Anything beyond this level can have harmful effects.
- EAR (Estimated average requirement)—This intake level has been judged to satisfy the daily nutrient needs of fifty percent of healthy people.

The main objective for referencing DRIs is to ensure that appropriate daily values are being consumed but preventing intake that goes beyond the levels that have been judged to be safe. Some nutrients, while necessary, can be toxic when consumed beyond certain levels.

Trainers must remember that DRIs are guidelines for healthy people and that there are no perfect amounts established for the intake of nutrients. Requirements vary from person to person. If a client has any health conditions or is on any type of medication, they are no longer considered to be healthy individuals that the guidelines are meant for. Advice on nutrient intake and supplementation should then be provided by health professionals who understand the interactions between nutrients and drugs and have knowledge of how nutrients can affect the body systems and organs.

It should be noted that while some nutrients may not have a UL listed, harmful effects are still a possibility, and the lack of a UL may be due to lack of information on that particular nutrient. The UK's Safe Upper Levels for Vitamins and Minerals is a source that may be used to find safe upper levels or guidance levels for nutrients that don't have established ULs in the DRIs.

USDA Food Patterns

There are three USDA Food Patterns included in the 2015–2020 Dietary Guidelines: Healthy U.S. Style Eating, Healthy Mediterranean Style Eating, and Healthy Vegetarian Style Eating. One eating pattern is not necessarily superior to another; it is more of a preference. However, a vegetarian lifestyle has been associated with a decreased risk for some chronic diseases such as heart disease and certain cancers. The USDA Food Patterns are all based on systematic review from scientific research, food pattern modeling, and analysis of intake of the U.S. population. Each USDA Food Pattern is based on the five food groups—vegetables, fruits, grains, dairy, and protein—and can be customized to meet an individual's needs based on age, sex, height, weight, and level of physical activity.

The Healthy U.S. Style Eating Pattern is based on typical foods consumed in Americans' diets with a focus on nutrient-dense foods in portions that are appropriate for the desired caloric intake. The Healthy Mediterranean Style Eating Pattern is based on the Healthy U.S. Style Eating Pattern but adjusted to align with the eating patterns of the Mediterranean diet, which have been associated with positive health outcomes. Specifically, the Healthy Mediterranean Style Eating Pattern has more fruit and seafood but less dairy than the U.S. Style Eating Pattern. The Healthy Vegetarian Style Eating Pattern is also based on the Healthy U.S. Style Eating Pattern but is adjusted to reflect the eating habits of self-reported vegetarians, as identified in the National Health and Nutrition Examination Survey (NHANES).

DASH Eating Plan

The DASH Eating Plan is based on clinical research trials that found that the plan helped individuals lower their blood pressure and low-density lipoprotein (LDL) cholesterol and improve heart health while meeting nutrient requirements. The DASH Eating Plan emphasizes whole grains, poultry, fish, and nuts along with food sources of potassium, calcium, and magnesium. Individuals are encouraged to consume as much as seven to eight servings of grains and four to five servings of fruits and vegetables per day on a 2000-calorie diet. Individuals using the DASH Eating Plan may need to gradually increase the intake of whole grains, fruits, and vegetables since the increased fiber of these foods can lead to bloating and diarrhea.

MyPlate

MyPlate is a tool developed by the USDA that is based on the five food groups and healthy eating. It is focused on variety, appropriate portion sizes, nutrient-dense foods, and low saturated fat, sodium, and added sugar intake. The MyPlate Daily Checklist and the SuperTracker are two specific online tools that allow individuals to customize nutrition planning for their specific needs.

Food Exchanges

Food exchanges are used for meal planning purposes, especially for those with diabetes and/or seeking weight loss. Food exchanges divide food into six categories based on the amount of carbohydrate, fat, and protein they contain: starches/breads, fruits, milk, vegetables, meat, and fat.

- Starches and breads contain 15 grams of carbohydrate, 3 grams of protein, and 80 calories per exchange.
- Fruits contain 15 grams of carbohydrate and 60 calories per exchange.

- Milk exchanges contain 12 grams of carbohydrate; 8 grams of protein; 3–8 grams of fat depending on whether the milk exchange is a low-, medium-, or high-fat choice; and 90–150 calories depending on the fat content.
- Vegetable exchanges contain 5 grams of carbohydrate and 25 calories per serving.
- Meat exchanges contain 7 grams of protein per ounce; 0–8 grams of fat, depending on whether the source of the meat exchange is very lean, lean, medium fat, or high fat; and 35–100 calories.
- Fat exchanges provide 5 grams of fat and 45 calories.

Glycemic Index

Finally, the glycemic index and glycemic load offer insight as to how foods affect blood glucose and insulin levels. Glycemic index and load can be useful tools in meal planning to help individuals better understand the impact specific foods may have on their blood sugar. Carbohydrate counting may also be a useful tool in helping individuals monitor and understand the impact various carbohydrates have on their blood sugar.

Meal Planning Approaches

Each of these meal planning approaches are useful in working with clients to guide them toward healthy eating. The most appropriate meal planning approach depends on the client's nutrition goals and personal preferences. For example, a client wanting to lower blood pressure and blood lipids may be best served with the DASH approach. Another client who would like to adopt a vegetarian lifestyle may be more interested in using the USDA Healthy Vegetarian Style Eating Pattern, while a client interested in lowering blood sugar might be interested in food exchanges and/or the glycemic index as a meal planning approach.

Nutritional Needs of Clients

Nutritional requirements for clients are typically higher than nonclients and vary depending on the type of activity.

Health Risk Factors Associated with Dietary Choices

Dietary choices affect health risks associated with some chronic health conditions.

Saturated fats

Saturated fat is associated with an increased risk for cardiovascular disease, so the Dietary Guidelines for Americans recommends consuming no more than 10% of caloric intake from saturated fats An emphasis should be made on replacing saturated fats with unsaturated fats, especially polyunsaturated fats, as this substitution is associated improved total and LDL cholesterol.

Triglycerides

Circulating triglycerides are also affected by diet. Limiting refined, sugary foods; replacing saturated fats with unsaturated fats; and increasing fiber intake can help to keep triglycerides in the normal range of less than 150 milligrams per deciliter. High triglycerides can lead to increased risk of heart disease and diabetes.

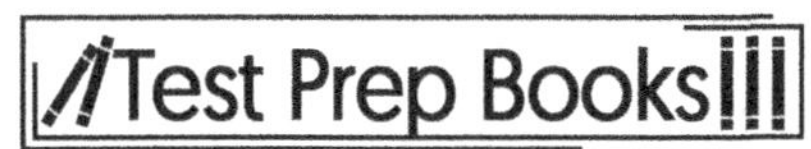

Trans fats

Trans fats are produced through a process called *hydrogenation,* which makes packaged foods (such as coffee creamer, snack foods, store-bought baked goods, vegetable shortening, stick margarines, fast foods, and refrigerated dough products) more shelf stable. In recent years, manufacturers have begun limiting or removing trans fats per the Food and Drug Administration regulatory requirements because these fats have been shown to pose a significant risk for heart disease and should be eliminated from the diet.

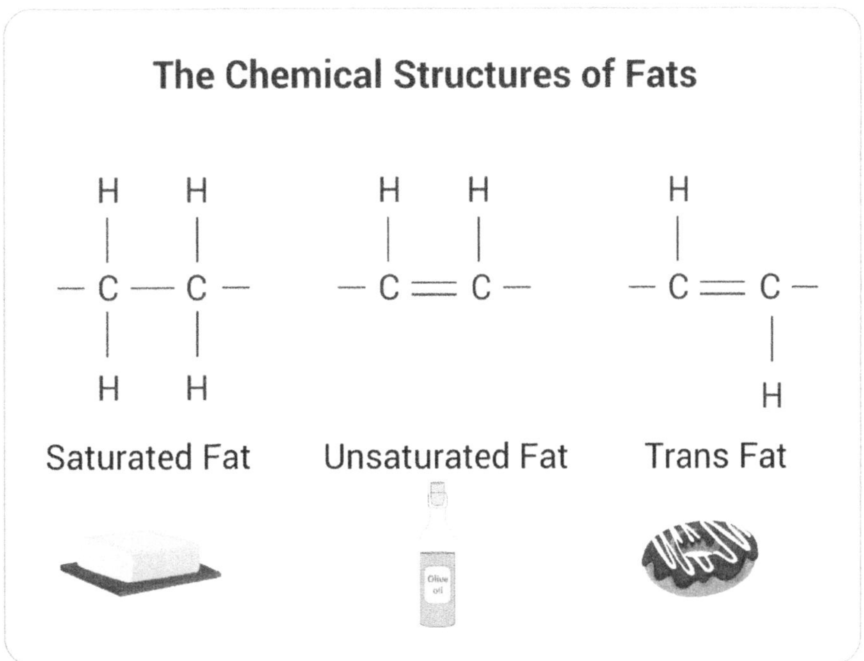

Cholesterol

Cholesterol is required for various physiological and structural functions, such as the production of cells and hormones. However, these requirements are met by the cholesterol produced in the body; little to no additional dietary cholesterol is needed. The upper limit for healthy levels of cholesterol is 200 milligrams per deciliter; high cholesterol is a risk factor for heart disease. The 2020–2025 Dietary Guidelines recommend that cholesterol intake should be minimal. The Institute of Medicine (IOM) still recommends limiting the intake of cholesterol-laden foods such as high-fat meats and dairy, which also contain high amounts of saturated fat.

Calcium

Calcium plays important physiologic roles including vascular contraction, vasodilation, muscle contraction, and nerve impulse transmission. The majority of calcium in the body is stored in bones and teeth. To support bone mineral deposition and avoid bone resorption, it is important to have adequate calcium intake. This is especially true at certain stages of the life cycle, when bones are forming or have the tendency to demineralize, as well as for clients, who may lose additional calcium through perspiration. Postmenopausal women need to obtain adequate amounts of calcium in the diet to decrease the risk for osteoporosis. Signs and symptoms of calcium deficiency may be absent or may include muscle weakness, cramping, and increased susceptibility to fractures. Recommended intake varies by gender and throughout the lifespan, with increases for females, adolescents, lactating mothers, and postmenopausal women.

Iron

Iron in the body is primarily combined with hemoglobin, in an iron-protein compound that increases the blood's oxygen-carrying capacity sixty-five times, as well as in muscle myoglobin. Intensive workout programs put individuals at risk for developing iron-deficiency anemia, which decreases aerobic capacity since less oxygen can circulate to working tissues, leading to fatigue and reduced athletic performance. Other symptoms of iron-deficiency anemia include brittle nails, sluggishness, headaches, pale skin, and dizziness. Iron recommendations are 1.3-1.7 times higher for clients than nonclients and another 1.8 times higher for vegetarian clients in comparison to those who consume animal protein, due to the lower bioavailability of nonheme iron sources in the vegetarian diet. The Recommended Dietary Allowance (RDA) for iron is as follows:

- 8 milligrams per day for men over the age of 18
- 18 milligrams per day for women ages 19–50
- 8 milligrams per day for women ages 51 and older

Females of childbearing age are at a higher risk for iron-deficiency anemia due to red blood cell loss during menstruation. Females often tend to consume less dietary iron as well. Endurance clients may require additional iron due to foot-strike hemolysis, loss of hemoglobin in urine from strenuous training, and the small amount of iron lost in sweat. Heme sources of iron are more easily absorbed and include beef, pork, and beef liver. Nonheme sources include oatmeal, lentils, dark green leafy vegetables, and fortified cereals. Vitamin C intake can increase the absorption of iron in the small intestine; a glass of orange juice increases nonheme iron bioavailability by three times. It should be noted that excessive iron intake, especially in males, can be toxic.

Portion Sizes, Meal Timing, and Meal Frequency

The USDA publishes Dietary Guidelines for Healthy Americans every several years, with changes as nutrition science advances. The Food Guide Pyramid has been replaced by ChooseMyPlate.gov and provides tips and guidelines for portion sizes and relative amounts in each food group to strive for, as well as recommended amounts of physical activity. The full report and printable resources that trainers can share with clients are available at: cnpp.usda.gov/2015-2020-dietary-guidelines-americans.

Composition and Timing of Nutrient and Fluid Intake

The body's preferred source of energy comes from muscles and liver glycogen stores; however, these stores are limited and not sufficient for sustained high-intensity athletic performance. Nutrient timing refers to effectively altering the content and timing of dietary intake—particularly carbohydrates and protein—to deliver optimal health and performance. Nutrient timing can involve the use of whole foods, isolated nutrients from food sources, and synthetic compounds, and it may vary by sport and among individuals. Research results have found that appropriate nutrient timing provides superior health and athletic performance compared to unplanned or traditional intake strategies.

Carbohydrate Loading

Carbohydrate loading is one specific nutrient timing strategy used by endurance clients to help maximize glycogen stores. Recall that glycogen is glucose that has been converted from carbohydrates and stored in the muscles and liver. It is the body's preferred fuel source during moderate- and high-intensity activity. For optimal performance, it is important for clients to have adequate stores of glycogen before beginning an endurance activity lasting 2 hours or more. To accomplish carbohydrate loading, clients first deplete their carbohydrate stores by reducing carbohydrate intake while maintaining exercise volume and intensity about 5 days out from the event and then increase carbohydrate intake (to 8–10 grams per kilogram of body weight) and taper training volume for several days just before the event. Carbohydrate loading is typically recommended for activities that last longer than 120 minutes because this is roughly the threshold for depleting glycogen stores during intense exercise.

Nutrient Timing—Before, During, And After

Nutrient timing recommendations can be divided into three categories: before, during, and after exercise recommendations. The International Society of Sports Nutrition (ISSN) recommends 8–10 grams of carbohydrate per kilogram of body weight alone or with protein before resistance exercise to maximize glycogen stores. During exercise, 30–60 grams of carbohydrate per hour in 8–16 ounces of fluid should be consumed every 15 minutes or so. The addition of protein at a ratio of 3–4 grams of carbohydrate per 1 gram of protein may support endurance and the formation of glycogen after the activity. For resistance exercise, the intake of carbohydrates alone or combined with protein improves muscle glycogen, minimizes muscle damage, and supports strength training efforts.

Within 30 minutes after exercise, ingestion of carbohydrates and protein helps to rebuild glycogen stores; the ISSN recommends an intake of 8–10 grams per kilogram of body weight for carbohydrates and 0.2–0.5 grams per kilogram of body weight of protein in the post-exercise meal. The ISSN posits that the intake of essential amino acids (EAAs) stimulates muscle protein synthesis; adding carbohydrates to the amino acid intake may further help increase muscle protein synthesis. Finally, during bouts of continuous, prolonged strength training, consuming carbohydrates and protein together has been demonstrated to improve strength and body composition, typically in a 3 to 1 or 4 to 1 ratio of carbohydrates to protein.

Nutrient and Energy Density

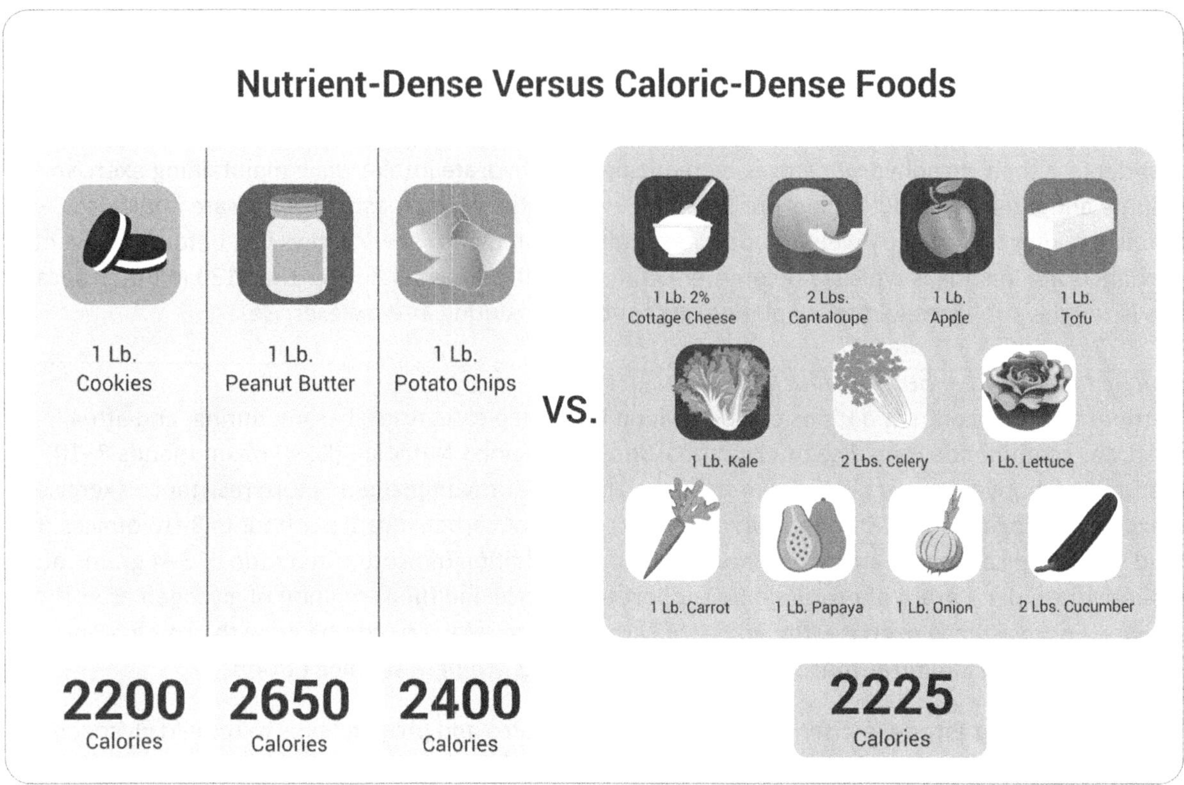

Nutrient-dense foods are rich in essential nutrients, vitamins, and minerals but low in calories, especially in comparison to calorically-dense or energy-dense foods. Calorically-dense foods provide few essential nutrients relative to the number of calories they provide. When focusing on weight loss or optimal health, it is important to focus on nutrient-dense foods. Sources of nutrient-dense foods include fresh vegetables and fruits, specifically dark green leafy vegetables like kale, spinach, and collard greens and fruits like berries, melon, mangoes, and citrus. Other nutrient-dense foods include lean sources of protein, dairy, legumes, and whole grains that have been enriched with vitamins and minerals. Calorically-dense foods include cookies, cakes, pastries, soda, chips, high-fat meats, and fast foods and other highly processed, highly caloric foods.

There are a number of systems that can be used in nutritional profiling or rating to support choosing nutrient-dense foods. Nutritional rating systems, which offer guidance on the nutritional value of food to make selection easier, differ from nutrition labeling, which provides detailed nutrient content on the specific food item according to serving size. Some nutritional rating systems include the Glycemic Index, the Guiding Star, Nutripoints, Nutrition IQ, the Naturally Nutrient Rich Score, the NuVal Nutritional Scoring System, the Aggregate Nutrient Density Index (ANDI), the ReViVer score, and the Points Food System by Weight Watchers. The Dietary Guidelines, to some extent, can also be considered a nutritional rating system.

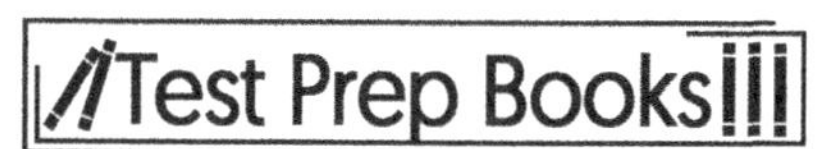

Inappropriate Weight Loss Methods

Unfortunately, fad diets are popularized in the media on a daily basis. The weight-loss industry is a multi-billion-dollar industry for a reason: people are desperate to lose weight and are often looking for a "quick, easy fix," which many of these diets and exercise gadgets promise. However, many of these fad diets are dangerous or not developed by consummate professionals with any scientific research to validate their safety or efficacy, eliminating entire food groups or claiming the diet to be some sort of health panacea. Other unhealthy methods promising rapid weight loss in popular culture include exercising in saunas or steam rooms to "sweat off pounds," starvation or liquid diets, cleanses, and mega dosing dietary supplements. These can cause dangerous dehydration, overdose on certain supplements, electrolyte imbalances that can cause arrhythmias, and loss of resting metabolic rate when the body senses starvation, making subsequent weight loss harder. Trainers should be aware that clients may inquire about such diets and fitness gadgets. When they do, trainers should remember that it may take patience as well as targeted and thorough education to convey the danger and ineffectiveness of such methods and provide the alternative realities for healthy weight loss.

Ergogenic Aids and Nutritional Supplements

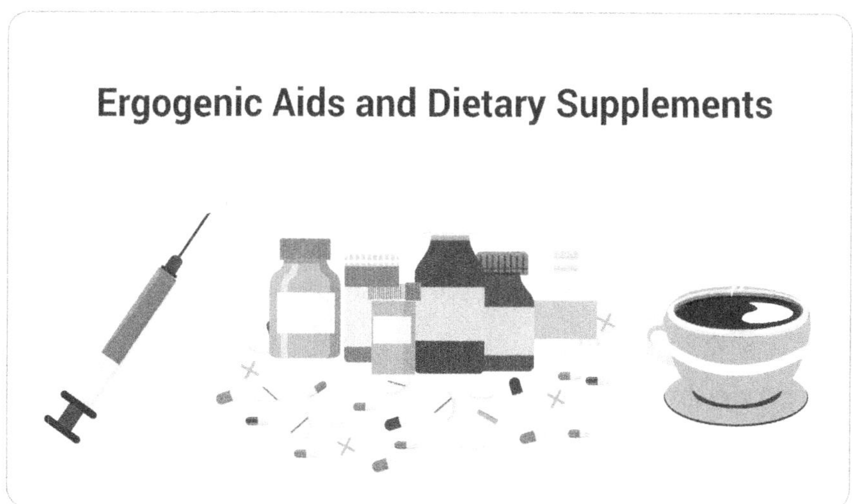

There are a variety of ergogenic aids and dietary supplements on the market available to clients, and the options continue to grow as more supplements are created. Ergogenic aids are considered to be any substance, device, or practice that has the ability to enhance or improve an individual's performance. They can be categorized as nutritional, pharmacological, physiological, psychological, or mechanical. Availability and use of ergogenic have increased tremendously in the last 10 years, and research indicates that about half of the general population, 76% of college clients, and nearly all clients engaged in strength building use ergogenic aids. Some popular ergogenic aids for increasing muscle mass and strength include creatine, beta-hydroxyl beta-methylbuteric acid (HMB), protein and amino acids, and beta-alanine. Popular aerobic endurance nutrition supplements include branched-chain amino acids (BCAAs), caffeine, sodium tablets, glutamine, high molecular weight carbohydrates, protein, sodium bicarbonate and citrate, and sports beverages.

Ergogenic Aids for Increasing Muscle Mass and Strength

Creatine

Creatine is a naturally occurring substance that is found in the kidneys, liver, and pancreas. It consists of the amino acids glycine, arginine, and methionine and can be found in protein sources such as meat and fish. Creatine supplementation is used to improve strength, increase lean body mass, and potentially aid in rapid muscle recovery during exercise. Creatine converts to creatine phosphate in the body, which is needed to make ATP, the energy molecule for muscle contractions. While research indicates that creatine can improve performance in high-intensity exercise, evidence does not support its use in endurance sports because it does not appear to affect aerobic metabolism.

Creatine monophosphate supplements are considered to be safe if used in recommended amounts by healthy individuals. The ISSN position on creatine monophosphate supplements concludes that creatine is an effective ergogenic nutrition supplement in clients to enhance high-intensity exercise and lean body mass. The recommended regimen by the ISSN to increase muscle creatine is to take 0.3 grams per kilogram of body weight per day of creatine monohydrate for at least 3 days, then 3–5 grams per day to maintain the increased stores. Creatine at the rate of about 0.1 grams per kilogram of body weight per day added to a protein supplement may help further facilitate resistance training. The ISSN concludes that creatine monophosphate supplements may be used in youth clients under proper guidance and supervision.

Beta-Hydroxyl Beta-Methylbuteric Acid

Beta-hydroxyl beta-methylbuteric acid (HMB) comes from the amino acid leucine. HMB plays a role in the prevention of protein breakdown, or proteolysis. As a result, it is used in individuals with muscle wasting conditions and by clients to enhance performance. HMB may be useful for individuals who are starting a strength training program and seeking to increase lean body mass. HMB can be safely used by youth and adults. Although HMB is commonly used as a supplement, it can be found in citrus fruits, catfish, and milk.

Protein and Amino Acids

Protein is needed to prevent muscle atrophy, even during strength training. The body needs to remain in positive nitrogen balance to prevent muscle atrophy and catabolism, which is the breakdown of muscle that occurs when protein is inadequate. Resistance training, along with positive nitrogen balance, is needed to build muscle. As such, protein or its building blocks (amino acids) must be present to ensure positive nitrogen balance. The RDA for protein of 0.8 grams per kilogram of body weight may be sufficient as a minimum for individuals not engaged in strength training; however, individuals engaged in strength training require at least 1.2–1.7 grams per kilogram of body weight.

When considering protein intake, it is important to consider the type of protein—complete or incomplete. Complete proteins contain all of the EAAs and usually come from animal sources. Incomplete proteins contain some of the essential nutrients and are found in foods such as beans, nuts, seeds, and grains. Incomplete proteins can be combined with other incomplete proteins or complete proteins to provide a complete amino acid profile. Clients may also use other sources of protein isolates such as whey, casein, or soy in the form of powders, bars, drinks, etc.

Beta-alanine

Beta-alanine is used to enhance athletic performance, particularly high-intensity, anaerobic activities. Beta-alanine, a non-EAA, is a component of carnosine, along with histidine, and is produced in skeletal

muscle. Carnosine is an essential buffering substance in skeletal muscle. If beta-alanine is not present, carnosine production cannot occur. Beta-alanine supplementation increases muscle carnosine content, which helps to improve performance during high-intensity exercise by neutralizing acid production. Beta-alanine is usually supplemented in amounts of 3-6 grams per day for clients engaged in anaerobic activity who are seeking performance enhancement.

Ergogenic Aids for Increasing Aerobic Endurance

Branched-Chain Amino Acids

Branched-chain amino acids (BCAAs), sometimes called the *proteinogenic amino acids,* are essential nutrients for building protein and include leucine, isoleucine, and valine. The term *branched-chain* refers to the chemical structure of the nutrients. BCAA usage is becoming increasingly popular with clients engaged in aerobic activity, as they are believed to enhance recovery from exercise, reduce muscle damage, and decrease central fatigue. Research studies have used a range of doses for BCAAs; however, the optimal dose is not clear. Dosing for BCAAs should be based on body weight and intensity and duration of exercise.

Caffeine

Caffeine is the most widely used stimulant in the world. Research on the use and potential benefits of caffeine and athletic performance has continued to evolve, but current prevailing studies indicate that caffeine enhances endurance and alertness and reduces muscle soreness. Caffeine is known to be a mild diuretic, and as such, can potentially lead to dehydration during exercise activity if consumed in large amounts; however, this problem has not been widely cited in literature. The International Olympic Committee allows clients to have up to 12 micrograms per milliliter of caffeine in their urine, and the National Collegiate Athletic Association (NCAA) allows 15 micrograms per milliliter in urine before any violation is cited. Optimal dosing of caffeine ranges from 3 to 6 milligrams per kilogram of body weight. Some individuals believe that caffeine should be eliminated from a client's diet prior to competition and that, because it is considered a gateway drug, youth should not be allowed to use caffeine.

Sodium Tablets

Sodium tablets for electrolyte replacement help prevent hyponatremia during exercise. The tablets usually contain sodium chloride, which is a dissolved salt in the body. Clients who have hypertension or kidney disease should not take sodium supplements.

Glutamine

Glutamine is a nonessential amino acid, and it is the most abundant amino acid. It is found in the blood and muscles. Dietary sources of glutamine include beef, pork, chicken, fish, eggs, and dairy products. It has been shown to be effective in preventing illness and infection and reducing or preventing muscle soreness.

High Molecular-Weight Carbohydrates

High molecular-weight carbohydrates help clients by replenishing glycogen stores and increasing gastric emptying, compared to other starches such as maltodextrin and dextrose. Waxy maize is an example of a high molecular-weight carbohydrate that does not contain sugar and is rapidly absorbed. Protein, as mentioned earlier, can be used in conjunction with carbohydrates to rebuild glycogen stores after exercise and has been shown to be more efficacious than high molecular-weight carbohydrates alone.

Sodium Bicarbonate

The use of sodium bicarbonate with caffeine 70–90 minutes before exercise has been shown to reduce fatigue. Sodium bicarbonate is essentially a buffer, which helps to prevent the acidic environment associated with fatigue during anaerobic activity. Sodium bicarbonate with citrate may lead to gastrointestinal discomfort, so it may not be the best solution for clients.

Sports Beverages

Sports beverages support hydration, prevent hyponatremia through the maintenance and restoration of electrolytes, and help reduce fatigue during prolonged aerobic activity. Sports beverages can be divided into three categories: isotonic, hypertonic, and hypotonic. Isotonic beverages contain sodium and sugar in physiologically similar levels; hypertonic beverages contain more sodium and sugar than the body; and hypotonic beverages contain lower amounts of sodium and sugar than the body. Some believe that sports beverages with higher amounts of sodium and sugar are not needed unless clients are engaged in activity lasting over 90 minutes. Sports beverages should ideally contain about 6–8% carbohydrates and be ingested at a rate of 3–8 ounces every 10–20 minutes for activities lasting around 90 minutes or longer.

Signs and Symptoms of Ergogenic Aid Abuse

Since ergogenic aids can enhance athletic performance, there is potential of abuse. However, ergogenic aids can adversely affect major body systems including the cardiovascular, endocrine, genitourinary, dermatological, hepatic, musculoskeletal, and psychological systems. Signs and symptoms of ergogenic aid abuse include changes in blood lipids, increased blood pressure, and decreased myocardial function; gynecomastia (enlarged breasts), decreased sperm count, shrunken testicles, impotence, and infertility in men; menstrual irregularities, enlarged clitoris, deepened voice, and a more masculine appearance for women; acne and baldness; increased chance for liver tumors and damage; increased risk of tendon tears, intramuscular abscesses, and early epiphyseal plate closure; and depression, mood swings, hostility, and aggressive violent behavior.

Specific ergogenic aids banned by the Olympics and/or the NCAA include amphetamines, anabolic steroids, androstenediol, androstenedione, blood doping, dehydroepiandrosterone (DHEA), ephedrine, and human growth hormone. The Drug Enforcement Agency (DEA), the agency in the United States responsible for controlling the issues associated with controlled pharmaceuticals and chemicals, prohibits the sale or possession of anabolic steroids without the prescription of a physician. Violators may be subject to fines and/or imprisonment.

The World Anti-Doping Agency has a complete list of performance enhancement substances (PES) that are prohibited at their website (https://www.wada-ama.org/); the major categories of PES that are prohibited include anabolic agents; peptide hormones, growth factors, related substances, and mimetics; beta-2 antagonists; hormone and metabolic modulators; diuretics and masking agents; stimulants; narcotics; cannabinoids; and glucocorticoids.

Food and Supplement Label Reading

Food and supplement labels are broken into four categories: serving size, calories, key ingredient potency, and additional ingredients. The number of calories contained in each food product is listed per serving size; for example, if there are 260 calories per serving of baked beans, and there are four servings per can, then there are 1,040 calories per can. Food labels also show how many calories derive

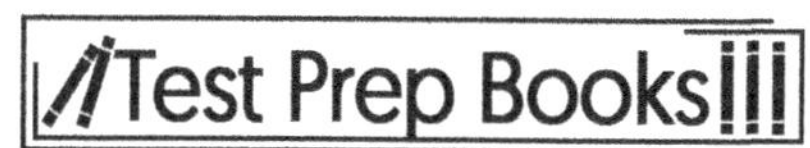

from fat and from which type of fat (i.e., from saturated or unsaturated fat). The section on key ingredients shows the quantity of each ingredient per serving and its ratio relative to daily values. Note that these daily value percentages correspond to a 2,000-calorie diet. The section on additional ingredients indicates ingredients without nutritional value, such as casings on sausages. Information on allergens and potential allergens is also found in this section. Supplement labels will include additional information on both dosage frequency and quantity.

Factors Influencing Weight Management

The First Law of Thermodynamics asserts that energy is neither created nor destroyed; it simply changes form. In other words, the total amount of energy in a system, such as a body, is constant. Applied to weight loss and weight management, this law serves as the basis for two sides of a heated debate over the efficacy of diet and exercise.

In broad strokes, the debate plays out as follows. The first camp asserts that exercise is the key to weight loss. Citing the First Law of Thermodynamics, proponents of this theory argue that a person loses weight by burning more calories than they put into their body. The belief that all calories are created equal informs this perspective. A calorie burned through exercise is equal to a calorie consumed. In short, if a person consumes 2,000 calories and burns 2,100 calories each day, then over the course of time that person will lose weight.

The second camp asserts that all calories are not created equal, and that some calories are lost more easily. For example, energy from inefficient calorie sources (such as protein) is lost during the metabolic process, so those calories are burned more easily through exercise. This second camp still bases its hypothesis on the First Law of Thermodynamics, but it believes that different calories produce heat differently. Therefore, a balanced system does not depend solely on the number of calories consumed; rather, it depends on the number and type of calories consumed.

Beyond caloric intake and expenditure, other factors, like sleep and medication, also impact weight management. Ghrelin and leptin, two hormones responsible for regulating hunger, are affected by poor sleep, so when a person does not get enough sleep, they may feel the need to eat more. Additionally, fatigue plays a factor since a tired person will likely engage in less physical, calorie-burning activity than a well-rested person.

Medications may be prescribed to people who are obese or have a large body mass index. These medications may make a person feel less hungry, feel full sooner, or limit the amount of fat stored in the body. Medication is designed to supplement lifestyle changes. When lifestyle changes alone are insufficient, physiological conditions, such as endocrine abnormalities, may be part of the problem.

The endocrine system influences some aspects of the metabolism. For example, an underactive thyroid may cause hormone imbalances, which affect the metabolism. Underproduction of leptin may keep a person from feeling full. Insulin imbalances may adversely affect the regulation of blood sugar and fat.

Practice Quiz

1. High-intensity resistance training causes all muscle fibers to hypertrophy because of the order of motor unit recruitment. What is the name of this phenomenon where smaller motor units are recruited first, followed by the recruitment of larger units when more force is needed?
   a. Selective recruitment
   b. The size principle
   c. Maximal recruitment
   d. Synchronization of motor unit activation

2. High-intensity anaerobic training causes changes to connective tissue growth and structure. Which of the following is NOT a change that occurs in tendons in response to this training?
   a. Increased collagen fibril diameter and number
   b. Increased tendon flexibility
   c. Increased formation of long filaments
   d. Increased collagen fibril packing density

3. An acute bout of anaerobic resistance exercise significantly impacts the cardiovascular system. During resistance exercise, which cardiovascular responses occur?

   I. Increased heart rate and systolic blood pressure
   II. Increased cardiac output
   III. Increased peripheral blood flow
   IV. Increased stroke volume

   a. I, II
   b. I, II, III
   c. I, II, IV
   d. I, II, III, IV

4. Increased tendon stiffness is associated with which of the following?
   a. Greater muscular recoil and power production
   b. Decreased ability of the tendon to withstand tensional forces
   c. Enhanced muscular flexibility
   d. Increased risk of injury

5. A client would like to start using creatine as an ergogenic aid. The athlete should receive which of the following advice?
   a. Creatine can be made in the body and supplementation is not safe for athletes.
   b. Research indicates that creatine is best suited for endurance sports.
   c. The ISSN has concluded that athletes should consider other ergogenic aids.
   d. Creatine can be started at 0.3 grams per kilogram of body weight.

See answers on the next page.

Answer Explanations

1. B: As part of the neural response to high-intensity resistance training, the recruitment of motor units in an orderly manner is controlled by the size principle. The size principle is a method used by motor units to modulate force production, and it is dependent upon how many motor units are activated. If more force is needed for an activity, a greater number of motor units will be recruited. The smallest motor units are recruited first, and as more force is needed, larger motor units are sequentially activated. These strategies are designed to help the body be as efficient as possible.

2. B: Tendon stiffness increases in response to anaerobic training, and therefore, tendons become less flexible. While this may sound negative, stiffer tendons have a better mechanical advantage and are more efficient at transferring muscular work to the connected joints to produce powerful movements. High-intensity anaerobic training causes connective tissue growth and structural changes. Specific changes within a tendon include an increase in collagen fibril diameter, number, and packing density.

3. C: Choice *C* is the only answer containing the three correct functions while excluding option III (increased peripheral blood flow). Muscular contractions greater than 20% of maximum voluntary contraction slow peripheral blood flow during a set, but during rest, blood flow increases to levels above baseline. Acute anaerobic exercise increases cardiac output, heart rate, stroke volume, and systolic blood pressure.

4. A: Anaerobic training increases tendon stiffness, which is directly associated with greater muscular recoil and power production because a stiffer tendon is better able to transfer forces from muscular contractions to the joints the muscles control, resulting in better efficiency and, thus, higher power. Flexibility is not improved. Decreased ability to withstand tensile forces and increased risk of injury do not necessarily occur due to increases in tendon stiffness; many other factors, such as biomechanics, proper load selection, fatigue, training status, and hydration, are involved.

5. D: A recommended regimen by the ISSN to increase muscle creatine is to start taking 0.3 grams per kilogram of body weight per day of creatine monohydrate for at least 3 days. Creatine is a naturally occurring substance that is found in the kidneys, liver, and pancreas, and the ISSN states that it can be safely and effectively used to enhance high-intensity exercise and lean body mass. Evidence does not support the use of creatine in endurance sports because it does not appear to have an effect on aerobic metabolism.

Client Relations and Behavioral Coaching

Keeping the client motivated in his or her exercise program and applying behavioral change are keys to adherence. Trainers can foster a positive, supportive environment by using a variety of verbal and nonverbal communication techniques. Use of S.M.A.R.T. (Specific, Measurable, Attainable, Realistic, and Timely) goals and tapping into sources of intrinsic and extrinsic motivational aids, helping ensure the client has a dependable support system, giving frequent reinforcement and feedback, and identifying and tackling barriers to adherence can bolster client success.

Communication Methods

Phone calls, emails, text messages, newsletters, and websites are all useful tools that facilitate frequent conversations with clients, although each client may have his or her communication mode preferences. The trainer can likely find ways to incorporate a variety of these methods. Electronic or digital means such as text and email are convenient and fast. They may be used in ways such as to remind clients of upcoming sessions, notify clients to bring something to a session, such as an extra water bottle, or as a way to offer friendly and quick praise after a great session. Phone calls may work better for longer discussions, perhaps when a client is sick and the trainer is giving return-to-activity advice, or if the client is not easily reachable by digital means.

Confidentiality principles should always be practiced. Trainers should not send sensitive or personal messages through any method that may breach this need. Newsletters and websites are geared more toward a wider audience, rather than the individual client, although clients may use these resources to learn more about nutrition, exercises, or other informative articles the trainer prepares. These communication channels can also be used as marketing tools for the trainer to recruit new clients. Plus, the trainer can employ metrics to analyze the reach and return-on-investment for such sources.

Verbal and Nonverbal Behaviors

Verbal and nonverbal behaviors are equally important in setting a positive, educational, and supportive environment for the client. The trainer should follow these behaviors:

- Look professional and fully attentive
- Give eye contact
- Use encouraging facial expressions and body language
- Augment interaction with positive verbal feedback, demonstrations, instructions, and cueing

Body language such as hands on hips or crossed over the chest may appear standoffish. Conversely, smiling and nodding enhance client comfort and satisfaction. The trainer should refrain from checking phone messages, complaining about his or her life, or acting distracted in any number of ways.

Active Listening Techniques

Active listening is a process of trying to understand the underlying meaning in a client's words, which builds empathy and trust as well as greater client satisfaction and compliance. Asking open-ended questions and repeating or rephrasing what a client said in a reflective or clarifying manner is a form of active listening that builds a positive, trusting relationship. The client may indicate he or she would like to "lose a few pounds," and, in response, the trainer could ask, "Okay, so just to make sure we are in the same page, it sounds like you are hoping to lose a little weight?" The trainer should encourage the client

with verbal and nonverbal cues, eye contact and undivided attention, look engaged and non-judgmental, and not rush the client.

Learning Styles

There are different learning styles that can vary with each client. The trainer should be aware of these learning styles because a client will greatly benefit from instructions during sessions that are tailored to his or her specific learning style. Auditory learners learn through hearing, so the trainer can explain exercises and give verbal cues about form. Visual learners learn through seeing, so the trainer can demonstrate and exercise for the client to observe and give printed illustrations of exercises for the client to take home and review. Kinesthetic learners learn through movement, involvement, and experience. The trainer can demonstrate and then have the client try an unweighted trial of the exercise or a partial range of motion to demonstrate understanding before trying the full resistance or movement.

Goal Setting

Effective goal setting requires a systematic approach to ensure the goals positively impact both the physical and psychological development of the client. For goal setting to be successful, goals need to be specific, challenging but attainable, and outcome- and process-oriented, and include interdependent short- and long-term goals.

S.M.A.R.T. Goals

- Specific: clearly-defined (who, what, when, where, why, how)
- Measurable: a way to track progress and determine when the goal is achieved
- Attainable: make sure the goal is not out of reach
- Realistic: similar to attainable, but also making sure that goals are compatible with client's lifestyle, health, injury history, injuries, and time to train
- Timely: a specific date or timeframe for goals, which gives structure to the goal, helps it to be more measurable, and provides an appropriate sense of urgency, while still being practical and feasible in the allotted timeframe

Setting Effective Client-Oriented Behavioral Goals

Goal setting is a strategic approach to address and implement positive behavioral changes through which progressive standards of success (short term goals) are set en route to a desired standard of achievement (long term goal). This systematic approach aids in a feeling of mastery, which increases motivation and commitment, leading to improved behavioral change. The personal trainer needs to take an individualized approach to the goal-setting process with clients, taking into account the person's interests and needs and not just relying on the results of testing to set goals.

Short- and Long-Term Goals

A staircase is a useful metaphor for understanding short- and long-term goals. Each individual step is a short-term goal, and the top of the staircase is the long-term goal. The client's current ability level is the bottom step, and each step moving toward the top is a series of progressively more challenging short-term process-oriented goals that are linked to the top step, representing the long-term outcome goal.

Process Goals

Process goals are focused on the actions that are required to execute a skill or perform well. Focusing on the actions rather than the final result increases the client's control over achieving the desired results. Obtaining a process goal is dependent on expenditure of effort by the client to alter his or her actions.

Outcome Goals

Outcome goals usually focus on a result of a competitive event, such as setting a world record. Obtaining these goals is not under the client's control because these outcomes are dependent on the effort and performance of both the client and others. Using process goals to achieve outcome goals can facilitate the development of obtainable daily goals. This can help to lessen the focus on the end result and help the client maintain the motivation and effort required to reach the final result.

Client Expectation Management Related to Client-Trainer Relationship and Overall Training Goals

First and foremost, the client-trainer relationship is a business relationship. A client pays a trainer to receive a service and results. As with any business, the quality of the service a trainer provides depends on the trainer's business practices.

Developing trust between a trainer and a client is one of the best ways to manage expectations in the client-trainer relationship. Trainers build trust with their clients by keeping appointments and arriving early. Clients want to see that trainers are as committed to their fitness goals as they are. Arriving early to sessions, greeting clients with enthusiasm, and showing genuine interest in a client throughout the session are keys to building trust. If a trainer must break an appointment with a client or if a trainer arrives late to a session, they should communicate with the client directly, apologize for any inconvenience, and reschedule the appointment if necessary. Life happens, and most clients will understand if schedule changes are communicated effectively and a trainer demonstrates that their clients are a priority.

While courtesy and integrity are two important elements of quality service, a client will also want to see results. Trainers manage client expectations of overall training goals by helping a client set clear and realistic goals at the start of their fitness program. Since body types vary, trainers may help a client set realistic goals according to the client's particular body type. Clients often begin fitness programs with unrealistic goals and perhaps an exaggerated impression of their own physical abilities. Naturally, a client who believes anything is possible will demand impossible results, and this may create tension between client and trainer when unrealistic expectations are not met. Trainers manage client expectations of overall training goals by educating clients and working within a manageable program to meet realistic goals.

Transtheoretical Model of Behavior Change

Trainers can employ a variety of techniques to facilitate client motivation, depending on the client's personality and challenges as well as his or her stage of readiness (transtheoretical model). In earlier stages, rewards may need to be more tangible and frequent. As the client moves more from the preparation and action stage to the maintenance stage, the focus can shift to more of the rewarding

aspects of exercises such as enjoyment, improvements in health, and a break from the workday. Some motivational techniques include the following:

- In early stages of a program: use of a points system, competitions, recognitions (Athlete of the Month bulletin board), trophies
- Personal contracts
- Varied routines to prevent boredom and burnout or exercise challenges
- Reminders of the benefits of exercise or the negatives of inactivity
- Well-rounded S.M.A.R.T goals that are both long-term and short-term, addressing all five areas of health-related fitness
- Social support such as group classes, buddy systems, periodic telephone calls or emails, support from family and friends
- External rewards such as new exercise clothes, playlists, spa treatments if certain weekly physical activity recommendations are met
- Reduced fees or free sessions based on adherence

Evaluating Behavioral Readiness to Optimize Exercise Adherence

The trans-theoretical model describes the client's process of getting ready to start exercise and consists of five stages:

- Precontemplation: Client is not intending to take action toward changing physical activity and is not considering becoming physically active.
- Contemplation: Client intends to increase physical activity within the next six months.
- Preparation: Client has developed a plan of action toward behavior change and will be making changes in the immediate future (next thirty days) and/or is inconsistently engaging in some amount of physical activity, but not at least thirty minutes of moderate-intensity activity for five or more days per week.
- Action: Client engages in at least thirty minutes of moderate-intensity activity for five or more days per week, but for less than six months.
- Maintenance: Client actively maintains changes made during the action stage, and new behaviors are established for six months or more; client is working to prevent relapse.

Behavioral Coaching Methods

Health Coaching Principles

Research has found that motivational interviewing is a successful tool for improving readiness for changing health behaviors such as engaging in or increasing exercise. This technique involves acknowledging and slowly working through a client's challenges concerning regular activity, stressing the fact that it is his or her choice to be active while also encouraging the change. Motivational interviewing requires clients to reflect on what may happen if they do not change their current habits and weighs the pros and cons of activity and inactivity. Personal trainers can also use the Five A's Model when counseling clients to create a physical activity plan:

- Address why the client is there. What is the agenda?
- Assess current health and activity and readiness for change
- Advise clients of the benefits of activity and consequences of inactivity
- Assist clients in creating a plan for exercise and conquering barriers
- Arrange for follow-up after plan implementation

Ideal Performance State

Often referred to as "the zone," clients report the ideal performance state is characterized by several components including 1) a sense of personal control, 2) a feeling of effortless performance, 3) an absence of a fear of failure, 4) attention focused on the activity being performed, 5) performing the activity without having to think about or analyze it, and 6) a feeling that time slows down.

Motivational Techniques

Motivation, a psychological construct, is the direction and intensity of a client's effort. There are several forms of motivation including intrinsic and extrinsic motivation, achievement motivation, and motivation associated with skill development. It should be noted that clients generally experience more than one type of motivation, and these can vary depending on the activity being performed, perceptions of competency, the level of importance the client places on the activity, and other factors.

Intrinsic Motivation

Intrinsic motivation is a client's internal desire for his or her behavior to be competent and self-determined. It originates from the client's love and interest in the sport and personal satisfaction (inherent reward) in performing the activity. Intrinsic motivation is generally considered the best form of motivation. It can help a client maintain focus on achieving short-term goals that require consistent effort to enhance the client's performance level.

Extrinsic Motivation

Extrinsic motivation, used extensively in sports, comes from external sources (e.g., trainers, teammates) in the form of individualized rewards such as praise from trainers and teammates, medals, social acceptance, avoidance of punishment, and the desire for positive reinforcement.

Achievement Motivation

Achievement motivation reflects a client's effort to master a specific task, achieve excellence, perform better than others, and overcome obstacles. Clients with high levels of achievement motivation are more competitive and generally perform better than clients with lower levels of achievement motivation. There are two types of achievement motivation. The motive to achieve success (MAS) is characterized by a desire to challenge and evaluate one's ability and be proud of accomplishments. Clients with greater MAS like challenging situations, where the likelihood of success or failure is approximately the same. The motive to avoid failure (MAF) is characterized by the desire to avoid being perceived as a failure, preserve one's ego and self-confidence, and minimize shame. Clients with greater MAF prefer either easy situations where they will likely succeed and avoid shame or difficult situations where success is unlikely and feelings of shame are minimized.

Reinforcement Strategies

Positive Reinforcement

The goal of positive reinforcement is to increase the occurrence of a favorable behavior (e.g., skill, movement, appropriate teamwork) or outcome (e.g., improved performance). Immediately after the positive behavior occurs, the client or team is given a positive incentive. This incentive is something that the client/team values (praise, more playing time, starting position, extra rest between sets, etc.) to encourage continued occurrence of the desired positive behavior.

Negative Reinforcement

Similar to positive reinforcement, negative reinforcement provides a "reward" after the occurrence of the desired behavior or outcome. This reward is the removal of a stimulus the client/team views as aversive. A trainer might remove the regularly performed sets of push-ups after the entire team performed an exercise using the correct technique.

Positive Punishment

Positive punishment is used to deter undesirable behavior by presenting an action, object, or event after the unwanted behavior occurs. Positive punishment might take the form of a client running extra sprints after practice because he or she was late or a team receiving a reprimand from the trainer after incorrectly running a specific play.

Negative Punishment

Negative punishment involves the removal of a highly valued positive stimulus after an unwanted behavior or outcome occurs to deter future occurrences of the behavior. A team that is joking around during a resistance training session may receive negative punishment when the trainer turns off the music for the remainder of the training session.

Extrinsic and Intrinsic Reinforcement Strategies

Rewards and reinforcements may help in motivating clients to make and keep positive behavioral changes. Extrinsic rewards are factors outside of the exercise itself that help to support the desire to be physically active, and may be especially important in the earlier stages of programs when the exercise itself is more painful due to discomfort and lower fitness levels. Extrinsic rewards include things like a free t-shirt or iTunes gift card for workout music, which can be given after completing a certain number of sessions. It is important that such rewards are not counterproductive to accomplishing health goals — for example, high-calorie milkshakes or candy bars. Intrinsic rewards are ones the client feels directly from the exercise itself, such as improved self-esteem or fitting into their favorite jeans. These rewards remain important long after goal achievement. Intrinsically motivated clients or those with self-determination enjoy the process of the exercise itself and therefore may maintain their health behaviors more easily than externally motivated clients who exercise for the sake of achieving some sort of reward. As the client's fitness level improves, it is likely that extrinsic rewards may become less important.

Imagery Techniques

Imagery techniques utilize mental visualization of specific athletic situations such as the performance of a targeted event/race. The benefits of vivid imagery include providing a client with exposure to the successful execution of a specific skill under a stressful competitive situation (e.g., sinking a putt on the 18th hole); allowing the client to "experience" the sights, sounds, smells, and physical exertion associated with the competitive environment on a regular basis and at a much greater frequency than actual competitions during the season; and the client feeling (or watching) himself or herself perform successfully and gaining confidence in the ability to perform optimally.

Methods that Enhance Motor Learning and Skill Acquisition

Instruction

There are three main types of instruction that can be used with clients: explicit instruction, guided discovery, and discovery. *Explicit instruction* facilitates the client's learning by providing the most information about the task in a prescriptive manner, aimed at guiding the client through the entire movement, often in a step-by-step fashion. *Guided discovery* gives less information to the client than explicit instruction but provides a more holistic description of the overall movement. By providing the goal of the task and some details about the movement, the client has to integrate the information provided with the movement pattern being practiced to understand how the goal is related to the movements performed. *Discovery* provides no instructions, but rather presents the overall goal of a movement. Using discovery-oriented instruction gives the client an opportunity to explore various methods to achieve the movement goal; however, it can be time-intensive.

Feedback

Feedback plays a critical role in the acquisition and refinement of new motor skills. In general, when learning a new movement skill, it is beneficial to provide more frequent feedback that decreases over time as mastery is reached. The client has readily accessible *intrinsic feedback* provided by his or her body and sensory systems. A client kicks a soccer ball, and sensory information from the client's eyes, proprioceptors, mechanoreceptors, and joint receptors in the foot provides intrinsic feedback that the he or she can utilize to refine the movement. *Augmented feedback* originates from an external source, such as a trainer, other observer, or technology (e.g., video, heart rate monitor, laboratory equipment). Two types of augmented feedback are *knowledge of results* and *knowledge of performance*. The difference between these two forms of feedback is whether information provided to the client is about the completion of a movement task (i.e., the amount of time the task took) or the client's performance of the movement task (e.g., the position of the client's feet).

Whole vs. Part Practice

When learning a complex motor skill, there are two different strategies: whole vs. part practice. *Whole practice* is required with complex motor skills because the component movements are interrelated (such as in archery or performing a jump shot). It also works well for skills that are not particularly complex. *Part practice* is best used to teach clients complex skills with subcomponents that are less interrelated, such as a gymnastics floor routine.

Behavior Change Strategies

Behavioral coaching occurs when trainers help clients improve their habits. Behavioral coaching is a holistic approach to personal training that recognizes the role of lifestyle in the advancement or deterioration of fitness goals. Behavioral coaching strategies aim to add healthy, positive habits to a client's lifestyle and mitigate—if not replace—unhealthy, negative practices.

Habit stacking is a behavioral coaching strategy that seeks to add positive habits to a client's lifestyle without necessarily removing negative habits. This strategy is based on the science of habit formation, which articulates the brain's ability to develop neurological connections based on behavior. For

example, the brain develops strong connections between the parts of the brain that are responsible for catching a baseball or high jumping when a person makes such habits a part of their routine.

Alternatively, neurological connections between the parts of the brain that are responsible for catching or jumping deteriorate if a person does not regularly practice catching or jumping. This is an example of synaptic pruning, which is the brain's process of maintaining efficient connections between various parts of the brain. These connections are determined by one's habits. The brain of someone who works out regularly will maintain efficient connections between the parts of the brain that are responsible for exercise. Alternatively, the brain does not maintain efficient connections between parts of the brain that are responsible for actions that are not done regularly.

The brain's natural function of regulating connections between different parts of the brain provides the basis for habit stacking and other behavioral coaching strategies. Habit stacking helps clients reduce stress when they start a new diet or fitness program. For example, rather than tell clients not to eat pizza, a trainer may encourage them to order a side salad whenever they order a pizza. This way healthy habits are introduced without encouraging clients to give up things they enjoy. People feel stress when they are asked to give up things they like.

Habit stacking is an effective way to reduce the stress clients feel when they complete a fitness program. People become stressed when they must abandon their favorite vices and when life's natural stressors—trouble at work, family pressure, and so on—occur. When stress compounds, people often fall back into negative habits, but if those negative habits are not prohibited in the first place, then people find ways to deal with stress in less self-destructive ways.

Health Behavior Change Models to Support Exercise Adherence

An understanding of behavioral change models will assist personal trainers in reinforcing positive behaviors and help clients avoid sabotaging progress toward behavioral goals. While there are many health behavioral change models, several common ones and the ways in which they can be used to support exercise adherence are as follows:

Health Belief Model: The perceived seriousness of a potential health problem is the main predictor of behavioral change, aided by discussions of the physical and psychological benefits of exercise and the consequences of inactivity.

Theory of Planned Behavior: The client's level of motivation for behavioral change is shaped by his or her attitudes, subjective norms, and perceived control. The intention to engage in a behavior will ultimately result in that behavior. Plans such as carrying extra exercise clothes and shoes in the car to be ready when opportunity strikes, formally scheduling workouts into a calendar, and planning for high-risk relapse situations (like packing exercise DVDs and a resistance band for work travel) use this model to encourage adherence.

Social Cognitive Theory: Behavioral change is influenced by the triad of interactions of the environment, personal factors, and behavior itself. It relies heavily on the idea of self-efficacy. Self-regulatory strategies such as self-monitoring physical activity, setting personal goals and rewards, planning activity in advance, and having reasonable expectations are methods using this theory to improve adherence.

Socio-Ecological Model: Addresses relationships. Behaviors, such as a client's motivation to exercise, are shaped by interpersonal relations, the surrounding environment, community, policy, and law. To improve adherence, make sure the client has a good social support system, perhaps has an exercise buddy, goes to a gym in a convenient location to work or home, or perhaps joins a local sports league.

Strategies to Increase Non-Structured Physical Activity

Trainers can encourage clients to add unstructured physical activity throughout the day by making "healthy swaps," which means replacing a sedentary behavior with a healthy, active one. Some suggestions include:

- Wearing a pedometer or using a phone app to track activity with the goal of increasing steps per day
- Engaging in active play with children or grandchildren
- Keeping an extra pair of workout clothes and sneakers in the car for spontaneous opportunities to be active
- Walking a dog, walking at lunch, getting up to walk around a few minutes every hour
- Performing yard work such as gardening, raking, shoveling, pruning, cleaning gutters
- Performing housework such as vacuuming, mopping, dusting, rearranging furniture
- Walking or biking to the corner store for milk or small groceries instead of driving
- Walking to local establishments for food instead of ordering delivery
- Walking or biking to work if the commute is reasonably short
- If taking public transportation, getting off a few stops early to a destination to walk the remainder
- Refraining from emailing or calling coworkers and walking to their desk instead
- Taking stairs instead of elevators
- Parking farther away from the entrance at stores or work

Behavioral Strategies to Enhance Exercise and Health Behavior Change

Feedback leads to the knowledge of results and is important in the progress toward goal achievement and evaluation of success or failure. Setting goals that are both appropriately difficult and personally motivating for the client will enhance commitment. Reinforcement can occur on a psychological level (influencing behavior and self-esteem or self-efficacy) and a neurobiological level (with the release of dopamine, which strengthens the synaptic pathways involved in learning a behavior).

The personal trainer should use feedback and positive reinforcement to enhance a client's self-efficacy and motivation towards health improvement. Positive, encouraging social support from peers, family, friends, or community can also enhance behavior change and goal achievement. Negative social support can cause feelings of doubt and inadequacy and lower self-esteem. The personal trainer should ask each client about the social support system he or she has and realize that many clients need the trainer to play a significant role of support.

Barriers to Behavior Change

Barriers to exercise adherence and compliance can be personal (fear, embarrassment, injury), behavioral (lack of motivation, unhealthy habits in times of stress, time management), environmental (no safe parks near client's home, inconvenient gyms), social (lack of support or someone sabotaging progress), and programmatic (lack of knowledge, too intense of a previous plan that caused injury or failure). Trainers should help clients identify the barriers in their own lives and brainstorm solutions such as designing home exercise programs or "on-the-road" workouts for traveling, eliciting social support,

offering helpful rewards and incentives, and educating clients on alternative workout locations or dietary substitutions. The solutions should be mutually evaluated, since some will be more realistic than others. The trainer should aid the client in developing a plan for implementing solutions to the identified barriers. After that step, the plan may need to be fine-tuned.

Relapses

Some breaks in an exercise routine are inevitable, such as with injury, illness, travel, or holidays, but it may be possible to circumnavigate others, such as inclement weather or a busier work schedule. Interruptive events can cause relapse, but if psychological, behavioral, or physical strategies are employed in advance to ensure such breaks are only temporary and do not become full-blown lapses, the client can continue training and resume a path toward success of his or her fitness goals. Trainers should emphasize that these breaks or relapses are not failures as long as the routine is picked up again as soon as possible. If not, arrangements and modifications to the plan can be made to accommodate some of these challenges, enabling the client to stay focused and remain motivated toward achieving his or her goals.

Trainers should remind clients of the physical and psychological benefits of exercise, possibly implement reward strategies, and ensure that the client has the social support to get back on the program. Sometimes perceived failure or lack of progress can cause a client to relapse into a sedentary lifestyle. If so, it might be necessary to re-evaluate the goals and shift focus to something more rewarding or tangible in the short-term. This will instill a feeling of success before moving back toward tackling a particularly challenging goal.

Psychological Responses to Exercise

One of the most obvious psychological responses to exercise is increased self-esteem. This response isn't immediate, as progress has to be made before a client will see the physical effects of exercise. However, it is a factor that contributes to whether a client adheres to an exercise program. For clients who begin an exercise program for medical reasons, the changes that result from exercise can positively influence their state of mind regarding their health. Other psychological effects such as better sleep and reduced stress, anxiety, and depression can be enjoyed sooner. Individuals find that they easily fall asleep, have deeper sleep, and wake up feeling like they have experienced a more restorative sleep when they have a consistent exercise schedule. Being able to sleep well provides additional advantages for clients in exercise programs. Clients wake up rejuvenated and energetic, making exercise less of a struggle. Adequate sleep also improves the immune system and can reduce stress-related health problems. Additionally, exercise has been found to have similar effects as medication and therapy on depression.

Since an exercise program will be most successful if the client experiences desired results, it's important for the trainer to be able to communicate well with the client in order to personalize the workouts to address individual client needs. Not all clients are looking to only lose weight or build strength. It is widely known that exercise has psychological benefits, therefore many clients may turn to exercise as a way to handle anxiety, depression, stress, or even to get better sleep. It only takes about 5 to 10 minutes of moderate exercise to induce a positive change in mood. Being aware of these advantages and having good communication skills will allow the trainer to facilitate the changes that the client desires. It will also give the trainer insight into areas of the client's life that could benefit from the positive psychological responses to exercise. If the client is looking to reduce stress through exercise, a good trainer will communicate with the client and schedule exercise sessions to produce the effect that's needed. For instance, if a client usually goes home from work stressed out and can't fall asleep, the trainer might recommend workouts after work, but before going home. Trainers need to be able to recognize when clients need the psychological benefits of exercise and know to design and schedule programs to meet those needs.

Arousal and Anxiety

In sports, arousal is the intensity of motivation, anxiety, and focus experienced by a client and is the result of physiological and psychological activation. Arousal can be understood as a continuum of activation from deep sleep to very intense excitement. A highly-aroused client may experience an increased heart rate, sweating, and anxiety, while the client with low arousal may be lying down and feel tired and unfocused. Optimal arousal is often described as an inverse "U," wherein the ideal performance occurs with moderate levels of arousal, while either extreme can detract from performance. Arousal can be associated with both pleasant and unpleasant situations and interpreted as being a positive or negative to a client.

Anxiety is perceived as a negative emotional state, associated with the body being physiologically aroused, which is generally characterized by worry, nervousness, apprehension, and fear. The thought process responsible for the perception of anxiety as negative is a result of *cognitive anxiety*, while its counterpart, *somatic anxiety*, is the physical symptoms (e.g., increased heart rate, upset stomach) of anxiety. Previous negative outcomes (e.g., false start on a relay) and negative thoughts may manifest physically, negatively impacting the physical performance of the client. Recognizing how negative physical and psychological arousal impacts a client's mental state and performance can provide an opportunity to assist the client in understanding his or her reaction to anxiety in stressful situations. The client can begin working on perceiving the stressful situations more positively and to control the anxiety.

Additionally, anxiety can also be categorized as trait or state anxiety. *Trait anxiety* is considered to be part of one's personality, predisposing a client to perceive many situations as being threatening when in fact, no physical or psychological danger exists. In general, clients with high trait anxiety generally experience higher levels of state anxiety. *State anxiety* is a continually changing component of mood that is the subjective perception of tension and apprehension associated with increased arousal of the autonomic and endocrine systems. A client's level of state anxiety may change throughout a soccer game with changing situations and may have a positive, negative, or no impact on performance, depending upon the client's skill level, difficulty of tasks being performed, and his or her level of trait anxiety.

Drive Theory

Drive theory considers the relationship between arousal and performance to be linear; the more arousal experienced by the client, the better the he or she will perform. Clearly, this is not the case, as too much or too little arousal can negatively impact performance. Two factors that significantly impact how a client's level of arousal influences performance are *skill level* and *task complexity*. Clients at lower skill levels need less arousal to perform than their highly skilled counterparts because less skilled or new clients must concentrate on the actions being performed; too many apprehensive thoughts can interfere with the unskilled client's ability to concentrate. Lower levels of arousal are also advantageous for clients attempting difficult tasks that require a lot of conscious attention. For example, hockey goalies perform better with lower levels of arousal that clients whose tasks do not require an extensive amount of attention. In contrast, long-distant runners can perform well at a higher level of arousal because the

biomechanical task (running, in this case) is somewhat automatic and does not require a significant amount of conscious attention.

Inverted-U Theory

The inverted-U theory posits that too little or too much arousal negatively impacts athletic performance, and there is an optimal level of arousal that facilitates optimal performance. The inverted-U graphically shows this (x-axis is level of arousal; y-axis is performance), as the shape demonstrates that low levels or high levels beyond the optimal level of arousal result in worse performance, and somewhere between low and high arousal is the range of arousal associated with optimal performance (the top of the inverted-U). At this point, the internal and external stimuli experienced by the client generate the optimal amount of arousal required to enhance performance. For example, if the heart rate is not fast enough, the body might not be physiologically ready to perform, but a heart rate that is too fast can cause fatigue too early in the competition, negatively impacting performance. As mentioned, clients vary greatly in the level of arousal needed for optimal performance depending on a variety of factors.

Individual Zones of Optimal Functioning (IZOF) Theory

This theory recognizes that there is a continuum of state anxiety that varies across clients and that emotions can also impact a client's optimal zone of functioning. It is the role of the trainer to help the clients identify and reach their optimal level of state anxiety. This can be accomplished by quantifying state anxiety and mood using specific assessments. By quantifying state anxiety, it is possible to identify each client's ideal range of state anxiety needed to enhance performance and optimize the client's abilities.

Catastrophe Theory

Catastrophe theory recognizes that cognitive and somatic anxiety, along with physiological arousal, can negatively impact optimal arousal levels, leading to an abrupt decline in athletic performance. Cognitive anxiety taking effect after the arousal threshold has been reached can quickly and detrimentally impact a client's thought process, causing the client to focus on and doubt his or her ability to perform, resulting in a devastating performance decline.

Reversal Theory

Reversal theory simply states that high levels of arousal and anxiety experienced by a client can be perceived positively as an indication that the client is excited and ready to compete, or negatively as unpleasant, as demonstrated by a lack confidence. For the client to perform optimally, arousal must be interpreted positively. This theory is novel because 1) the client's interpretation of the arousal—not the amount felt—is important, and 2) the client has the ability to change negative interpretations of arousal into positive interpretations, thus controlling the response to high levels of arousal.

Stress

Stress is the result of a psychological and/or physical demand placed on a client who does not have the ability to respond to the demand. The situation causing this imbalance of demand and response – an environmental or cognitive stressor – causes a stress response. Stress can be positive *(eustress)* or negative *(distress)* for a client. Training places a physiological stress on the body that is required for a client to improve performance.

Confidence and Positive Self-Talk

Self-Confidence

Self-confidence is the belief in one's ability to perform a specific behavior such as hitting a baseball or completing a marathon. In the realm of sports, research has identified several types of self-confidence including self-confidence in performing physical skills, in one's ability to use psychological skills (e.g., self-talk) and perceptual skills (e.g., visual scanning), one's learning potential (needed to improve skills), and confidence in one's training and level of fitness.

Self-Efficacy

Self-efficacy (SE) is the client's perception of his or her ability to perform a situation-specific task successfully. The personal trainer should recognize that his or her actions can improve the client's SE by targeting the multiple sources that influence SE. The first and most significant source of SE is the client's past performance experiences. Helping the client set challenging but attainable short-term goals can provide performance success, which can have a positive impact on SE. The second source is vicarious experiences where the client watches/models a similar client's successful performance (e.g., "If someone similar to me can complete that new drill, so can I."). Verbal persuasion, the third SE source, can include encouragement from trainers, teammates, oneself, and other external sources (e.g., Nike's "Just Do It" slogan). The fourth source of SE is physiological arousal and emotional/mood states. For example, helping a client interpret pre-competition "jitteriness" as excitement to compete because the client knows he or she can successfully achieve a specific performance goal can positively influence SE, as opposed to the interpretation of the "jitteriness" as a sign of being nervous or unprepared to compete.

Self-Talk

Positive self-talk provides motivation ("I can get my personal best time in this race!"), encouragement ("Get ready to swim fast!"), and reinforcement ("I am prepared for this race!") and often is used to increase effort, energy, and a positive attitude. When a client uses *instructional self-talk*, he or she generally focuses on technical and task-related aspects of performance ("Streamline off the wall!") or strategy ("Maintain my race pace for this 800-meter run."). *Negative self-talk* typically denotes anger ("Can't believe I missed that putt. I'm such an idiot and will never win now."), doubt ("I can't do this."), negative judgment ("That was not good enough."), or discouragement ("There is no way I can win this race.").

Practice Quiz

1. Although Robert is not the runner in the road races he enters, he loves participating in the races and having the opportunity to work on his areas of weakness. He also is good at maintaining his focus on achieving his short-term goals. What type of motivation is driving Robert's behavior?
   a. Extrinsic motivation
   b. Achievement motivation
   c. Outcome motivation
   d. Intrinsic motivation

2. The ideal performance state can be characterized by all BUT which of the following?
   a. The absence of fear
   b. A high level of arousal
   c. A sense of personal control
   d. A narrow focus of attention on the activity

3. Beth has elevated levels of psychological arousal prior to competing that have been detrimental to her performance. She recently learned a new relaxation technique that involves alternating between tensing the muscles and relaxing the muscles in succession over the entire body. What specific technique is Beth using to reduce arousal?
   a. Diaphragmatic breathing
   b. Imagery
   c. Progressive muscular relaxation
   d. Systematic desensitization

4. A client is getting ready to perform a heavy set of squats and blocks out the other exercisers in the gym and noisy conversations and sounds of weights hitting the floor in order to focus on performing the lift. This behavior is an example of which of the following?
   a. Internal attention
   b. Selective attention
   c. Focus
   d. Optimal functioning

5. A client obtained her best performance on a step test at the beginning of the current training block. This is an example of what type of self-efficacy source?
   a. Vicarious experience
   b. Mastery performance accomplishment
   c. Verbal persuasion
   d. Physiological states

See answers on the next page.

Answer Explanations

1. D: Robert's behavior is driven by intrinsic motivation. He loves the running and racing, gets personal satisfaction out of participating, and is continually working on his weaknesses and improving. With achievement motivation, clients are looking to master a specific task, outperform their previous levels of achievement, and overcome obstacles. Extrinsic motivation typically comes in the form of individualized rewards such as praise from coaches and teammates, medals, social acceptance, avoidance of punishment, the drive for positive reinforcement, and other sources outside of the client. The construct of outcome motivation does not exist.

2. B: The ideal performance state is referred to as "the zone" in many sporting applications. It is characterized by a sense of personal strength and effortless performance and control, increased attentiveness and focus on the activity at hand, confidence and feelings of capability, and mental clarity. Arousal that is too high leads to anxiety and can impair performance.

3. C: Progressive muscular relaxation is used by athletes to control anxiety. It is particularly useful for controlling pre-competition levels of somatic and cognitive anxiety and regulating levels of physical and psychological arousal. This relaxation technique consists of tightening and relaxing muscle groups throughout the body in succession until the entire body is relaxed.

4. B: Selective attention is the ability to focus on relevant, task-oriented cues while ignoring other stimuli and thoughts unrelated to the athletic performance. The client performing squats who is blocking out external distractions while focusing on the lift is utilizing selective attention.

5. B: Self-efficacy (SE) is the client's perception of his or her ability to perform a situation-specific task successfully. There are numerous sources that influence SE, especially the client's past performance accomplishments and experiences. The client's successful performance in the previous step up test is an example of past performance accomplishments. Vicarious experience refers to the client watching someone similar achieve a successful performance and then deciding that he or she, too, can have a successful performance. Verbal persuasion refers to encouragement from trainers, athletes, teammates, oneself, and other external sources. Physiological states refer to whether a client interprets his or her arousal as facilitative or detrimental.

Assessment

Components and Preparation for the Initial Client Consultation

The initial client consultation is the first scheduled meeting between the client and the personal trainer and is intended to assess compatibility between trainer and client, determine client goals, develop an appropriate exercise/training program, and establish the client-trainer agreement. There are several key components and preparatory steps that a personal trainer should have in place for a new client prior to beginning an assessment or engaging in the actual exercise program. This preparation sets the groundwork for safe exercise, a positive and compatible client-trainer relationship, mutually agreed upon goal development, and the setting of appropriate expectations for both the trainer and the client. Specific documentation should be completed and reviewed. There should be a thorough discussion and written agreement related to pricing, policies (e.g., cancellations and missed sessions), where and when sessions will take place, what equipment is needed/provided by each party, and whether medical clearance from a physician is needed prior to commencement of the exercise training program.

Necessary Paperwork to be Completed by Client Prior to Initial Client Interview

There are several required documents to be completed initially by the client in order to proceed to the interview. Each of these forms warrants an in-person discussion of the content of the forms during the initial client consultation.

The Informed Consent Form gives clients information about the procedures and processes of the exercise program. This form should include a detailed description of the planned exercise program, a confidentiality clause (keeping pertinent client information private or for intended parties only), risks and benefits associated with participation, responsibilities of the client, and documentation of acknowledgement and acceptance of the stated items in the form.

The Client Intake Form includes basic identifying demographic information about the client, including contact information, height/weight, goals, reasons for starting an exercise program or seeking personal training, and any concerns.

The Health/Medical Evaluation Form assesses the appropriateness of moderate and vigorous levels of exercise by identifying positive risk factors associated with coronary artery disease (CAD), existing diagnosed pathologies, past surgical history, medications, orthopedic conditions, and lifestyle management. This form is used to help stratify the level of risk for the patient and the suitability of exercise testing and programming.

The Client/Trainer Agreement Form reinforces that the personal trainer and client are under contract law. It is a written document signed by both parties describing the services, the involved parties and expectations of each, as well as a timeline of delivery, cost, and payment, including aspects such as the cancellation policy and contract termination.

The Physical Activity Readiness Questionnaire (PAR-Q) is a questionnaire of self-recall, referring to signs and symptoms experienced by the client as well as information referring to diagnosed conditions. The purpose of this form is to screen and identify clients that require additional medical screening prior to exercise participation, while not excluding those who should be safe to start a low-intensity exercise program without physician approval (due to the known inherent benefits of physical activity and their low-risk stratification).

The Medical Clearance Form is a form signed by the client's physician after his or her evaluation. If the PAR-Q or other health appraisal screening information reveals that the client requires medical referral and physician clearance (e.g., one or more questions have been answered "yes" on the PAR-Q, client is over the age of forty and has not participated in regular physical activity for a substantial period of time), then additional attention may be required.

Components and Limitations of a Health/Medical History

The trainer should be aware that there are some limitations inherent to the health appraisal forms and screening tools. For instance, the PAR-Q is designed to determine the safety of exercise, but it does not necessarily identify any disease risks. The Informed Consent Form does not inherently relieve the personal trainer of the responsibility to perform in a competent manner under his or her scope of practice.

Sometimes these forms are augmented by the addition of a Release/Assumption of Risk Agreement. This form may be used for apparently healthy individuals with no known risk factors who want to begin an exercise program, but who decline to complete the necessary health appraisal forms. The Release/Assumption of Risk Agreement must identify the potential risks in participating in the exercise program and validate that the client understands these risks and voluntarily chooses to assume responsibility.

Lastly, the PAR-Q and certain medical history forms filled out by the client, rather than the physician, are based on client recall and self-support, leaving room for intentional or unintentional error. It is important to ensure that all forms including a clause are filled out as true and with full disclosure. They should also include the client's signature.

Essential Elements of Personal, Occupational, and Family Medical History

Trainers collect subjective details about their clients by gathering personal, occupational, and family medical histories. Elements of personal, or lifestyle, history include the client's habits, such as smoking, alcohol consumption, and sleep and exercise habits; athletic recreational activities they regularly participate in; and any other hobbies they have. These factors help to determine what level of activity the client is accustomed to, what types of exercises might be useful in the client's recreational activities, and what barriers there may in performing exercises or achieving goals. The client's occupational history is gathered to find out what types of body movements occur on a regular basis and whether the job causes stress. The customary questions in the occupational history inquire about prolonged periods of sitting or performing repetitive movement, shoes with heels being worn daily, and stress or anxiety caused by the job. The answers to these questions give the trainer clues to areas of the body that may be imbalanced. The family medical history asks for information on immediate family, such as whether there's been heart disease, diabetes, or stroke, and at what age the condition occurred in the family member.

Risk Factors and Associated Risk Thresholds

One of the main functions of the health appraisal process is to identify any potential risk for cardiovascular, pulmonary, and metabolic diseases for the client based on his or her current health. Personal trainers need to be familiar with the American Council on Exercise (ACE) guidelines and risk factors for these diseases so they can appropriately stratify risk and, if needed, refer clients to medical specialists prior to engaging in an exercise program.

Possible Symptoms of Chronic Cardiovascular, Metabolic, and/or Pulmonary Disease

Chronic Cardiovascular Disease

Coronary artery disease (CAD) is associated with atherosclerosis: a progressive, degeneration of the endothelial lining and resultant hardening of the arterial walls. Arteries become less elastic and more narrow as plaque builds up inside, reducing blood-carrying capacity to the heart. While exercise can be protective against this disease process, if clients are already at increased disease risk, exercise may result in adverse coronary episodes due to the increased demand exercise places on an already compromised system.

Extensive research on CAD has identified positive risk factors: aspects of behavior, lifestyle, environmental exposures, or inherited traits that may increase the potential to acquire CAD. The greater the number of positive risk factors, the higher the risk of CAD and resultant issues with exercise. Positive risk factors include the following:

- History: family history of myocardial infarction, coronary revascularization, or sudden death in a first-degree relative before age fifty-five in males or sixty-five in females
- Cigarette smoking: current smoker or one who has quit in the previous six months
- Hypertension: taking antihypertensive medications or systolic blood pressure ≥ 140 mmHg or diastolic pressure ≥ 90 mmHg, confirmed by at least two separate measurements on different occasions
- Hypercholesterolemia: current use of lipid-lowering medications or total cholesterol > 200 mg/dL, LDL > 130 mg/dL or low HDL < 40 mg/dL
- Impaired fasting blood glucose: ≥ 100 mg/dL, confirmed by at least two separate measurements on different occasions
- Obesity: waist circumference of > 100cm (39 inches) or BMI ≥ 30 kg/m^2
- Sedentary lifestyle: little to no exercise or failure to meet the U.S. Surgeon General's report's minimum physical activity recommendations of thirty minutes or more of moderate-intensity physical activity on most, if not all, days per week

Chronic Metabolic Disease

Diabetes mellitus is the primary metabolic disease of concern, affecting the body's ability to metabolize blood glucose. It is an independent risk factor for cardiovascular disease. There are two types of diabetes. In Type 1, there is a problem with insulin secretion, and patients are insulin dependent, requiring insulin injections for glucose metabolism. This is an autoimmune disease that typically presents early in life. In Type 2, patients produce enough insulin, but glycemic control is abnormal because the tissue does not respond adequately to the circulating insulin. Symptoms indicative of possible metabolic disease include the following:

- Excess abdominal fat (men: waist circumference > 100 cm or 39 inches; women: waist circumference > 88 cm)
- Elevated triglyceride levels (> 150 mg/dL)
- Low HDL cholesterol (< 40 mg/dL)
- Elevated fasting glucose levels (> 100 mg/dL)
- Elevated blood pressure (> 140 mmHg systolic and > 90 mmHg diastolic)

Chronic Pulmonary Disease

Pulmonary diseases affect the ability of the respiratory system to transport oxygen to the tissues during exercise via the cardiovascular system, resulting in inadequate oxygen supply and reduced exercise capacity.

Pulmonary disease symptoms mirror many of those for cardiovascular disease and include the following:

- Shortness of breath with mild exertion or even at rest
- Dizziness or syncope (fainting)
- Water retention or swelling in the ankles (edema) or calf cramping (intermittent claudication)
- Irregular heartbeat (palpitations) or rapid heartbeat (tachycardia) or known heart murmur
- Chest, neck, jaw, or arm pain due to limited blood flow (ischemia)
- The need to sit up to breathe easily (orthopnea)
- Unusual fatigue
- Breathlessness, especially at night (nocturnal dyspnea)

While not diagnostic in and of themselves, it is important that trainers be aware of these symptoms and refer clients to physicians for formal evaluations.

Risk Stratification

Risk stratification is the process of classifying clients into one of three risk strata or levels (low-risk, medium-risk, or high-risk) based on the risk factors identified in the health screening process along with age, health status, and symptoms. Stratifying health concern risks is an important preliminary step in determining whether a client needs further professional medical clearance and the overall appropriateness of physical exercise, yet the personal trainer should understand that risk assessment needs to be an ongoing process. The three strata and criteria for each are as follows:

Low risk: younger (males < 45 years of age; females < 55 years), asymptomatic, and have ≤ 1 risk factor for cardiovascular or pulmonary disease

Moderate risk: older (males ≥ 45 years of age; females ≥55 years) and have ≤ two risk factors for cardiovascular or pulmonary disease

High risk: diagnosed cardiovascular, pulmonary, or metabolic disease or ≥ 1 symptom of cardiovascular or pulmonary disease (e.g., dizziness or syncope; ankle edema; palpitations; pain in the chest, neck, jaw, arm; heart murmur)

Medical Clearance, Exercise Testing, and Supervision Recommendations Based on Risk Stratification

A personal trainer should require medical clearance for clients who answer "yes" to any PAR-Q questions, experience any signs or symptoms of cardiovascular or pulmonary disease, or want to participate in vigorous exercise as a moderate risk stratification or moderate exercise with a high risk stratification.

- Low risk: medical exam not needed prior to moderate or vigorous activity; physician supervision not necessary for maximal or submaximal testing
- Medium risk: medical exam not needed prior to moderate activity, but recommended for vigorous activity; physician supervision not necessary for submaximal testing, but recommended for maximal testing
- High risk: medical exam recommended prior to moderate or vigorous activity; physician supervision recommended for maximal or submaximal testing

Determining Risk and Stratifying Clients in Accordance with NASM Guidelines

The personal trainer should use NASM's guidelines to determine risk and stratify clients for their safety as well as to limit liability. When in doubt, it is better to err on the side of caution and obtain written physician clearance (prior to exercise participation) and include physician monitoring of exercise testing, particularly at maximal levels.

Pregnancy

Pregnancy itself is not a contraindication to exercise, and many women continue to enjoy working out while pregnant. However, there can be some risks involved in exercising while pregnant, and trainers need to be knowledgeable about the changes that occur in a pregnant woman's body and how exercise should be modified to accommodate the changes and prevent complications. During pregnancy, the supply of oxygen is reduced, blood circulation is increased, and there are changes in the regulation of body temperature. Pregnant women are more likely to experience dizziness or fainting and nausea. Trainers working with pregnant clients need to inquire about high-risk conditions and contraindications to exercise, such as incompetent cervix, preterm rupture of membrane, continued bleeding, previous miscarriages, and history of preterm labor. Additional risks include diabetes, obesity, and pregnancy past the age of 35. Trainers should know all of the proper adjustments and modifications to make when conducting assessments and designing fitness programs for both healthy pregnant women and pregnant women with high-risk pregnancies.

Eating Disorders

It's very common for people who have eating disorders to exercise excessively, which can be dangerous for many reasons. Energy expenditure and the fuel required to perform activities become unbalanced, leaving the body systems with less energy for proper functioning. Exercising too much can lead to heart problems, affect the balance of electrolytes, contribute to wasting of muscle, and cause injuries due to overuse of muscles or joints. Individuals with eating disorders also have a greater risk for bone fractures. It's important that a trainer can recognize signs of an eating disorder and refer the client to the appropriate health professional for help. Some of the signs include low BMI, rapid weight loss, and exercising for an extended amount of time, although these signs aren't always indicative of an eating disorder.

Trainers can work with clients who have eating disorders if they work as a team with the client's physician, dietitian, or eating disorder specialist. While bone mineral density is decreased in individuals with eating disorders and exercise can lead to fractures, trainers can help the client regain some of the bone mineral density with appropriate exercises. Exercise can also help with anxiety and depression, which commonly occur alongside eating disorders.

Elements of a Lifestyle Questionnaire

Personal trainers are health and fitness professionals who use an individualized approach to assess, educate, train, and motivate clients. They help clients identify reasonable and measurable goals, then design safe and effective exercise programs to achieve those goals. Personal trainers have the responsibility of interviewing potential clients prior to beginning a program in order to gather pertinent information regarding health, lifestyle, and exercise readiness. They also follow a health appraisal process to screen clients for risk factors and symptoms associated with cardiovascular, metabolic, pulmonary, and orthopedic conditions. This pre-participation health appraisal process optimizes the safety of exercise testing and programming.

Common Assessments

- Cardiovascular fitness: YMCA 3-minute step test, Rockport Walk Test, Astrand-Rhyming VO2 Max or YMCA Cycle Test, 1-mile run, rate of perceived exertion
- Movement: overhead squat, push/pull, single leg squat
- Muscular strength: bench press or leg press 1 repetition max (RM), 3RM, vertical jump test
- Muscular endurance: push-up test, one-minute sit-up test
- Body composition: skinfold, BOD-POD, DEXA, circumferences
- Flexibility: sit-and-reach test
- Speed and Agility: 40-yard dash, 5-10-5 drill, box drills
- Physiological: resting heart rate, blood pressure, waist-to-hip ratio

Recommended Order of Fitness Assessments

After the client has completed the health questionnaire, provided informed consent, completed the initial interview to discuss goals, fitness level, and any injuries, and has received any necessary medical clearance, testing can begin. There is not a mandated sequence of assessments that the personal trainer must follow, and often, the exact order is determined by the setting and available equipment. If possible, it is often best to do resting measures prior to exertional ones to avoid assessments being negatively affected by fatigue. In order to prevent injury, flexibility should be done at the end after muscles have had adequate warm-up time.

- Resting measurements (heart rate, blood pressure, and weight to get a resting baseline)
- Body Composition (circumference measurements, skinfolds, BMI)
- Cardiovascular Fitness (Step Test or one mile run)
- Muscular strength and endurance assessments (Push-ups)
- Flexibility (Sit and Reach Test or V-Sit Test)

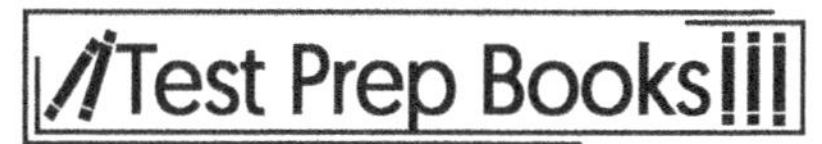

Cardiovascular Assessments

There are a variety of cardiovascular assessments trainers can choose from, depending on client age, fitness level, health, interests, and testing environment. Field tests typically require minimal equipment and occur outside (i.e., "in the field"), such as the Rockport walk test, 1-mile run, or Step Test. Laboratory tests, such as the YMCA Cycle Ergometer test, require equipment. Health, fitness level, and injuries also factor into assessment selection. It may be safer and more successful for a sedentary client to do a submaximal test like the YMCA Cycle Ergometer test rather than a VO_2 max treadmill protocol, and a client with a sore knee would be better suited for a cycle rather than running test as well. Normal acute responses to cardiovascular exercise include increases in heart rate, blood pressure, stroke volume, respiration, and body temperature.

Assessing Intensity During Exercise

Personal trainers can assess peripheral pulses, typically at either the carotid or radial arteries, and teach clients how to palpate these areas for a pulse correctly. The common carotid artery is located on the side of the neck in the groove between the trachea and hyoid muscles. The pulse can be palpated just under the anterior edge of the sternocleidomastoid. The radial pulse is taken on the thumb side (lateral side) of the wrist.

After the pulse location is correctly identified, the index and middle fingers are placed over the site, counting pulsations for a given time interval (ten, fifteen, thirty seconds) and extrapolating this number out for a one minute interval. Pulse counts are more accurate for longer intervals, but also slow down more noticeably the longer the interval since ceasing activity. The more intense the activity, the shorter the counting interval should be for greater accuracy. While less common in a fitness setting, heart rate can be measured at the brachial, femoral, popliteal, tibialis posterior, and dorsalis pedis arteries.

Rate of perceived exertion (RPE) can be used during exercise and testing as a subjective indicator of effort level, especially with older adults, those on HR-altering medications, and those in whom measuring heart rate is difficult. A six to twenty ("no exertion at all" to "maximum exertion") Borg scale is most commonly employed, with studies indicating that the threshold for improvements in cardiorespiratory fitness are at an RPE between twelve and sixteen ("hard" range).

3-Minute Step Test and Rockport Walk Test

Cardiorespiratory assessments are used by trainers to determine the level of workout intensity that is suitable for a client. The 3-minute stress test and the Rockport walk test are practical ways to estimate a client's VO_{2max}:

- 3-minute step test: Using a 12 inch step, the client performs 24 steps per minute at a set rhythm per step. Next, the client's heart rate is taken for 1 minute, starting within 5 seconds of completing the last step. This final recovery pulse is recorded and found on the chart to determine which category (poor, fair, average, good, or very good) the client is in. The category helps to determine which training zone should be used for the client's starting program. Finally, the client's age is subtracted from 220 to calculate their maximal heart rate, and the maximal heart rate is multiplied by a certain percentage according to which zone they fall into in order to find the heart rate range for that zone.

- Rockport walk test: The Rockport walk test is similar to the 3-minute step test, but instead of finding and using the client's recovery pulse rate, the client's VO2 is calculated and used to find the client's category and zone for a starting program. The VO_2 score is found by having the client walk as fast as they can on a treadmill for 1 mile and plugging the heart rate that is recorded immediately after and the time it took to finish the mile into the following formula:

$$132.853 - (0.0769 \times weight) - (0.3877 \times age) + (6.315 \times gender) - (3.2649 \times time) - (0.1565 \times heart\ rate) = VO_2\ score$$

(Weight in pounds, age in years, Male = 1, Female = 0, time in minutes and 100ths of minutes)

Physiological Assessments

Physiological assessments provide trainers with information about a client's current condition. Physiological assessments track a client's progress throughout the fitness program and monitor their health. Resting heart rate measurements should be taken when the client is relaxed and well rested, perhaps first thing in the morning. Trainers place their first two fingers below a client's wrist. Trainers count and record beats per minute, but if a client is shy or does not like to be touched, heart beats may be counted for ten seconds and multiplied by six.

Trainers use a sphygmomanometer to measure an athlete or client's blood pressure. The top number indicates a client's systolic reading, and the bottom number indicates a client's diastolic reading. Systolic readings should fall between a range from 90 to 120, and diastolic reading should fall between a range from 60 to 80.

Trainers may also use body composition assessments to assess weight ratios between parts of the body, and trainers and clients may use this information to set fitness goals. For example, by measuring the circumference of a client's waist and hips, fitness trainers utilize waist-to-hip ratio assessments, and they compare these measurements to help clients develop reasonable fitness and weight loss goals.

The risk of developing a chronic disease is increased in individuals who have more fat accumulated in their midsection. Waist-to-hip ratios of more than 0.80 in women and more than 0.95 in men indicate risk. This ratio is calculated by dividing the waist circumference by the hip circumference. To get accurate measurements, the measuring tape should be pulled firmly with no slack and wrapped level around the area being measured. The waist should be measured between the ribcage and the hipbones at the narrowest part. If no part of the waist is narrowest, measuring at the navel is sufficient. To get the hip measurement, the measuring tape should be wrapped around the buttocks at the widest point.

Kinetic Chain Checkpoints

Many movement assessments are based on evaluations of the five kinetic chain checkpoints. The five kinetic chain checkpoints are at the (1) ankles and feet, (2) knees, (3) lumbo-pelvic-hip, (4) shoulders, and (5) head and cervical spine. Muscle and joint imbalances may occur between the muscles and joints that comprise each kinetic chain, and these imbalances may cause improper movements of the human movement system.

Assessments of the kinetic chain may begin with an evaluation of a client's static posture, which is an evaluation of a client's posture while standing still. Trainers compare a client's posture to a body's ideal posture, which occurs when all kinetic checkpoints are in line. Trainers may also prompt clients to complete an overhead squat assessment, which will reveal imbalances in a client's neck, shoulders, back, and legs. Additionally, trainers may evaluate a client's range of motion by observing the range of

motion available to a client at a given joint. Trainers usually measure range of motion by observing their clients, but measuring tools, such as goniometers or inclinometers, allow trainers to quantify range of motion, especially in clinical settings. Finally, trainers may utilize manual muscle tests, which reveal the ability of muscles at the five kinetic chains to generate power against resistance.

Applicability of Assessments from Other Health Professionals

Trainers may request that new clients undergo preliminary screening assessments before starting a fitness program. Trainers will often complete some of these assessments themselves, especially those measuring body fat. Body mass index (BMI) is especially easy for trainers to measure without additional equipment or specialized training. A client's BMI indicates the level of exercise that they are equipped to perform.

Trainers should never complete physical assessments for which they are not certified. One common test that trainers should utilize assesses blood pressure. After trainers complete their certification requirements, they may acquire blood pressure testing kits and administer blood pressure assessments to their clients. Blood pressure assessments give trainers a better understanding of client risk factors and allow trainers to develop safer fitness programs for at-risk clients.

Trainers who are not certified to complete blood pressure assessments may request that clients share their medical records. Results from medical assessments are both relevant and applicable. Trained health professionals like doctors and nurses can complete assessments that analyze a sample of the client's blood or urine, which can provide the trainer with important information such as blood sugar and glucose levels. This information will alert trainers to client health conditions and allow trainers to devise safer fitness programs.

During screening assessments, trainers may request more information about a client's medical history from at-risk clients than they would from those without observable medical conditions like obesity or breathing issues. Applicable information includes results from cholesterol tests, as well as family and medical history. Neither high cholesterol nor adverse family medical history are observable to the naked eye, but both factors impact client safety during fitness programs. This information helps trainers monitor client safety and plan individualized fitness programs.

Body Composition Assessments

Body composition assessments are an important parameter to track and measure, particularly because some clients may lose body fat, but make gains in lean body mass through training. Thus, they see little progress on the scale, despite larger improvements in health. There are varieties of techniques for assessing body fat, each inherent with its own set of pros and cons:

Skinfold measurements: caliper measurements of subcutaneous fat from pinches of skin at specific body sites, plugged into equations to estimate body fat percentage

> Pros: easy to conduct in the field, more accurate than BMI, inexpensive
>
> Cons: uncomfortable for clients emotionally (given some immodest access sites) and somewhat physically, requires trainer skilled in obtaining accurate measurements

Plethysmography (BOD POD®): special laboratory tool, uses air displacement to calculate volume of the body along with weight to determine body fat

Pros: highly accurate, as much so as hydrostatic weighing, but easier to administer and fast

Cons: not highly available, more expensive than field tests, can be impractical for regular reassessments

Bioelectrical impedance: uses the principle that fat mass and fat free mass have different resistances to electrical current, which can be measured to report body fat percentage

Pros: very inexpensive devices, non-invasive, comfortable for clients, fairly accurate

Cons: sensitive to body hydration status, requiring restrictions on client's eating/drinking (shouldn't eat or drink for at least thirty minutes), exercising (none for at least twelve hours), drinking alcohol (none for at least 48 hours), and caffeine intake (abstain prior to test)

Infrared: fat mass and fat-free mass assessed via a specialized infrared-light-emitting probe placed against an area of the body

Pros: non-invasive, top-of-the-line laboratory devices, very accurate

Cons: may overestimate body fat in lean people and underestimate in overweight, commercially available devices not as accurate

Dual-energy X-ray absorptiometry (DEXA): measures bone mineral density fat mass via a specialized infrared-light-emitting probe placed against an area of the body.

Pros: most accurate and easy to administer, done in clothes, quick results, also assesses bone mineral density, measures entire body, not just estimating based on certain sites

Cons: requires trip to physician/laboratory, can be expensive, not recommended for pregnant women due to x-ray

Circumference measurements: measurements with measuring tape at specific body sites, plugged into equations to estimate body fat percentage

Pros: can be more accurate than skinfolds on very obese clients, easy to administer in the field, less skill involved than skinfold measurements so often less measurement error, inexpensive

Cons: typically not as accurate of an estimate as skinfold or laboratory tests

Circumference Measurements

Circumference measurements should be taken with a flexible plastic tape that is taut, but does not indent the skin. The personal trainer should measure all sites, record the values, and measure each specific area in order once, and then in the same order again.

Waist circumference (smallest circumference between xiphoid and umbilicus) alone has health-related criterion standards as abdominal obesity carries a greater risk for high blood pressure, metabolic syndrome, type 2 diabetes, high cholesterol, CAD, and premature death. The standards for high risk are

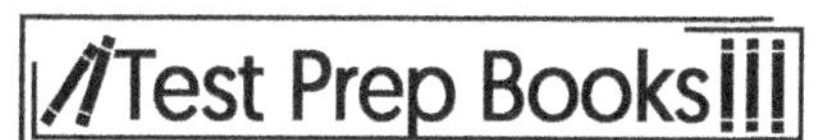

≥ 102 cm for men and ≥ 88 cm for women. The standards for low risk are < 80 cm for men and < 70 cm for women.

Waist-to-hip ratio is another commonly used marker of health. Other circumference sites are often taken to monitor over time with exercise training and to assess how body shape changes. Such sites include the upper arm, buttocks, calf, forearm, abdomen, and mid-thigh. The personal trainer should be consistent with measurement sites to avoid contributing to error.

Skinfold Measurement Sites

Skinfold measurements should be taken precisely, on dry skin, and with an experienced tester. Two measurements should be taken per site, both on the right side of the body, with values no more than 2 mm or 10% difference. The following sites are typically used:

- Chest: diagonal fold halfway for men and one-third for women of the distance from anterior axillary line and nipple
- Midaxilla: vertical fold on midaxillary line at xiphoid level
- Triceps: vertical fold on midline of triceps, halfway between acromion and olecranon with elbow extended and relaxed
- Subscapula: diagonal fold on line connecting inferior angle of scapula to a point 0.8 inches from the medial border
- Abdomen: vertical fold one-inch lateral to umbilicus
- Suprailium: vertical fold above iliac crest in line with anterior axillary line
- Thigh: anterior vertical fold halfway between hip and knee joints

Static Postural Assessment

Trainers use the static postural assessment to screen for any imbalances in the muscles that could be addressed and corrected with exercise. The client is examined, while standing, from anterior, posterior, and lateral views. The focus is on identifying three possible postural distortions—pronation distortion syndrome, upper crossed syndrome, and lower crossed syndrome. The trainer looks over the kinetic chain checkpoints assessing for symmetry, alignment, balance of muscle tone, and deformities of the posture.

Trainers can screen for postural abnormalities such as kyphosis, lordosis, and scoliosis using a posture chart (a grid that the client stands in front of) or a plumb line. Scoliosis is a lateral curvature of the spine. A client with scoliosis will display unequal heights of posterior landmarks such as shoulder height or iliac crests. The posture grid helps provide an objective background for this assessment. Lordosis and kyphosis are exaggerated curves in the lumbar and cervical spine respectively and are best viewed from the side. A curvature of twenty to forty-five degrees is normal; beyond forty-five degrees is abnormal. Lumbar lordosis greater than sixty degrees is considered abnormal.

Performance Assessments

Performance parameters can be measured in some of the following selected examples:

- Muscular strength: 1RM bench press for upper body and 1RM leg press for lower body
- Anaerobic capacity or power: Wingate cycle ergometer test, vertical jump test, Margaria-Kalamen stair sprint test, medicine ball throw
- Muscular endurance: Push-up test, curl-up test
- Aerobic endurance: Cooper 12-minute run test, 1.5 mile run test
- Agility: 25-yard shuttle test, zig-zag test, quadrant jump test, hexagon test, box drill
- Speed: Line drills, 300-yard shuttle test, sprint tests like 50m sprint, plate tapping test for upper body speed
- Flexibility: sit-and-reach test

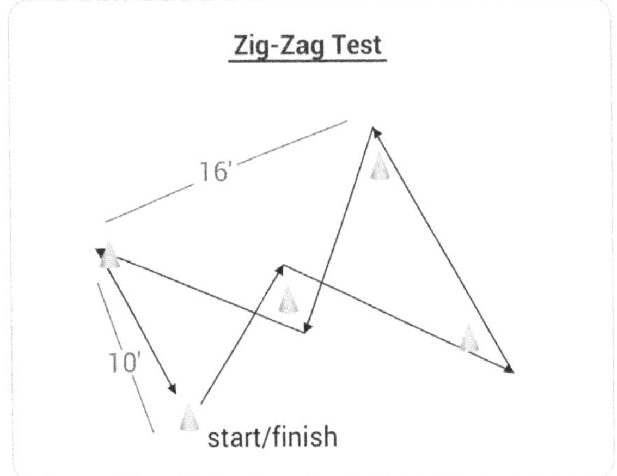

The 1 Repetition Maximum test (1RM) determines the highest amount of weight a client can safely move using the range of motion and proper form for the exercise. The test is used with both upper body and lower body strength exercises, utilizing the bench press and leg press, respectively, to help a trainer design a program that best suits the client's abilities, strengths, and weaknesses. Before performing the test, the trainer can calculate an appropriate starting test weight by multiplying the client's weight by

65% and using the resulting number as a starting weight. For example, a 170-pound client would start a 1RM test at 110.5 pounds (170 x .65 = 110.5).

Movement Assessments

Movement assessments allow trainers to evaluate whether a client can activate the correct muscles to complete a workout. Rather than measure strength, speed, or performance, movement assessments measure form. Movement assessments are often prescribed at the beginning of a fitness program. Fitness instructors and personal trainers use movement assessments as diagnostic tools to check for muscle imbalances. Muscle imbalances could stunt a personal fitness program and cause injuries.

A personal trainer often assigns an overhead squat assessment at the beginning of a fitness program because it is a simple motion that gives the personal trainer information about that client's body movements. Trainers instruct clients to extend their hands straight over their heads and hold their squats at the bottom of the motion. Trainers check for several dysfunctional motions in the shoulders, back, knees, and feet, which indicate improper movement patterns. Trainers may use push/pull movement assessments, including one-arm cable rows and the overhead press, with an overhead squat assessment to gain additional information about a client's movement patterns. Push/pull movement assessments measure curvature in the back, shoulders, and neck. A trainer may even deploy a single-leg squat movement assessment to evaluate the likelihood that a client, particularly one involved in competitive sports, will suffer a major knee injury.

Strength, Muscular Endurance, and Power Assessments

One-repetition maximum strength tests measure the maximum weight that a muscle or group of muscles can handle in one repetition. This is an evaluation of a muscle's isotonic strength, which refers to the strength of a muscle when tension is equivalent, whether the muscle is shortened or lengthened, (i.e., when completing a single bench press repetition). One-repetition maximum strength tests are popular in high school weight rooms because they measure isotonic strength gained over the course of a fitness program. Weight is added incrementally until an individual is only able to complete one repetition with correct form. Results over time are compared with an initial baseline.

While one-repetition maximum strength tests measure strength, push-up tests measure both strength and endurance. Push-up tests are simple, and they are used to track progress in a fitness program as well as compare one's strength and endurance to the average strength and endurance for one's age and gender. Finally, vertical jump tests measure lower body muscle power. A test subject stands on the side of a wall and extends a hand at the height of his or her jump. The highest point that the subject reaches on the wall is recorded, and progress is tracked throughout the duration of a fitness program.

Speed, Agility, and Quickness Assessments

The 40-yard dash is a classic fitness assessment that measures an athlete's speed. An athlete stands at a starting line, usually on a track or a measured field like a football field, and they sprint 40 yards straight ahead when prompted. A test administrator stands at the finish line with a stopwatch, and when the athlete crosses the finish line, the test administrator records the athlete's time. The time it takes for an athlete to complete the sprint provides a good indication of their speed.

Other fitness assessments measure an athlete's agility and quickness. The 5-10-5 drill is especially popular for football players because it gives coaches a good impression of a player's ability to change directions swiftly, an indication of the player's ability to run effective pass routes and cover opposing receivers. The 5-10-5 drill measures lateral quickness. While both quickness and agility refer to an athlete's ability to change direction, quickness refers to an athlete's ability to change direction effectively, with maximum power. Both 5-10-5 and box drills measure elements of both quickness and agility. The 5-10-5 drill requires that athletes run five yards in one direction, ten yards in the opposite direction, and five yards back in the initial direction. Each time the athlete changes directions, they decelerate and accelerate (agility) and use maximum force (quickness).

Considerations for Selection of Assessments

Test selection, proper administration that adheres to the set protocol, and trained raters influence the reliability and validity of any given test for a client. Some tests are only valid for certain populations, such as the 8 Foot Up and Go test of agility in the elderly. All tests are valid only if they are conducted according to the specified protocol, and tests are significantly less reliable if the rater is unfamiliar with test administration, such as a trainer performing skinfold measurements without practice at selecting the correct sites and pinching the tissue appropriately.

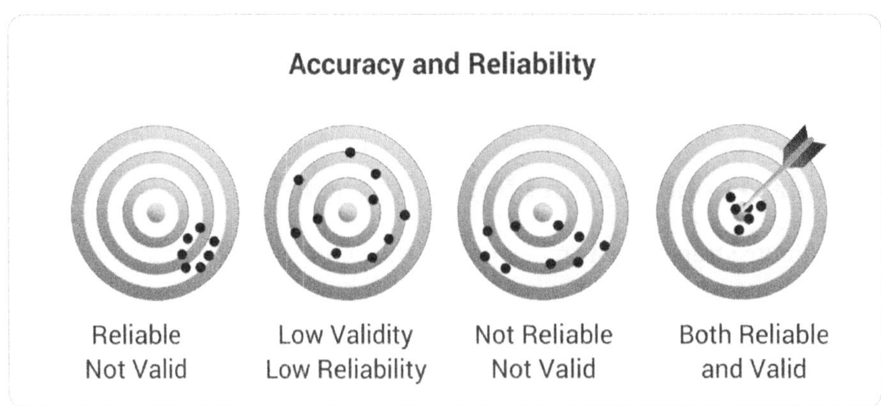

Selecting the appropriate tests involves considering the physiological energy systems required by the client's physical needs and fitness goals compared to the test, movement specificity, and the client's experience with training and testing. To choose the most appropriate tests, trainers should perform a needs analysis of the client's vocation and avocation (sports and fitness hobbies) to determine what aspects of fitness are most important (speed, power, strength, agility, etc.) and therefore should be tested. From there, tests should be selected based on their validity for such fitness components as well as the client's training status. For example, a VO_2 max running assessment should be selected rather than a cycle protocol for a distance runner. long axis of fascicles is parallel to long axis of muscle reduce overall performance and achievement of a true maximal result. By the same reasoning, a Wingate test of anaerobic power is probably not a good choice for a basketball player who never cycles; the vertical jump test is preferable.

Determining Appropriate Physical Assessments

The initial paperwork and interview yield information about the client's current health, physical fitness level, health/injury risk, and unique goals that can guide decisions about appropriate physical assessments. It is important to choose assessments that are safe, keeping in mind that depending on a client's stratification, physician supervision may be required and/or submaximal assessments should be used. Ideally, assessment selection should match goals or be something that can be monitored for improvements caused by targeted training during subsequent reassessments. For instance, if a client is going to be focusing primarily on a strength/resistance training program, using only an endurance assessment may not be the optimal choice.

Test Administration Procedures that Use Equipment, Personnel, and Time Efficiently

When testing individual clients, trainers have more flexibility in test selection because equipment usage, personnel to score or observe tests, and time efficiency are less of a concern. Many sport coaches, however, will need to test entire teams or multiple athletes at one time, so these become factors of consideration. With the current trend toward increasing small group training rather than the individualized session model, personal trainers should consider the implications of testing multiple people simultaneously. Field tests typically require minimal equipment and occur outside "in the field" such as the Rockport walk test, 1-mile run, or step test, while laboratory tests such as the Wingate test of anaerobic power require equipment. When testing multiple clients, field tests may be more appropriate because they do not usually require much equipment. In addition, these tests can be conducted more efficiently by having clients complete them at the same time.

Exercise Testing Precautions

In certain circumstances, testing is not safe, and there are absolute contraindications. It is important for the personal trainer to heed the advice of medical professionals and work with physicians specifically trained in exercise testing in those cases where physician supervision of assessments is recommended. It is prudent to err on the side of caution, such as choosing submaximal tests over maximal tests.

Absolute Contraindications	**Relative Contraindications***
Post myocardial infarction (two days)	Electrolyte abnormalities
Inability to obtain consent	Atrial fibrillation or high-degree AV block
Physical impairment that would preclude safe testing	Coronary stenosis, valvular heart disease

Absolute Contraindications	Relative Contraindications*
Acute illness (myocarditis, endocarditis, infection, pulmonary embolism, renal failure) that could be aggravated by exercise	Tachycardia or Bradyarrhythmia, hypertrophic cardiomyopathy
Uncontrolled cardiac arrhythmias, aortic stenosis, symptomatic heart failure	Inability to cooperate or mental impairment affecting comprehension/informed consent
Unstable angina	

* If benefits are deemed to outweigh risks, relative contraindications can be superseded.

Test Termination	
Absolute Indications	**Relative Indications**
Drop in systolic BP below baseline despite workload increase	Increasing chest discomfort
New or increasing chest pain	Fatigue, breathlessness, wheezing, cramping
Client's request to stop	Minor heart arrhythmias
Serious arrhythmias	EKG changes such as QRS axis shift
Technical difficulties with EKG or BP monitoring	Bundle branch block
CNS symptoms: dizziness, ataxia, etc.	Perceived maximal effort or achievement of clinical end points
Signs of poor peripheral perfusion, cyanosis	

After sudden test termination, place patient supine or seated and continue to monitor blood pressure and EKG for six to eight minutes. If test ends comfortably and normally, the patient should walk or slowly and gradually cool down to bring physiologic parameters back to resting value.

Selecting Safe Muscular Assessments

Trainers should carefully review medical history and all of the prescreening stratification for any contraindications to testing and review any necessary safety precautions, such as physician supervision, during testing. The benefits of selected tests must always outweigh potential risks. Client factors—including health status, such as any current illness or injuries, functional capacity, age, sex, and pre-training status—should be considered when selecting an appropriate assessment. For example, a bench press 1RM test may not be appropriate for an older adult with shoulder pain. In such a case, a test at submaximal workloads to predict maximum would be a safer choice. It is normal for heart rate and blood pressure to increase during resistance exercise as the heart works to oxygenate and fuel the working muscles.

Selecting Safe Flexibility Assessments

To avoid injury, the muscles, ligaments, and tendons should be fully warmed-up prior to flexibility assessments. Pushing joints beyond the comfortable and normal range of motion can also cause injury, so clients should be instructed on how to complete the assessments and stretches, prior to attempting them. Flexibility will tend to improve with conditioning and consistency, although temperature, genetics, sex, and age determine certain limits of flexibility. Ballistic stretching should be avoided as it can injure muscles and tendons. With the sit-and-reach assessment, a moderate stretch may be felt in the low back, hamstrings, arms, and calves, but it should not feel painful.

Considerations and Modifications for Performing Assessments with Special Populations

Special populations, including clients with chronic conditions, require individualized fitness programs. As with any client, trainers must adjust fitness plans to meet the needs and abilities of the individual, though these clients may require additional special modifications and precautions. Long-term goals should be realistic while prioritizing safety during workouts.

Trainers should conduct careful assessments of their clients from special populations and help them establish realistic goals that meet their needs. Losing five pounds and developing healthier eating habits are perhaps two realistic goals for clients with chronic conditions, like obesity. For elderly clients, a realistic fitness plan might include two or three days of low-impact forms of cardiovascular and strength training.

Trainers typically consult a client's health history before they begin physical assessments. Trainers must ensure that clients with underlying conditions, like cardiovascular disease and hypertension, utilize heart rate monitors or pacemakers during exercise. Prenatal clients may also utilize these devices as their bodies may strain during exercise. These devices help to ensure client safety.

During initial assessments and throughout fitness programs with clients from special populations (including elderly, youth, and prenatal clients), trainers monitor the client's physical responses to exercise. Shortness of breath and other physical limitations may indicate an issue with one of the major systems responsible for facilitating physical activity, so trainers should remain alert to indications of physical strain or discomfort.

When performing assessments with special populations some modifications may need to be made. One common adjustment for various special populations is allowing a single-leg balance to replace a single-leg squat. For obese clients, skin fold measurements may be uncomfortable and inaccurate, so circumference measurements and weight can be used to track progress. Clients with PAD should be able to perform movement assessments but with fewer repetitions. Movement deficiencies should be the focus of youth assessments. Seated and standing assessments are appropriate for prenatal and senior clients and clients with coronary heart disease or osteoporosis. Flexibility should be assessed in seniors. Clients with cancer should be assessed according to their level of ability. When assessing a client who has arthritis, trainers should observe for the range of motion that is painless.

Standards for Assessments and Outcome Expectations for Special Populations

When working with clients from special populations, safety is a trainer's top priority. Trainers design assessments according to risk considerations related to a client's underlying health conditions. Aside from evaluating a client's eligibility for fitness training, trainers also use health and fitness assessments to help clients develop safe and realistic training goals.

Complete rehabilitation is often an unrealistic goal for clients with underlying health conditions because some conditions are simply uncurable. For clients with chronic conditions, improved quality of life is a common goal. Regular, low-impact strength and cardiovascular exercises prevent muscle atrophy and increase positive feelings of self-worth and accomplishment. As clients age, mobility often decreases, so a well-designed fitness program will aim to help an elderly or aging client sustain his or her current range of mobility.

Other clients, like children or prenatal clients, temporarily belong to special populations. They have short-term conditions, rather than chronic conditions, that qualify them for specialized assessments and fitness programs. Typically, the fitness goals of a prenatal woman apply only so long as she is pregnant. Pregnant women may strive to achieve some form of light to mild exercise six to seven days a week. Her goals are related to preventing complications related to her short-term condition such as swelling or constipation.

Medical Clearance and Referral to Another Professional

A client must obtain medical clearance from a physician if he or she answers "yes" to any PAR-Q questions, experiences any signs or symptoms of cardiovascular or pulmonary disease, wants to participate in vigorous exercise (as a moderate risk stratification) or moderate exercise (with a high risk stratification). Additionally, previously inactive men over age forty and women over age fifty must obtain clearance.

Personal trainers are allied health professionals, and to avoid operating outside their scope of practice, they should refer clients to physicians and other healthcare clinicians when clients display or mention certain signs and symptoms of orthopedic, cardiorespiratory, metabolic, and neurologic issues. When in doubt, it is prudent for the trainer to seek the advice of healthcare professionals. Any and all documentation of symptoms (e.g., knee pain with squatting, dizziness with exertion) and objective measurements (e.g., heart rate or blood pressure before, during, or after exercise) should be sent with the referral along with a clear, concise narrative detailing the concern.

Trainers should be prepared to refer clients to local physicians for a variety of issues clients may experience, ranging from medical clearance to musculoskeletal issues. HIPAA policies and confidentiality should be exercised while communicating the pertinent health information. After the referral has been established, the trainer and physician should have ongoing communication about the client's ability to participate in the exercise program as well as to provide updates and any necessary modifications.

Reassessment

Goals and progress can be measured at regular intervals to be compared to a baseline, typically every four to twelve weeks, depending on the frequency of sessions, goal difficulty, and client personality. Trainers should track workouts and record detailed information about sessions, including weights, reps, rest intervals, RPE, modifications made to workouts or exercises based on pain, and fatigue. Trainers should be mindful of reassessing each component of fitness (cardiovascular, muscular strength/endurance, flexibility, and body composition), noting which areas are in need of renewed focus.

Practice Quiz

1. Which of the following does NOT typically affect the validity of an assessment?
    a. Population tested
    b. Order of tests conducted
    c. Test selection
    d. The rater's skill level

2. What type of score is VO_2 max?
    a. Norm-referenced score
    b. Criterion-referenced score
    c. Reliability-referenced score
    d. Validity-referenced score

3. Body fat assessments include all EXCEPT which of the following?
    a. Skinfold measurements
    b. DEXA scans
    c. BMI
    d. Bioelectrical impedance

4. How can the following image be described?

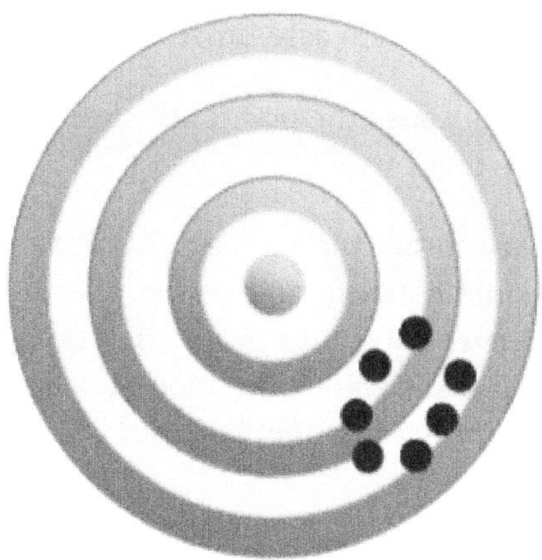

    a. High reliability, low validity
    b. High validity, low reliability
    c. High reliability, high validity
    d. Low reliability, low validity

5. Which of the following is a field-based body fat assessment?
    a. Skinfold measurements
    b. DEXA scans
    c. BMI
    d. Plethysmography

See answers on the next page.

Answer Explanations

1. D: The rater's skill level typically affects the reliability or consistency of a test score. Validity refers to a test measuring what it is intended to measure—such as a strength test actually measuring force production. Reliability of a test refers to its ability to produce consistent measures. Selecting the appropriate test for a client affects the validity of a test; some tests are valid only for certain populations. Oher tests are valid only for certain measures (for instance, a 1RM bench press measures upper body strength but should not be used as a measure of upper body endurance). The test order matters in that fatiguing tests should not be conducted prior to less fatiguing tests, or they can confound the results.

2. A: VO_2 max is a norm-referenced score. Norm-referenced standards compare the client's performance against that of other similar people (in terms of demographics) and scores are presented in percentiles. The 50th percentile indicates the client performed better than half of the comparative population and worse than half. It is important that the personal trainer reports not just the percentile score, but educates a client on his or her score's relative value. Criterion-referenced standards are derived from research- and normative-based achievement levels of health and fitness that, if reached, predict lower disease risk for the clients. These may be lower standards than those likely achieved by athletic populations.

3. C: BMI is a measure of weight relative to height and not a direct measure of body fat. Skinfolds, DEXA scans, and bioelectrical impedance are common assessments for body fat.

4. A: This image shows high reliability because the points are consistently in the same area, but low validity because they are not near the bullseye.

5. A: Skinfold measurements are easily conducted on the field with a pair of calipers. With experience, the coach can conduct 7- or 3-site skinfold measurements on individual athletes in just a few minutes, making it an efficient measurement, even for a large group. BMI does not directly measure body fat, but rather weight relative to height. DEXA scans and plethysmography are common assessments for body fat, but they take place in medical facilities and not in the field.

Program Design

Periodization

Periodization is a training plan that uses logical phases of training, during which training variables are manipulated to produce physiological adaptations, manage fatigue, minimize overtraining, and promote maximum athletic performance. The periodization plan includes all aspects of training that are planned over a specific period of time (typically one year or, in some cases, two to four years). The preplanned training loads, load volumes, and training intensities are designed to apply the training stress necessary to cause adaptive responses in the client. Periodized training consists of segments that are organized around the client's sport season and sport activities in a way that will allow training adaptations to occur at appropriate times, thereby improving the client's competitive performance.

Macrocycle

The macrocycle is the primary periodization component consisting of the entire annual training program. A macrocycle is typically a year but can be several months or, in rare cases, up to a four-year developmental plan (e.g., Olympic training cycle). The macrocycle consists of smaller segments that are used to focus on specific aspects of training in order to develop the specific athletic qualities required for the client to peak and perform optimally during competition. A common macrocycle divides the client's training year into off-season, preseason, in-season (i.e., competition), and postseason periods.

Mesocycle

A mesocycle is a segment of the macrocycle that is generally a block of two to six weeks (four weeks is the most common length). This time frame has been shown to optimize adaptations to training.

Microcycle

A microcycle is the shortest training segment, lasting from several days to weeks. Variables like intensity and volume can be manipulated to alter the client's training within the microcycle segment. The manipulation of the microcycle training is an important part of tapering clients for competition. A client's training progress can be consistently monitored and altered across the microcycle.

Preparatory Period

The preparatory period is usually the starting point of the periodization training plan. It is usually the longest period and most often corresponds to the off-season when there are no competitions. This period establishes a base level of conditioning that will provide the client with the ability to tolerate increased training intensity. The preparatory period is divided into the general preparatory phase and the specific preparatory phase.

General Preparatory Phase

The general preparatory phase takes place during the early part of the preparatory period and focuses on developing the general physical conditioning that will be required for the client to handle more intense training. The conditioning during this phase consists of high-volume and low-intensity training and includes activities like slow distance swims, resistance training using high repetitions and light to moderate loads, and low-intensity plyometrics.

Hypertrophy/Strength-Endurance Phase

The hypertrophy phase, also known as the strength-endurance phase, takes place during the general preparatory phase. The two primary goals of the hypertrophy phase are to develop the client's physical endurance base and increase lean body mass. This phase uses low to moderate intensity and high volume. For example, exercises might consist of three to six sets of eight to twenty repetitions at 50–75% of 1-RM.

Specific Preparatory Phase

The specific preparatory phase builds on the general conditioning base and begins to focus on more sport-specific training.

Basic Strength Phase

The basic strength phase occurs during the specific preparatory phase and focuses on increasing the strength of primary sport-specific muscle groups. This is achieved by using higher-intensity and moderate-volume training. For example, exercises might consist of two to six sets of two to six repetitions at 80–95% of 1-RM.

First Transition Period

The first transition period is the training segment between the preparatory phase and the competitive period. This "precompetitive" period focuses on converting strength into power. The last week of the first transition period focuses on recovery with reduced work volume and intensity, thus allowing the client to recover from training in preparation for the competitive period.

Strength/Power Phase

Definitions:

- Strength: The ability to produce force
- Power/Explosive Strength: The time rate of doing work (power = work x time)
- Work: The product of the force exerted on an object, and the distance the object moves in the direction in which the force is exerted (also called displacement; work = force x displacement)

The strength/power phase is the primary phase of the first transition period (the second segment of the preparatory period). The focus during the strength/power phase is on increasing the intensity of training to pre-competition levels. Resistance-training exercises consist of low to very high loads and low volumes. For example, exercises might consist of two to five sets of two to five repetitions at 30–95% of 1-RM.

Competitive Period

The focus of the competitive period (also called the competition period) is preparing the client for competition. This is achieved by increasing strength and power. Training intensity increases and volume decreases. Resistance-training exercises consist of moderate and high intensities and moderate volumes. Individual sports with a competition period of several weeks (e.g., fencing or judo) will use a peaking program, while team sports with competition periods of several months will use a maintenance program.

Peaking Programs: The objective of a peaking program is to get the client in peak performance condition for one to two weeks. To reduce fatigue, the training progressively shifts from higher-intensity to lower-intensity training as the client goes through the taper prior to competition. Resistance-training exercises consist of very high to low intensities and low volumes. For example, exercises might consist of one to three sets of one to two repetitions at 50–93% of 1-RM. Trying to extend a peak beyond one to two weeks will decrease fitness and reduce performance capacity.

Maintenance Programs: The extended duration of the competitive period requires training to be manipulated across microcycles. Alterations in training intensity and volume effectively maintain strength and power while simultaneously controlling the fatigue that results from frequent competitions. Resistance-training exercises will be modulated between moderate to high intensities and moderate volumes. For example, resistance exercises would consist of approximately two to five sets of three to six repetitions at 85–93% of 1-RM. It should be noted that the two-to-five-set recommendation does not include warm-up sets and is the target number of sets for core exercises only.

Second Transition Period

The second transition period (also called active rest or restoration period) is between the competitive period and preparatory period of the next macrocycle and is typically one to four weeks in duration. During this period, intense training is avoided in order to allow clients to recover from injury and get both physical and mental rest. If this period lasts longer than four weeks, the preparatory phase will need to be longer to allow enough time for the client to regain a conditioning base. During this period, clients can participate in other recreational sports and resistance training, if desired, using very low volumes and loads.

Unloading/Deloading Week

The second transition period can be designed to have one-week rests between three-week training phases. The week of rest allows the body to "unload" in preparation for the upcoming training.

Periodization Models

Linear Periodization Model: This is the "traditional" resistance-training periodization model. It is called linear because of the gradually progressive increases in mesocycle intensity, but this is actually a misnomer because the linear model has substantial amounts of variation in intensities and volumes at the microcycle level and across the mesocycle. Resistance-training exercises will consist of the same number of sets and repetitions daily over a certain span of time, but the load will vary. This type of training results in volume-load changes.

Undulating Periodization Model: Also called the nonlinear periodization model by individuals in the fitness industry, the undulating periodization model has daily fluctuations in training intensities and volumes for core resistance-training exercises. During a training week, one day may be focused on strength (four sets with a 6-RM load), the second day might focus on power (five sets with a 3-RM load), and the third set might focus on hypertrophy (three sets with a 10-RM load).

NASM's Optimum Performance Training (OPT™) Model

NASM's exclusive Optimum Performance Training (OPT™) model is one of the fitness industry's first comprehensive training systems. It is based on scientific, evidence-based research and NASM believes this model provides superior programming and results for clients and eliminates the guesswork for trainers.

The OPT™ model was developed to concurrently improve all functional abilities, including flexibility, core stabilization, balance, strength, power, and cardiorespiratory endurance. The model helps guide NASM personal trainers to make the most scientifically-sound, personalized training plan that considers the client's unique needs and goals and also the environment in which the client is training to maximize program effectiveness and reduce injury risk. The foundation of the model is assessment, and proper assessment of intangibles like goals and tangibles like muscle imbalances and movement dysfunctions must be evaluated prior to any program development. For example, asking a client to perform a simple bodyweight overhead squat can reveal important information about asymmetries and weaknesses that must be addressed early in a training program to prevent injury. The OPT™ Model has five phases:

- Phase 1: Stabilization Endurance
- Phase 2: Strength Endurance
- Phase 3: Hypertrophy
- Phase 4: Maximal Strength
- Phase 5: Power

The first phase is part of the Stabilization Level. In this level, the focus is on endurance, joint stabilization, and posture, to help develop a good stable foundation, particularly for deconditioned athletes. Stabilization is important before moving on to the Strength Level, which is composed of the second, third, and fourth phases. In the Strength Level, the focus is moved to adding load and intensity to resistance exercises. In the Power Level, speed and more advanced movements are added to the exercises. A client is only progressed from phase to phase or level to level when he or she is ready. In that way, it is a very individualized and safe programming philosophy. A wide variety of modalities are encouraged throughout the model, such as core training, balance, agility, plyometrics, speed training, resistance training, and cardiovascular training.

Specificity, Variation, and Overload

All exercise training programs should be designed based on a client's fitness and health goals, taking into account all components of health-related fitness as well as areas of greatest deficit. Then, progressive overload, specificity, and program progression should be determined in order to plan a program that will help a client work towards their goals. When modifying a client's program following regular assessments that help a trainer determine when a client has progressed to a point where frequency, intensity, duration, or type of exercises should increase, trainers should consider progressive overload. Not only does appropriate program progression ensure that the client remains challenged and on track toward their goals, but it also minimizes the chance of plateauing in a program that is too consistent and lacks sufficient training stimulus.

All effective exercise-training programs should consider the principles of specificity and program progression. Specificity is the focus on exercises that utilize muscle groups and functions that directly relate to a client's goals. Program progression refers to regular assessments of a client that allow a trainer to reevaluate and modify a training program to include exercises that continue to challenge the client as they increase their fitness level; in order to avoid plateaus in training, trainers should make consistent modifications to the client's exercises' frequency, intensity, duration, and type to ensure the client remains challenged and continues toward their specific goals.

Variations in Exercise Orders

Power, Other Core, Assistance Exercises

Training sessions typically order the exercises from the most metabolically demanding and technical (i.e., power exercises) to the least demanding exercises (i.e., core and assistance exercises). For example, Olympic lifts are the most demanding power exercises because they place large metabolic demands on the client's body, require excellent technique and concentration, and are the most affected by fatigue. Accordingly, power exercises would be completed first during a training session. Non-power core exercises (i.e., multi-joint exercises) are completed next because they require quality technique, load the spine, and place large metabolic demands on the client's body. Finally, assistance or single-joint exercises are performed last because they are less technical and the least demanding resistance exercises. The personal trainer must consider both the technique and effort required when ordering resistance exercises because fatigue can cause clients to use poor technique and increase their risk for injury.

Alternated Upper- and Lower-Body Exercises

Alternating upper- and lower-body resistance exercises allows for greater recovery between exercises. This training order is useful when training time is limited, because it minimizes the rest needed between exercises while maximizing the rest for the upper- and lower body between sets. When minimal rest is provided between sets, the method is called circuit training. Because circuit training requires a client to train with minimal rest between sets, this training style helps to improve mental focus. Also, the lack of rest requires the client to perform more exercises in a shorter period of time, and therefore helps to reduce body fat by imposing significant metabolic demands on the client.

Alternating "Push" and "Pull' Exercises

This variation alternates between pushing resistance exercises, such as shoulder presses or triceps extensions, and pulling exercises, such as bent-over rows and biceps curls. Alternating push and pull exercises improves recovery and recruitment between the exercises by ensuring that the same muscle group is not used in two consecutive exercises. Examples of push-pull exercise arrangements for the lower body include back squat (push) and leg (knee) curl (pull) and leg press (push) and stiff-leg deadlift (pull). Circuit training often uses alternating push and pull exercises. This ordering method can be used with clients starting or returning to resistance exercise training.

Supersets

A superset is the performance of two resistance exercises sequentially. The first exercise stresses an agonist muscle or muscle group and the second exercise stresses the antagonist muscle or muscle group. An example of a superset is ten repetitions of triceps pushdowns followed immediately by ten repetitions of barbell biceps curls. Supersets efficiently use training time but may not be appropriate for unconditioned clients or those needing significant training instruction.

Compound Sets

A compound set is the performance of two different resistance exercises in a row in order to stress the same muscle or the muscle groups. For example, a set of barbell biceps curls is followed immediately by dumbbell hammer curls. Compound sets are time-efficient and demanding, causing greater stress to the muscles. This type of training is not appropriate for unconditioned clients.

- oxidative system's energy production, work-to-rest ratios for training should be 1:1 to 1:3.

Variations in Exercise Modes

Explosive Training can include power exercises (structural exercises performed very fast) and various plyometric exercises (e.g., box jumps, drop jumps, loaded jumps).

Strength Training can include the use of free weights, resistance machines, bodyweight, variable-resistance training methods (e.g., chain-supplemented exercises and resistance-band exercises), Strongman training (e.g., tire flipping, log lifting, farmer's walk), and kettlebell training.

Cooldown: This is a period of low-intensity exercise such as stretching that allows the body's physiological parameters to return to their normal levels.

Energy-System Training Prioritization

As mentioned, specific types of training can affect the phosphagen system, glycolytic system, and oxidative system in various ways. Carbohydrates, fats, and proteins can be metabolized for energy, but carbohydrates are the only macronutrient that can be metabolized without oxygen.

- Phosphagen System: The phosphagen system provides energy via anaerobic metabolism for brief, high-intensity activities (i.e., up to 6 seconds of extremely high-intensity exercise or 6–30 seconds of very high-intensity exercise). Modes of exercise that can be used to train the phosphagen system include doing resistance exercises in which each set has a low number of repetitions, sprinting less than 200 meters, and performing some types of plyometrics. To improve the phosphagen system's energy production, work-to-rest ratios for training should be between 1:12 and 1:20.

- Glycolytic System: The glycolytic system provides energy during moderate- to high-intensity and short- to medium-duration activities (i.e., 30 seconds to 2 minutes of high-intensity exercise or 2–3 minutes of moderate-intensity exercise). Glycolysis provides energy by breaking down muscle glycogen or blood glucose. Modes of exercise that can be used to train the glycolytic system include sprinting for 200 meters to 800 meters, doing high-intensity interval training, and performing some types of plyometrics. To improve the glycolytic system's energy production, work-to-rest ratios for training should be between 1:3 and 1:5.

Oxidative (aerobic) System: This system is the primary source of energy during low-intensity and long-duration exercise (i.e., more than 3 minutes). The oxidative system uses carbohydrates (glucose and glycogen) and fats (triglycerides) to produce energy. Aerobic exercise at low to moderate intensities can be used to train the aerobic system.

General Adaptation Syndrome

The stages of adaptation that the body goes through when confronted with stress are part of a syndrome referred to as the general adaptation syndrome (GAS). There are three stages:

- Alarm reaction
- Resistance development
- Exhaustion

The alarm reaction stage occurs when the body is first exposed to stress, which in the case of resistance training would be weight. The body begins to respond to the uncommon pressure put on it. Blood and oxygen amounts are raised and neural recruitment is activated. The unusual activity results in pain, stiffness, and fatigue. The soreness that occurs 2–3 days after the workout is known as DOMS (delayed onset muscle soreness). It can be reduced if overload and intensity are kept to a minimum and progressed slowly.

The resistance development stage is when adaptation to stress occurs. At this point, muscles are easily recruited, the body can utilize the supply of blood and oxygen appropriately, and acute variables can be modified to add new levels of stress.

If there is too much stress, either in volume or length of time, the body reaches the exhaustion phase. This is the phase in which clients are likely to suffer from injuries such as sprains, strains, and fractures. Clients can also suffer from emotional fatigue if allowed to reach this stage.

Outcomes Associated with the Manipulation of Training Volume

Training volume is one variable that can be manipulated in order to progress an exercise-training program. Increasing training volume can result in physiological adaptations to increased physical stress. General adaptation syndrome (GAS) occurs when the body is subjected to external loading. Firstly, the client will experience soreness, stiffness, and decreased performance (alarm phase). Secondly, the body will return to normal (resistance phase). Thirdly, the body will adapt and the client's muscle mass and strength will increase (exhaustion phase). If training volume is increased and the client is unable to adapt, the client may experience overload resulting in overtraining syndrome.

Decreasing training volume and intensity – called *tapering* – is a key part of an endurance client's preparation for important competitions. A taper may last between seven and twenty-eight days and it allows the client's body to completely recover from training and build muscle and liver glycogen storage. The elevation of the client's performance capacity resulting from tapering is sometimes referred to as supercompensation. In contrast, if exercise volume and intensity decrease (resulting from illness, injury, etc., the client will begin to lose the physiological adaptations achieved from training, which is called *detraining.*

Flexibility Training

Flexibility consists of static and dynamic components and is a measure of range of motion (ROM). ROM is the degree of movement that occurs at a joint.

Static flexibility is the amount of movement around a joint during a passive movement. Static flexibility is not dependent on voluntary movement. A partner, gravity, or a machine provides the force required for the stretch.

Dynamic flexibility is the ROM during active movements that require voluntary muscle activity. In general, dynamic ROM is greater than static ROM.

Active-isolated stretching involves isolating one muscle and stretching it repeatedly for only two seconds at a time.

For flexibility and performance, the type of sport-specific movements that clients must perform dictates the level of flexibility they need. The personal trainer needs to base a client's flexibility training on the requirements of the sport, as well as the force patterns required through the ROM. Injury risk may increase if a client is unable to obtain the level of flexibility required by the sport. Likewise, hyperflexibility can also increase the risk for injury.

Factors affecting flexibility include:

- Joint Structure: The type and shape of the joint (e.g., ball-and-socket, ellipsoidal, hinge) and its surrounding tissue affect its ROM.
- Muscle and Connective Tissue: Many body tissues (e.g., tendons, muscle, fascial sheaths, skin, joint capsules, and ligaments) can limit ROM. Stretching takes advantage of the plasticity and elasticity of connective tissues and can affect ROM.
- Muscle Bulk: ROM can be negatively affected by substantial muscle bulk. The specific requirements of the sport (e.g., large muscles versus joint mobility) should be considered when determining a flexibility program for a client.
- Neural Control: ROM is controlled by the central and peripheral nervous systems, so an effective flexibility program needs to affect both systems.
- Stretch Tolerance: How well clients can tolerate the discomfort of stretching influences their ROM. Clients with a greater stretch tolerance generally have a greater ROM.
- Resistance Training: Heavy resistance training can decrease ROM; however, an appropriately planned resistance-training program can actually increase ROM. Increased ROM can enhance the development of force capacity.
- Activity Level: Active individuals are generally more flexible than inactive individuals, particularly if the activity includes flexibility exercises.
- Age and Sex: Young people are generally more flexible than older people, and women are generally more flexible than men.

Flexibility can be practiced in a variety of ways, including traditional methods such as stretching and yoga, or less traditional ways such as self-myofascial release (SMR), which involves using an external object such as a foam roller to massage the muscles.

Resistance Training

Chronic resistance training affords strength, power, and coordination improvements as well as greater efficiency of the anaerobic systems. Nervous system adaptations occur quickly with training as motor units (an alpha motor neuron from the spinal cord and all of the skeletal muscle fibers it supplies) become conditioned to activate more efficiently, more quickly, and more often. These adaptions increase the neural stimulation for muscle fibers to contract. As more motor units activate and coordinate with each other, a higher percentage of fibers in a muscle contract simultaneously, which increases contractile strength. In fact, many of the earliest strength improvements noticed in resistance training programs are due to these neural adaptations rather than muscle hypertrophy, which takes approximately 4–8 weeks to occur. A client can quickly experience increases in strength and power as a result of training. Over time, muscle fibers increase in size while bone mineral density increases in load-bearing bones, helping mitigate age-related bone and muscle loss.

Free Weight Training Equipment

Dumbbells and barbells are the most commonly used free weight training equipment. While both involve "lifting weights," this equipment differs from resistance machines in that weight plates, dumbbells, and barbells are used in varying weights for any number of exercises being typically held in the hands of the client. Conversely, machines are prearranged setups where the client simply adjusts the weight and machine height. With machine equipment, a client can typically perform a minimal number of designated movements per machine, which are specifically designed for that exercise.

Resistance Machines

Resistance machines typically enable the proper form to be achieved more easily for exercises because they only allow movement in certain planes of motion based on the mechanical setup of the levers, hinges, pulleys, and movable pieces. However, this guidance, restriction, and stabilization make exercises completed on resistance machines less sports-specific than free weight, plyometric, or body weight exercises in which the client must stabilize the body while moving through the range of motion.

Weight machines can be a good starting place for beginners and also for senior clients and others who have poor balance and coordination, and for certain exercises for individuals recovering from injuries. This is because these machines are generally safer to use and usually only isolate one movement, which makes them easier to use and a good way for beginners to grasp one specific movement at a time. Resistance machines can be helpful for rehabilitating certain body parts because they generally isolate a specific muscle group. In general, this is not advantageous for overall strength-training, especially for sports-specific work important to competitive clients.

However, resistance machines have their place, particularly in injury rehab, solo sessions, rapid circuit training, and reaching higher maximal lifts. For heavy weights and maximal efforts, most machines have the advantage of not requiring a spotter, although clients should still always exercise caution when attempting any lift. Some machines force the correct movement for the lift, which may help reduce the risk of injury and ensure that the client is moving through the entire range of motion for each repetition. Machine workouts can be more efficient because they are generally organized in a circuit in the layout of the gym, so the client can easily move from one to another. With that said, if clients prioritize saving time and they do not properly adjust the settings to fit the machine to their body, clients can "cheat" in the movement and increase injury risk.

As mentioned previously, most weight machines require the client to move the weight in a predetermined path, making it difficult to strengthen the stabilizer muscles. Similarly, usually only one exercise can be completed on each machine, making it cumbersome to keep getting up, moving to another machine, and adjusting the settings accordingly. Most machines are designed for the average-sized adult, so small youth clients, slight women, or significantly taller and larger clients may find the fit less than ideal, even when adjusted as much as possible, resulting in a fit that is not only uncomfortable, but may cause difficulty performing the exercise correctly.

Preparatory Body and Limb Position

Proper form with a good neutral erect spine, chest up and out, feet flat on the floor, and shoulders back should be used on machines. The height of the bench or chair portion can usually be adjusted so that the knees are flexed to 90 degrees and the feet are flat on the floor. For machines such as the leg press, the feet should be placed on the platform slightly wider than hip-width. Knees should flex in alignment with the ankles, refraining from any tendency to deviate them laterally, which internally rotates the hips and places undo stress on the lateral compartment of the knee. Hand grip should be neutral and evenly spaced in most cases, unless a narrow or wide grip is specifically introduced as a modification. Most machines have pictures of proper alignment and positioning of pads and bars so that clients can adjust the machine to fit their bodies. Clients should align their joint axes with the axis of rotation of the machine to optimize joint function and prevent any incongruity in the moving axes, which can induce injury.

Execution of Technique

As with free weight exercises, proper technique on resistance machines is imperative, both to prevent injury and to maximize the benefit of the exercise. The proper execution of lifting exercises with free weights should be demonstrated and explained thoroughly by strength trainers. Each exercise obviously has its own set of procedures to carry it out properly, but in general, emphasis on form and breathing technique will lead to successful execution. Many resistance machines execute the movement in the seated position. As mentioned, exercises in the seated and supine positions require five points of contact for optimal body support: the head is firmly on the bench or back pad, the shoulders and upper back are evenly placed and firmly on the bench or back pad, the buttocks are positioned evenly on the bench or seat, and both feet are placed flat on the floor. The same general guidelines for execution that have been previously discussed should be employed with machine-based exercises as well.

Correction of Improper Technique

One of the benefits of resistance machines is that they make it more challenging to have improper technique compared to free weights and alternative strength-training modalities because of the constraints imposed by the design of the machines. Nevertheless, strength trainers should monitor clients on the training floor and quickly correct any deviations from optimal form to prevent injury and to maximize training benefit. Clients should be instructed to adjust settings on the machine, both in terms of sizing and resistance, to meet their individual bodies, even if working with a partner in a circuit when it would be more time-efficient to share the same setup. Mirrors work well to provide visual feedback to clients, but their effectiveness is limited by the client's understanding of proper form, attention to detail, and the desire to perform exercises correctly. For this reason, strength trainers still need to heed attention to clients using resistance machines.

Alternative Modes of Training

Alternative modes of training include core work, stability, balance, calisthenic, and bodyweight exercises. Such exercises augment training and may help prevent injuries. Plyometric training such as pull-ups, push-ups, chin-ups, squat thrusts, lunges, yoga, jumping jacks, and planks provide resistance in the form of bodyweight. These exercises improve relative strength, core strength, and body control, and they are low-cost. Many of these activities can be performed outside on the field or in an open gym with an entire team. Some trainers find that adding body work such as yoga to a client's regime improves flexibility, focus, breathing, core strength, and supports athletic goals in a less intense fashion. Strength trainers should educate clients unfamiliar with these practices on their benefits to help improve acceptance and adherence. Calisthenics can be used in conjunction with dynamic warm-ups to prepare the clients for practice and competition.

Preparatory Body and Limb Position

For push-ups and pull-ups, arms should be roughly shoulder-width apart, although modifications affecting hand spacing are often introduced to provide variable challenges to the muscles. For example, diamond push-ups have the client place his or her hands together, directly under the chest, with the index fingers and thumbs of each hand touching to form a diamond. This modification places extra emphasis on the triceps rather than the chest muscles, such as the pectoralis major, that are emphasized during a regular push-up. With core exercises, it is important that the spine stay neutral and that clients do not pull up on their neck while doing crunches or sit-ups.

They should use their core muscles to lift the shoulder blades off of the surface, with their hands simply supporting the weight of the head rather than pulling it upward. Yoga and Pilates incorporate many poses and positions and should be guided by a trained and certified professional. Lunges and squats require an athletic stance, feet slightly wider than hip-width apart and flat on the floor. For clients who are limited in squat depth due to tight Achilles tendons, elevating the heels on a weight plate or other incline will help achieve a deeper squat, despite limited range of motion in the ankles. These clients should be guided through a regular static stretching routine to help improve ankle mobility.

Execution of Technique

Bodyweight exercises improve relative, but not absolute, strength. With these exercises, clients are often able to safely complete a higher number of repetitions than more traditional "weight lifting" exercises. This can improve muscular endurance and help prevent fatigue during long-duration activities. Clients should inhale during the concentric or challenging phase through the sticking point and exhale on the eccentric or easier phase. The spine should stay neutral, with shoulders, hips, and ankles in alignment. While risk of injury is often lower with bodyweight-only exercises due to smaller loads than those imposed by external weights, proper form should still be followed.

Correction of Improper Technique

Strength trainers should pay close attention to clients' form and technique for common mistakes such as a swayed back on push-ups or planks or raised buttocks above the plane of the body. Other issues to note include clients using momentum during core work or craning and pulling the neck, and knees coming over the ankles with hips not sitting far enough back during squats and lunges. Because of the lack of external weights used during bodyweight exercises, it is sometimes easier to perform them with improper form without the client receiving any obvious physical signs of discomfort that are commonly experienced with weighted exercises. As with other forms of exercise, strength trainers must correct improper technique as early as possible in the learning process in order to prevent the development of bad habits as well as to reduce risk of injury. Even advanced clients may demonstrate poor technique when fatigued, distracted, or unmotivated, so observing and giving cues on preparatory and execution form and technique should be the constant focus of strength trainers.

Non-Traditional Implements

In recent years, there has been an increased interest by clients and trainers to implement non-traditional equipment for strength and resistance training, power and speed training, and overall conditioning. Tires, logs, water-filled pipes, sandbags, kettle bells, heavy battle ropes, and a variety of medicine balls have entered the training arena, popularized by some adventure races, CrossFit, and other innovative or rogue training programs. Such implements are creative ways to essentially add tools to the tool bag of a trainer, while accomplishing similar physiologic goals for the clients. Still, trainers must be aware of when and how to properly use this equipment and be sure to educate and supervise clients in their use. Much of the non-traditional equipment is best reserved for advanced clients who have the basic foundations of movements, such as a well-mastered squat and deadlift, because programs with non-traditional equipment tend to use heavier implements in power movements that can induce injury if the exercise is not performed properly.

Preparatory Body and Limb Position

Some non-traditional training implements can be used to improve grip strength. Heavy ropes require the client to grip very tightly while forcefully swinging the ropes. Similarly, some sandbags lack traditional handgrips, so the client must squeeze the material tightly while powerfully moving it. A client's stance and core engagement should be emphasized for all training exercises. For tire-flipping activities, clients should use a wide base of support when squatting and keep the spine in the neutral lumbar lordosis position to protect the lower back and knees. A weight belt can help support the lumbar spine. Kettlebells offer somewhat of an exception to the rule against swinging weights and harnessing momentum, and in fact, many exercises specific to kettlebells, such as kettlebell swings, rely on swinging for proper form. In this exercise, power should come from thrusting the hips forward and not from the shoulders lifting the implement.

Execution of Technique

Many of the non-traditional exercise tools provide a challenge for anaerobic and strength-building workouts. Strength trainers should demonstrate the proper execution of each movement and should consider the use of mirrors so that clients can monitor their own form. Weight belts can be helpful in certain cases with maximal loads. As with traditional resistance exercises, clients should exhale through the more challenging phase of the exercise, including the "sticking point," and then inhale slowly after the "sticking point" through the completion of the movement. The Valsalva maneuver is likely inevitable when loads are greater than 80% of maximum, but it does help stabilize the spine and decrease intradiscal pressure. When activities require speed, force, or a combination of the two (power), clients should be prepped, focused, and ideally aroused to bring about optimal performance.

Correction of Improper Technique

Particularly when using a training implement for the first time, clients will need extra supervision and critique of form. Strength trainers should be prudent to work with only a few clients at a time so that clients can get individualized attention, instruction, clarification if they have questions, and correction of improper form. While non-traditional equipment can bring fresh variety into a training program, it does have the potential for increased risk of injury if clients are not properly trained, both in terms of their skill level as well as the particular instruction on the equipment usage.

Resistance Training Modalities

As a client progresses in their exercise-training program, the trainer can implement more advanced modalities of resistance training. Specialized equipment such as kettlebells, TRX straps, and medicine balls, as well as external and static resistance devices, add a variety of resistance training modalities to a challenging exercise program. Using different equipment and exercises can help clients improve fitness level, strength, and power, while preventing boredom, burnout, and injury. Trainers should repeatedly demonstrate proper form and technique, providing detailed descriptions of the exercise's goals and common mistakes that pose risk of injury. Spotting and consistently providing verbal and nonverbal cues will help to ensure that the client masters the techniques and performance of exercises.

Free Weights

The source of resistance for free weights is gravity. Free-weight exercises are often performed in a standing position, which places more stress on the body's muscles and bones than weight-stack machines. Free weights require muscles to support and stabilize the body. Lifting free weights is a closer replication of the movements required in sports, because it involves the coordination of multiple muscle groups (as opposed to machines, which typically isolate single muscle groups).

Weight-Stack Machines

The source of resistance for weight-stack machines is gravity; however, these machines utilize cables, pulleys, cams, and gears that allow increased control over both the pattern and direction of resistance. Weight-stack machines are safer than free weights, in part because less skill and muscle coordination are needed for control, and the design of the machines provides resistance to body movements that are difficult to duplicate with free weights (e.g., hip adduction and abduction, or leg curl). Machines also can be readied more quickly than free weights because weight selection only requires inserting a pin into the weight stack.

Circuit Training

The use of circuit training during resistance-training sessions condenses the time needed to complete a specific amount of work. The client goes from one exercise to the next with limited rest between the movement sets. Circuit training can be used with any type of resistance exercise movement, but the most demanding movement sets (i.e., power movements) should be completed before less demanding movement sets (i.e., core and assistance movements). There are several benefits to using circuit training, including improved time efficiency, enhanced cardiorespiratory functioning, and increased muscle endurance. Circuit training increases metabolic costs and can be beneficial for clients interested in reducing body fat.

In a single set circuit, each set of repetitions is completed only once, whereas in a multiple set circuit, each exercise is completed in more than one set of repetitions. In a super set, trainees will go from one exercise to the next with no break in between. A pyramid set utilizes the same exercise, but gradually increases weight while simultaneously decreasing the number of repetitions.

Circuits can be loaded either horizontally or vertically. Horizontal loading refers to the client performing all required sets of a particular exercise for a particular area of the body in immediate sequence before starting another exercise for a different area of the body. Vertical loading refers to the client starting with one set of the first exercise, moving on to the first set of a different exercise for a different area of the body, and advancing in this fashion through each area of the body before going back to the first exercise and repeating the circuit.

Bodyweight-Training Methods

Bodyweight training is a basic resistance-training method that utilizes an individual's bodyweight as resistance. This training helps to develop core muscles and, as a result, may decrease injury risk. Benefits of bodyweight training include the following: bodyweight training is specific to the client's anthropometrics; it incorporates many closed chain exercises; it improves body control and relative strength while strengthening multiple muscle groups simultaneously; and it is a low-cost form of training. The limitations of bodyweight training include the following:

- The load is limited by the athlete's weight.
- Absolute strength is not substantially improved by training.
- Changing movement patterns or repetitions are required in order to increase intensity.

As the number of repetitions increases, the outcome focus of training will change from strength-to-strength endurance. Examples of bodyweight-training exercises include:

- pull-ups
- sit-ups
- push-ups
- squat thrusts
- chin-ups
- calisthenics
- yoga
- gymnastics

Variable-Resistance Training Methods

Types of variable-resistance training methods include the following:

- Constant External Resistance: Constant external resistance involves free weights and traditional resistance exercises where the external load remains constant throughout the movement. This type of movement better replicates real activities and promotes more realistic movement patterns and skeletal muscle coordination.

- Accommodating Resistance: Also known as semi-isokinetic resistance applications, accommodating resistance controls the speed of movement (i.e., isokinetic resistance) throughout a range of motion (ROM). This type of training requires specific devices that generally have poor external validity and provide an inadequate training stimulus in comparison with constant external resistance exercises.

- Variable Resistance: Variable resistance training utilizes devices that apply varied resistance as the joint angle changes in an attempt to maximize forced application across the full ROM. Fitness facilities commonly combine chains or rubber bands with traditional free-weight resistance-training methods in order to alter the loading profile, thus allowing varied resistance across the ROM.

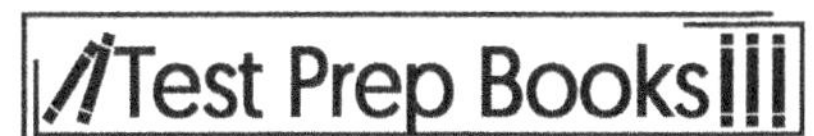

- Chain-Supplemented Exercises: Variable resistance can be applied by the addition of chains to resistance exercise activities (e.g., back squat or bench press). The size (e.g., diameter, length, density, or number of links) of the chain controls the amount of resistance it provides. The use of chains results in a linear increase in the applied resistance. Two ways to apply chains are to let them touch the floor from the fully extended position of the movement or to hang them from lighter chains so they only touch the floor when the lowest portion of the movement pattern (e.g., bottom of the squat) is reached.

  Note: Determining the Barbell Load to Use with Chains: First, a client must determine what the barbell load should be without chains. Second, the client should take the average of the chain resistance at the top and bottom of the movement. Third, the average chain resistance should be subtracted from the desired barbell load to determine the final barbell load. For example, a client who wants to train at a 5-RM (repetition-maximum) load on bench press must first determine the 5-RM load without the chains. If the 5-RM load without chains is 120 kg, then subtract the average chain resistance from this load. If the bottom position has a chain resistance of 0 kg and the top position has a chain resistance of 11.1 kg, the average chain resistance is 5.55 kg ($11.1 \div 2$). The client would need to subtract 5.55 kg from 120 kg to have appropriate barbell loading.

- Resistance-Band Exercises: There is some research supporting the efficacy of using resistance bands in combination with traditional resistance exercise. The personal trainer needs to be aware that the make-up of the resistance bands can affect their tension (resistance), and the stiffness of the band affects the amount the band can stretch (deformation). Note that the tension of a resistance band is equivalent to the product of its stiffness (k) and deformation (d), so $tension = k \times d$. Increased stretching of the band results in a linear increase in the band's tension. Note that two similar bands can be different (3.2–5.2%), which will increase the amount of mean tension by 8–19%.

  A resistance band can either be attached to a barbell and then attached to a heavy dumbbell or attached with a customized attachment to a squat rack. The resistance will be greatest when the band has the highest amount of tension. At the top position and the bottom position, there will be no resistance from the band because it is no longer stretched. Thus, the stretch load increases when the client is ascending from the bottom position and the load decreases as the client descends from the top position. Once the loads at the top and bottom positions are determined, those values are averaged. If a client wants to use a 5-RM load of 150 kg using bands, the average of bands at the two positions is subtracted from the original load on the bar. If a client is doing a bench press and the load at the bottom is 0 kg and the load at the top is 26.6 kg, the average is 13.3 kg. This average would be subtracted from the total weight on the bar (without bands), so the client would put between 136 kg and 137 kg on the bar, attach the bands, and complete the resistance exercise.

Cardiorespiratory Training

Cardiorespiratory training is best done in zones, or stages, in which clients gradually work towards higher goals. At first, workouts should be shorter and less intense. Clients progress as they are able to handle longer, more intense workouts.

Pace/Tempo Training Method

This training method is a type of aerobic endurance training that utilizes an intensity consistent with or slightly higher than race or competition intensity. The goal of pace/tempo training is to replicate the pattern of muscle fiber recruitment and physiological stress during competition in order to improve running economy, increase aerobic- and anaerobic-energy production, and increase the lactate threshold. The intensity in this type of training—sometimes called threshold training or aerobic-anaerobic interval training—corresponds to the lactate threshold and improves the aerobic- and anaerobic-energy systems, which are both active during a race. Pace/tempo training can either be steady or intermittent. Steady training consists of a twenty- to thirty-minute bout of continuous training at the client's lactate threshold.

During exercise, muscle cells release lactate into the blood. Resting levels of blood lactate range between 0.8 nM (nanomolar) and 1.5 nM, and lactate levels can be greater than 18 nM during intense exercise. The lactate threshold is the amount of work (i.e., percentage of VO_2 max) that causes blood lactate concentrations to increase above resting levels. In aerobic training, lactate threshold can refer to the speed of movement or exercise intensity that is associated with a specific concentration of lactate in the blood. When clients exceed their lactate threshold during exercise, they experience substantial physical and mental fatigue. Intermittent training is similar to the steady pace/tempo approach, except that the work intervals are separated by short recovery periods. When doing pace/tempo training, it is important that the work is done at the prescribed intensity. Clients should avoid working at a more intense pace. This type of training is generally done one to two times per week for twenty to thirty minutes, at the client's normal race pace.

Long, Slow Distance (LSD) Running

LSD training is usually done one to two times per week at an intensity of approximately 70% of VO2 max and 80% of maximal heart rate. This type of training is slower than race pace. The distance covered should be longer than the race distance and the training duration should be 30 minutes to 2 hours. Several physiological adaptations arise from LSD, including improved thermoregulation, cardiovascular function, mitochondrial energy production, and use of fat as energy. Lactate threshold may also increase as these adaptations make clearing lactate from the blood easier. Too much LSD can be detrimental to race performance, because neuromuscular adaptations may be made to a running intensity that is significantly lower than that required during a race.

Fartlek Training

Fartlek literally means "speed play." It combines several types of endurance training and can be used for runners, swimmers, and cyclists. Fartlek training low-intensity exercise (approximately 70% of VO2 max) with short bursts of high-intensity (85–95% of VO2 max) exercise at more irregular points, lengths, and speeds than in interval training. Fartlek training can provide an opportunity for clients to challenge themselves on a weekly basis and help relieve the monotony of a single type of training session. It is best used during periods of heavy training leading up to an event. This type of training challenges all body systems and can improve VO_2 max, lactate threshold, energy consumption, and exercise economy. Fartlek training is generally done once per week for 20–60 minutes. The intensity varies from LSD to pace/tempo.

High-Intensity Interval Training (HIIT)

This training uses repeated high-intensity (≥90% of VO_2 max) exercise bouts with rest periods in between. Depending on the desired training response, desired training response, short exercise bouts of

45 seconds or less or long bouts of 2–4 minutes can be used. As the duration of the high-intensity exercise gets longer, blood lactate levels will increase because energy will come from anaerobic glycolysis. The length of the rest periods between the intervals is important. Rest periods that are too short will not allow the client to recover enough to put forth the required effort necessary to complete the remaining high-intensity bouts. If the rest period is too long, the client's body may not require energy from anaerobic glycolysis and the training response will not occur. An example of appropriate work-to-rest time periods would be 2–3 minutes of high-intensity exercise followed by a rest period of 2 minutes. Running economy and speed may be improved by HIIT. This type of training is typically done once per week.

Interval, Continuous, and Circuit Training Programs for Cardiovascular Fitness

The trainer can design a workout routine that best benefits the client by applying the basics of interval, continuous, or circuit-training methods. Because each training method implements a different approach to the progression of the workout, it's best to consider the client's abilities, restrictions, and goals to determine the advantages and disadvantages of each. The trainer should remain aware of the client's program progression and improved fitness level, adjusting as needed to ensure that the client doesn't plateau as a result of continuous training with the same method.

Interval Training

Interval training requires the client to work at a high level of exertion for brief periods with intermittent periods of rest. By challenging the cardiovascular and musculoskeletal systems to their maximal potential, providing only short rest periods, and then returning to high intensity, interval training can condition the cardiovascular system, improve endurance, and maximize metabolic functioning for improved weight loss. One benefit of interval training is that intensity is relative for each client. Therefore, with medical clearance, typically even clients with poor fitness, arthritis, or even many cardiorespiratory conditions can enjoy the variety and challenge of interval training. In these cases, trainers should keep in mind that simply walking at a faster rate, or getting up and down from a chair, may be maximum effort. Trainers should consult medical professionals if any questions arise about the safety of such workouts.

Continuous Training

Maintaining a steady speed and intensity throughout cardiovascular exercise falls into the category of continuous training, also known as steady state. With the cardiovascular system challenged at a continuous pace for an extended duration, the benefits to the entire body include improved endurance, prolonged conditioning of muscle groups, and improved aerobic metabolic functioning. For clients who require low- to moderate-impact workouts, this mode of training can be an effective introduction to cardiovascular exercise that minimizes risk of overtraining, illness, or injury.

Circuit Training

Circuit training implements periods of cardiovascular exercise with intermittent strength training exercises. By challenging the cardiovascular system followed by musculoskeletal activities focused on muscle strength, circuit training improves cardiovascular endurance and the strength of major muscle groups that support cardiovascular function by improving the efficiency of oxygen delivery and utilization.

Core and Balance Training

The scientific definition of the anatomical core is the axial skeleton (which includes the shoulder and pelvic girdles) and all of the soft tissues (i.e., muscles, articular cartilage, tendons, fascia, ligaments, and fibrocartilage).

Core Exercises

A strengthened core is important to succeed in many other areas of fitness. There are several exercises that can be utilized to stabilize and strengthen the core. Stabilizing exercises include planks, bird dog exercises, and bridges, among others. Strengthening exercises include crunches of several varieties (regular, reverse, ball, and bicycle) and cable rotations. Some examples of exercises that help increase core power include the medicine ball pullover throw, rotation chest pass, and soccer throw).

Also called multi-joint exercises, core exercises involve two or more primary joints and recruit one or more large muscle areas (e.g., shoulder, thigh, back, etc.). Multi-joint exercises stimulate muscles the most because they recruit all of the large muscle groups associated with the involved joints. As a result, they allow for the greatest amount of loading during resistance training. These exercises should be used for clients who have a limited amount of time to train.

Examples:

- Bench Press: Sternal pectoralis major, clavicular pectoralis major, anterior deltoids, triceps brachii
- Front Squat: Biceps femoris, gluteus maximus, rectus femoris, vastus intermedius, semimembranosus, vastus lateralis, semitendinosus, vastus medialis
- Deadlift: Vastus intermedius, gluteus maximus, vastus lateralis, biceps femoris, semimembranosus, rectus femoris, semitendinosus, vastus medialis

Isolation Exercises

These exercises usually are dynamic or isometric muscle actions that isolate the specific core musculature. The upper and lower extremities do NOT contribute to the muscle actions. These exercises can improve spinal stability because there is increased muscle activation. Performance improvements may be seen in untrained clients as well as clients recovering from injury; however, research suggests that these exercises generally do not improve sport performance in other client populations. Research indicates that ground-based free-weight exercises (e.g., snatch, deadlift, squat, push-press, and trunk-rotation exercises) produce the same or greater levels of core-musculature activation. Examples of isolation exercises include:

- side plank
- prone plank

Instability Devices

Effects of Instability-Based Exercises

Instability-based exercises utilize unstable surfaces devices to cause imbalances that require increased stabilization functioning of the core musculature. While using these devices, the application of external forces to an individual's center of mass, called perturbations, can cause balance challenges that require

core musculature to activate to make postural adjustments and maintain balance. Evidence indicates that core-musculature activation may increase with the use of instability devices. However, the agonist muscle has reduced force generation and a reduced rate of force development. Also, the overall power output and overall force-generating capacity may be 70% or less than that produced during exercise under stable conditions.

Effectiveness of Instability-Based Exercises Versus Ground-Based Exercises

The use of instability devices during static balance activities can help to improve balance and core stability before starting ground-based free-weight exercises done on stable surfaces. Ground-based free-weight exercises (e.g., Olympic lifts, squats) are a better exercise stimulus for developing core stability. These exercises have some inherent instability that facilitates the development of the links of the kinetic chain, which helps improve sport performance to a greater extent than instability-based exercises.

Examples of instability devices include:

- physio balls
- hemispherical physio balls (BOSU)
- inflatable disks
- balance boards
- wobble boards
- foam tubes and platforms

Balance Training Exercises

Balance is important for any client that a trainer works with because proper balance reduces the risk of injuries, particularly to the lower extremities, and improves performance. Being able to make movements and move the body in different directions on various surfaces is referred to as dynamic balance. Neuromuscular skills such as flexibility, endurance, speed, and strength play a role in dynamic balance. Neuromuscular, joint, and muscular components are all in use when maintaining balance. Issues with balance, along with neuromuscular inefficiency, can be the result of imbalances in the kinetic chain. Training programs should be designed to include balance exercises that improve both dynamic balance and neuromuscular efficiency. The goal of balance training is to get the client to the point where they can stabilize their body in various planes of motions by activating the appropriate muscles exactly when needed.

An effective and safe balance training program will progress through the stabilization, strength, and power levels of the OPT™ Model. Variables such as surfaces, positions of the body, or opening or closing of the eyes can be changed as needed for progression or regression, but no more than one variable should be altered at any given time. Stabilization exercises improve the stability of joints and include exercises such as the single-leg balance, single-leg balance reach, and single-leg windmill. Neuromuscular efficiency is increased by strength level exercises with more movement being involved in the balance leg. Exercises include the single leg squat and the lunge to balance. Speed and specificity are incorporated more at this level. At the power level, exercises such single-leg hops, single-leg box hops, and single-leg hop downs increase reactive stabilization of joints, eccentric strength, and dynamic neuromuscular efficiency.

Depending on which level the client is at, the trainer should be knowledgeable about the number and types of exercises to use and which variables to adjust for progression. Benefits to both static and dynamic balance have been seen after 4 weeks of exercise at a rate of 10 minutes per day for 3 days per week.

Proprioceptive Progression and Regression

Often likened to a sixth sense, proprioception is the body's ability to know where it is in space. Human beings use proprioception all the time; it allows them to walk down a street without looking at the ground to see where their feet should go, and it allows them to sit down in a chair without twisting their necks to see precisely where the chair is located behind them.

Problems with proprioception may occur because of injury or illness, and trainers may use balance and coordination exercises to help athletes and clients recover their proprioceptive capacities. Proprioception rehabilitation exercises typically involve a progression from simple to more complex exercises. For example, a client may begin by standing on a solid surface with their feet shoulder's length apart. If they easily maintain this stance, a trainer may prompt a client to position their feet one in front of the other, heel to toe, or stand on one foot. If a client performs well on a solid surface, a trainer may increase the complexity of the exercises by prompting the client to stand on uneven surfaces. Foam pads, wooden teetering beams, and air-filled balls are good uneven surfaces. Trainers further complicate proprioception balancing exercises by integrating coordination exercises, like throwing and catching, and trainers may prompt clients to complete balance and coordination exercises with their eyes closed. The elimination of sight further challenges a client's proprioception.

Reactive Training

Lower-Body Plyometrics

Including lower-body plyometric exercises in a client's training program can improve sport performance by increasing the client's ability to produce greater force in a shorter period of time. Lower-body plyometric exercises are appropriate for almost every sport, including track and field events, sprinting, soccer, volleyball, football, baseball, basketball, cycling, distance running, and triathlons. Different sports require different movement patterns. Lateral and horizontal movements are used in baseball, football, and sprinting, while volleyball requires vertical and horizontal movements. Some sports like soccer and basketball require powerful and quick movements with changes in direction and planes. In addition to improving the force and velocity of movement, endurance clients also benefit because lower-body plyometric training improves muscle efficiency by training muscles to produce more force using less energy. Lower-body plyometric exercises that can be included in a client's training program from lowest to highest intensity include jumps in place, standing jumps, multiple hops and jumps (also called countermovement jumps), bounds, box drills, and depth jumps. Training adaptations can be obtained over relatively short periods of time (six to ten weeks), but clients can benefit from plyometric training throughout the macrocycle.

Upper-Body Plyometrics

Upper-body plyometric exercises use the same neuromuscular mechanisms as lower-body plyometric exercises to produce sports movements. Upper-body plyometric exercises should be included in training programs for clients participating in sports that require fast and powerful upper-body movements. These sports include tennis, softball, golf, baseball, field throwing (e.g., shot put, discus, and javelin),

lacrosse, swimming, and other sprint and endurance activities. Sports that require tackling, catching, and holding off opponents can also benefit from upper-body plyometric training. Although upper-body plyometric exercises (e.g., throwing and catching a medicine ball and plyometric push-ups) are an essential training component for clients requiring upper-body power, these exercises are not as commonly used as lower-body plyometric exercises.

Modifications for Performing Trunk Plyometrics

It is difficult to perform a true plyometric trunk exercise because the mechanical and neurophysiological mechanisms necessary for the stretch-shortening cycle may not be present. Although some elastic energy may be stored during plyometric trunk exercises, research suggests that the stretch reflex is not sufficiently involved for potentiated muscle-contraction activity to occur. The abdominal muscles are close to the spinal cord, which may result in shorter latencies for the abdominal stretch reflex. The large range of motion and time associated with the trunk movements inhibit the potentiation of the abdominal muscles. However, altering the exercise movements so that they are shorter and quicker may cause rapid eccentric muscle loading that elicits the stretch reflex and results in potentiated contraction of the muscle.

Frequency of Plyometric Training Activities

The frequency of plyometric training is primarily influenced by the client's sport, previous experience with plyometric training, the phase of training in a cycle or season, and the intensity and volume of daily workouts, including plyometrics, resistance training, sport practices, and aerobic training. For most sports, a client can perform one to training sessions per week with 48–72 hours of recovery time between plyometric training sessions. In order to determine plyometric training frequency, the personal trainer must evaluate the intensity of the plyometric exercises performed, the number of repetitions completed for each exercise, and the total volume of all other types of training. Because there is very limited research about the frequency of plyometric training, guidelines for the frequency of training do not exist.

Plyometric Training Volumes

Plyometric exercise volumes are commonly determined as the number of repetitions and sets that are completed during a single training session. Training volumes for lower-body plyometric exercises are expressed as the number of foot contacts during a session. For example, if a client is doing bounding exercises, volume may be expressed as a total distance covered. Training volume for upper-body plyometrics is typically expressed as the number of catches or throws during a training session. A client's level of plyometrics experience is used to provide a suggested training volume.

- Beginner: 80–100 repetitions per session
- Intermediate: 100–120 repetitions per session
- Advanced: 120–140 repetitions per session

Age Considerations and Possible Limitations for Plyometric Training Activities

A wide variety of ages – not just the elite adult client – can safely benefit from plyometric and plyometric-like exercises if appropriate guidelines are followed. This is particularly true for prepubescent and adolescent children who gain muscular power and bone strength from participating in an appropriately designed plyometric program. Young clients who regularly participate in plyometric training gain enhanced neuromuscular control and performance, helping to prepare them for the demands of sport competitions and practices. Plyometric programs designed for children should focus on developing correct technique to ensure quality movements while performing the plyometric activities and should progress from simple to more difficult plyometric exercises. Among prepubescent clients, depth jumps and high-intensity lower-body exercises are contraindicated because they can cause the epiphyseal growth plates to close prematurely, resulting in the stunting of limb growth.

Adequate recovery time of two to three days should separate the plyometric training sessions for young clients. Master clients also benefit from plyometric training but the goals of the program and preexisting orthopedic and joint degeneration must be considered when designing the plyometric training program. With a few exceptions, the same general program development guidelines used for adult clients can be used for developing training programs for older clients. The program should not include more than five low- to moderate-intensity exercises, the volume should be lower, and there should be three to four recovery days between training sessions.

SAQ Training Exercises

SAQ (speed, agility, and quickness) training programs can be designed for any client who could benefit from improvements in coordination and nervous system responses. SAQ exercises can increase the body's ability to speed up, slow down, and adjust the direction of movement with quickness and ease. The continuous demand for reactions and adjustments in the exercises increases the efficiency of body mechanics as well as the neuromuscular system. Connective tissue becomes stronger, the body stands up to eccentric forces more easily, and individuals will find that they have better core strength, dynamic flexibility, and postural control. This leads to less risk of injuries, which is important for seniors and athletes, including youth. SAQ training can improve clients' reaction times to stimuli and enhance speed. Clients of all types, from athletes to seniors, can find SAQ training a beneficial addition to their exercise program. After a full evaluation, a trainer should be able to construct an appropriate SAQ training program or incorporate SAQ drills into an exercise program. The exercises will challenge speed, agility, and quickness using equipment such as cones and speed ladders.

When designing programs for clients that include SAQ training, exercises need to be specific to the client's capabilities and correspond to their goals and expected outcomes. SAQ training programs for youth will involve exercises such as Follow the Snake and Red Light, Green Light. Seniors will benefit from exercises that decrease the loss of bone density (osteopenia) and muscle mass (sarcopenia). Bone density can be improved with exercises that add to the load on the skeleton, and muscle mass can be improved with exercises involving greater force and speed. SAQ training also improves the ability to maneuver in daily life, whether it's walking around furniture or being able to sit down and stand up easily. Some SAQ drills that would be appropriate for seniors include Stand-Up to Figure 8s and Varied Size Cone/Hurdle Step-Overs. It has also been found that SAQ training is just as effective for weight loss as long-duration exercises of moderate intensity. Programs for clients who want to lose weight might consist of circuits of exercise such as jump roping, cone shuffles, and various ladder drills. The drills should increase the heart rate to adequately burn calories and oxidize fat. Even healthy clients can further improve their health by participating is SAQ exercises.

Speed/Sprint Training

Important Definitions

- Rate of Force Development (RFD): The change in force divided by the change in time; a sprinter wants to generate maximal force in minimal time.

- Impulse: The product of the amount of time that force is applied to the ground and the amount of force applied.
- Momentum: The relationship between the mass of an object and the velocity of movement; an increased impulse (due to greater force generation) results in either an increase in momentum (acceleration or reacceleration) or a decrease in momentum (deceleration).

Methods for Improving Sprinting

Method #1: Sprinting

The best way to improve speed (i.e., running velocity) is to do maximum-velocity sprint training. Sprinting relies on a client's ability to produce high forces in a short period of time. Inclusion of maximum-velocity sprinting in long-term training plans can produce neurological adaptations that can improve RFD and impulse generation. Resisted and assisted sprint training techniques are commonly used to enhance force production or specific neuromuscular adaptations in order to enhance sprinting performance.

Resisted Sprint Training Techniques for Speed Development: Resisted sprint training techniques include modalities such as using harnesses for sled and parachute towing, uphill running, weighted vests, wind resistance, and sled pushing. The objectives of resisted sprint techniques are to enhance the acceleration phase biomechanics and to produce greater propulsive forces so that the client can cover longer distances faster. The trainer should be aware that loads used for training are sport-specific. Sprinters should use lighter loads (i.e., loads that do not decrease velocity by more than 10% to 12%) while field clients who are exposed to external resistance may use loads that are 20% to 30% of the client's body weight.

Assisted Sprint Training Techniques for Speed Development: The goal of assisted sprint training techniques is to produce an overspeed effect that causes the client to run at a faster pace than normal. This increased pace supports adaptation of the client's neuromuscular system to contract at faster rates, thus allowing clients to increase their stride rate and maximum sprint velocity. Assisted training techniques include pulling the client with cords (e.g., rope towing, elastic-band/surgical-tubing pulls), high-speed treadmill sprinting with a specialized treadmill, and downhill running. Personal trainers should recognize that running mechanics can be difficult to regulate at high speeds. The maximum speed should be no greater than 110% of the client's known maximal speed.

If speed is too great, it can lead to the following issues:

- Rushing the stance phase, which lessens the time available to produce propulsive force production
- Increasing braking forces while being towed due to the client's inability to handle the increased velocity
- Exposure to significant eccentric forces during downhill running due to the modified mechanics of altered foot placement

Because assisted sprint training can have detrimental effects, it is critical to consider the client's biomechanics and training status when deciding whether to implement assisted sprinting techniques.

Method #2: Strength

Sprint speed is dependent upon the ability to produce large forces in a minimal period of time. Weight training plays a critical role when training sprint clients. One issue that personal trainers need to be aware of is the importance of being able to transfer the strength qualities from the weight room to the track. Making the movement pattern, RFD, peak force, and acceleration and velocity patterns in a weight-training program specific to the demands of the sport can facilitate this transfer of the training effect.

Method #3: Mobility

Mobility Training: Mobility (the client's ability to move a limb through a specific range of motion) and mobility training are part of dynamic flexibility training programs. Mobility and flexibility are both important components of correct agility and sprinting mechanics because maximum range of motion is needed to perform these activities. Common sprinting mechanics issues include improper arm swinging, premature upright posture, neck hyperextension, and bouncing. A personal trainer can correct these errors to improve mobility. Helping the client to lengthen the push-off and stride can help vertical bouncing; keeping a steady eye level can help premature upright posture; and keeping eyes focused on the ground will improve neck hyperextension. The recovery phase is key because the sprinter's body is aligned in a way that will enhance speed.

A client's speed and agility may also be limited by compromised joint mobility or flexibility. Joints with poor mobility and flexibility produce improper forces, reduce sprinting speed and agility capabilities, and increase the risk for injury. Optimal mobility and flexibility allow the client to have fluid movements, which can help to increase turnover rates during the phases of sprinting and agility activities. Personal trainers need to be aware of a client's mobility or flexibility limitations so that they can design programs that will increase mobility and flexibility and enhance sprinting and agility. Assessing the client's muscular balance, activity levels, and range of motion can help identify issues that can be improved and corrected through a focused training program.

Mobility Drills: Dynamic stretching is sometimes referred to as mobility drills. Mobility drills emphasize sport-specific movement requirements instead of individual muscle movements. Mobility drills increase not only range of motion, but also blood flow to muscle tissue, synovial fluid circulation to the joints, body temperature, and central nervous system activity, which are all beneficial for pre-sport activity (i.e., training or competition). These physiological changes are consistent with those that occur when a client goes from a resting to an active state. Mobility drills are the ideal pre-activity stretching method because static stretching does not produce the aforementioned physiological changes, and ballistic stretching is not as safe as mobility drills. Mobility drills for swimmers may include shoulder raises and arm swings, while drills for runners may include walking knee lifts, inverted hamstring stretches, and lunge walks.

Agility Training

Agility is a multicomponent skill that is used in response to a sport-specific stimulus. It includes the ability to change direction, velocity, or mode in response to a stimulus. Agility also requires perceptual-cognitive skills such as pattern recognition of players on a playing field, visual scanning, anticipation, accuracy, and reaction time.

Reaction time allows the client to make quick decisions based on how the nervous system and muscular system react to a stimulus. Because a client's ability to process a stimulus cannot be trained,

improvements to reaction time will be small regardless of the training. Also, faster reaction times only result in better decision-making; they do not affect performance in explosive activities.

Agility-drill types include continuous drills, discrete drills, and serial drills. Continuous drills have no beginning or end, and they are helpful for improving running and jumping. Discrete drills help to develop movement patterns and improve a client's strength and power. Serial drills are sport specific and combine continuous and discrete drills. Together, these drill types can improve strength, change-of-direction (COD) ability, and perceptual-cognitive ability.

Methods for Developing Agility

Method #1: Strength

Dynamic Strength: This is the base strength that is needed for all other strength training. Dynamic strength can help provide mobility during bodyweight-only and loaded training. Examples of dynamic strength exercises for clients include calisthenics, squats, pulls, and change-of-direction drills.

Eccentric Strength: Developing eccentric strength improves the ability to effectively absorb load during the brake phase of a COD. Examples of eccentric strength exercises for clients include drop landings, receiving strength required during catch phase of Olympic lifts, accentuated eccentric training, and deceleration drills (high velocity, various angles).

Multidirectional Strength: This type of strength improves the client's ability to hold the body position during movement demands. Examples of such exercises include lunges, Z-drills, unilateral lifts, high-velocity COD drills, and cutting-angle COD drills.

Reactive Strength: Having reactive strength enhances the client's ability to transfer from high eccentric load to concentric explosiveness. Examples of reactive strength exercises include plyometrics, drop jumps, and loaded jumps.

Concentric Explosive Strength: Clients need concentric explosive strength to reaccelerate after the braking phase. This type of strength is required for the maintenance of a strong position through the transition phase of COD and agility. Example exercises include box jumps, acceleration drills, loaded squat jumps, sled pushes, and Olympic lifts.

Method #2: COD Ability

The progression of closed-skill COD drills is similar to the progression of plyometric exercises: it is based on the difficulty and intensity of each drill. The following list provides examples of progressing deceleration drills for clients at various levels:

- Beginner Level: The client would start with forward deceleration drills and progress with a higher entry velocity or shorter stopping distance.
- Intermediate Level: The client would do lateral deceleration drills and progress with a higher entry velocity or shorter stopping distance.
- Advanced Level: The client would do a drill requiring deceleration to reacceleration in forward and lateral directions.

Method #3: Perceptual-Cognitive Ability

Perceptual-cognitive ability can be trained by increasing the demands of the task in order to improve performance. Within-sport skills include visual scanning and pattern recognition. Drills to improve agility focus on improving accuracy, anticipation, and decision-making time.

The following list provides examples of progressing agility activities to improve perceptual-cognitive abilities for clients at various levels:

- Beginner Level: Closed-skill COD drills with an added perceptual-cognitive element can become agility drills by including a generic stimulus such as a trainer's instruction, flashing light, or whistle blow.
- Advanced Level: Drills that use sport-specific stimuli (e.g., evasive drills, small-sided games) have been shown to have a greater effect on performance.
- Note: By progressively increasing the time (temporal) or spatial stress on the client, generic and specific stimuli within an agility skill can both be made more difficult.

Determining and Assigning Exercise Progression

Determining and assigning exercise progression for an aerobic-exercise program requires the manipulation of the following variables:

- Exercise Mode: The specific type of activity the client is doing (examples include swimming, running, cycling, resistance exercise, and plyometrics)
- Training Frequency: The number of exercise sessions completed daily or weekly
- Exercise Duration: The length or amount of time of the training session or bout of aerobic exercise
- Training Intensity: The amount of effort expended during a training session

Aerobic-Exercise Progression

Progression starts with increases in the frequency, intensity, and/or duration of aerobic endurance exercise; however, these increases should not be greater than 10% per week. Elite clients reach a point where it may not be feasible to increase the frequency or duration of exercise, so progression will involve the manipulation of the intensity of the exercise. Exercise intensity should be monitored using RPE, heart rate, or METS (if machines provide this information) depending on which method was originally used to determine the original exercise intensity prescription. At least one recovery day, or active recovery day, should be included each week.

Plyometric-Training Program Length and Progression

Most plyometric-training programs are six to ten weeks in length; however, a four-week plyometric program has been shown to improve vertical-jump height. Similar to many of the other plyometric-training variables, there is limited research examining the effectiveness of programs having varying lengths, so the optimal program length has not been determined. It should be noted that doing plyometric training throughout the season can be beneficial for clients in sports that require quick and powerful movements. Because plyometrics are a type of resistance training, program progression should

follow the principles of progressive overload, which systematically increase training intensity, volume, and frequency in varying combinations. The personal trainer develops the training schedule and progressive overload based on the sport, training phase, and design of the fitness program. Client experience, sport requirements, and sport season are used to determine the length and progression of the plyometric-training program. Remember that plyometric training is added to a client's strength and conditioning program in order to develop more power.

Resistance-Training Progression

Timing of Load Increases

Two-for-Two Rule: The two-for-two rule provides a conservative guideline of structure and consistency for determining when a client's training load should be increased across training sessions. Using the rule allows clients to understand how their training load progresses for each exercise and that sustained performance is needed for progression to occur. The rule indicates that when a client is able to do two additional repetitions during the last set of the exercise and the client does this in two consecutive sessions, the weight should be increased at the next training session.

Quantity of Load Increases

Making the decision to increase load can be difficult. The personal trainer must consider the client's physical condition as well as the body area where the load increase will occur. A client who is sleep deprived or who has a poor diet will not be able to increase the training load as readily as a client who is well rested and eats balanced meals. Also, a client who trains too frequently will not be able to progress as quickly as a client who gets an appropriate amount of rest between training sessions.

There are general guidelines for increasing load; however, the amount of variation in the exercises and volume loads will significantly affect what load-value increases are appropriate for a specific client. Guidelines for specific load increases, as well as relative load increases, can be used to determine load progression. The general recommendations for absolute load increases for weaker, smaller, or less-trained clients are 2.5 lb to 5.0 lb (1 kg to 2 kg) for upper body exercises and increases of 5 lb to 10+ lb (2 kg to 4+ kg) for lower body per week. Stronger, larger, or more-trained clients may increase upper body loads by 5 lb to 10+ lb (2 kg to 4+ kg) per week and lower body loads by 10 lb to 15+ lb (4 kg to 7+ kg) per week. Relative load increases of 2.5% to 10.0% for all clients can be used rather than absolute load-increase values.

Regression

While progression is typically the goal in exercise programs, trainers must watch for circumstances that require regression. Any exercise that the client performs should be executed with the proper technique and postural alignment. If this can't be done, the exercise needs to be regressed. Adjustments can be made to the intensity of the exercise, repetitions and sets can be reduced, periods of rest can be increased, or the trainer could choose to have the client perform a different exercise that fits better with their capabilities. If the trainer and client are following the OPT™ Model, a step back in the progression continuum may suffice.

Depending on the exercise, common regressions might involve having a client stand on both legs instead of balancing on one or decreasing the range of motion in order to maintain proper form during an exercise. If needed, a wall can be used for push-ups or planks or the knees can remain on the floor. Shorter steps/boxes can be used for exercises involving stepping or hopping up or down. The trainer should be aware of all compensations that may occur with particular exercises and make corrections any time a client appears to be compensating. Additionally, a client's heart rate could be an indicator that the intensity of the exercise is too great for the client. Any exercise can be modified by making adjustments to the acute variables.

Acute Variables

Acute variables are aspects of a workout that change, including the number of repetitions per set, number of sets per exercise, speed of each exercise, type of exercise completed, and amount of rest between exercises. Acute variables change according to fitness goals.

Best understood within the context of the Optimal Performance Training (OPT) model, acute variables determine the intensity of a workout. Broken into three levels and five phases, the OPT™ Model helps athletes and clients develop prerequisite stability and endurance before advancing to higher level strength and power workouts. Stability/endurance, strength, and power categorize the three levels of the OPT™ Model. The strength phase is broken into three sub-categories: strength endurance, muscular development, and maximal strength. Acute variables vary within each level and phase.

The OPT™ Model provides an intuitive method for achieving fitness goals. The organization of acute variables reflects fitness goals at each level and phase. At the first level, acute variables match stability and endurance goals. Each exercise may last between one to three sets, and each set may include 12 to 25 repetitions. The speed of each repetition is slow, and rest intervals range from half a minute to a full minute. Acute variables at the second level—the strength level—of the OPT vary according to each strength phase. In the preliminary phases of the second level, repetitions per exercise range between eight and twelve sets, and sets per exercise range between three and four. Both the speed of each repetition and the rest intervals between sets remain consistent throughout this level, however. From the first level to the second level, the speed of repetitions increases and the interval of rest between sets increases by about thirty seconds.

Regardless of whether or not a fitness routine follows the OPT™ Model, acute variables change as clients make progress toward their fitness goals. FITT stands for frequency, intensity, time, and type, and trainers use these acute variables to develop fitness programs that work for their clients. *Frequency* indicates the number of days per week for each workout, and this number is established based on the client's fitness goals and availability. *Intensity* indicates a client's rate of exertion relative to their maximum effort level. *Time* indicates a workout's duration. In general, fitness routines establish an inverse relationship between duration and intensity. If a workout has a longer duration, then clients should spend a proportionately reduced amount of time near their maximum exertion levels. Finally, *type* indicates which exercises comprise a workout. These acute variables factor into the construction of a safe and effective fitness routine.

Risks and Rewards of Different Exercises

Resistance Training Exercises

For each major muscle group, resistance-training exercises can improve strength, endurance, and metabolic function, resulting in increased fat and calorie burn. By showing clients how to perform the exercise correctly and with proper form using a suitable weight, a trainer can target specific muscle groups individually. Shoulders and arm muscles benefit from biceps curls, dips, and overhead presses. Back and chest muscles are challenged with bench presses, push-ups, flies, rows, and pull-ups. Leg and

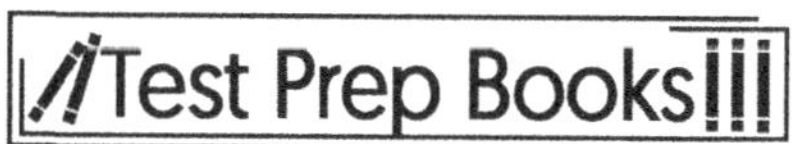

glute exercises include squats, lunges, deadlifts, and leg extensions. Abdominals respond to core-focused exercises such as crunches, leg raises, and plank exercises. Trainers must be aware of risks and contraindications inherent in these exercises, such as previous injuries that could interfere with a client's ability to perform a specific exercise correctly, pregnant women beyond their first trimester, or clients suffering from conditions related to the bones and joints.

Range of Motion Exercises

Range of motion exercises should be implemented in every exercise-training program with the goal of strengthening and stretching muscles and their related joints. Clients of all ages can suffer from limited range of motion due to lack of use, repetitive tasks, or illness or injury. A trainer can help a client improve the ability to perform exercise properly and perform daily tasks without risk of injury. Active range of motion exercises can be performed outside of formal training sessions; yoga and tai chi promote stretching in fluid motions that strengthen muscles and joints and limit the risk of injury that can be posed by explosive or "jerky" stretching movements. Alternatively, passive range of motion exercises are those in which a force, other than the client's own strength, is used to move a joint; assistance from a partner or machines, such as in Pilates, provide the client with the force used to move the joints and muscles. Clients with injuries or existing conditions that limit mobility may benefit from passive forms of exercises, with a focus on gradually increasing range of motion.

Cardiovascular Training Exercises

Cardiovascular exercise plays an important role in improving a client's level of fitness and overall health. Because clients have unique abilities and goals, each requires a varied approach to the cardiovascular component of their exercise-training program. By considering a client's current level of fitness, experience, daily activities, skill level, and specific training goals, the trainer can design an effective cardiovascular training routine. Clients who are healthy and able to exercise regularly at moderate to high intensities can benefit from running, cycling, and swimming. Clients who have restrictive conditions such as previous injuries, chronic conditions, or even those who have previously engaged in minimal or mostly sedentary activities, should refrain from high-impact and high-intensity cardiovascular exercises, instead engaging in light- to moderate-intensity, low-impact cardiovascular exercises such as walking or swimming. Special populations such as pregnant women, those with serious health conditions, and children and adolescents can greatly benefit from cardiovascular activities specifically tailored to the individual client.

Overtraining

If clients don't allow the time for proper rest and recovery, overtraining will occur as cortisol levels remain elevated. Some signs of long-term overtraining include fatigue, muscle loss, fat gain, diminished performance, injuries, and abnormal soreness in muscles after workouts. Overtraining can also be a singular occurrence if the client hasn't slept well, hasn't had the proper intake of nutrition, or is attempting to perform high-intensity exercises for too long. High-intensity exercises always need to be balanced with less training volume. To avoid overtraining, clients who have progressed to Stage III of cardiorespiratory training should alternate the stages for each of their workouts and not move to zone 3 during a workout if it takes more than one minute for their heart rate to return to a suitable level after completing zone 2. Overtraining can also be avoided by following the OPT™ Model or using a periodization plan that schedules periods for rest and recovery. Keeping accurate records of and regularly monitoring a client's resting heart rate, resting blood pressure, and recovery heart rate can help to identify overtraining. When a client is overtraining, it takes longer for the heart rate to recover after exercise and resting heart rate and resting blood pressure tend to increase. If there is evidence that a client is overtraining, the trainer should encourage sufficient sleep and nutrition and balance the stress that training puts on the body with adequate rest and recovery periods.

Rest and Recovery

The length of rest periods between sets and different resistance exercises depends on three variables: the goal of training, the relative load lifted, and the client's training condition. Clients in poor condition need longer rest periods when starting a resistance-training program. Generally, the amount of rest between sets is positively associated with the load (i.e., heavier loads require more rest, lighter loads require less rest).

Different rest period lengths can lead to a variety of physiological changes and should be considered in the context of the client's goals. Longer rest periods promote nervous system and muscular system recovery, while shorter rest periods promote cardiovascular conditioning.

Recommended Rest Period Length Per Training Goal

Muscular Endurance: It is recommended that rest periods between workloads are less than 30 seconds. Because muscular endurance training uses light loads and many repetitions, only a short amount of rest is used. Circuit training typically uses rest periods of 30 seconds or less between resistance exercises.

Hypertrophy: It is recommended that rest periods between workloads are between 30 and 90 seconds. To increase muscle size, research suggests that it is best to use a limited rest period that does not allow the client to fully recover before starting the next set. Personal trainers should recognize that resistance exercises using large muscle groups might require extra recovery time because of the metabolic demands of the exercises.

Strength: It is recommended that rest periods between workloads are 2–5 minutes. Maximal or near-maximal repetitions require longer rest periods, particularly for lower-body and all-body structural exercises.

Power: It is recommended that rest periods between workloads are 2–5 minutes, which is similar to the rest periods for developing strength. Maximal or near-maximal repetitions (i.e., heavy load) require longer rest periods, particularly for lower-body and all-body structural exercises.

Metabolic Conditioning: The work-to-rest ratios should be based on the specific energy system stressed. For the phosphagen system, ratios of 1:12 to 1:20 are best. Fast glycolysis should use 1:3 to 1:5 work-to-rest ratios. The glycolytic (fast glycolysis) and oxidative systems together use ratios of 1:3 to 1:4. The oxidative only is optimized with a ratio of 1:1 to 1:3.

Plyometric Exercises: Plyometric exercises involving maximal effort can improve *anaerobic power*, but adequate recovery time is needed for full recovery. The time between sets is based on a work-to-rest ratio that depends on the volume and type of drill. Work-to-rest ratios are often 1:5 to 1:10. Rest periods between repetitions of certain exercises (e.g., depth jumps) may be five to ten seconds.

Recommended Recovery for Various Types of Training

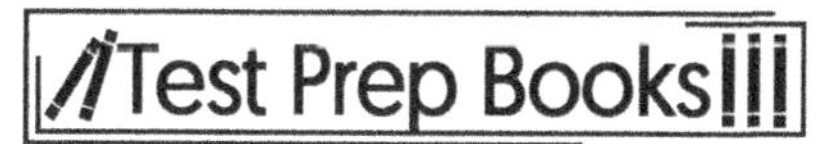

Resistance Exercise: Typically, one to three days of rest is recommended between resistance-training sessions that focus on the same muscle groups.

Plyometrics: Generally, two to four days of recovery is needed between plyometric-training sessions. This specific number of days will depend on the client's sport and the sport season. A specific body area should not be trained on consecutive days.

Aerobic Endurance Exercise: At least one rest day, or active rest day, per week is recommended with endurance-training programs.

Current Trends and Their Applicability to Individual Training Programs

Popular fitness technology, like smart watches, can help people manage their fitness goals everywhere they go. Increasingly, people achieve fitness goals away from the gym with help from fitness trackers and online workout sessions. Accessibility to affordable home gym equipment, like dip stations and barbells, have made home gyms more popular. While these trends may seem to suggest that people are moving away from gym memberships and active participation in local gyms, the opposite is often true.

Smart watches and other forms of fitness tracking technology encourage user commitment to fitness goals that are often set with the help of trainers in gyms. While frequently offered to gym members and non-members alike, online workout programs tend to lead existing members back to gyms and prospective members into new subscriptions. Even home gyms connect people to traditional gym settings because they can easily supplement services offered by traditional gyms.

Current trends toward remote workouts and hybrid training programs indicate an increased emphasis on personal wellness. Clients have found new ways to stay engaged with fitness programs and make progress toward their goals. Commitment to personal wellness integrates elements of traditional exercise, along with focus and consideration on nutrition, sleep, and mental health.

Types of Fitness Technology

Fitness technology can help clients track their workouts and pursue long term fitness goals. Fitness devices measure everything from heart rate to calorie intake per day. Clients often measure several health variables with downloadable applications and smart watches.

Heart rate monitors are among the simplest forms of fitness technology available. At-risk clients—those with a history of cardiovascular disease, obesity, and other health conditions that cause significant cardiovascular strain—may use heart rate monitors during workouts to track their active heart rates and ensure that they never reach dangerous levels. Many fitness and performance trackers measure heart rate in addition to several other fitness, health, and performance variables, though some clients may prefer to use a simple heart rate monitor during their workouts. Tracking active heart rates can help to ensure the safety of at-risk clients.

Other clients use more comprehensive forms of fitness technology. Smart watches are popular examples of fitness hardware that measure multiple health, fitness, and performance variables. Clients who want to engage with workout and nutrition goals outside of the gym may find these forms of fitness technology especially useful. Comprehensive fitness and performance trackers measure everything from calories burned in a day to blood oxygen levels. Clients with specific health conditions, as well as those who want to optimize their daily routines to provide the best fitness results, may choose to utilize these types of trackers.

Clients may also track diet and nutrition goals through downloadable applications and websites. Clients set nutrition goals, including daily calory intake, and they record their meals online or in their app. Clients who want to consume specific types of calories and avoid other types utilize these resources daily. These resources also provide guides to refueling after workouts.

Considerations for Selection of Exercises Based on Client

For healthy and ambitious clients, a well-designed individual fitness program balances challenging exercises with moderate or mild exercises. Challenging exercises push clients beyond their current limits. Moderate exercises help clients achieve prerequisite and intermediary levels of strength and balance. Mild exercises facilitate rest and recovery. When trainers work with healthy and ambitious clients, they may assign fitness assessments to determine which exercises will challenge their clients and which exercises will facilitate recovery.

Not every client seeks to make large or ambitious gains, however. Trainers base exercise selections both on clients' goals and on their level of personal fitness. Some clients begin fitness programs with the goal of maintaining their current levels of fitness, range of motion, or activity. Trainers will avoid selecting high-intensity workouts for such clients.

Other considerations may present themselves during assessments. Movement assessments reveal muscular imbalances, which may affect high-intensity and low-intensity clients alike. Trainers will seek to correct improper form before advancing to high-intensity exercises or avoid workouts that might aggravate known imbalances. Results from physiological assessments, like heart rate assessments, may also impact the selection of certain exercises.

Certain variables prohibit clients from participating in either fitness programs or physical assessments, so trainers complete screening assessments, usually in the form of a dialogue, with new clients before beginning any physical assessments or exercise. Screening assessments include questions about a client's medical history. Trainers are on the lookout for contraindications, which refer to medical conditions that may prohibit a client from starting a fitness program.

There are two categories of contraindications: absolute contraindications and relative contraindications. Absolute contraindications include recent heart attacks, as well as major heart-related diseases, severe infections, severe illness, and intense mental or emotional distress. Clients who exhibit absolute contraindications should not participate in exercise while these conditions persist. On the other hand, relative contraindications represent a wider category of potentially dangerous conditions, including prior history of heart disease, high blood pressure, back injuries, and pregnancy. Clients with these conditions may participate in exercise. Trainers are responsible for creating safe fitness programs for clients with relative contraindications, and they must provide increased supervision for such clients.

Considerations for Exercise Program Design for Special Populations

The term *special populations* indicates clients with underlying chronic or short-term health conditions who require specialized fitness programs that are catered to their individual needs and abilities. Trainers carefully design fitness programs for clients from special populations because these clients are prone to medical complications and other issues that may threaten their safety. Trainers must consider each

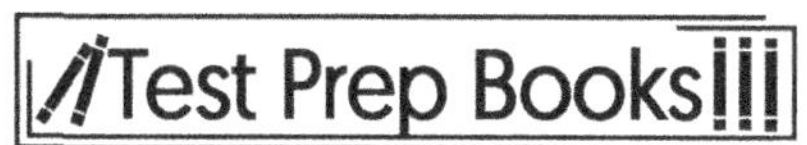

client's particular needs and abilities when designing fitness programs for children, seniors, prenatal clients, clients in clinical settings, and clients with chronic health conditions.

Fitness programs for elderly clients aim to help them maintain current levels of physical fitness and mobility while improving well-being through regular, light exercise. During workouts, trainers should remain alert to possible side effects caused by medication. Since the side effects of medication vary widely based on the individual client and prescription type, trainers, especially those in clinical settings, should be aware of the side effects their clients might experience. This information is communicated to trainers through the evaluation of the client's health history, and trainers should access this information before beginning a new fitness program with their clients.

Underlying health conditions may also jeopardize the safety of clients with chronic conditions. For example, clients with obesity may experience shortened breath during exercise, which may derive from complications related to any of several bodily systems, including the respiratory system and the cardiovascular system. Trainers must allow clients with underlying medical conditions enough time to recover between sets, and trainers must adjust workouts according to how clients react.

Trainers who work with clients from special populations should always weigh decisions by considering the inherent risks attached to each exercise. Trainers should avoid risky, high-intensity exercises with clients from special populations. In general, clients from special populations aim to develop healthy habits, limit adverse effects of chronic or short-term conditions, and maintain current levels of personal fitness. Trainers should always keep the individual goals of their clients in mind, even if their goals seem modest.

Selecting Appropriate Exercises and Training Modalities Based on Different Factors

In designing an effective exercise training, the trainer is responsible for selecting exercises and training modalities that best suit the client's abilities and restrictions. The training programs for a twelve-year-old would be far different from one for a seventy-year-old. Age impacts the recommended type, duration, and intensity of exercise. More so than age, the client's functional capacity (or training age), shown in their exercise test results, will provide the trainer with a clearer picture of a client's strengths and weaknesses. For example, clients who need to improve their flexibility would benefit from a training program implementing range of motion, strength, and endurance exercises. Those requiring improvements in strength and power might benefit from a more anaerobic-focused cardiovascular routine, with strength-training exercises using high weight and low repetitions and with less focus on flexibility.

Guidelines for Exercise Training for Clients with Chronic Disease

Some clients require special attention in developing and implementing an exercise program even after receiving medical clearance. While these general guidelines apply to clients with chronic disease, the trainer may find it necessary to make modifications as the client progresses. Constant awareness and open communication about the client's heart rate and perceived level of exertion is essential throughout each session, as are frequent breaks for hydration and rest.

Clients with stable chronic heart disease should engage in cardiovascular activity of moderate intensity for thirty minutes three to seven days per week, ideally performing five to seven hours of cardiovascular activity weekly as the client progresses in ability and endurance. Clients should perform an extended warm-up of five to ten minutes in duration prior to engaging in cardiovascular activity, and the program should also include low-impact resistance exercises two to five days per week focusing on all major muscle groups; these exercises should include five to ten exercises with one to three sets of five to fifteen repetitions. Flexibility and stretching exercises should be performed daily, with each stretch being performed two to four times, held for fifteen to thirty seconds each.

Clients with diabetes mellitus should engage in physical activity daily. Low-impact cardiovascular activities of light to moderate intensity should be performed for a duration of twenty to sixty minutes, three to four days per week; the form, intensity, and duration of the cardiovascular exercise should be prescribed in accordance with the client's abilities and comfort level in consideration. Strength training and resistance exercises should be performed three to five days per week (with forty-eight hours of rest between) and consist of one to two sets of five to twenty repetitions, focusing on each of the major muscle groups. Flexibility and stretching exercises should be performed daily, with each stretch being performed two to four times and held for fifteen to thirty seconds.

Clients with obesity should be encouraged to engage in physical activity daily. Cardiovascular exercise should be performed at a moderate intensity for forty-five to sixty minutes, five to seven days per week; these exercises should be low-impact (such as swimming or walking), gradually including a wider variety of activities and progressing in intensity as the client achieves a greater level of fitness and ability. Strength training and resistance exercises focusing on all major muscle groups should be performed three to five days per week, including five to ten exercises of fifteen to twenty-five repetitions using a moderately challenging starting weight that allows for proper form. Flexibility and stretching exercises should be performed daily, with each stretch being performed two to four times and held for fifteen to thirty seconds.

Clients with metabolic syndrome should engage in physical activity daily. Cardiovascular exercise should be performed for twenty to sixty minutes, three to four days per week, gradually increasing in frequency and intensity as the client's level of fitness and ability improves. Strength training and resistance exercises should be performed with a focus on low resistance and low intensity as the client gradually increases in strength and endurance. Programs should include one to two sets of ten to fifteen repetitions for each of the major muscle groups, increasing to fifteen to twenty repetitions as the client's program is revised. Flexibility and stretching exercises should be performed daily, with two to four stretches focusing on all the major muscle groups held for fifteen to thirty seconds each.

Clients with hypertension should engage in physical activity daily. Cardiovascular activities should be performed for thirty to sixty minutes, three to seven days per week. Strength training and resistance exercises should be performed four to seven days per week, focusing on low weight and high repetition exercises in order to avoid significant increases in systolic pressure. Flexibility and stretching exercises should be performed daily, with two to four stretches focusing on all the major muscle groups held for fifteen to thirty seconds each.

Clients with osteoporosis, chronic pain, and arthritis should engage in physical activity daily while paying attention to discomfort. If, and when, the client experiences difficulty during or following exercise, adequate rest and possible modifications should be considered before engaging in exercise again. Low-impact cardiovascular exercise should be performed at light to moderate intensity for twenty to sixty minutes, three to five days per week, gradually increasing in intensity and duration as the client's fitness and ability improve. Strength training and resistance exercises should be performed two to three days per week focusing on all major muscle groups, including one to two sets of three to twenty repetitions.

Flexibility and stretching exercises should be performed daily, including two to four stretches held for fifteen to thirty seconds each.

Considerations for Exercise Program Design for Special Populations

Youth

Regular exercise and physical activity are important factors in the health of children as it improves bone and muscle strength and also provides exposure to good habits that can be carried on throughout life. Fitness programs for youth should focus on fun resistance and aerobic activities that result in developmentally appropriate adaptations. It's recommended that youth participate in at least 60 minutes of exercise per day for 5–7 days per week. When designing programs for youth, there are some characteristics specific to children that need to be considered when choosing exercises and their duration and intensity. Children's bodies don't have the same thermoregulatory abilities as adult's bodies, so hydration and rest must be allowed when exercising when it's hot or humid. In this type of environment, intense exercise should not last more than half an hour. Additionally, due to having fewer glycolytic enzymes, children can't participate in high-intensity exercises for as long as adults can. Trainers should plan programs for youth that include various games, sports, and activities, as well as jogging, walking, and appropriate resistance training exercises and SAQ drills. Resistance training in the Phase 1 level of the OPT™ Model is advised. Postural control and skill should be the focus. Any exercise program must be safe, so before planning a fitness routine, a movement assessment should be performed to identify any flaws in movement.

Seniors

Although some physical changes are expected in older adults, exercise can be just as beneficial in the senior years as it is when younger. Exercises that are selected for fitness programs for older adults should focus on preventing or reversing issues such as sarcopenia and osteopenia and improving balance and coordination, focusing on movements that are used daily. The objective should be on increasing the client's ability to be self-sufficient. Resistance and SAQ training can be used to slow down sarcopenia and osteopenia and can even result in improvements in muscle and bone density. SAQ drills might include Varied Size Cone/Hurdle Step-Overs and Stand-Up to Figure 8 exercises. Resistance exercises for seniors should begin with lighter weights and in seated positions. An adequate amount of training for seniors would be 20–30 minutes of resistance exercises, performing 8–10 exercises, with 1–3 sets of 8–10 repetitions. Seniors can participate in resistance training 3–5 days per week, but any progressions should be made gradually. Cardiorespiratory training in Stages I and II at a rate of 3–5 days per week is suggested for seniors, but trainers should observe closely if the client is on any medication or has chronic conditions. Aquatic exercises and stationary or recumbent cycling are recommended for seniors. Walking on a treadmill is a good choice for seniors if a rail is provided for support. Flexibility is also a concern with seniors because connective tissue loses elasticity with age. Therefore, stretching and self-myofascial release should be incorporated in exercise programs for seniors. Any exercises or stretches should be planned according to the capabilities of the client. Seniors can be expected to exercise 30–60 minutes a day, and workouts may be broken up into 8–10 minute intervals.

Obese Clients

When designing an exercise program for an obese client, one important consideration is the client's ability and motivation to adhere to the program. The environment as well as the exercises might need to be planned to provide privacy and comfort. Obese clients may prefer to perform certain exercises at home where they can have more privacy. The use of exercise machines should be avoided because obese individuals have difficulty with properly positioning themselves in or on exercise machines. Exercises that utilize dumbbells or cables are better options for obese clients. Exercises that provide support for the client's weight, such as water exercises or cycling, are also good choices. Obese clients do best with seated or standing exercises instead of exercises that must be performed in prone or supine positions.

In addition to adherence, an important consideration when designing a fitness program for obese clients is the effectiveness of the workout for weight loss. The program should incorporate aerobic activities and resistance training. More calories are burned through aerobic activity, but resistance training has positive effects on metabolism and lean body mass. Circuit training is a fun and effective way to add resistance training to the program. To lose weight, 200–300 kcal need to be burned during each session. Obese clients can be expected to exercise 5 days per week with sessions lasting 40–60 minutes. Participation in resistance training can occur 2–3 times per week. Workouts should start out at a low intensity with a goal of burning 1,250 kcal each week and progress in intensity and duration with a final goal of burning 2,000 kcal each week. To make sure the client is eating the appropriate amounts and types of food to assist with weight loss and body composition goals, collaboration with a dietitian is advised.

Prenatal Clients

Although there are some contraindications to exercising while pregnant, most women can benefit from exercising during pregnancy. The effects of core exercises on the muscles of the pelvic floor are especially beneficial to prenatal clients. Prenatal clients can participate in resistance, balance, flexibility, and cardiorespiratory training, but since woman have a lower work capacity during pregnancy, the intensity of exercises should be less than 40–50% of peak work capacity. Cardiorespiratory training should remain in Stage I, but with physician approval, Stage II can be safe. Circuit training can also be safe if approved by a physician. For exercises involving the OPT™ Model, prenatal clients should only participate in Phase 1 exercises throughout the pregnancy. Phase 2 exercises as well as plyometric exercises and exercises done in the supine or prone positions cannot be performed after the first trimester. Prenatal clients should exercise 15–30 minutes per day 3–5 days per week. Low-impact and light-load exercises are advised. Appropriate forms of exercise include step aerobics, stationary cycling, and walking on the treadmill.

Practice Quiz

1. Healthy clients should have an initial basic training load of which of the following?
    a. 55% to 85% of 1RM
    b. 10% to 25% of 1RM
    c. 90% to 100% of 1RM
    d. 15% of 1RM

2. For endurance, clients should perform two to three sets of which of the following?
    a. Fifty or more reps
    b. Fifteen or more reps
    c. Two to three reps
    d. One rep at 1RM

3. For muscle mass gain, clients should perform three to six sets of which of the following?
    a. Six to twelve reps
    b. Fifteen to twenty-five reps
    c. Fifty or more reps
    d. One to two reps at 1RM

4. Training programs implementing endurance activities requiring oxygen would be classified as which of the following?
    a. Anaerobic
    b. Aerobic
    c. Power-lifting
    d. One Repetition Maximum

5. If a client reports new-onset discomfort in the chest and arms, the appropriate action of the trainer would be to?
    a. Continue exercise for the full session
    b. Seek medical assistance
    c. Call the client's physician
    d. Send the client home

See answers on the next page.

Answer Explanations

1. A: Clients can generally benefit from a basic training load of 55% to 85% of their one-repetition maximum. Modifications should be made to limit the risk of injury. In order to design an effective exercise-training program, a trainer must be able to determine the appropriate repetitions, sets, loads, and rest periods for exercises based on the client's skills, abilities, restrictions, and goals.

2. B: For improving endurance, the general recommendation is to perform two to three sets of fifteen repetitions or more within the weight load range of 55% to 65% of the client's 1 repetition maximum. All sets should be performed with a rest interval of two to four minutes between sets.

3. A: For muscle hypertrophy, three to six sets of six to twelve repetitions at 75% of the 1 repetition maximum is recommended. For increases in strength, two to six sets of fewer than six repetitions performed at 75% to 85% of the 1 repetition maximum is effective. Power training entails three to five sets of one to two repetitions performed at 90% to 100% of 1 repetition maximum. All sets should be performed with a resting period of two to four minutes between, with exception of power-related sets, which require one minute of rest between.

4. B: Aerobic exercises, such as running, swimming, and endurance cycling, require oxygen in order to perform for extended periods of time. Anaerobic exercises include explosive exercises performed for only short durations and require little-to-no oxygen delivery to the muscles throughout the performance.

5. B: If a client reports new-onset discomfort in the chest and arms, the appropriate action of the trainer would be to seek medical assistance. While this symptom can be considered a fairly normal physical response to vigorous exercise, trainers are responsible for recognizing when a client's symptoms may indicate a serious medical complication. When in doubt, trainers should err on the side of caution and refer the client to a physician for approval to continue with the exercise program. This prioritizes the client's health and minimizes the risk of liability for the trainer.

Exercise Technique and Training Instruction

Demonstrating Proper Exercise Techniques

A trainer must ensure that every exercise included in a client's training program has been effectively described and demonstrated for the client. Cardiovascular activities should be modeled for the client, explaining proper form and contraindicated postures that can pose risk of injury; trainers should offer tips to minimize risk in running, walking, cycling, and swimming. Strength training routines also must be demonstrated, ideally with the client mimicking the trainer's example, to ensure that proper form and posture are maintained throughout. Range of motion exercises should be demonstrated for the client with an emphasis on the extent to which clients should stretch, the duration of each stretch, and avoidance of explosive movements.

Providing Feedback

Written reports and verbal feedback are important in the process of goal achievement. They also correct and teach proper form. They should be given at frequent intervals so the client can have knowledge of his or her progress and stay motivated toward the goals. Feedback should be timely while the movement or assessment is fresh in the client's mind. Feedback should always be given in positive language and never come across as threatening.

The following are common forms of feedback and how they might be used in sessions:

Evaluative feedback: guides the client to make improvements on incorrect movements or form and understands what parts he or she is mastering. Example: "Your back is perfectly straight now, but let's see if you can bring your hands closer to shoulder-width apart."

Supportive feedback: often given during particularly difficult parts of a workout as a means of encouraging the client. Example: "I know it's challenging, but if you can push through three more reps, you will break your record!"

Descriptive feedback: given at the completion of a movement or workout in a clean, concise fashion that provides a summary of what was seen and what can be improved or changed. After completing biceps curls, the trainer may remark, "It's exciting to see you working hard on these curls. I notice as you get tired, there's a tendency to swing the weights forward and use momentum. Let's see if we can use a little bit of a lighter weight next set and try to focus on isolating your biceps to bring the weight up."

Corrective feedback: should be given immediately, especially if something is unsafe. Example: "It seems like you are yanking up on your neck during these crunches, but your hands should just be supporting your head, not pulling it up."

Flexibility Training Methods

Flexibility exercises can help improve range of motion, prevent injury, and prevent muscle, ligament, and tendon tightening. They also have a positive impact on elements of the nervous system, such as the Golgi tendon organs, and they prepare the body to recruit the necessary motor units for optimal athletic performance. Clients should receive coaching on proper and improper stretching techniques, including how to hold a position in a comfortable and moderate stretch without causing pain.

Static Stretching Exercises

Static stretches should follow the completion of the workout, especially for excessively stiff clients or those with previous injuries. Static stretching exercises can improve the muscle tension and joint relationship over time. Static stretches done prior to exercise can reduce explosive power and increase joint laxity when stiffness is required for energy conservation, placing a client at greater risk of injury.

Preparatory Body and Limb Position

Static stretching should take place after the workout while the muscles are warm. There is a variety of static stretches, most targeting the major muscles of the body. Some can be completed standing, such as the standing quadriceps stretch with the foot coming up behind the buttocks, stretches for the shoulders and chest, and standing hamstring and calf stretches. Seated stretches are mostly for the hips, glutes, and hamstrings. Supine stretches can be for the quadriceps, low back, and abdominals. During all static stretches, the client should be instructed to maintain good posture and joint alignment to keep joints within their normal range of motion (ROM) without hyperextension, and to keep them within their typical planes of motion (i.e., sagittal plane for flexion) without undue twisting and contorting.

Execution of Technique

Stretches are typically held at the end range of motion for 30 seconds, followed by a brief rest, then repeated for two to three total sets. The body should be held as still as possible, refraining from any bouncing or excessive reaching and relaxing. The joints should always be in safe, anatomically-normal positions (i.e., without hyperextending or twisting out of typical planes of motion). For example, the traditional hurdler's stretch, with one leg extended in front of the body and the other knee bent with the foot back behind the buttocks, twists the knee and can damage ligaments and is therefore contraindicated. Breathing should be smooth and steady, and clients should focus on the tension in the muscles and imagine elongating and releasing the tension.

Correction of Improper Technique

To correct improper technique and prevent injuries, strength trainers should watch for ballistic, bouncing movements, joints that are twisted or hyperextended, and clients who are grimacing or otherwise showing signs of excessive stretching.

Proprioceptive Neuromuscular Facilitation (PNF) Stretching Exercises

Proprioceptive Neuromuscular Facilitation (PNF) is a technique that uses the neuromuscular responses to specific feedback from isometric and concentric contractions performed both actively and passively. These actions and responses result in changes in the muscle/joint tension relationships and enable greater ROM to be achieved. In this way, PNF uses neurological phenomena to facilitate muscular inhibition in a specific protocol designed to improve flexibility and decrease discomfort from stretching. PNF relies on autogenic inhibition whereby inhibitory signals from the Golgi tendon organs override the excitatory impulses from the muscle spindles, resulting in gradual relaxation of the muscle. PNF is typically completed with a partner.

Preparatory Body and Limb Position

PNF stretching can be used for a variety of muscle groups such as the hamstrings, quadriceps, chest, and shoulder muscles. Positions vary depending on the muscle being stretched. For example, hamstrings are done with the client in the supine position.

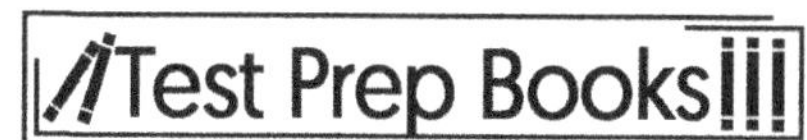

Body Mechanics to Perform PNF Stretching on a Client

The partner or trainer must not only apply appropriate resistance for the stretching client, but also must be in the correct position, typically at the end range of the desired movement with the facilitator's shoulders and hips facing the direction of movement. How the facilitator moves directly influences how the client moves. The desired movement should bisect the facilitator's midline and center of gravity. The trainer's body should be positioned in such a way that the resistance applied to the client should come from the trunk and hips, not the extremities.

Execution of Technique

There are three forms of PNF stretching: hold-relax, contract-relax, and hold-relax with agonist contraction, which all begin with 10 seconds of passive pre-stretch held at the point of mild discomfort. In the hold-relax form, after the pre-stretch, the partner applies a flexion force while the client holds and tries to resist the force, creating an isometric contraction for 6 seconds. The client then relaxes back into a passive stretch lasting 30 seconds, which is now a deeper stretch than the initial pre-stretch due to autogenic inhibition. Using the hamstrings as an example, in the contract-relax method after the pre-stretch, the client extends the hip while the partner resists this extension so that a concentric contraction occurs throughout the full ROM. After this, the client relaxes back into a passive hip flexion stretch of 30 seconds in duration, again deeper than initially performed due to autogenic inhibition (in this case, activation of the hamstrings). The hold-relax with the agonist contraction uses the idea of reciprocal inhibition, whereby the contraction of the agonist muscle causes relaxation of the antagonist so that after the regular hold-relax protocol, the second passive stretch is replaced with an active stretch to further increase the stretch.

Here are some examples:

Correction of Improper Technique

It is important that both the client and the partner or trainer are in the proper positions and using correct techniques to effectively and safely use PNF. Trainers can get injured as well, if they attempt to provide resistance from their extremities rather than through the hips and trunk. They also must be sure to keep the hips and shoulders squarely facing the direction of movement to not induce any twisting of the spine. Clients should be instructed to breathe and only push stretches to the point of mild discomfort to prevent overstretching. Because PNF relies on overriding neural regulation of the stretch reflex, it is important to exactly follow the protocols to protect the tendons and muscles. Strength trainers should pay extra attention to clients nursing injuries or those with hypermobile joints.

Dynamic Stretching Exercises

Dynamic stretching or mobility drills emphasize the required movements of the planned activity, rather than individual muscles, by actively moving the joint through the ROM encountered in a sport prior to the sport. Dynamic stretching occurs before the activity as part of the warm-up routine to increase heart rate, temperature, and blood flow as well as CNS (central nervous system) and PNS (peripheral nervous system) activity to prepare the body. It promotes dynamic flexibility and mimics the movement patterns

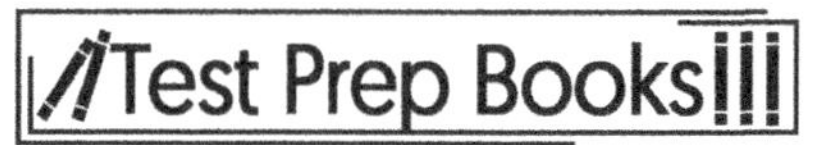

and ROM needed in sports activities without ballistic movements. It is less effective than static PNF stretching on increasing static ROM.

Preparatory Body and Limb Position

A neutral erect spine and athletic posture should be maintained in dynamic stretching or mobility drills. Drills such as walking lunges and hip mobility drills should use proper squatting form.

Execution of Technique

Clients typically complete 5-10 repetitions of each movement, either in place or over a given distance with a progressive increase in the ROM and/or speed on each repetition or set. The movement mechanics of the sport should be reinforced in the mobility drill, along with the predominant joint positions, such as ankle dorsiflexion on a high knee drill for sprinters.

Correction of Improper Technique

Trainers should ensure that clients move deliberately and progressively through the ROM, but in a controlled fashion that does not include bouncing. The focus should always be on proper technique and form while warming up the body and perfecting sport-specific movements.

Core Exercise Technique

The core is the region of the body containing the lumbar spine, pelvic girdle, abdomen, and the hips. It's also known as the LPHC (lumbo-pelvic-hip complex). The core muscles are part of either the global or local stabilization systems.

The proper technique for many core exercises includes drawing in and/or bracing. Both of these actions provide stabilization to the spine and the pelvis. Drawing in is accomplished by pulling the navel in toward the back, which utilizes the local core stabilizers. Bracing involves the global stabilization system and is accomplished by contracting the abdominal, gluteal, and lower back muscles. These maneuvers help to prevent overload to the tissues and contribute to the desired neuromuscular adaptations. A neutral position of the cervical spine and the pelvis are also required in many core exercises. Core stabilization exercises, such as marching, plank, and floor bridge, are performed without a lot movement of the pelvis or spine:

- Marching: With the pelvis neutral and drawing in the abdominal muscles, the client lies supine on the floor with the knees bent and feet pointed ahead and planted on the ground. One foot is lifted as far as possible while keeping the pelvis neutral and abs drawn in. After holding this position for 1–2 seconds, the foot is lowered to the floor and the exercise is continued with the other leg.
- Plank: Beginning in the prone position on the floor with the feet next to each other, the forearms are placed on the ground with the elbows under the shoulders. The body is lifted and held, using the forearms and toes for support. While holding this position the back is straight and the chin is kept tucked.
- Floor bridge: Keeping the feet planted at the same width as the shoulders on the floor, the client lies in the supine position with the knees bent. The pelvis is raised off the floor to create a straight line between the hips, knees, and shoulders, being sure to contract the gluteal muscles and not overextending the lower back. The pelvis is lowered back to the floor.

Drawing-in, bracing, and making sure the lower back isn't hyperextended are necessary when performing these exercises.

Core strength exercises, such as ball crunches, cable rotations, and reverse crunches, require more motion than stabilization exercises:

- Ball crunches: While lying with the lower back on a stabilization ball, the knees are bent to 90 degrees with the feet planted on the ground and pointing straight forward. The hands can be positioned behind the head or at opposite shoulders with arms crossed. With the chin tucked, the shoulder blades are lifted off of the ball with a forward movement of the upper body and then back down onto the ball.
- Cable rotations: Standing with the feet the same width as the shoulders and the knees bent just a bit, the client will retract and depress the shoulder blades while holding the cable with both arms extended to the front. The movement is made away from the exercise machine, keeping the arms extended and turning onto the back toes to allow triple extension of the hip, knee, and ankle, and then rotating back to the beginning position.
- Reverse crunches: While lying supine on a bench, the knees and hips are bent to 90 degrees, positioning the feet in the air. Holding onto the bench near the head for reinforcement, the hips are lifted, bringing the knees in to a crunch position, and the return to the beginning position is made slowly. It's important to not use the legs to create momentum.

Tucking the chin during ball crunches protects the cervical spine. In cable rotations, the lower back needs to be protected so the turn is made using triple extension of the hips, knees, and ankles. Using the correct muscles for the movement and not using the swaying of the legs for momentum during the reverse crunch helps to prevent injury.

Power exercises are performed with more force and speed to generate power. Core power exercises should be performed using as much speed as possible without losing correct form, so core stabilization and strength must be established before moving to this level. Core power exercises include the rotation chest pass, the ball medicine ball pullover throw, and the soccer throw:

- Rotation chest pass: The client holds a medicine ball while standing with feet facing forward and at the same width as the shoulders. Powerfully, the body is turned 90 degrees while the back foot turns, creating the triple extension of the ankle, knee, and hip, and by the generation of force from the back arm the ball is thrown. After catching the ball, the exercise can be performed again.
- Ball medicine ball pullover throw: While lying with the lower back on a stability ball with knees bent to 90 degrees and feet planted on the ground, the client will hold a medicine ball with both hands as the arms extend over the head creating a straight line between arms, shoulders, hips, and knees. In a fast crunch motion, the client will throw the ball, allowing the arms to move through the entire range of motion to land at their sides near the stability ball. The ball is then caught after being thrown back by a partner or bounced off a wall back to the client.
- Soccer throw: Starting in a standing position a medicine ball is held above the head. With both arms coming forward the ball is thrown to the ground. The arms should continue through with the motion after the ball leaves the hands.

Balance Exercise Technique

Balance exercises are performed using controlled instability with the goal of improving balance and neuromuscular efficiency. By repeatedly enduring unstable conditions, the client's body learns to react properly and activate the muscles required to sustain balance. Trainers should have clients progress through a balance training program using the OPT™ Model, progressing from stabilization to strength and ending with power. Many of the exercises performed for balance training start with the client in the same position. They will begin by standing with their hips neutral and feet pointing ahead, at about shoulders-width distance. Stabilization exercises include the single-leg balance, the single-leg balance reach, and the single-leg windmill:

- Single-leg balance: Continuing from the beginning stance, the client lifts one leg and holds it for 5–20 seconds, then releases the leg back to the ground and repeats with the other leg.
- Single-leg balance reach: This exercise begins like a single-leg balance but adds an extension of the leg before holding and releasing.
- Single-leg windmill: This exercise begins like a single-leg balance but adds a windmill rotation of the arms that are positioned in a T-shape.

When performing these exercises, it's important that the knee of the balancing leg is in alignment with the toes, and the hips need to remain level. Additionally, in order to stabilize the balancing leg, the gluteal muscles need to be contracted.

Balance strength exercises include the single-leg squat, the single-leg dead lift, and the lunge to balance. All begin in the same starting position as mentioned above:

- Single-leg squat: This exercise consists of squatting while one leg is lifted and holding that position for a few seconds before returning to standing and contracting the gluteal muscles.
- Single-leg dead lift: One leg is raised and extends back while the client hinges at the hips and reaches toward the toes. Hinging at the hips should help to avoid hunching the shoulders and keep the spine straight. The gluteal and abdominal muscles are used to return to the standing position, and the exercise is repeated on the other side.
- Lunge to balance: From the starting position and keeping the knee aligned with the toes, the client lunges forward, then using the heel of the front foot, pushes back to standing, keeping that foot lifted while balancing on the opposite leg.

Balance power exercises include the single-leg hop, the single-leg box hop, and the single-leg hop down:

- Single-leg hop: From the starting position, one leg is lifted and then the client hops onto the other foot. After 2–3 seconds of sustaining that pose, they hop back onto the other leg and sustain that pose for 2–3 seconds. This exercise is repeated as required.
- Single-leg box hop: This exercise requires the client to stand in the starting position with a box in front of them. The client lifts one leg and jumps and lands with the balancing leg on the box and remains balancing on that leg for a few seconds before stepping and down repeating the exercise with the opposite leg.
- Single-leg hop down: This exercise is performed similarly to the single-leg box hop, but the starting position is on the box and one leg is lifted and the jump is made to the floor, landing on the balancing leg and maintaining balance on that leg for a few seconds.

It is important that when performing any of the balance power exercises the landing is made as softly as possible, maintaining alignment between the knees and toes.

When appropriate, the trainer can have the client make progressions with some of these exercises. A single-leg balance reach may be altered by extending the leg to the side or back. Single-leg deadlifts can be modified by having the client reach toward either the knees, shins, or feet. Progressions for lunging and hopping exercises include performing lunges and hops in various planes of motion, such as side-to-side or while turning.

Speed and Agility Technique

Agility

Agility is loosely defined as a client's collective coordinative abilities and technical skills used to perform the wide range of motor tasks of the sport from fine motor control to gross, powerful, and dynamic tasks. Agility is an important component of many athletic endeavors and relies on perceptual-cognitive ability as well as the ability to decelerate and re-accelerate in the intended directions and as quickly and seamlessly as possible. Combined with speed, agile clients are able to outperform competitors with quicker ball-handling skills, breakaways, and tactics. Agility is not simply just about the change of directions, but involves changes in speed, decision-making, cognitive development, and biomechanical and metabolic efficiency. The following factors influence agility:

- Adaptive ability: how well the client can respond to observed and anticipated changes in the condition or sports situation and modify his or her actions accordingly
- Balance: the ability to establish and maintain static and dynamic equilibrium in the body
- Combinatory ability: ability to coordinate movements of the body during a given action
- Differentiation: the ability to accurately adjust body motions and mechanics in an efficient, economic way
- Orientation: location, control, and movements of the body within spatial and temporal parameters
- Reactiveness: the rapid, correct response to various stimuli
- Rhythm: ability to respond and implement appropriate timing and variation of dynamic motor patterns

These parameters vary in their degree of modifiability through training, depending on the client's age and skill level. Preadolescent clients are generally in a time period considered to be critical and sensitive for skill development. During this time, the coordinative abilities are thought to be the most trainable. Training should center on more basic movement patterns to establish competency and build a strong baseline level of fitness. Younger clients may not yet specialize in just one sport, which is actually advantageous for preventing injuries and developing a well-rounded client with the basic abilities needed for most athletic endeavors. During adolescence, clients begin to lose some of this plasticity for skill development and should turn to specific skills and abilities for their targeted sport of focus. Agility training can include ladders, directional drills, cone drills, speed changes, line sprints, and other technique-driven footwork.

Preparatory Body and Limb Position

Preparatory body positioning for agility training depends on the exercise or drill to be performed. Nearly universally across exercises, clients are standing with their gaze forward or slightly downward to keep

targets in their peripheral vision. Arms should be relaxed in the athletic position; hands should be positioned with somewhat of a slight lateral angle that is deviated in some cases for additional balance; and bodyweight should be concentrated on the midfoot rather than the heel. This allows for quicker turnover and more precise movements. There is a tendency for the client to slouch or drop the shoulders downward while concentrating on the ground below the foot in some situations, such as when using agility ladders. However, it is important, as with all athletic activities, to attempt to maintain as much of an upright posture as possible, with a neutral spine that is in alignment with the head and the neck. Agility training requires tremendous visual and mental focus. Clients should be reminded to breathe in a controlled and purposeful manner. Much of the training is not particularly demanding in a cardiovascular sense, but proper breathing mechanics are always important.

Execution of Technique

Agility training requires clients to use quick, light steps so that they are able to change directions and speeds readily. Body weight should be concentrated on the forefoot, and knees should come up toward the chest by firing hip flexors and core muscles. Clients should visualize the movement patterns prior to execution to strengthen the cognitive aspects of the agility training. For sports requiring a high degree of agility, it's usually most effective to incorporate agility work on most days of an athletic training program, but only for a short time due to the technique and focus required.

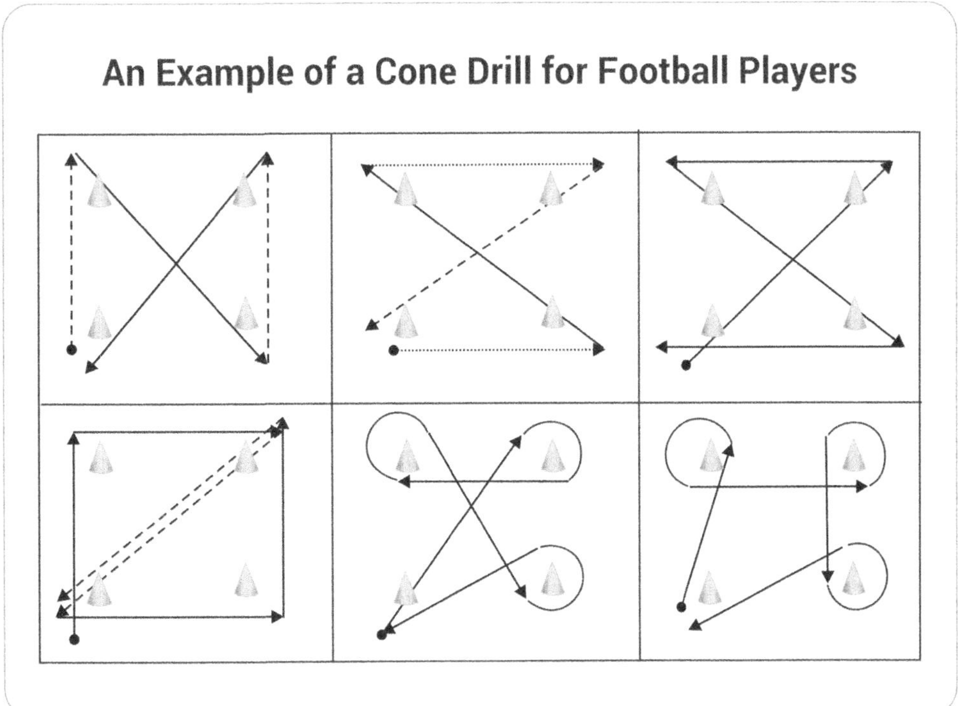

As a client fatigues, the completion time for various agility exercises will increase due to slower physical performance as well as reduced mental capacity, which causes an increase in both reaction time and decision-making time. In almost all sports, agility and changes in direction or speed are not pre-planned or programmed, but must be made as instantaneous decisions. Clients have to react to the environmental conditions, the game play, the movement and position of defending clients, and ball position. Aspects of this on-the-fly decision-making ability are affected and improved simply with game experience over time, but some degree of rapid decision-making skills can be improved through agility drills.

Correction of Improper Technique

Strength trainers can use verbal cues and video analysis to help guide technique issues. Agility practice takes time and focus, and improvements can be slow. It is important for both the client and trainer to set reasonable goals and be patient. A lack of agility for skills such as cornering, backward running, and certain maneuvers such as crossovers and sidestep cutting has been implicated as a mechanism of injury in clients. Therefore, it is important that strength trainers take the time to work with clients to improve agility, reaction time, coordinative abilities, and rhythm. As with all fitness modalities and aspects of training, strength trainers should correct improper technique as early as possible in the learning process and all form correction feedback should be positive, supportive, and instructive in order to foster a warm learning environment and keep the client motivated and comfortable.

Speed

Many clients can benefit greatly from improving sprint and speed technique, which increases the maximal velocity with which they can accelerate and move. Strength, in the sense of sprinting, is somewhat different than with resistance training. Force application in sprinting enables the client to accelerate, reach high velocities, and maintain these speeds. Force is defined as mass multiplied by acceleration. For athletic endeavors, the rate of force development (RFD) combined with impulse is important since force must be generated in a short time interval. Rate of force development is an index of explosive strength, referring to the development of maximal force in the minimal time interval, while impulse is the generated force multiplied by the time required for its production. Speed can be improved with sprint training, downhill and uphill training, and technical foot drills. Sprint training with resistance is often performed using sleds or parachutes.

Fundamental training objectives for increasing running speed center on the following:

- Minimizing ground contact braking forces: This can be accomplished by maximizing the backwards velocity of the foot and leg at touch-down and by working on creating this touch-down moment with the foot firmly under the center of gravity of the body.
- Emphasizing the brevity of ground support time: This helps bring about rapid stride rate, which takes explosive strength and can be improved through careful and specific plyometric exercise.
- Prioritizing functional training of the hamstring muscles: These muscles act simultaneously as concentric hip extensors and eccentric knee flexors: as the leg swings forward, the eccentric knee flexor strength has the greatest impact on the leg's recovery.

Preparatory Body and Limb Position

Track sprinters use blocks to help them accelerate rapidly by enabling a powerful push-off. These clients essentially pre-load the leg like a spring by pressing backwards onto the block with their flexed leg and dorsiflexed foot, storing potential energy in the series elastic components of tendons and muscles. This enables a rapid transfer to kinetic energy when the race begins. The front knee is flexed about 90 degrees and the rear knee is flexed from 110–130 degrees. Hip angle varies with sprinting ability and experience. The front hip is flexed at 40 degrees in elite sprinters and 50 degrees in sub-elite sprinters. Additionally, the rear hip is at 80 degrees in elite sprinters and at 90 degrees in sub-elite sprinters. The client should place his or her hands just behind the starting line slightly wider than shoulder-width apart

and the fingers held together. Each thumb should bridge out to the side and should be directly under each shoulder, ready to support the bodyweight. Gaze should be downward, with the back of the head and spine in alignment.

Execution of Technique

Speed is influenced by stride rate and stride length, so clients should focus on quick turnover and powerful steps. Of these factors, stride rate has a greater impact on speed and should be the focus when designing programs for improving sprinting speed. Elite sprinters are able to perform about 5 strides per second. As running speed approaches maximal for a given client, stride frequency increases more than stride length to contribute to additional speed gains. Ground contact time decreases about 50% from the acceleration phase to maximal velocity running. Impulse production becomes more and more dependent on the client's ability to generate explosive ground reaction forces (GRFs). The single leg support phase of running includes the eccentric braking component and the concentric propulsion.

The flight phase of running is comprised of the recovery and ground preparation. Stride rate and stride length typically increase over the first 15-20 meters or 8-10 strides. During this time, forward lean decreases from about a 45-degree angle to fully upright by about 20 meters. Gaze should be directly forward, arms forcefully pumping at the sides with a lightly closed, relaxed fist or an open hand. Knees should drive upwards toward the chest. The core should be engaged to limit trunk rotation, support the diaphragm, and keep movement efficient. Arms should be flexed about 90 degrees and swing toward the forehead to help overcome inertia and to increase momentum. At the start of the sprint, runners push explosively out of the blocks. The rear leg produces the greater initial force but loses ground contact earlier. However, the front leg assumes a greater influence on starting velocity and exerts force for a longer duration. In elite clients, the peak initial forces can exceed 1500 N and impulses can exceed 230 newton-seconds. In the final amount of extension in the front leg, the rear leg swings forward for the subsequent stride.

During the acceleration stage, the swinging leg's thigh is perpendicular to the trunk, and the lower leg is parallel to the trunk. At maximal velocity, the flexed leg acts like a pendulum and thrusts forward at the maximal speed to assist with leg power at push-off. The lower leg swings forward passively when the thigh reaches its maximal possible knee lift. When the forward leg starts to make contact with the ground at the toe, it makes light contact with the ground slightly in front of the body's center of gravity. As weight is transferred to this leg in the forward support phase of the body, the ball of the foot fully supports the body weight, and the trunk is fully upright or assumes a 5-degree forward lean.

In the rear support phase, triple extension helps the body push up and propel forward in a hip-knee-ankle angle of 50–55 degrees, with propulsion velocity dependent on push-off impulse and direction. In the maximal velocity phase, leg drive ability is facilitated by explosive arm action, somewhat like hammering, where the hands swing forward above shoulder height and the upper arm is parallel to the trunk. Then the arm swings downward and backward past the pocket area and the hips. The shoulders should be held steady, with the elbows flexed to 90 degrees and the hands lightly cupped. The mouth should be left open and relaxed to prevent any unnecessary muscular fatigue.

Correction of Improper Technique

Trainers can help guide clients to correct form and technique with drills such as high knees, bounding, turnover drills, resisted sprints, and assisted sprints (downhill). Video analysis and playback as well as practicing with blocks can be helpful. It can be difficult to truly change running form in a radical way, but athletes can significantly improve speed and other aspects of technique through appropriate drills and a scientific approach to training. Parachutes and sled pulls provide added resistance to sprinting and strengthen the client's muscular and cardiovascular systems as well as force and power. However, they should be reserved for more trained and experienced clients, particularly sled pulls, which can cause injury if form and technique are poor or if a client is fatigued, weak, prone to injury, pre-pubescent, or elderly. For children, parachutes are a safer choice but should still be used with caution. Deep-water running and shallow-water sprinting drills can also be used to provide added resistance with the goal of improving strength, stamina, and ability.

Reactive Exercise Technique

Reactive training, such as plyometrics, involves jumping and power exercises such as box jumps, squat thrusts, burpees, and hurdle drills to train the muscles to achieve maximal force in the shortest time. These explosive activities help strengthen a client's ligaments, tendons, joints, and muscles for sports-specific movements in order to better tolerate the physiologic demands of competition. Clients who are susceptible to injury – particularly those with poor bone density, prior ligamentous or tendon injuries especially to the knees, or post-surgical individuals – should only do plyometric under carefully monitored and modified conditions due to the strains and forces induced by such explosive jumping. Young clients and senior clients can safely do plyometric training, but in a more modified fashion to control the load on the body. For example, box jumps or depth jumps are likely not safe for these populations, but bounding or skipping drills and one-legged hops can be implemented into programs in healthy clients. However, the frequency of such activities should be limited to a day or two per week, with several rest days in-between. Even at such infrequent intervals, plyometrics can play a role in improving fitness and power without posing a substantial injury risk.

Preparatory Body and Limb Position

Plyometric exercises usually involve some sort of jumping, so clients should be taught proper landing. This involves using the arms to reduce momentum and flexing the knees to attenuate the landing forces. Clients should engage their core muscles to help brace the torso and to provide support to the intervertebral discs. It is imperative that clients focus their eyes where they intend to jump to and maintain mental focus during each individual repetition to prevent tripping and accidental injuries. It is best not to engage in such activities late in a workout when the neuromuscular system and mental focus might be fatigued. Most plyometrics are performed with the hands either relaxed or open and flat in the neutral position, with the palms facing the body such as in sprinting form.

Execution of Technique

Plyometrics use quick, powerful movements that involve a pre-stretch or countermovement. This serves as a stretch-shortening cycle and increases the power of subsequent movements by harnessing the stretch reflex. It also uses the natural elastic components of tendons and muscles. With the stretch-shortening cycle, rapid eccentric contractions elicit the stretch reflex and the storage of elastic energy, which increases force production of the subsequent concentric contraction. Plyometrics can be completed for the lower body, trunk, and upper body areas and can include depth jumps, medicine ball throws, catches, pushups, box jumps, and bounding drills. Adequate rest is needed between repetitions and between sets, such as 5–10 seconds between box jumps and 2–3 minutes between sets. Depending

on the sport and skill level, these exercises should only be completed one to three times per week in training.

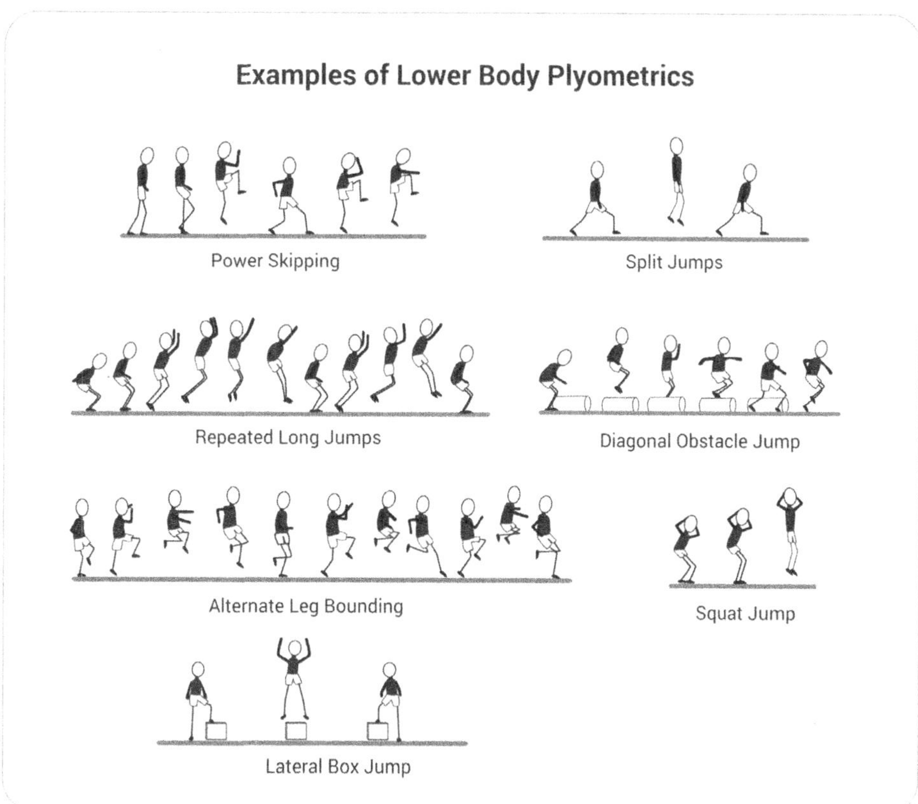

Correction of Improper Technique

Because of the demand on the body during plyometric exercises, proper technique is imperative to avoid injury. Also, heavier clients (over 220 pounds) should be constantly monitored for any joint tenderness. Special care also must be considered for previously injured clients, senior clients, youth, and clients with balance issues. Proper footwear and soft, rubberized flooring or grass should be used to reduce landing forces. With plyometrics, it is especially imperative that strength trainers correct improper technique as early as possible in the learning process in order to prevent the development of bad habits and to reduce the risk of injury. Even advanced clients may demonstrate poor technique when fatigued, distracted, or unmotivated, so observing and giving cues on preparatory and execution form technique needs to be a constant focus. For maximal effectiveness, feedback should be as specific and timely as possible, and it should be either visual, auditory, and kinesthetic, depending on each client's learning style.

Resistance Training Technique

Resistance exercises are performed using weight to put stress on the body in order to cause adaptations that create the client's desired results. The trainer should be aware of proper techniques required for all the exercises chosen for clients. There is a wide variety of stabilization, strength, and power exercises that can be performed for the chest, back, shoulders, arms, and legs. Each exercise will follow particular movements and techniques, but there are some standard rules that should be followed for various positions and types of exercises. Most exercises require the client to stand or sit with their feet facing straight ahead at the same width as the shoulders. For some exercises, it's important for the knees to be bent to a 90-degree angle, and others require just slightly bent knees. Maintaining alignment in the lower extremities is necessary for certain exercises, such as lunges or squats. Alignment is also important when using a stabilization ball, whether in a prone or supine position, for exercises such as prone ball dumbbell triceps extensions or ball dumbbell chest presses. Alignment should be sustained between the ears, shoulders, elbows, hips, knees, and ankles. These parts of the body should also remain level. In the prone position, the cervical spine must be protected by allowing the head to lie on the stability ball. Tucking the chin will also protect the cervical spine when performing certain exercises. The trainer needs to observe for any arching or hyperextending of the back and make sure clients are drawing in at the navel when necessary. When performing an exercise that involves hopping or jumping, the client should land on the middle of the foot as gently as possible. Regardless of the particular exercise or technique, the client needs to be in control of all movements and the trainer needs to watch for compensation.

Preparatory Body and Limb Position

Proper form, including position and stance, varies depending on the free weight exercise. There are also modifications of basic exercises that alter grip position as a way to provide a different challenge to the muscles and to stress particular fibers. For example, typical dumbbell curls can occur in a standing or seated position, depending on the workout and goal of the exercise. The standing position recruits additional muscles, such as those in the core, to stabilize the body. When the exercise is done in a seated position, core muscles do not need to work as hard because the body's weight is supported by the chair, but this modification does require the targeted muscles (in this case, the biceps) to be more isolated and consequently work harder to lift the weight unassisted by any momentum that may be gathered while standing and swaying the body.

Even with very skilled and disciplined clients the weight lifted during a seated curl may be less than the weight lifted while standing due to this muscle isolation. Therefore, trainers must consider the trade-offs of the two positions: adding a core workout component to a standing exercise versus truly isolating the primary muscle more directly by sitting. Whether standing or sitting, clients should be mindful to maintain proper posture with an erect spine, the shoulders back, chest out, and eyes gazing straight forward. Feet should be shoulder-width or slightly wider apart, and knees should have a slight bend when standing. During a seated curl, feet should be positioned flat on the floor under the knees, which are flexed to 90 degrees.

- *Grips*: As mentioned, grip position can also be tweaked. In a standard biceps curl, the client holds the dumbbell in the middle of the bar with a *supinated grip*, allowing muscle fibers to work equally and in the typical sagittal plane of motion for flexion. In a variation called *hammer curls*, the client holds the dumbbell in the middle of the bar but with a 90-degree internal rotation of the wrist so that palms are facing the hips, which is called a *neutral grip*. This places slightly more of the workload on the lateral fibers of the biceps, working the lateral head more than the standard grip position.

  Pronated grip is also called *overhand grip* and occurs when the palms face the floor and the knuckles face the ceiling. In contrast, the supinated grip is also called *underhand grip*, and the palms face up while the knuckles face the floor. *Alternated grip* is when one hand is pronated and the other is supinated; *closed grip* is when the thumb is wrapped around the bar; and *false*

grip is when the thumb does not wrap around the bar. Another grip pattern is the *hook grip*. It is similar to a pronated grip, but the thumb is moved under the index and middle fingers.

- *Squats*: Feet are typically slightly farther than shoulder-width apart, and toes should be pointing straight forward. As the client lowers the body into the squatted position, the hips should go backwards as if they are reaching to sit back in a chair, and the flexed knees should not come forward beyond the toes. Clients should visualize pushing up through their heels to return to the fully upright position. Before performing squats, when facing the bar, it should be racked prior to execution at mid- to upper-chest level.
- *Free Weight Exercises*: Significantly more focus should be placed on proper form and stability of the body when performing free weight exercises than when using resistance machines, which typically support the body in the correct position and only allow movement in the desired plane. Because of this, particularly in less experienced clients, the weight lifted in free weight exercises may be lower for any given exercise than that successfully attempted with the equivalent resistance machine. Strength trainers should pay attention to lifting form to ensure that clients are not swinging the weights, attempting to lift weights that are too heavy and relying on momentum for assistance, or using improper form, all which can increase injury risk.

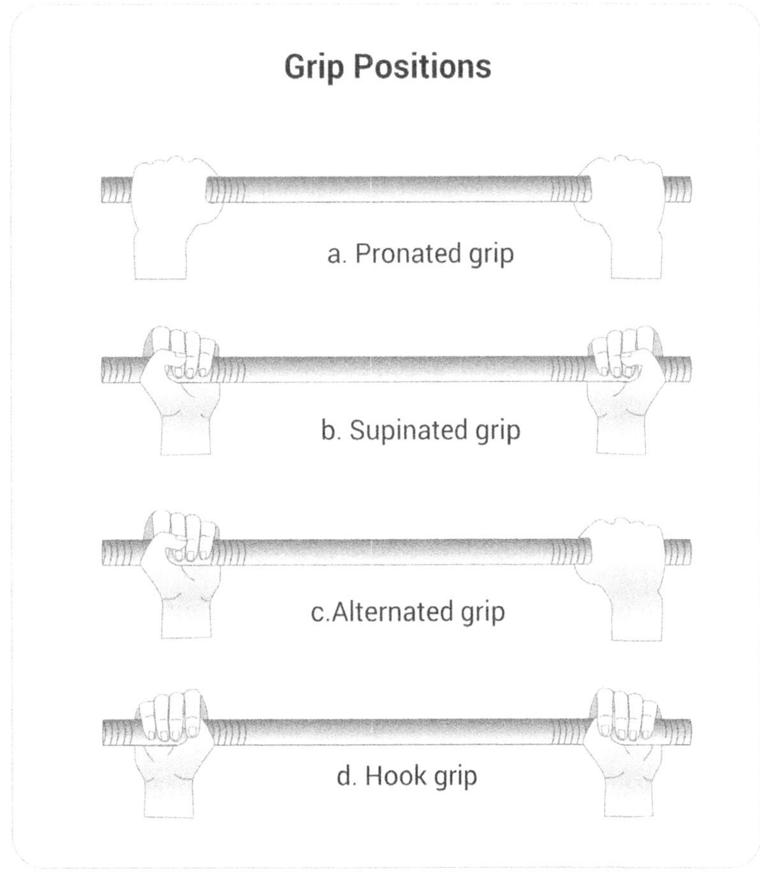

Execution of Technique

The proper execution of lifting exercises with free weights should be demonstrated and explained thoroughly by strength trainers. Clients often have different learning styles, so the execution and explanation of proper form and technique in exercises is imperative to convey this information to each client. Each exercise obviously has its own set of procedures for proper execution, but in general, emphasis on form and breathing technique will lead to successful execution. With exercises that are completed in a standing position, knees should be slightly relaxed and not locked, feet should be facing forward, and a strong core should be engaged to support the erect spine. Exercises in the seated and supine positions require five points of contact for optimal body support: the head is firmly on the bench or back pad, the shoulders and upper back are evenly placed and firmly on the bench or back pad, the buttocks are positioned evenly on the bench or seat, and both feet are placed flat on the floor.

In American society today, daily activities tend to focus on forward posture such as typing on a computer or holding a cell phone in front of the face and hunching over to type on it. This chronic slouched posture can lead to tightness in the anterior muscles of the chest and a stretching and weakening of posterior muscles of the shoulders, neck, and upper back. Strength trainers often need to remind clients to pull their shoulders back and engage their rhomboids and keep their chest up and out, which opens it up for both improved breathing mechanics and a healthy posture. In all standing exercises, swinging the weights should be avoided, and clients should attempt to hold their bodies as still in the upright position as possible, refraining from swaying and rocking, which uses momentum to augment the lifting motion.

Clients should be instructed to exhale, mostly through the mouth, during the concentric or more challenging lifting portion of the movement through the sticking point (the hardest point of the exercise). They should then inhale slowly through the nose during the eccentric or easier phase, depending on the motion. In most cases, holding the breath such as in the Valsalva maneuver is contraindicated, and it can greatly increase blood pressure and cause dizziness and disorientation. However, it can be used in certain core exercises, with care, as a way to increase torso rigidity and aid support of the vertebral column. This lessens compressive forces on the intervertebral discs and supports the normal and neutral lordotic lumbar spine. These same benefits can be achieved using a weight belt, which should be used for exercises that stress the lower back, especially at near maximal loads.

With the exception of power exercises, free weight exercises should use a minimum of one or two spotters when a client moves the bar over the head or face, has it on the front of the shoulders, or positioned on the back during the execution. When performing an incline bench press, the weight bar should make contact with the upper chest at the sticking point. In contrast, with a flat or decline bench press, the bar should make contact slightly lower—at or below the nipple line. There are a variety of squats, depending on the location of the bar, including front squats, back squats, and split squats (similar to a stationary lunge). With deadlifts, the conventional lift has the feet spaced about hip-width apart and hands outside of the stance. The sumo modification places the feet wider than a conventional squat, outside of shoulder-width, and the hands are inside of the stance. Romanian deadlifts are similar to conventional ones in that the feet are hip-width apart and the hands are outside of the stance.

- *Common Mistakes*: Clients should only lift the weight that they are able to manage while safely completing the exercise with proper form through the entire range of motion, maintaining control of the weight during the lowering, eccentric phase. A common mistake is selecting a

weight that is too heavy for the client, so it cannot be lifted through the full range, and then is dropped quickly when being lowered with gravity in a hurried, uncontrolled manner. For example, if a client is doing a dumbbell chest press, the weights should be pushed all the way up until the elbows are straight (but not locked), with the arms fully extended up and away from the chest. If the weight is too heavy, the client cannot fully extend the arms and noticeable flexion will remain in the elbows. As the weights are brought back down to either side of the chest, the trainer may notice the weights plummet precipitously and may even drop to the floor. This is not only dangerous, but negates the muscular work of slowly lowering the weight, so the client misses out on this training effect and strength benefit.

- *Arousal*: For maximal benefit from any resistance exercise, clients should dedicate their focus on form and breathing, concentrating on the workout, keeping distracting conversations to a minimum. There is an optimal point on the arousal-relaxation curve, also known as the "Inverted U" due to its shape, for best performance — somewhere in the middle of the two extremes of being too lackadaisical and too anxious about the lift. Some anticipation, anxiety, and arousal can increase levels of epinephrine, which actually primes the system for increased strength performance. On the other hand, too much stress and arousal can flood the system with epinephrine and increase heart rate and blood pressure beyond helpful levels.

  This can lead to a detrimental state where the exercise on top of the increased sympathetic nervous system response drives these physiologic variables too high, resulting in the body reducing its physical output during the exercise. These clients may need trainers to calm them, working on relaxing visualizations, and working to reduce pressure to lower their arousal state so that excess epinephrine does not negatively impact performance. A client that is too relaxed and unfocused does not reap the benefit of this hormonal influence on performance, and these clients may need cheering, motivation, verbal "pumping up," and some small stimulus of external pressure to increase their arousal.

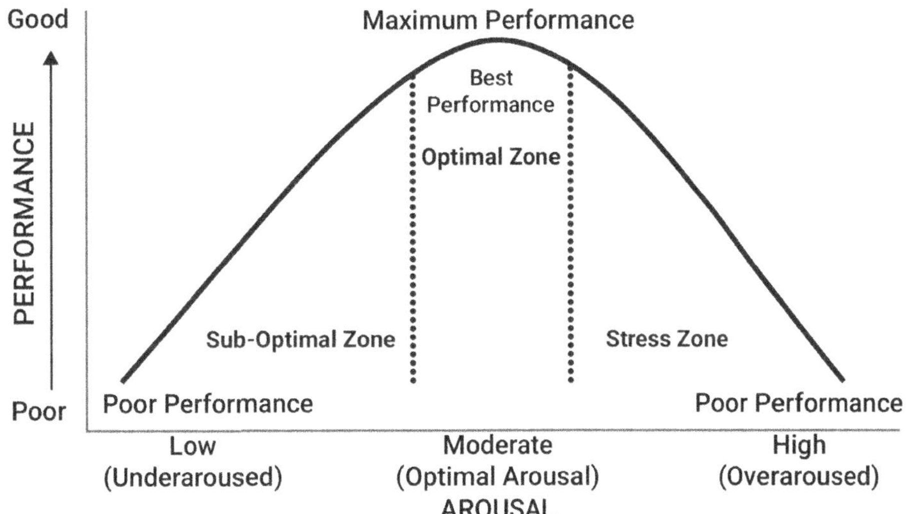

Correction of Improper Technique

Strength trainers must correct improper technique as early as possible in the learning process in order to prevent the development of bad habits and to reduce the risk of injury. Even advanced clients may demonstrate poor technique when fatigued, distracted, or unmotivated, so observing and giving cues on preparatory and execution form techniques need to be a constant focus of strength trainers during workouts. For maximal effectiveness, feedback should be as specific and timely as possible, and it should be either visual, auditory, and kinesthetic, depending on each client's learning style. Strength trainers may position clients in front of the mirror so they can observe and self-correct deviations in form, sometimes concurrent with a proper form demonstration alongside the client for comparison.

Trainers can also pair up clients with differing skill levels to promote a learning/teaching mentorship. This can also help more experienced clients develop leadership roles while also finding a reason to focus on their own form, which may need some fine-tuning as the client becomes complacent with experience. Strength trainers can use videos and handouts to supplement learning or break down exercises into smaller movement steps for kinesthetic learners. Regardless of the delivery method, all form correction feedback should be positive, supportive, and instructive in order to foster a warm learning environment and keep the client motivated and comfortable.

Warm-Up and Cool-Down Protocol

Warm-Ups are usually 10–20 minutes and consist of two specific periods, or they may be structured based on the raise, activate and mobilize, and potentiate (RAMP) protocol. The general warm-up period is 5 minutes of slow aerobic activity (e.g., jogging) followed by general stretching that focuses on ROM of the upcoming activities. This is followed by the specific warm-up period, which consists of movements that replicate those required for the upcoming activity. The RAMP Protocol consists of the following:

- Raise: Phase 1 of the protocol consists of activities that raise various physiological parameters like heart and respiration rates, body temperature, and blood flow. The activities simulate movement activities associated with the upcoming activity or develop skill patterns required for the specific sport.
- Activate and Mobilize: Phase 2 of the protocol focuses on mobility and may include dynamic stretching for muscles and mobility exercises for joints.
- Potentiation: Phase 3 of the protocol is sport specific, with a focus on progressing the intensity of the activity to the intensity required for the training or competition.
- Note: This is followed by the planned workout, which may include resistance training, plyometrics, speed and agility, aerobic endurance, etc.

The cool-down is an essential final stage of any workout, and an effective one plays a distinctive role in any well-designed workout. While a warm-up prepares the body for the main phase of a workout, the cool-down helps the body recover afterward.

The first step of an effective cool-down involves light exercise. Ideally, the form of light exercise will mimic the intensive exercise completed during the main stage of the workout. For example, walking is a common light exercise that follows a full running or sprinting exercise. Excess blood is pushed away from exerted muscles, where it may otherwise congeal and cause inflammation.

Deep breathing, which gets oxygen to all parts of the body, is another important aspect. Clients and athletes should regulate their breathing during light exercises in the cool-down phase and through the stretches that follow. The goal of cool-down stretches is not to overstretch the muscles; instead, cool-down stretches aim to lengthen muscles that were previously contracted. Finally, no cool-down is complete without proper nutrition and hydration. Fruits and vegetables provide valuable nutrients after a workout.

Kinesthetic, Auditory, and Visual Cueing Techniques

People learn and absorb information in many ways. Auditory learners learn best by following verbal instructions; visual learners learn best by observing a demonstration of proper form; and kinesthetic learners learn best by completing an action. Since trainers work with clients and athletes with various learning styles and preferences, they should vary instructional tactics to serve their clients in the best way.

Group fitness instructors may find that varying instructional techniques throughout a session determines the success of that session. Group fitness instructors who rely too heavily on demonstrating proper form without using supplementary auditory cues may find that the auditory learners in their classes struggle to complete exercises with proper form. Alternatively, visual learners may struggle to master proper form or know which direction to move in big classes or in rooms where they do not have a good view of their instructor. Trainers assist visual learners by positioning themselves where they are visible to all participants, and trainers use deliberate finger and hand motions to guide participants in the correct directions.

In individual training sessions, trainers may work with a client who has a difficult time completing an exercise even after the trainer articulates directions clearly and completely. These clients may benefit from a demonstration. Additionally, some kinesthetic learners simply need to complete an exercise before they fully understand it.

While many people undoubtedly learn more effectively from seeing, listening, or doing, most people learn best when trainers use a combination of visual, auditory, and kinesthetic instructional techniques. Therefore, trainers should deploy all techniques throughout fitness sessions.

Trainers improve delivery of auditory instruction by changing the inflection of their voices. They make themselves sound calm during yoga sessions and upbeat during high-intensity sessions. When trainers adjust the delivery of auditory cues to match the level of each workout, they do much to help participants improve their performance.

Safe Training Practices

Maintaining a safe exercise environment comes down to two factors: foresight and vigilance. Foresight means that trainers anticipate safety concerns before something dangerous happens, and vigilance means that trainers remain alert to possible dangers. Foresight involves planning; vigilance involves daily practices.

Trainers maintain a safe environment by instituting proper client intake procedures. Clients should complete consent or waiver forms before they access a gym. Trainers should keep a record of client health conditions that may jeopardize client safety. Clients should complete a screening test before they begin rigorous fitness programs. These standard operating procedures help trainers anticipate client safety needs and prevent dangerous situations.

Once clients start in a new gym or begin a new fitness program, trainers should monitor the intensity of their exercises. Trainers should never prompt a client to complete an exercise that a trainer cannot demonstrate themselves. Trainers should provide clear verbal instructions when clients begin new exercises. If a client feels dizzy, nauseous, or lightheaded during a workout, that client should refrain from exercise until symptoms subside. While trainers develop a fair sense of client abilities and limitations through screening assessments, clients may still experience worrying symptoms during intensive exercise. Trainers should never push clients beyond their means, and trainers should always remain alert to danger.

Training Modification Based on Physical Signs and Symptoms

In addition to being knowledgeable about chronic conditions and certain populations that require modifications for exercise programs, there are signs and symptoms that trainers should be aware of that would indicate the need to modify or stop exercise. Any time a client is experiencing severe pain or fatigue, the exercise should be discontinued. For clients who have arthritis, stopping or modifying the exercise is necessary if the exercise causes pain that lasts longer than 60 minutes after ending the exercise. Exercises need to be completely put on hold during arthritic flare-ups. Pain in the abdomen of prenatal clients is a definite sign that exercise should cease. If a prenatal client is leaking amniotic fluid, bleeding, or experiencing dyspnea, they should stop exercising right away. Clients with lung disease should be monitored for dyspnea and oxygen desaturation, both of which would indicate that exercise must be discontinued. They may also experience fatigue more easily, requiring modifications to exercises. With any client, the amount of exertion may be too much, and the trainer can observe this by performing the Talk Test or having the client rate their exertion level. These methods work great for obese clients and clients with coronary heart disease. Trainers should also be aware of the signs of hypoglycemia, such as dizziness and weakness. Trainers will notice that clients struggle to maintain proper technique during an exercise when modifications and regressions are necessary. Thus, unlevel positions and compensation are signs that training should be modified.

Application and Modalities of Exercise Regressions and Progressions

Exercise regressions and progressions occur during any effective fitness program. When a client amplifies acute variables, like weight or intensity, it's called progression, and when a client decreases acute variables, it's called regression. Both progressions and regressions are necessary parts of effective fitness programs. Sometimes a client must take one or two steps backward in order to take several steps forward. Trainers must determine when to increase the severity of exercises and when to make exercises milder.

The OPT™ Model is designed for clients to progress through different levels as they improve stability, strength, and power. These levels are applied to various forms of training, such as cardiorespiratory, core, and balance training. The general progression for any client in these levels is as follows:

- Stabilization: The progressions in this level are made by increasing the instability of the environment.

- Strength: The progressions in this level continue with changes to stability, but adjustments to load and volume are added.
- Power: The progressions in this level involve increases in load and speed.

The changes in stability are made progressively by moving from workouts on the floor to workouts on balance beams, half foam rolls, foam pads, balance disks, wobble boards, and Bosu balls. With each of these changes, progressions are made from using both legs to one leg. Stability may also be adjusted in some exercises by switching from a bench to a stability ball, or moving from a stability ball to standing. Exercises involving the upper body can start with the use of both arms at the same time and progress to alternating the arms and finally to using only one arm. Turning of the torso can then be included with the one-arm movement. Cardiorespiratory exercises can progress by reducing the amount of time for rest and increasing the amount of time performing high intensity activities. Regressions can be made to any exercise by going back to the simpler form of the exercise.

Trainers will need to determine which acute variables to change when progression or regression is necessary. The acute variables that can be modified are as follows:

- Particular exercises
- Periods of rest
- Number of repetitions
- Pace of repetitions
- Number of sets
- Intensity
- Duration of sessions
- Frequency of sessions
- Training volume of sessions

Only one variable should be modified at one time.

Progressions will always involve adding some form of challenge by increasing the difficulty, complexity, instability, or speed of an exercise. Regressions will remove a challenge. For example, a progression for dumbbell chest presses might involve alternating the arms, while a regression might have the client perform the exercise on a more stable surface such as a bench rather than on a stability ball. Other methods for progressing or regressing exercises include changing the plane of motion (sagittal, frontal, or transverse), adjusting the height of a box for jumping exercises, and choosing either machines or free weights. Movements in the three different planes would be performed as follows:

- Sagittal—the body moves forward.

- Frontal—the body moves side-to-side.

- Transverse—the body turns or rotates 90 degrees.

Additionally, the use of supports, such as rails on a treadmill, can either be added or removed as necessary. Rest periods should also be modified when needed.

Trainers determine when to make progressions or regressions based on safety. For example, a trainer may notice that their client struggles to maintain proper form when completing an exercise with increased weight. Improper form may cause injuries, so the trainer may decide to make that exercise easier for their client by either reducing weight or offering ancillary support during an exercise.

Just as effective trainers should know when to make exercises easier for a struggling client, they should also know when to make exercises more challenging. Trainers should never hold a client back from timely progressions, on the condition that they help clients implement those progressions safely. Effective trainers use a combination of long-term planning and regular observation to make safe decisions about when to implement progressions.

Effective fitness programs progress according to a documented fitness plan, but fitness plans are not written in stone. Reassessments should occur at regular intervals because they help trainers determine whether clients have progressed according to their original fitness plan. Flexible fitness plans provide opportunities for both progressions and regressions, according to clients' needs and abilities.

When trainers allow clients to progress beyond their abilities, trainers harm their clients more than they help. Trainers must actively observe clients during training sessions and take time to demonstrate proper techniques when clients fail to perform. Trainers allow clients to succeed by providing consistent, constructive feedback throughout a fitness program.

Spotting Techniques

Spotting procedures help clients complete exercises safely and efficiently. Not only do trainers need to know how to execute correct spotting techniques, but they must also be able to demonstrate and teach the techniques to clients so that they can spot one another during partner activities. Spotting also helps monitor a client's lifting form and movement execution, allowing the spotter to give verbal cues and help correct any errors in execution. It also allows for motivation, instruction, encouragement, feedback, and certain exercise modifications that would otherwise be dangerous and physically impossible without spotters. An example is negative resistance training, wherein clients can handle greater weight on the eccentric or lowering portion, but need spotters to help raise the weight in the concentric phase. Spotters should be prepared to offer as much help as needed. Clear communication between the lifter and spotter is required for safety, and the pair should discuss the lift before it occurs. The spotter should ensure that the weights are evenly spaced and equally loaded on the bar and that the collars are properly used.

Number of Spotters Needed for Given Situations and Exercises

The required number of spotters is determined by the load being lifted, the experience and skill of the client and spotters, and the physical strength of the spotters. The spotters must be strong enough to handle the load that the client is lifting with little notice and sometimes in less-than-ideal angles and positions. Therefore, it is crucial that spotters are honest with themselves and lifters about their abilities. It is better to err on the side of caution and use multiple spotters when necessary, as long as they can be accommodated spatially around the lift without being overly cumbersome.

Apart from power exercises, free weight exercises should use a minimum of one or two spotters when a client moves the bar over the head or face, or has it on the front of the shoulders or positioned on the back during the execution. During power exercises, client should be instructed to push the bar away or drop it when the bar is in front and to release it or jump forward when the bar is missed behind the head. A spotter should not be used. Two spotters are sometimes needed with heavy lifts, especially bar lifts, where one spotter should be at each end of the bar.

Spotter Location

The location of the spotter or spotters depends on the lift being attempted. For exercises with heavy weights on a bar such as a front squat, often two spotters are needed, with one at each end of the bar, to help balance the weight with the client and lift from either side, should an issue occur. For standing exercises such as squats and deadlifts, spotters should stand behind the lifter while the bar is still on the rack and as the lifter gets into position. They should then move as close as possible toward the lifter without touching them, as the lifter steps away from the rack with the bar.

The spotter's hands should be in the ready position near the bar while the lifter raises and lowers the weight. Once the set is complete or when failure is indicated by the lifter, the spotter should assist the lifter in returning the bar to the rack by holding on to the bar and guiding it back to the racked position. During exercises such as a dumbbell bench press, spotters should keep their hands near the lifter's forearms, close to the wrists. For a seated overhead triceps extension with a barbell, spotters should straddle the flat bench.

Body and Limb Placement Required When Spotting the Lifter

Once the spotter and the lifter are in the correct positions, the spotter needs to pay attention to their body and limb placement for their own safety during the lift as well as that of the client. When spotting over-the-face barbell exercises, the spotter should grasp the bar with an alternated grip, usually narrower than that of the client's grip. The spotter also should use a solid, wide base of support and a neutral spine position. Spotters should use an athletic stance, with feet slightly wider than hip-width apart, knees flexed, arms and hands up and in a ready position that is close to the bar and client without touching them.

Bodyweight should be equally and soundly distributed on both feet, which should be firmly planted on the ground. Spotters must follow the movement of the client and the bar with their eyes as well as their hands and remain intensely focused on the task at hand until the bar is re-racked. Spotters and lifters should communicate throughout the lift if anything changes, but it is the spotter's job to verbally motivate and check in with the lifter, since the client is likely less physically and mentally able to talk during maximal exertion.

Proper Breathing Techniques During Exercise

Proper breathing techniques during exercise help clients achieve fitness goals. Breathing during exercise moves oxygen to exerted muscles, which allows clients to complete difficult workouts. Knowing when to inhale and exhale is key to utilizing proper breathing techniques.

Clients should exhale when muscles contract and inhale when muscles lengthen in the direction of their resting position. For example, when a client completes a set of ten biceps curl repetitions at a weight consistent with their hypertrophic exertion level—three to four sets, eight to twelve repetitions per set—they should exhale when the biceps reaches maximum tension. Maximum tension occurs as the client raises the dumbbell toward their shoulder. Alternatively, a client should inhale as they release tension in the biceps (i.e., as the client lowers the dumbbell back to a resting position). Proper breathing technique involves timing inhalation and exhalation with each repetition.

While everyone should use proper breathing techniques during exercise, people with underlying medical conditions, like cardiovascular disease, should pay special attention to their breathing. Trainers should monitor their clients' well-being by encouraging them to stop when they feel dizzy or lightheaded. Any time clients complete high-intensity workouts, they should maintain proper focus on breathing techniques.

Kinetic Chain Checkpoints

The kinetic chain is the term used to refer to the human movement system, which consists of the muscular, skeletal, and nervous systems. The kinetic chain checkpoints are the areas of the body containing joints that trainers use to detect abnormalities in the posture. These checkpoints consist of the following areas:

- Feet and ankles
- Knees
- Lumbo-pelvic-hip-complex
- Shoulders
- Head and cervical spine

The checkpoints need to be observed while clients are performing exercises to make sure that the clients are not compensating or at risk for injuries. Exercises require correct posture, and trainers should be aware of the necessary alignment throughout the body for each exercise. Some signs to look for are shoulders that are elevated, neck and head that are extended forward, lower back that is hyperextended, femur that is adducted, and feet that are rotated externally. Modifications may be needed if any abnormalities are seen.

Practice Quiz

1. Tire flipping, kettlebells, sandbags, and battle ropes are implements best reserved for which of the following?
    a. Highly trained athletes
    b. Younger athletes
    c. Athletes rehabbing injuries
    d. Newer athletes

2. Which type of stretching should be done prior to workouts, and which type of stretching should follow the workout?
    a. Static (prior to workouts), dynamic (following workouts)
    b. Dynamic (prior to workouts), static (following workouts)
    c. Flexibility (prior to workouts), dynamic (following workouts)
    d. Dynamic (prior to workouts), flexibility (following workouts)

3. Which of the following factors is most influential in improving sprinting speed?
    a. Leg length
    b. Stride length
    c. Stride rate
    d. Impulse time

4. A client has medial tibial stress syndrome, which of the following cardiovascular equipment is NOT a wise choice?
    a. Arm ergometer
    b. Elliptical
    c. Spin bike
    d. Treadmill

5. Which of the following exercises should spotters NOT be used for?
    a. Dumbbell chest press
    b. Incline barbell bench press
    c. Front squat
    d. Power jerk

See answers on the next page.

Answer Explanations

1. A: Tire flipping, kettlebells, sandbags, and battle ropes are implements best reserved for highly trained athletes. Such implements are creative ways to add variety to workouts while accomplishing similar physiologic goals. Personal trainers should still be aware of when and how to properly use this equipment and be sure to educate and supervise clients in their use. Much of the non-traditional equipment is best reserved for advanced athletes who have the basic foundations of movement, such as a well-mastered squat and deadlift, because programs with non-traditional equipment tend to use heavier implements in power movements, which can induce injury if not carried out safely.

2. B: Dynamic stretching should be done prior to workouts and static stretching should follow the workout. Dynamic stretching occurs before the activity as part of the warm-up routine to increase heart rate, temperature, and blood flow, as well as CNS and PNS activity to prepare the body. Static stretches should follow the workout, especially for excessively stiff athletes or those with past injuries. Static stretching can improve the muscle tension and joint relationship over time. Static stretches performed prior to exercise can reduce explosive power and increase joint laxity, placing a client at greater risk of injury.

3. C: Speed is influenced by stride rate and stride length, so clients should focus on quick turnover and powerful steps. Of these factors, stride rate has a greater impact on speed and should be the focus when designing a program for improving sprinting speed. Leg length cannot be readily modified, especially after growth has ceased.

4. D: Medial tibial stress syndrome, or shin splints, is an overuse injury made worse by pounding or impact, so treadmill running should be avoided. Non-weight-bearing cardiovascular equipment such as an arm ergometer or bike is ideal. The elliptical can be a workable option as long as it does not cause pain. It is weight-bearing, but non-impact.

5. D: Spotters are not used in power exercises such as the power jerk. With the exception of power exercises, free weight exercises should use a minimum of one or two spotters when an athlete moves the bar over the head or face, has it on the front of the shoulders, or on the back during the execution. During power exercises, clients should be instructed to push the bar away or drop it when the bar is in front, and release it or jump forward when the bar is missed behind the head; a spotter should not be used.

Professional Development and Responsibility

Professional Standards

Safeguard Client Confidentiality

All sensitive and identifying client information should be safely stored and kept confidential and private, unless clients formally waive these privacy rights in writing or if this information must be accessed in emergency situations.

Systems for Maintaining Client Confidentiality

Trainers and facilities should have systems in place to ensure sensitive client information is kept confidential. Hard copy files should be locked in file cabinets, with key accessibility for intended audiences only. When trainers wish to communicate about a client with a physician, healthcare professional, other trainer, or a client's family member, they must obtain written and signed permission from the client and add this form, along with a timeframe beyond which this authorization is no longer valid, to the chart.

Importance of Client Privacy

Client files should be kept private to protect clients from identity or credit card theft, respect medical laws of confidentiality, and protect the trainer from legal liability by breaching these privacy laws.

FERPA and HIPAA Laws

The Family Educational Rights and Privacy Act (FERPA) relates mainly to protected information involving education, particularly in school settings. The Health Insurance Portability and Accountability Act (HIPAA) of 1996 defines individually identifiable health information such as demographics, prior and current health history, social security number, etc. The purpose of these laws is to protect sensitive client information and ensure this identifiable and personal information is kept only for the intended professionals. Trainers and fitness facilities must be sure to comply with these laws and lock up and otherwise encrypt all client files.

Rapid Access to Client Information

A client's file with all health, demographics, prior workouts, and emergency contact information should be with the trainer during testing and training sessions with that client. Should an emergency arise, trainers and staff need to have quick and easy access to pertinent information on the client such as emergency contact numbers, physician's name and number, and allergies. To abide by the laws of confidentiality and patient privacy, trainers should be sure to keep this file safely out of the hands of other people during sessions. If the trainer stores this information digitally, a computer or tablet should be turned on and accessed in the event of an emergency.

Professional Communication Health Professionals

Trainers are allied health professionals, and as such, are part of the medical community. They need to be able to communicate effectively with physicians and other health professionals on an ongoing basis to follow up on client referrals and progress using adherence to HIPAA and confidentiality guidelines. Trainers should be mindful to use proper medical and anatomical terminology so they do not lose credibility and are effective communicators.

Providing a Comfortable Environment

Training sessions are physically and mentally (and sometimes financially) challenging for clients, so trainers should strive to provide a conducive and comfortable environment, prioritizing the client's preferences over his or her own. Clients may have music type and volume preferences, temperature needs, and sensitivities to scents. Trainers should also be mindful of cultural differences with hygiene, dress, and even gum-chewing. They should inquire respectfully how to make each client feel most comfortable. Client compliance and satisfaction may decrease in the absence of these somewhat sensitive but helpful conversations.

Avoiding Distractions

To optimize client safety, reduce liability due to negligence, and treat clients with respect, trainers should give clients their undivided attention and avoid distractions during training sessions and conversations with clients. Trainers should refrain from using cellphones to text, make calls, or check emails. They also should avoid talking to other people in the fitness facility. Eye contact, active participation and demonstration, and verbal and non-verbal communication should all be directed toward the client.

Medical Clearance Requirements

To optimize client safety and minimize liability, personal trainers must adhere to NASM's Guidelines for obtaining medical clearance prior to participation in exercise testing and programming. The following people must obtain medical clearance prior to starting an exercise program:

- Previously inactive men over age forty and women over fifty
- Clients who answer "yes" to any PAR-Q questions and who experience any signs or symptoms of cardiovascular or pulmonary disease or want to participate in vigorous exercise as a moderate risk stratification or participate in moderate exercise with a high risk stratification

Positive Role Model for Clients

Trainers should be positive role models of healthy lifestyle behaviors for clients and should embody an attitude and practice of wellness. They should engage in an active lifestyle and fitness program, eat a nutritious diet, abstain from smoking and drug use, and lead by example, striving to be ambassadors of healthy choices.

Professional Behavior

Clients pay trainers for exercise programming and therefore trainers should bear in mind that behavior and dress should always be professional. Trainers should keep the environment smoke- and substance-free; give clients undivided attention; use active listening skills; wear appropriate attire that is neither too tight, too casual, or too revealing; and use polite language and professional topics of conversation. Although trainers may develop friendly relationships with clients over time, the trainer's responsibility is to be a health and fitness professional. Inappropriate jokes, swearing, offensive music, or other unprofessional behavior is not appropriate.

Scope of Practice

Certified Personal Trainers are involved in the education, motivation, assessment, and training of clients toward health and fitness goals and should refer clients to other health professionals when working with

issues outside of this scope of practice. It is imperative that trainers respect the boundaries of their scope of practice and do not attempt to diagnose, treat, counsel, or prescribe, or they may be subjected to liability and malpractice. While "exercise is medicine" is a common idea and has truths to it, trainers should refrain from using terms like "exercise prescription" or "this exercise will treat your condition," and instead refer to the "exercise program." While clients may rely heavily on the advice and expertise of trainers, often asking questions outside of a trainer's scope of practice, the trainer can educate on topics within his or her scope. However, they must refer to appropriate sources for all else.

Conducting Activities within the Scope of Practice

NASM trainers develop and implement individualized programming to clients based on sound exercise science principles. Under the scope of practice, trainers lead and demonstrate safe and effective exercise methods, write appropriate program recommendations, and motivate clients to begin and maintain healthy behaviors. NASM trainers should always act professionally and within this scope of practice.

Collaboration with Healthcare Professionals

Trainers should form a network of various types of healthcare providers such as physicians, physical therapists, mental health professionals, chiropractors, and nutritionists in order to provide clients with comprehensive, reputable care. Appropriate referrals minimize liability by ensuring the trainer acts only within his or her scope of practice. It also maximizes program effectiveness by addressing the many concerns and challenges faced by clients, which may otherwise prevent full exercise participation and goal achievement.

Reputable Referral Sources

Trainers should ensure referrals to other professionals are reputable and competent. Professionals should carry current certification or licensure from industry leaders. When networking with such professionals, trainers should be aware that referrals can work both ways, and that through professional and positive relationships with other local clinicians, they may get referrals back for exercise programming. It is prudent to either read reviews or speak to a trusted individual or practice about any new provider before adding him or her to a referral list. In the personal training industry alone, there are an increasing number of uncertified trainers or those with overnight "certifications" from websites that do not necessarily ensure competency.

Developing and Growing a Business

Business Models

There are several legal structures for personal training businesses, depending on if the trainer plans to work independently, as an employee in a fitness center, or manage a larger company with employees. He or she may use one of the following:

Sole proprietorship: a one-person business in which the owner/worker owns all business assets and since there is no separate legal entity, is responsible for all liabilities. These are easy to set up and terminate and often just under the owner's name. All profits are added to personal income, expenses are deducted, and owner must pay self-employment tax.

Partnership: two or more people agree to create a business. Assets, profits, and liabilities are split among those in the partnership, so a great deal of trust and thought must go into entering a partnership. Profits and expenses are divided among partners, and each partner pays taxes and self-employment tax on his or her share.

Corporation: separate legal entities with owners and shareholders. They are more time-consuming, costly, and harder to set up and terminate but hold a higher level of professionalism, have an easier time receiving loans, and risk less personal responsibility for liabilities and debts. The business pays taxes on profits, and individual owners also must pay taxes on their dividends from the payment from their shares.

Developing a Business Plan

Developing a sound business plan takes time, thought, research, and sometimes professional guidance. It should include the vision, mission, values, and goals of the company. The plan also should have the business legal structure fully detailed, all job descriptions detailed with expected salaries and required experience, as well as policies of the business such as cancellations or late arrivals. It should include a thorough financial plan, explaining startup costs for things like equipment, location, or supplies, expected revenue sources (what services are offered) and prices, payment methods, funding, and sometimes financial projections for a certain number of years. Business plans should be updated when changes occur and are required when negotiating funding or loans and for some rental agreements.

Ethical Business

Trainers must adhere to ethical business models, treating clients fairly and being transparent in financial obligations for clients and expected outcomes. It is beneficial to gather testimonials and reviews from real clients as well as keep thorough records. Although there are fitness and diet claims that over promise and under deliver, Certified Personal Trainers should operate with integrity and present realistic expectations. Whether trainers work independently or as an employee, they must fully and honestly report income and expenses, pay appropriate taxes, use just hiring practices, and abide by the laws in their state. NASM offers ethics courses for CECs, which can be helpful to refresh ethical principles.

Business Objectives

Similar to goal setting with fitness clients, business goals should be S.M.A.R.T. and cover various domains of the business such as financial, client outcomes, business growth, marketing/reach, and personal goals. All business partners must collaborate and define business objectives and how these will be measured to monitor success. Methods of continuous quality improvement (CQI), such as client surveys of program evaluation that are then reviewed and examined for improvements to be implemented, is an example of goal assessment and business improvement to better achieve goals.

Mission Statements

The mission statement defines the aspirations, mandates (required functions), constituents (who will be served), and values of the company. Values are important key organizational attitudes and beliefs used to guide behavior and decision-making. Mission statements should guide your daily activities and purpose, and be measurable and distinguishable from other organizations, helping define the company's niche within its given market. Most companies readily publish their mission statement on their websites, promotional materials, and even physically in-house for customers to read.

Financial Planning

Many personal trainers work as independent contractors for at least part of their income. While some personal trainers may earn a regular wage—as employees of a fitness center, for example—most

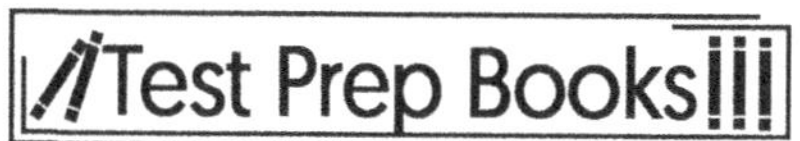

personal trainers experience regular changes in their weekly or monthly income. For personal trainers, successful financial planning depends on foresight and flexibility.

In the world of personal fitness, some seasons are busier than others. Over time, personal trainers learn to identify high and low calendar periods, and they make themselves available to new and existing clients when their services are in demand. Personal trainers can respond to unexpected lows by ramping up marketing campaigns. They may reach out to new and former clients with personalized messages and special promotions.

Ultimately, personal trainers deal most effectively with low periods by anticipating them. Personal trainers save their money during high periods, and they stay focused on income and expenses. Unexpected drops in weekly or monthly income will not break the banks of personal trainers who prioritize expenses and plan for low periods.

Maintaining Professional Credentials

Requirements for Certification and Recertification

To be eligible for certification as an NASM personal trainer, the candidate must be at least eighteen years of age, have current CPR/AED certification, and be within 90 days of earning a high school diploma or the equivalent prior to testing. The candidate must have a passion for health and fitness and helping others with their fitness goals. After passing the test, the certification is valid for two years, provided the trainer adheres to the scope of practice of a trainer, maintains CPR/AED certification, earns the required twenty hours of continuing education credits (CECs), and pays the recertification fee or retakes the certification exam.

CEC Requirements

In addition to keeping current CPR and AED certification, personal trainers must earn 2.0 CECs (equivalent to twenty hours) every two years as part of the recertification process. CECs may be earned in a variety of ways, including taking one of NASM's specializations, authoring a book, attending conferences, workshops or training courses, taking quizzes from NASM's publications, and completing certain university courses. The NASM maintains a list of approved continuing education course providers on its website. Random audits are conducted in which the certified professional has thirty days to submit all necessary documentation to the NASM Recertification Department.

Resources Regarding Rules and Regulations

Certified personal trainers (CPTs) are among the most under-regulated professionals in the workforce. As such, certified personal trainers may face uncertainty about where to turn when they decide to reach out for legal or ethical advice. In most cases, certified personal trainers defer to the rules and protocols outlined by the fitness club or gym where they are currently employed. This does not mean, however, that certified personal trainers should base their own ethical and professional standards solely on those expressed by their employer. Fitness clubs and gyms may inadequately express rules and protocols, so every certified personal trainer employed by a fitness club or gym should have a strong professional and ethical compass.

Every personal training certification course articulates professional and ethical standards, which cover everything from client-trainer relationships to business and marketing. When certified personal trainers enter the workforce, they should keep these standards in mind. Certified personal trainers may access these standards through their certification programs directly.

Since rules and regulations applicable to certified personal trainers are often unclear, certified personal trainers often rely on one another for guidance. Communication between certified personal trainers in a fitness club or gym is crucial, and consultation of online resources, like blogs, is often a great way to find answers.

Marketing Concepts and Techniques

In order to grow the business and build a client base, trainers need to develop and distribute marketing materials and spend time networking with other professionals and businesses in the community to promote their services.

Word of mouth advertising is one of the greatest marketing techniques. Personal trainers benefit from the positive things family members and friends tell each other about their experiences working with a personal trainer. Since trainers help clients achieve meaningful health goals that improve—and perhaps extend—the lives of clients, client-trainer relationships are intensely personal. Clients only hire trainers with whom they feel comfortable working.

This type of passive business-to-customer networking helps build and maintain a trainer's brand. A trainer's brand depends as much on what clients say about a personal trainer as on what types of fitness classes they offer or which areas of personal fitness, wellness, and nutrition they specialize in. Although much of the work of brand development occurs naturally—the result of customer feedback in public spaces and word of mouth advertising—trainers can do much to actively promote their brands.

A trainer's brand is established through a variety of sources. Trainers increase their business-to-customer advertising by maintaining an active social media presence. Facebook and Instagram are popular social media sites for personal trainers and fitness enthusiasts to share and engage with content. For example, trainers can generate leads on new clients by maintaining a strong social media presence.

Since most trainers and gyms maintain at least some form of social media presence, social media also provides an excellent forum for business-to-business networking. Businesses may reshare each other's content or coordinate joint social media campaigns. Additionally, business-to-business networking takes place at conferences, fitness competitions, and other events. On-brand public events provide trainers an excellent way to connect with one another. From these events, concrete professional relationships may spring. Trainers may decide to grow a common brand together, or they may discover a business willing to sponsor them in exchange for recommending the business's product or service.

Pricing

The law of supply and demand in the trainer's given geographical area largely dictates the price range for services. Trainers should research the fees that Certified Personal Trainers in the area charge, and aim to price themselves accordingly, justifying potentially higher fees for experience, educational level, or provided services. When setting fee structures for services, trainers should also consider weekly income goals and all associated expenses as well as the expected volume (number of sessions per week). It is somewhat customary in the industry to offer discounts if sessions are purchased in bulk at one time (packages). Trainers may also consider offering special promotions at certain times of the year,

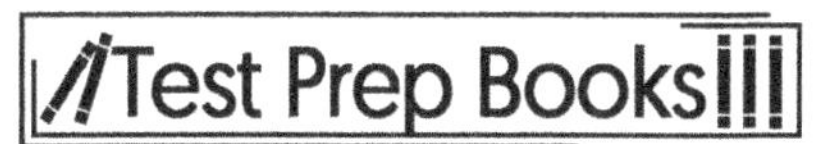

which offer lower prices for a certain commitment of sessions. This can be especially beneficial in slower times to attract new clients or when other competitors drop prices, often at the beginning of the year or during summer.

Marketing Materials

Trainers can promote their business through the use of marketing materials such as brochures, flyers at local health food stores or markets, maintaining a web page, and updating a blog or posting video clips with fitness, nutrition, or motivation tips. There are an increasing number of e-marketing methods. These include posting Google banner ads and updating social media accounts such as Facebook, Twitter, and Instagram with special deals, exercise news, and client successes. Writing columns or guest posts on other health and fitness news sites and blogs provides are other promotional methods. Promoting the business helps attract new clients, educate them about available services, and increase profits. Trainers should carry professional business cards with contact information, website and physical training address, and qualifications with them during daily activities to hand to potential clients and contacts. Marketing materials should always be honest and ethical.

Computer Applications for Marketing Materials

Computer applications such as Microsoft Word, PowerPoint, or Publisher, or Adobe InDesign offer affordable methods to create professional marketing materials. There are also local printing and office supply stores such as FedEx or Staples that offer services. Additionally, a variety of online businesses provide ways for trainers to design and print their business cards, flyers, and promotional materials such as pens, water bottles, or banners.

Client Acquisition, Retention, and Ascension

Trainers often acquire new clients via social media. Trainers boost their social media presence by remaining active on various platforms. Trainers can make daily posts and reshare content relevant to their brands. When prospective clients engage with content shared by a trainer or gym, trainers and gyms can follow up with these individuals. Trainers and fitness centers observe activity on their social media accounts to identify leads, and they may send information about upcoming fitness classes and promotions. Such welcome and engaging methods often get new clients through the door.

Trainers and fitness centers should link their official websites with their social media accounts. This makes it easier for prospective clients to sign up for private sessions or gym memberships. Creating a seamless experience for prospective clients ensures that they follow through on their plans to sign up with either a personal trainer or a fitness center.

Once clients begin a new fitness program or membership, trainers and gyms work hard to retain those clients through open communication, feedback, and promotions. Trainers should establish a communication policy with their clients and maintain it faithfully. For example, trainers could have specified hours where they are available to answer calls or emails. They should strive to respond to missed calls and emails within a predetermined timeframe that they discuss with their clients.

Trainers should also ask for feedback to ensure they are listening to their clients' needs and addressing any areas in which they need improvement. Clients may provide feedback both online (such as a survey emailed to them) and in person (such as a paper form or face-to-face). Trainers may ask structured or open-ended questions, and they use the information they obtain to make decisions about how a fitness program should proceed. Trainers should always take this information seriously and use it to improve a client's experience. Satisfied clients are more likely to stay with a trainer. Clients who believe their concerns are unheard will explore other options.

Fitness centers and gyms may use promotions to attract new clients, retain existing clients, or both. Some promotions give existing members bonuses for referring friends and family members. Referral programs are often an effective method of client acquisition. Other promotions include a free month for new clients or yearly subscriptions at a discounted rate.

Since effective marketing campaigns depend on maintaining open channels of communication with existing and prospective clients, trainers and gyms utilize concise and engaging emails as part of a comprehensive marketing campaign. Weekly or monthly newsletters, which showcase fitness programs and highlight promotions, often facilitate client engagement. Trainers and gyms may also send personalized emails to valued clients.

Sales Concepts and Techniques

Identifying and responding to customer needs are important elements of effective sales, so salespeople should acquire as much information about prospective clients' needs as possible. Naturally, social media benefits salespeople because people share information on social media sites about their needs as consumers. Astute salespeople utilize this information to make more sales.

Like salespeople, observant and attentive trainers utilize information from social media to generate a deeper understanding of the needs of prospective clients. Trainers respond to comments on Facebook posts and send personalized messages to people they identify as prospective clients. Information gathered on social media provides the basis for effective sales presentations and pitches.

Trainers also utilize information they gain from in-person conversations to effectively pitch to prospective clients. The effective trainer-as-salesperson should begin every conversation with a prospective client by asking about the client's fitness goals. Equipped with a clear understanding of a client's goals, trainers sell prospective clients on personalized fitness programs and memberships. Knowledge of client goals leads to effective pitches and presentations.

Although selling clients on fitness programs and memberships may sound easy, much goes into how trainers present to prospective clients. *Prehandling* is a sales term that refers to how salespeople anticipate client objections to pitches. The effective trainer-as-salesperson phrases questions deliberately to address client objections before they get in the way of a successful sale. For example, rather than wait for a prospective client to explain that they are unwilling to begin a new fitness program or sign up for a new membership before the end of the holiday season, an effective trainer-as-salesperson will ask how soon a prospective client can begin training. *Prehandling* is about anticipating objections and overcoming them. The effective trainer-as-salesperson overcomes an objection about the cost of a gym membership or fitness program by making the sale about the client's personal goals, health, and wellness. Trainers overcome client objections to price by framing the program or membership explicitly in terms of its benefits to the client.

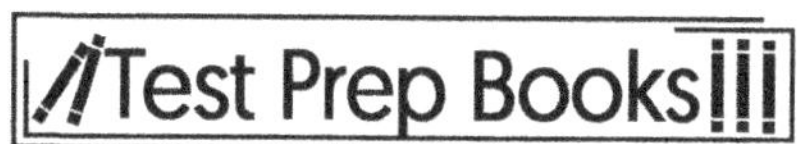

Equipment Maintenance and Safety Considerations

Equipment Maintenance

Daily inspection of equipment and routine maintenance by trained professionals in accordance to manufacturer's guidelines should be documented and conducted to decrease risk of injury and liability. Cables and bands should be checked for thinning or fraying prior to each use, and belts and safety stops on treadmills should be evaluated for wear and function. Weights should be racked and loose equipment put back and stored away after use to prevent trips and falls. Equipment and mats should be cleaned between clients with antibacterial wash to avoid the spread of germs. Safety equipment such as AEDs and fire extinguishers should be checked monthly and its proper function should be documented. Malfunctioning equipment such as broken bands should be removed from the floor if possible or clearly marked with an "Out of Order" sign if not mobile.

Safety Policies

Having comprehensive, well-thought-out and regularly rehearsed safety procedures decreases risk of unsafe behaviors, injury, and resultant liability. The absence of creating safety policies, training staff and clients in their use, and posting clear explanations of them (such as what to do in case of fire or power outage) in readily available places can result in negligence and legal responsibility on the part of the facility for any incurred injuries. Staff and clients should receive printed copies of all safety procedures, listen to a thorough explanation, rehearse them, and ask any questions for clarification. Incident reports should be completed and reviewed for every injury or safety issue that arises, looking for trends and better solutions for ongoing safety improvements.

Providing a Safe Exercise Setting

Precautions employed in the exercise setting can improve client safety. Trainers should ensure that routine maintenance is performed and documented on all equipment by trained professionals and that equipment is being used in the proper way. The surface floor should be tidy and free from potential tripping hazards. If exercising outside, trainers should heed warning to environmental conditions such as excessive heat, humidity, storms, cold, and wind, and terminate sessions or relocate indoors if any threats exist.

Spotting

Spotting clients while lifting weights and assisting clients with all types of equipment and exercises helps monitor form and effort to reduce injury risk and maximize training benefit. It helps prevent weights from dropping and rolling, which can distract and injure others in the vicinity.

Risk Stratification

As discussed before, risk stratification is the process of classifying clients into one of three risk strata or levels (low, medium, or high risk) based on the risk factors identified in the health screening process, along with age, health status, and symptoms. Stratifying health concern risks is an important preliminary step in determining whether a client needs further professional medical clearance and the overall appropriateness of physical exercise. It also helps safeguard the trainer from negligence and liability risk. The personal trainer should understand that risk assessment needs to be an ongoing process. The three strata and criteria for each are as follows:

Low risk: younger (males less than forty-five years of age; females less than fifty-five years), asymptomatic, and have less than or equal to one risk factor for cardiovascular or pulmonary disease

Moderate risk: older (males forty-five years of age or older; females fifty-five years or older) and have less than or equal to two risk factors for cardiovascular or pulmonary disease

High risk: diagnosed cardiovascular, pulmonary, or metabolic disease greater than or equal to one symptom of cardiovascular or pulmonary disease (dizziness or syncope, ankle edema, palpitations, pain in the chest, neck, jaw or arm, heart murmur, etc.)

Supervision-Based Risk Stratification

All clients with known diseases are automatically in the high-risk strata. Depending on risk level, supervision and monitoring may be required during exercise testing. Trainers should defer to physicians for guidelines regarding monitoring during sessions once appropriate testing is completed with proper supervision. Rate of Perceived Exertion (RPE) should be regularly assessed, particularly in cases where heart rate response may be altered.

- Low risk: physician supervision is not necessary for maximal or submaximal testing
- Medium risk: physician supervision is not necessary for submaximal testing but is recommended for maximal testing
- High risk: physician supervision is recommended for maximal or submaximal testing

Comprehensive Risk Management Program

Risk management reduces liability for trainers, but also raises the standard of care for clients and keeps their safety and health in the forefront. Clients should not only be properly stratified and have all necessary medical forms, consent, and waivers signed and on file, but they should also be educated on medical, environmental, and facility emergency procedures. All emergency procedures should be documented in written form, rehearsed and posted under each phone. An injury prevention program such as RICES (rest, ice, compression, elevation, stabilization) should be used.

Liability and Legality

NASM certified personal trainers can obtain personal injury and professional liability insurance through Forrest T. Jones & Company or other similar carriers. To reduce risk of liability and improve client safety, trainers should follow the professional, ethical, and business standards of the health and fitness industry.

Professional Liability and Negligence

- Personal injury liability insurance protects against libel, slander, and invasion of privacy.

- Professional liability insurance protects against injuries caused by services or negligence.

- Commercial liability insurance covers individuals and the business against incidents and accidents that occurred at the facility and must be purchased by trainers who own their own studios.

- Negligence is a failure to perform at the accepted standard (due care), while gross negligence is to do so willingly. In addition to carrying the necessary liability insurance, trainers can help defend against negligence claims by documenting all services daily and performing to the highest industry standards.

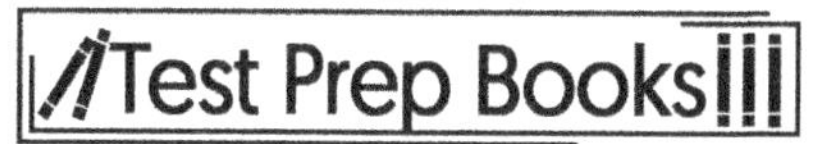

Legal Risk-Management Techniques

To reduce risk of legal issues, certified personal trainers should respect and always work within the boundaries of their scope of practice. Diagnosing or treating medical issues and injuries or prescribing diets are not functions of a personal trainer and must be correctly referred to the appropriately licensed healthcare professional. Certification requirements, medical clearances, signed informed consents, and proper personal injury and professional liability insurance should always be maintained and up-to-date. Trainers should always employ their best judgment and a scientific approach to exercise testing and programming, being mindful of each client's ability level and current health to avoid risky exercises. They also should avoid making significant leaps in intensity or skill level, which may injure clients. If home exercises or unsupervised sessions are expected of clients, trainers should fully explain and demonstrate exactly how to complete such tasks.

Safety Considerations

Exercise equipment poses safety risks to clients when not correctly organized. Trainers should place large machines like squat racks around the outside of the gym, against the wall, and trainers should secure these machines to the floor. Additionally, trainers should maintain space between pieces of medium-sized equipment, so spotters can easily access their partners in the event of an emergency. Clients should not feel crowded or have difficulty moving from one area of the gym to another. In the event of a fire or other similar emergencies, clients must have efficient access to exit doors.

Opportunities for Professional Development

Importance of Continuing Education

Trainers should regularly engage in NASM-approved continuing education opportunities to increase health and fitness knowledge in order to apply it to programming and maximize effectiveness as personal trainers and allied health professionals.

The Evolving Field of Health and Fitness

New health and fitness research is constantly being conducted and published, sometimes changing the prevailing ideas about proper training, exercises, nutrition, health, and performance. It is paramount that trainers stay curious and informed in order to apply the safest, most effective programming for clients and to participate in the research process, if possible, by constantly seeking to better their understanding, application, and science for clients.

Career Development Practices

Trainers should strive to continuously develop themselves and their careers as personal trainers. Attending continuing education seminars, reading fitness and health research journals and publications, learning about marketing and business, working with mentors, and aiming to stay on the cutting edge of the field are important keys to career growth. Trainers who manage or hire other employees and trainers should lead by example, modeling the level of professionalism and performance they expect from employees. Expectations, evaluation methods and frequency, and paths and criteria for promotion should be clearly conveyed.

Emergency Protocols

Responsibilities to Perform Emergency Procedures

Trainers are responsible and held liable for appropriately and safely caring for clients under their watch during emergency situations, both with the client directly and at the fitness facility. Trainers must be knowledgeable of and prepared to perform current emergency action plans and ensure client safety as much as possible.

Basic First-Aid

It is beneficial for trainers to get basic first-aid certification for proper knowledge and confidence of applying treatment to clients. Even in the absence of certification, trainers should be prepared to administer basic first-aid to clients during sessions in case injuries occur such as the following:

- Strains/sprains: Use RICES: ice for twenty to thirty minutes every two hours, elevate above the heart if possible, and use elastic wrap to apply compression for the first twenty-four to seventy-two hours.

- Fractures: Call EMS and, if possible, do not move client; calm and reassure them and provide an ice pack. Splints should not be used unless the client must be moved, in which case a proper splinting technique must be employed. Monitor for signs of shock, internal bleeding, or other emergencies.

- Exercise intolerance such as dizziness, syncope, and heat injury: Stop exercise immediately and try to get client supine. Provide water or sports drink if available. With suspected heat injuries, move client to shade or cooler environment, remove excess clothing, and apply cool water cloths on wrists, neck, and behind knees.

Emergency Procedures

Emergency procedures should be written and practiced every three months by all involved staff. It is important to keep emergency equipment up to date and documented as such, have established telephone procedures, required equipment, emergency response contacts, map of emergency exits and fire extinguishers, and specific documented responsibilities that are rehearsed by staff members. Trainers should explain the emergency procedures to each new client and remind him or her periodically or if changes are made.

Emergency Action Plan Components

Emergency plans should be written, explained orally, and practiced by staff and clients. Copies should be posted under each phone and distributed to staff and clients. As revisions are made, they should be explained and rehearsed. Emergency action plans should be comprehensive, clear, and concise and include things such as:

- Clearly marked exits with illuminated signs
- Fire extinguishers and a fire emergency safety plan, and emergency evacuation or shelter plans posted under each phone for things like floods, storms, and tornadoes
- Clearly delineated staff responsibilities
- Emergency Medical Services (EMS) contact activated on phones
- First aid kit, AED, latex gloves, blood pressure kit and stethoscope, CPR masks, etc.

Demonstrating Emergency Procedures During Testing

Staff and supervising physicians should be aware of all emergency procedures during testing and training. Clients should be instructed how to stop the test at any moment should the need or desire arise. Emergency stop switches and buttons, such as those on treadmills, should always be engaged, and clients should be instructed on their use during testing and training.

CPR and AED

Trainers must be trained in basic life support, and keep current CPR and AED (automated external defibrillator) certification and be prepared to respond with emergency cardiac care in cases of myocardial infarction (MI) or sudden cardiac arrest (SCA). It is beneficial if the facility has emergency oxygen and the trainer is versed in administering it during cases of suspected mild to moderate MI, while waiting for emergency medical personnel to arrive on scene. Failure to keep current CPR and AED certification is a liability risk for trainers and may also void personal training certification status.

Credible Resources of Information Regarding Health and Fitness Education

While the internet provides a wealth of information about health and fitness, websites and blogs are not always the most reliable sources of information for personal trainers. While much of the information on websites and blogs derives from scholarly articles, peer-reviewed articles, research, and case studies, information in non-academic articles is not always reliably transcribed. Professionals in every field must discriminate between credible and uncredible information, and fitness trainers are no exception. Fitness trainers do well to directly reference the sources of information, whether scholarly or peer-reviewed articles, rather than trending blogs. The information in both scholarly articles and peer-reviewed articles is validated by experts, whereas blogs are written and published without much editorial oversight. The level of professional and expert oversight demanded by publishers of scholarly articles and peer-reviewed articles guarantees reliable information.

Since the field of health and fitness is continually developing with new insights and theories, fitness trainers work hard to stay abreast of current trends. Fitness trainers attend conferences and workshops to obtain insight into developments in the field. Not all conferences or workshops are created equal, however. Fitness trainers should research information about panel members, topics, and sponsors before registering for a conference or workshop.

Practice Quiz

1. A mission statement should include all EXCEPT which of the following?
    a. Industry standards
    b. Values
    c. Mandates
    d. Constituents

2. Among many ways, CECs can be earned through which of the following ways?
    I. Teaching approved courses
    II. Authoring a book
    III. Passing grades in certain university courses
    IV. Turning in client exercise program records

    a. All of the above
    b. Choices I and II only
    c. Choices I, II, and III only
    d. Choices I, II, and IV only

3. If a piece of moveable equipment is broken, what should you do?
    a. Attach an "Out of Order" sign
    b. Let it be but avoid using it in a workout
    c. Remove it from the floor
    d. Unplug it

4. Music volume and type, hygiene, scents, and dress, as well as facility temperature all should be considered in regards to what?
    a. Providing a comfortable environment for the client
    b. Determining the intensity of the workout
    c. Relating it to the gender of the client
    d. Figuring the fee per session

5. RICES for acute injury treatment stands for?
    a. Rest, Ice, Compression, Elevation, Stabilization
    b. Rest, Ice, Compression, Elevation, Splint
    c. Rest, Injury, Compression, Elevation, Splint
    d. Rest, Injury, Compression, Elevation, Stabilization

See answers on the next page.

Answer Explanations

1. A: A mission statement does not include things about industry standards, but instead should help define the business's niche within the industry. It should also include the aspirations, mandates (required functions), constituents (who will be served), and values of the company.

2. C: Trainers need to keep detailed records of sessions and testing for clients, but this is simply a component of the job and does not earn CECs (continuing education credits). CECs may be earned in a variety of ways, including teaching approved courses, authoring a book, attending conferences, workshops or training courses, taking quizzes from ACE's publications, and completing certain university courses. The ACE maintains a list of approved providers on its website.

3. C: Because it was specified that the piece of broken equipment was movable, it should be picked up and removed from the floor so that it is not accidentally used, possibly leading to injury. Failing to do so would be an example of negligence, and gross negligence if the trainer was aware of the issue and left it there anyway. An "Out of Order" sign could be used for treadmills or large equipment that could not be easily removed, but it is safer to take the piece off the floor so the sign is not accidentally removed and the broken equipment used.

4. A: Providing a comfortable environment for the client includes details such as appropriate music volume and type, hygiene, scents, and dress, as well as facility temperature. Each client may have his or her preferences for such variables, and by discussing these factors with the client, trainers can ensure that the environment provided is conducive with the client's preferences. An uncomfortable environment can negatively impact adherence, particularly in instances where clients may have sensitivities to scents or temperatures or cultural differences with hygiene and apparel. To optimize client compliance and satisfaction, these somewhat sensitive, but helpful, conversations should take place in the initial sessions.

5. A: Acute injury treatment should employ RICES: Rest, Ice, Compression, Elevation, Stabilization

Practice Test #1

Basic and Applied Sciences and Nutritional Concepts

1. Which of the following is NOT a component of a sarcomere?
    a. Actin
    b. D-line
    c. A-band
    d. I-band

2. Which of the following best describes the likely ratio of Type I and Type II muscle fibers in a competitive tennis player?
    a. High Type I, low Type II
    b. High Type I, high Type II
    c. Low Type I, high Type II
    d. Low Type I, low Type II

3. Which of the following correctly lists the structures of a muscle from largest to smallest?
    a. Fasciculus, muscle fiber, actin, myofibril
    b. Muscle fiber, fasciculus, myofibril, actin
    c. Sarcomere, fasciculus, myofibril, myosin
    d. Muscle fiber, myofibril, sarcomere, actin

4. What is the purpose of sodium bicarbonate when released into the lumen of the small intestine?
    a. It works to chemically digest fats in the chyme.
    b. It decreases the pH of the chyme so as to prevent harm to the intestine.
    c. It works to chemically digest proteins in the chyme.
    d. It increases the pH of the chyme so as to prevent harm to the intestine.

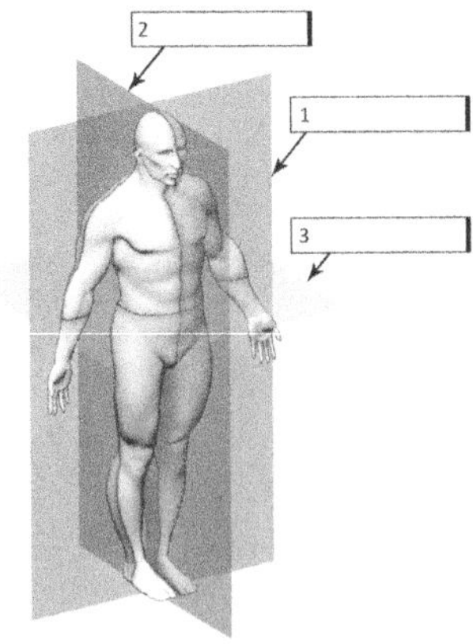

5. Which of the following is the correct sequence of the three primary body planes as numbered 1, 2, and 3 in the above image?
    a. Plane 1 is coronal, plane 2 is sagittal, and plane 3 is transverse.
    b. Plane 1 is sagittal, plane 2 is coronal, and plane 3 is medial.
    c. Plane 1 is coronal, plane 2 is sagittal, and plane 3 is medial.
    d. Plane 1 is sagittal, plane 2 is coronal, and plane 3 is transverse.

6. Which of the following are responsible for the exchange of nutrients, hormones, oxygen, fluids, and electrolytes between blood and the interstitial fluid of body tissues?
   a. Arterioles
   b. Venules
   c. Capillaries
   d. Hemoglobin

7. Myosin cross-bridges attach to the actin filament when the sarcoplasmic reticulum is stimulated to release which one of the following?
   a. Calcium ions
   b. Acetylcholine
   c. Troponin
   d. Adenosine triphosphate (ATP)

8. During heavy breathing, which of the following muscles do NOT help to elevate the ribs during inspiration?
   a. Sternocleidomastoids
   b. External intercostals
   c. Rectus abdominis
   d. Anterior serrati

9. If oxygen is available during glycolysis, what happens to pyruvate?
   a. It is converted to lactate.
   b. It is transported to the sarcoplasm for the Krebs cycle.
   c. It is transported to the mitochondria for the Krebs cycle.
   d. It is converted to lactic acid.

10. Cortisol is secreted by which of the following?
   a. Adrenal cortex
   b. Anterior pituitary
   c. Posterior pituitary
   d. Testes and ovaries

11. Which amino acid must be present for the development of carnosine, an essential muscle buffering substance?
   a. Histidine
   b. Beta-alanine
   c. Carnosine
   d. Leucine

12. What type of resistance exercise training promotes increased concentrations of growth hormone?
   a. 3 sets, high intensity, 1-minute interval
   b. 3 sets, low intensity, 3-minute interval
   c. 1 sets, high intensity, 1-minute interval
   d. 1 sets, low intensity, 3-minute interval

13. Soccer dribbling requires what joint movement at the ankle and in which movement plane?
   a. Eversion/transverse
   b. Inversion/frontal
   c. Eversion/frontal
   d. Inversion/transverse

14. Which one of the following answers provides the correct name and fascicular arrangement description associated with the biceps brachii muscle?
   a. Fusiform; spindle-shaped muscles
   b. Multipennate; tendon branches within the muscle
   c. Longitudinal (AKA: parallel); long axis of fascicles is parallel to long axis of muscle
   d. Radiate (AKA: convergent); muscle has broad origin (fan or triangular shape)

15. Which of the following characteristics of the mechanical load associated with resistance exercises are important for the stimulation of bone growth?

I. Speed of loading
II. Intensity of the load
III. Direction of the force
IV. Type of load

   a. I, III, IV
   b. II, III, IV
   c. I, II, III
   d. I, II, III, IV

16. Which of the following is the equation for power?
   a. $Force \times distance$
   b. $\frac{Work}{time}$
   c. $\frac{Work}{distance}$
   d. $Force \times time$

17. A collegiate track sprinter is doing interval training at a 1:12 work-to-rest ratio. This type of training is working what energy system?
   a. Fast glycolytic and oxidative
   b. Oxidative
   c. Fast glycolytic
   d. Phosphagen

18. A client would like to use an ergogenic aid to delay fatigue. Which of the following is a good option?
   a. Sodium tablets and/or sports beverages
   b. Glutamine and/or sodium tablets
   c. Branched-chain amino acids and/or caffeine
   d. Sports beverages and/or caffeine

Client Relations and Behavioral Coaching

19. Which of the following is NOT a way to foster a positive exercise experience?
    a. Using S.M.A.R.T. goals
    b. Using infrequent reinforcement and feedback
    c. Identifying barriers to adherence and strategizing solutions
    d. Building a support

20. What is motivational interviewing?
    a. An important part of the initial interview, it helps determine what motivates the client in his or her life.
    b. An important part of the initial interview when clients ask the trainer how he or she maintains an active lifestyle in an attempt to motivate the client.
    c. A helpful method of trainers to establish a points system to earn points for activity as a source of external motivation for a client.
    d. Acknowledging and working through a client's challenges concerning regular activity, stressing the fact that it is his or her choice to be active, while encouraging the change.

21. As a client's fitness level improves, what may become less important?
    a. Sources of external motivation
    b. Sources of internal motivation
    c. Setting S.M.A.R.T. goals
    d. Feedback

22. A visual learner would probably prefer which of the following?
    a. Reading about proper squatting technique
    b. Trying to squat back into a chair before a full body squat
    c. Watching video tutorials of squatting form
    d. Listening to you explain the major tips for the perfect squat form

23. Which is an example of active listening to a client who says, "I would like to lose a little weight and get in shape"?
    a. "Okay, good. Why don't you tell me what a typical day looks like for you?"
    b. "Okay, don't worry. That's certainly understandable."
    c. "Okay, so it sounds like you are interested in improving your fitness and losing a little weight. Can you tell me more about that?"
    d. "Okay. According to your BMI, I think we should aim for 40 pounds."

24. "I know it's challenging, but if you can push through three more reps, you will break your record!" is an example of what type of feedback?
    a. Evaluative
    b. Supportive
    c. Descriptive
    d. Corrective

25. "Your back is perfectly straight now, but let's see if you can bring your hands closer to shoulder-width apart." is an example of what type of feedback?
    a. Evaluative
    b. Supportive
    c. Descriptive
    d. Corrective

26. John is 5'10" and 210 pounds. According to the BMI, he would be categorized as which of the following?
    a. Underweight
    b. Normal weight
    c. Overweight
    d. Obese

27. "Feedback should be timely" is best described by which of the following statements?
    a. It should be given after every session
    b. It should be given after assessments only to explain results
    c. It should be given sporadically so it doesn't lose its meaning
    d. It should be given during or soon after a movement or assessment

28. Which of the following categories of barriers to a healthy lifestyle can trainers likely have the greatest impact on?
    a. Environmental
    b. Programmatic
    c. Social
    d. Personal

29. Ensuring the client has a good social support system, such as an exercise buddy, a gym in a convenient location to work or home, or a local sports league membership are methods to improve adherence based on which behavioral change model?
    a. Socio-Ecological Model
    b. Theory of Planned Behavior
    c. Social Cognitive Theory
    d. Health Belief Model

30. Which of the following is NOT a good way to prevent relapses in exercise behavior?
    a. Making goals easily achievable
    b. Assuring clients that short lapses are inevitable and not failures
    c. Ensuring a client's social support system is positive
    d. Making a list of possible causes of relapses and brainstorming solutions

31. Which of the following is NOT a reason that relapses in exercise behavior occur?
    a. Too much intrinsic motivation
    b. Lack of social support
    c. Illness or injury
    d. Perceived sense of failure

32. Tina is a new client who had a previously sedentary life. Which might be the best choice of a technique to facilitate motivation?
    a. Reducing session fees after she completes twenty sessions
    b. Reminding her of the benefits of exercise and the risks of inactivity
    c. Making S.M.A.R.T. fitness goals after assessment
    d. Establishing a points system to win prizes after completing sessions each week

33. Self-regulatory strategies such as self-monitoring physical activity and setting personal goals and rewards, planning activity in advance, and having reasonable expectations are methods to improve adherence based on which behavioral change model?
    a. Theory of Planned Behavior
    b. Social Cognitive Theory
    c. Health Belief Model
    d. Socio-Ecological Model

34. What is habit stacking?
    a. The process of adding new exercises to a workout program at regular intervals
    b. Pairing positive habits with negative ones to reduce client stress and promote healthier behavior
    c. Description of how one positive behavior leads to another
    d. Assigning specific exercises, which become the focus of fitness programs

35. How does synaptic pruning influence a client's ability to complete exercises?
    a. Excess nutrients are eliminated from synaptic systems to increase muscle efficiency.
    b. Habits build connections between parts of the brain responsible for completing certain actions.
    c. Negative habits are replaced with positive habits.
    d. Muscles develop elaborate protein structures that increase endurance.

36. How do trainers effectively manage client expectations?
    a. Cancel appointments with the same clients during peak seasons
    b. Build training programs around client ambitions
    c. Contact clients if they are going to be late for a session
    d. Assure clients that they will never let them down

Assessment

37. Which of the following is NOT considered one of the five main components of health-related physical fitness?
    a. Muscular power
    b. Flexibility
    c. Muscular endurance
    d. Body composition

38. Which of the following statements are true about medical clearance prior to participating in an exercise-training program?
    a. All clients need medical clearance from a physician prior to participation in an exercise-training program.
    b. Only clients with diagnosed cardiovascular, respiratory, or metabolic diseases need clearance prior to participation.
    c. Children, adolescents, men less than forty-five years, and women less than fifty-five years who do not have CAD risk factors/symptoms or known disease and who did not answer "yes" to any questions on the PAR-Q do not need clearance.
    d. Children, adolescents, men less than fifty years, and women less than fifty-five years who do not have CAD risk factors/symptoms or a known disease and who did not answer "yes" to any questions on the PAR-Q do not need clearance.

39. The Client-Trainer agreement form should include all EXCEPT which of the following?
    a. Cost-structure for sessions
    b. Cancellation policy
    c. Expectations of both parties
    d. Risk stratification information

40. What is the criterion of obesity that counts as a positive risk factor for CAD?
    a. Waist circumference of > 100 cm
    b. BMI ≤ 29 kg/m^2
    c. Waist circumference of < 100 cm
    d. BMI ≥ 29 kg/m^2

41. Which of the following is a positive risk factor for CAD?
    a. Blood pressure reading of 130/90 mmHg
    b. Fasting blood glucose of ≥ 90 mg/dL confirmed by at least two separate measurements
    c. Current use of lipid-lowering medications
    d. Death of father at age sixty-six from myocardial infarction

42. Which of the following is the best definition for intermittent claudication?
    a. Tissue swelling as a result of an imbalance between fluid coming out of circulation in blood vessels into tissues or back into circulation from tissue
    b. Dizziness upon standing that resolves with sitting or lying down
    c. Microscopic tissue damage from eccentric exercise that usually appears twenty-four hours after exercise
    d. An achy, cramping feeling typically of the lower legs that may come and go with exercise due to occlusion of blood vessels

43. In what region of the spine is the lordosis often exaggerated as an irregular spinal curve?
    a. Cervical
    b. Thoracic
    c. Lumbar
    d. Sacral

44. In order to be stratified as low risk, a client must meet which of the following conditions?
    I. Male less than forty-five years of age or female less than fifty-five years
    II. Asymptomatic
    III. Have no risk factors for cardiovascular or pulmonary disease
    IV. Have one risk factor for cardiovascular or pulmonary disease
    a. I and III only
    b. II and III only
    c. I, II, and III
    d. I, II, and IV

45. Which type of diabetes results from little to no insulin production?
    a. Type I
    b. Type II
    c. Both Type I and Type II
    d. Neither Type I nor Type II

46. Which of the following is NOT an absolute indication to terminate an exercise test?
    a. New chest pain
    b. Cyanosis
    c. Client's request to stop
    d. Increasing chest discomfort

47. Tom is a new client. He is forty-two years old, a non-smoker, and enjoys golfing. He is healthy except for mild lateral epicondylitis and takes a beta-blocker. He has done his initial interview, clearance, and assessments. Which of the following guidelines would you give him for target effort range for his cardiovascular workouts for gains in aerobic fitness?
    a. Aim for twelve to fifteen RPE
    b. Aim for fifteen to eighteen RPE
    c. Aim for a heart rate of 106-142 bpm
    d. Aim for a heart rate of 150-180 bpm

48. In which order would a strength coach recommend administering the following assessments?
    a. Skinfold, push-up test, step test, 1RM bench press, sit-and-reach
    b. Skinfold, step test, push-up test, 1RM bench press, sit-and-reach
    c. Skinfold, sit-and-reach, step test, 1RM bench press, push-up test
    d. Skinfold, 1RM bench press, push-up test, step test, sit-and-reach

49. How often is reassessment of fitness testing recommended?
    a. Every two to three weeks
    b. Annually
    c. Every three to four months
    d. Every four to twelve weeks

50. Tim is a twenty-one-year-old college student who plays on the baseball team. He is coming to you for strengthening. He is 70 inches tall and weighs 160 pounds. He doesn't smoke, and both parents are healthy. He was diagnosed with Type 1 Diabetes at age eight, but his blood glucose is normal with insulin injections. His blood pressure is 105/68 mmHg, and his total cholesterol is 170 mg/dL. He reports no symptoms and can train after practice and on weekends.
In what risk category is Tim?
   a. No risk
   b. Low risk
   c. Moderate risk
   d. High risk

51. Sarah is a twenty-three-year-old client, who lives with both parents. She is 64 inches tall and weighs 128 pounds. Her blood pressure today is 116/75 mmHg, and her total cholesterol is 170 mg/dL. LDL is 120, and blood glucose is 82 mg/dL. She dances or plays volleyball most days of the week and smokes, but only on the weekends with friends.
How many risk factors for CAD does Sarah have?
   a. Zero
   b. One
   c. Two
   d. Three

52. Tina is a fifty-eight-year-old sedentary female coming to you to "get in shape" since she "hasn't worked out since college." She is 180 pounds and 5'4," with a BMI of 30.9. She has no personal history of heart disease and quit smoking three years ago, but her mother had a myocardial infarction at the age of sixty-six. Tina's blood pressure is consistently 135/85 mm Hg, total cholesterol is 180 mg/dL with an HDL level of 30 mg/dL, and fasting blood glucose is 90 mg/dL.
How many risk factors for CAD does Tina have?
   a. Two
   b. Three
   c. Four
   d. Five

53. Which of the following skinfolds sites should be taken with a diagonal pinch/fold?
   a. Thigh
   b. Sub-scapula
   c. Triceps
   d. Abdomen

54. Which of the following is possibly a marker seen in someone with a risk of metabolic disease?
   a. Female waist circumference > 85 cm
   b. Triglyceride levels of 160 mg/dL
   c. HDL cholesterol of 50 mg/dL
   d. Fasting glucose levels of 105 mg/dL

55. Balance is facilitated by ____________ the base of support and ___________ the center of mass.
   a. widening, lowering
   b. widening, raising
   c. lowering, widening
   d. raising, raising

Program Design

56. Before designing a training program for a client, what step should the personal trainer take to get useful information about the client and his or her fitness goals?
   a. Create a long-term plan
   b. Begin selecting exercises
   c. Perform a needs analysis
   d. Determine the client's rate of perceived exertion

57. Which of the following shows the correct dynamic correspondence and training volume?
   a. 120 to 140 repetitions of lower-body plyometrics for a beginner basketball player
   b. 80 to 100 repetitions of upper-body plyometrics for a beginner baseball player
   c. 100 to 120 repetitions of lower-body plyometrics for an advanced volleyball player
   d. 80 to 100 repetitions of upper-body plyometrics for an intermediate soccer player

58. A client is performing three sets of chest presses with six repetitions per set. Using the two-for-two rule, how should the client increase his or her training load?
   a. By performing eight repetitions on the third set for the next two training sessions
   b. By performing five sets of six repetitions for the next two sessions
   c. By adding two additional training sessions every two weeks
   d. By performing the eccentric and concentric phases of the chest press for two seconds each

59. A 69-year-old woman would like to begin a resistance training program and knows that her physical inactivity has resulted in strength loss but does not know if it has impacted her bone mineral density. A bone density scan showed that her bone mineral density level was 1.5 standard deviations below the bone mineral density of young adults. Based on these results, what condition is the women experiencing?
   a. Reduced neuromotor functioning
   b. Osteopenia
   c. Sarcopenia
   d. Osteoporosis

60. Which physiological adaptation is expected after a client has participated in an aerobic-training program?
   a. Heart rate reserve decreases and resting-heart rate increases
   b. Heart rate reserve increases and resting-heart rate decreases
   c. Heart rate reserve increases and resting-heart rate increases
   d. Heart rate reserve decreases and resting-heart rate decreases

61. Which of the following statements about rest periods is FALSE?
    a. Longer rest periods promote nervous-system recovery
    b. Longer rest periods promote muscular-system recovery
    c. Longer rest periods promote cardiovascular conditioning
    d. Shorter rest periods promote cardiovascular conditioning

62. Which of the following is the method for organizing the strength program and preplanning a client's training load and volume to improve his or her physical ability over a certain amount of time?
    a. Training macrocycle
    b. Mesocycle
    c. Preparatory phase
    d. Periodization

63. Which of the following statements about kinetic chain movements is true?
    a. Pull-ups are a closed kinetic chain movement.
    b. Hamstring curls are a closed kinetic chain movement.
    c. Lunges are an open kinetic chain movement.
    d. Leg extensions are a closed kinetic chain movement.

64. A client wants to increase muscular hypertrophy for a bodybuilding competition. How many repetitions and exercises should be assigned to optimize success in the stated goal?
    a. Six to twelve repetitions per set; three exercises per muscle group
    b. Two to four repetitions per set; three exercises per muscle group
    c. Fifteen repetitions per set; three exercises per muscle group
    d. Six to twelve repetitions per set; one exercise per muscle group

65. Which of the following is true regarding muscle balance?
    a. The strength in opposing muscle groups must be equalized.
    b. The strength ratios in antagonist muscle groups must be improved.
    c. Muscle balance is not an integral part of a strength-training program.
    d. Even if a client has improper muscle balance, the body will maintain its normal movement patterns during exercises.

66. Which type of exercises give muscle tissue the most stimulation and are beneficial for limited training time, and which type of exercises involve the core muscles and should be the basis of training programs?
    a. Multi-joint; Assistance
    b. Structural; Primary
    c. Primary; Assistance
    d. Multi-joint; Structural

67. A client has limited time to train. She wants to improve mental focus and lose body fat. Which type of training would benefit her most?
    a. Split-routine training
    b. 1-RM
    c. Circuit training
    d. Percentage-based training

68. A client would like to improve strength and power for a weightlifting competition. In which order should she complete the following exercises?

I. Olympic lifts
II. Back extensions
III. Biceps curls

a. I, II, III
b. II, I, III
c. III, II, I
d. II, III, I

69. Which of the following agility-drill classifications is correctly matched with its description?
a. Serial drills combine continuous and discrete drills and are sport-specific.
b. Discrete drills are continuous in nature and are useful for developing running and jumping skills.
c. Continuous drills are helpful for developing specific movement patterns.
d. Continuous drills can make clients stronger and more powerful.

70. Which of the following is NOT an appropriate progression method for promoting physiological adaptations in a client during the training phase?
a. Increasing training-load intensities to improve speed
b. Increasing training density
c. Increasing training volume
d. Changing the duration of rest between sets

71. Which of the following approaches should be used to help a client recover from previous training sessions and improve neural patterns while promoting supercompensation?
a. Linear periodization
b. Unloading/deloading week
c. Undulating/nonlinear periodization
d. Rehabilitation

72. Which of the following exercises would help a client restore neuromuscular control after an injury?
a. Doing bodyweight squats on a flat surface
b. Jumping on a flat surface
c. Doing push-ups on a flat surface
d. Jumping on a trampoline

73. Which of the following movement combinations would be most appropriate for a complex-training model?
a. Bench press at 80% to 90% for two to three reps; plyometric push-ups for three to five reps
b. Chest press at 50% to 60% for fifteen to twenty reps; bodyweight sit-ups for twenty-five reps
c. Back squats at 70% for twelve to fifteen reps; maximum-height box jumps for six to eight reps
d. Leg press at 70% for twelve to fifteen reps; bodyweight calf raises for twenty-five reps

74. A marathon runner scores in the 40th percentile for 1RM bench press and the 70th percentile for VO_2 max, based on a 1.5-mile run. Which of the following should a trainer emphasize in a training program?
   a. Upper body strength
   b. Cardiovascular endurance
   c. Lower body strength
   d. Upper body endurance

75. Which of the following statements is true about recovery time and training frequency for endurance clients?
   a. Clients training at a low intensity need the same number of training sessions but more recovery time than those training at a high intensity.
   b. Clients training at a high intensity need the same number of training sessions but more recovery time than those training at a low intensity.
   c. Both clients participating in high-intensity training and those doing low-intensity training need the same amount of recovery time.
   d. Clients who are doing high-intensity training sessions should get more time to recover and should train less frequently than low-intensity clients.

76. Interval training for aerobic clients and anaerobic clients is similar in which way?
   a. Intervals last the same amount of time for aerobic and anaerobic clients.
   b. Rest periods last the same amount of time for aerobic and anaerobic clients.
   c. Both types of clients are training at higher levels of intensity compared with their VO_2 max.
   d. Both types of clients use a 2:1 work-to-rest ratio.

77. When a client performs biceps curls, which of the following is true regarding the phases of the stretch-shortening cycle?
   a. When the client raises the weight, the biceps are in the eccentric phase.
   b. The amortization phase is between the eccentric phase and the concentric phase.
   c. When the client lowers the weight, the biceps are in the concentric phase.
   d. The client is in the amortization phase after he or she begins the biceps curl.

78. What is true about muscle spindles?
   a. They are the most important feature in the stretch-reflex response.
   b. They are the primary baroreceptive structures in the muscle.
   c. They are sensitive to concentric muscle action.
   d. They are the secondary proprioceptive structures in the muscle.

79. What is the Karvonen method?
   a. When age is used to predict maximum heart rate
   b. When age is used to calculate target heart rate
   c. When resting heart rate is used to predict maximum heart rate
   d. When resting heart rate is used to calculate target heart rate

Exercise Technique and Training Instruction

80. Which of the following is NOT a benefit of resistance machines?
    a. They can be used easily without a spotter
    b. They can be particularly helpful for newer clients to learn proper form and control the motion within the desired plane of movement
    c. They can improve sports-specific movements and strength, incorporating core stability
    d. Clients can often lift higher maximal weights and isolate specific muscles, improving absolute strength

81. Benefits of the Valsalva maneuver include all EXCEPT which of the following?
    a. It increases blood pressure.
    b. It increases torso rigidity.
    c. It decreases compressive forces on the intervertebral disks.
    d. It supports the normal lordotic lumbar spine.

82. Box jumps, depth jumps, and medicine ball throws are examples of what type of training?
    a. Plyometrics
    b. Agility exercises
    c. Non-traditional modalities
    d. Speed training

83. During agility exercises, weight should be concentrated on what part of the foot?
    a. Forefoot
    b. Midfoot
    c. Hind foot
    d. Heel

84. Incorporating yoga training into a client's regimen can be beneficial in all BUT which of the following ways?
    a. It improves core strength.
    b. It improves flexibility.
    c. It improves mental focus and relaxation.
    d. It improves absolute strength.

85. Which of the following exercises would help an athlete restore neuromuscular control after an injury?
    a. Doing bodyweight squats on a flat surface
    b. Jumping on a flat surface
    c. Doing push-ups on a flat surface
    d. Jumping on a trampoline

86. What is the most challenging part of a strength exercise called?
    a. Eccentric phase
    b. Concentric phase
    c. Sticking point
    d. Maximal point

87. For most strength exercises, which of the following breathing patterns is optimal?
    a. Inhaling through the mouth during the concentric phase and exhale through the nose during the eccentric phase
    b. Exhaling through the mouth during the concentric phase and inhale through the nose during the eccentric phase
    c. Inhaling through the nose during the concentric phase and exhale through the mouth during the eccentric phase
    d. Exhaling through the nose in the concentric phase and inhale through the mouth during the eccentric phase

88. Mirrors and video analysis can be helpful in which of the following ways?
    a. Correcting improper form
    b. Allowing a trainer to focus less on monitoring clients
    c. Correcting improper technique
    d. Providing visual feedback regarding form and technique

89. After doing chest presses, an athlete complains of soreness, stiffness, and lower performance. What advice could a strength and conditioning professional give him?
    a. "You have trained too hard and will not be able to increase your performance beyond this point."
    b. "Keep training as hard as possible and eliminate your recovery time so that your body will experience super-compensation more rapidly."
    c. "You are experiencing the first phase of GAS. If you give your body time to recover, your symptoms will improve and you will eventually become stronger and have more muscle mass."
    d. "You're in the alarm phase of GAS. You should stop your training immediately and see a physician."

90. Depth achieved during a squat is often limited by which of the following?
    a. Knee injuries
    b. Hamstring tightness
    c. Achilles tendon tightness
    d. Gastrocnemius (calf) weakness

91. When using free weights, how many points of contact should be made for supine and seated exercises?
    a. 2
    b. 3
    c. 4
    d. 5

92. Which direction should the palms face when using a supinated grip?
    a. Upward toward the face
    b. Downwards toward the feet
    c. Inward toward the hips
    d. Out laterally away from the body

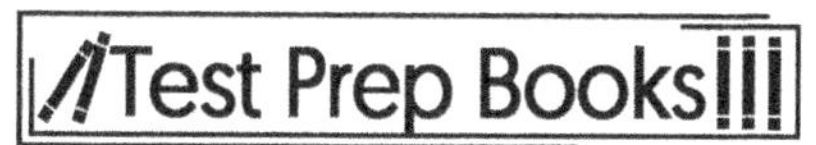

93. Negative resistance training is best described as which of the following?
    a. Reducing training volume prior to competition to taper and improve performance
    b. A detraining effect that occurs when clients fail to train with high enough frequency
    c. Lifting heavier weights on the lowering, eccentric portion and getting assistance during the lifting, concentric phase
    d. Lifting heavier weights on the lifting, concentric portion and getting assistance during the lowering, eccentric phase

94. Benefits of bodyweight exercises include all BUT which of the following?
    a. They increase relative strength
    b. They increase absolute strength
    c. They can be performed on the field or away from the gym
    d. Clients can often complete many repetitions, improving muscular endurance

95. What is the name for the grip pattern where palms face the floor and the knuckles face the ceiling?
    a. Pronated grip
    b. Supinated grip
    c. Hook grip
    d. False grip

96. Golgi tendon organs are stimulated in PNF stretching and cause relaxation of which of the following?
    a. The antagonist muscle by its own contraction
    b. The stretched muscle by its own contraction
    c. The antagonist muscle by contracting the stretched muscle
    d. The stretched muscle by contracting the antagonist muscle

97. Activation of muscle spindles is decreased in which of the following stretching methods?
    a. Dynamic
    b. Passive
    c. Static
    d. PNF

98. In order of decreasing percentage of total training volume, for a distance runner's program, which of the following would you suggest for the given activities?
    a. Cardiovascular/metabolic conditioning, muscular endurance, agility training, plyometrics
    b. Cardiovascular/metabolic conditioning, muscular endurance, plyometrics, agility training
    c. Cardiovascular/metabolic conditioning, agility training, muscular endurance, plyometrics
    d. Cardiovascular/metabolic conditioning, plyometrics, muscular endurance, agility training

99. In order of decreasing frequency for a tennis player's training program, which of the following should be suggested for the given activities?
    a. Speed training, cardiovascular conditioning, plyometrics, agility training
    b. Cardiovascular conditioning, speed training, agility training, plyometrics
    c. Cardiovascular conditioning, agility training, speed training, plyometrics
    d. Agility training, speed training, plyometrics, cardiovascular conditioning

100. During a heavy front-loaded squat, there should be how many spotter(s) positioned in what location(s)?
   a. One spotter should be in the middle of the bar in front of the lifter.
   b. One spotter should be in the middle of the bar behind the lifter.
   c. One spotter should be on either end of the bar, for a total of two spotters.
   d. One spotter should be in front of and one spotter should be behind the lifter, for a total of two spotters.

101. Which of the following is the correct protocol for the hold-relax PNF technique?
   a. 10-second passive pre-stretch, isometric contraction for 6 seconds, passive stretch for 30 seconds
   b. 10-second passive pre-stretch, isometric contraction for 6 seconds, passive stretch for 10 seconds
   c. 6-second passive pre-stretch, isometric contraction for 10 seconds, passive stretch for 30 seconds
   d. 6-second passive pre-stretch, isometric contraction for 10 seconds, passive stretch for 10 seconds

102. Benefits of static stretching include all EXCEPT which of the following?
   a. It improves muscle-joint tension relationship
   b. It can warm up muscles prior to workout
   c. It can increase joint laxity
   d. It can reduce risk of injury

103. With which of the following clients should you use extra precaution when programming plyometric exercises?
   a. A distance runner
   b. A 250-pound lineman
   c. A female client
   d. A figure skater

104. Which of the following anatomic structures detects rapid movement and initiates the stretch reflex?
   a. Extrafusal muscle fibers
   b. Mechanoreceptors
   c. Golgi tendon organs
   d. Muscle spindles

105. Static stretches should be held for about how many seconds and performed for how many sets?
   a. Thirty seconds, two to three sets
   b. Thirty seconds, three to five sets
   c. Ten seconds, two to three sets
   d. Ten seconds, three to five sets

106. Correct spotting position includes all BUT which of the following?
   a. Knees locked
   b. Feet flat on the floor
   c. Hands up in ready position
   d. Erect, neutral spine

107. Clear verbal instructions that instruct clients on the proper form of a new exercise are an example of which type of cueing technique?
   a. Visual
   b. Kinesthetic
   c. Comprehensive
   d. Auditory

108. Which term refers to intermittent assessments that measure a client's progress throughout a fitness program?
   a. Reassessments
   b. Screening assessments
   c. Program assessments
   d. Performance assessments

Professional Development and Responsibility

109. Which of the following is within the scope of practice of a certified personal trainer?
   a. Diagnosing a meniscal tear
   b. Making a customized nutrition plan for a client
   c. Giving a cross-friction massage for scar tissue
   d. Teaching the client exercises to do during work travel assignments

110. Recertification occurs every _________ years, and you need _______ CECs.
   a. two, 2.0
   b. three, 2.0
   c. two, 20
   d. three, 20

111. What kind of insurance protects against claims of libel, slander, and invasion of privacy?
   a. Personal injury liability
   b. Professional liability
   c. Commercial liability
   d. Negligence liability

112. Which of the following is one of the benefits of obtaining certification as an NASM personal trainer?
   a. You do not need to purchase liability insurance.
   b. Insurance companies recognize the certification and offer liability insurance.
   c. Certification comes with liability insurance as long as you maintain CPR/AED certification.
   d. You earn CECs for purchasing liability insurance.

113. Which of the following defines individually identifiable health information such as demographics, prior and current health history, social security number, etc.?

a. Health Insurance Portability and Accountability Act (HIPAA)
b. Health Insurance Portability and Privacy Act (HIPPA)
c. Family Exercise Rights and Privacy Act (FERPA)
d. Family Educational Rights and Privacy Act (FERPA)

114. When establishing a fee structure for services, it is helpful for trainers to do which of the following?

a. Charge as much as possible so you can work less
b. Explore what other trainers with similar education and experience are charging in the area
c. Survey friends or prospective clients about how much they are willing to pay
d. Have different prices for each client

115. To reduce liability risk, trainers should do all of the following EXCEPT?

a. Adhere to NASM risk stratification and guidelines for clearance and medical supervision
b. Rehearse emergency action plans and maintain CPR certification
c. Abide by the NASM Scope of Practice for certified personal trainers and adhere to the Code of Ethics
d. Model healthy lifestyle and behavior choices

116. To be stratified as low risk, a client must meet which of the following conditions?

I. Males less than forty-five years of age or females less than fifty-five years
II. Asymptomatic
III. Have no risk factors for cardiovascular or pulmonary disease
IV. Have one risk factor for cardiovascular or pulmonary disease

a. I and III only
b. II and III only
c. I, II, and III
d. I, II, and IV

117. Which of the following statements is true about medical clearance prior to participating in an exercise training program?

a. All clients need medical clearance from a physician prior to participation in an exercise training program.
b. Only clients with diagnosed cardiovascular, respiratory, or metabolic diseases need clearance prior to participation.
c. Children, adolescents, men less than forty-five years, and women less than fifty-five years who do not have CAD risk factors or symptoms, known disease, and who did not answer "yes" to any questions on the PAR-Q do not need clearance.
d. Children, adolescents, men less than fifty years, and women less than fifty-five years who do not have CAD risk factors or symptoms, known disease, and who did not answer "yes" to any questions on the PAR-Q do not need clearance.

118. When a certified personal trainer fails to perform what is typically considered to be a standard practice of care, it may be deemed to be which of the following?

a. Negligence
b. Malpractice
c. Liability
d. Scope of Practice

119. What pieces of equipment should be evaluated prior to every single use?

I. Medicine balls
II. Exercise bands
III. Cables on weight machines
IV. Emergency stop buttons on cardio equipment

a. All of the above
b. I, III, IV
c. II, III, IV
d. III, IV

120. Which of the following could breach the safety of privacy for paper client files?

a. Locking up paper files
b. Scanning and making digital copies for the facility computer
c. Carrying the paper file on your clipboard during sessions and keeping it on your person at all times
d. Making sure keys are only given to authorized individuals

Answer Explanations #1

Basic and Applied Sciences and Nutritional Concepts

1. B: A D-line in not a component of a sarcomere. Sarcomeres are the smallest functional unit of a muscle and contain the actin and myosin proteins responsible for the mechanical process of muscle contractions. Sarcomeres are divided into sections or regions based on the presence of the contractile proteins. The A-band, H-zone, I-band, and Z-line are defined regions within a sarcomere.

2. B: Tennis requires significant involvement of both Type I (slow-twitch) and Type II (fast-twitch) muscle fibers. Type I muscle fibers have a high capacity for aerobic energy supply and are fatigue-resistant—two traits that allow the player to maintain performance levels over multiple sets. Type II muscle fibers are easily fatigable but are capable of high force development, which is beneficial for short sprints to the ball, etc. Large locomotor muscles, such as the quadriceps, have a mixture of Type I and Type II fibers.

3. D: Muscle fibers (myocytes) are long, striated, cylindrical cells that are approximately the diameter of a human hair (50–100 micrometers), are multinucleated, and are covered by a fibrous membrane called the sarcolemma, which is similar in function to the cell membrane of other animal cells. Myofibrils, one of the smaller functional units within a myocyte, consist of long, thin (approximately 1 micrometer) chain proteins. The smallest functional unit of a muscle fiber, a sarcomere, contains the actin and myosin protein filaments that are responsible for the mechanical process of muscle contractions.

4. D: Sodium bicarbonate, a very effective base, functions chiefly to increase the pH of the chyme. Chyme leaving the stomach has a very low pH due to the high amounts of acid that are used to digest and break down food. If this is not neutralized, the walls of the small intestine will be damaged and may form ulcers. Sodium bicarbonate is produced by the pancreas and released in response to pyloric stimulation so that it can neutralize the acid. It has little to no digestive effect.

5. A: The three primary body planes are coronal, sagittal, and transverse. The coronal or frontal plane, named for the plane in which a corona or halo might appear in old paintings, divides the body vertically into front and back sections. The sagittal plane, named for the path an arrow might take when shot at the body, divides the body vertically into right and left sections. The transverse plane divides the body horizontally into upper or superior and lower or inferior sections. There is no medial plane, per se. The anatomical direction medial simply references a location close or closer to the center of the body than another location.

6. C: Capillaries are responsible for the exchange of nutrients, hormones, oxygen, fluids, and electrolytes between the blood and interstitial fluid in tissues. Hemoglobin helps carry oxygen and iron in circulating red blood cells. Arterioles and venules are intermediately-sized blood vessels, but their walls are too thick for cellular-level exchange.

7. A: During the excitation-contraction coupling phase, an electrical discharge at the muscle starts a series of chemical events on the surface of muscle cells. This causes the release of calcium ions (CA^{2+}) from the sarcoplasmic reticulum, resulting in the increase in intracellular calcium, which helps the myosin globular heads attach to the thin actin filaments.

8. C: Heavy breathing requires the movement of the ribs to accommodate lung expansion. The muscles that help to elevate the ribs during inspiration are the external intercostals, sternocleidomastoids, anterior serrati, and scalenes. The rectus abdominis consists of two superficial abdominal muscles that do not affect rib movement.

9. C: When sufficient oxygen is available, pyruvate is transported to the mitochondrial matrix to take part in the Krebs cycle. Pyruvate is converted to acetyl-coenzyme A (acetyl-CoA) by pyruvate dehydrogenase, resulting in the loss of CO_2, and the acetyl-CoA enters the Krebs cycle to resynthesize ATP. Under anaerobic conditions, fermentation occurs, pyruvate is converted to lactate, and NADH is reduced to NAD+

10. A: Cortisol is a glucocorticoid secreted by the adrenal cortex. The other structures listed also secrete hormones, but not cortisol.

11. B: Beta-alanine is the specific nonessential amino acid that must be present for the development of carnosine. Histidine is a component of carnosine; carnosine and leucine are not required for the development of carnosine.

12. A: Growth hormone concentration levels can be increased acutely by performing three high-intensity sets of each resistance exercise with short rest periods between sets.

13. B: Ankle inversion helps expose the inside of the foot for an adequate kicking surface, which is required for soccer dribbling. Inversion takes place in the frontal plane, which runs through the center of the body from side to side, dividing the body into front and back halves.

14. A:

Name of Fascicular Arrangement	Structure of Fascicular Arrangement	Muscle Example
Circular	Fascicles are arranged in a concentric ring	Orbicularis oris (muscles surrounding mouth)
Convergent (sometimes called radiate)	Muscle has a broad origin and is fan- or triangular-shaped	Pectoralis major; gluteus medius
Parallel/longitudinal	Long axis of fascicles is parallel to long axis of muscle	Rectus abdominis
Unipennate	Short fascicles insert obliquely into only one side of tendon	Extensor digitorum longus; tibialis posterior
Bipennate	Fascicles insert into opposite sides of one central tendon	Rectus femoris
Multipennate	Tendon branches within the muscle	Deltoid
Fusiform	Spindle-shaped muscles	Biceps brachii

15. C: The characteristics of mechanical load that stimulate bone growth are the speed of loading, the intensity of the load, and the direction of the force. In accordance to Wolff's Law, bone adapts to the stresses or lack thereof) placed upon it. The load type is not identified as a specific component of the mechanical load that is needed to stimulate bone growth.

16. B: Power (measured in watts [W]) is the rate that work is performed and, accordingly, is calculated as work divided by time. Power can also be calculated as the force applied to an object multiplied by velocity. Choice *A,* force × distance, is the equation for work.

17. D: The phosphagen system is the primary energy system stressed when using a work-to-rest ratio of 1:12 to 1:20. Additionally, an exercise duration of 5–10 seconds that uses 90–100% of maximum effort is used to stress this system. Energy is rapidly generated with this system because there are very few steps in the process, but only a small amount of energy is released, which is why exercise duration fueled with this pathway is so brief.

18. C: Branched-chain amino acids and caffeine is the best answer choice, since the other options do not represent combinations of ergogenic aids that are used to delay fatigue. Sodium tablets help to prevent hyponatremia during exercise. Glutamine is used typically to help prevent illness and infection and reduce or prevent muscle soreness. Sports beverages are used for hydration and the prevention of hyponatremia and fatigue; however, caffeine is used as a stimulant to enhance endurance, increase alertness, and reduce muscle soreness.

Client Relations and Behavioral Coaching

19. B: There are a variety of things the trainers can do to provide a positive, supportive training environment such as giving encouraging feedback and reinforcement that is frequent and timely. Trainers should help clients set SMART goals, identify sources of intrinsic and extrinsic motivational aids, help the client form a dependable support system, and identify and tackle barriers to adherence.

20. D: Motivational interviewing asks clients to reflect on what may happen if they do not change their current habits and weigh the pros and cons of activity and inactivity. It involves acknowledging and slowly working through a client's challenges concerning regular activity and stressing the fact that it is the individual's choice to be active.

21. A: As a client's fitness level improves, the act of exercising becomes less painful and more internally rewarding, so sources of external motivation may become less important. Intrinsic rewards are ones the client feels directly from the exercise itself and remain important long after goal achievement. They include things such as improved self-esteem or fitting into his or her favorite jeans. Intrinsically motivated clients, or those with self-determination, enjoy the process of the exercise itself, which tends to help them may maintain their health behaviors more easily than externally motivated clients, who exercise for the sake of achieving some sort of reward.

22. C: Visual learners ideally learn through observing, so Choice *C* would be best for these individuals. Kinesthetic learners learn best through movement, physical involvement, and experience. Trainers working with kinesthetic learners should demonstrate an exercise and then have the client try a simplified version of the movement such as completing an unweighted repetition of the exercise or moving through a partial range of motion. Before trying the full resistance or movement, these intermediate steps can demonstrate understanding while reducing injury risk. Auditory learners grasp information best through listening.

23. C: When using active listening, trainers try to understand the underlying meaning of what a client is saying and then demonstrate this understanding by paraphrasing and then confirming comprehension. Choice *C* is a good example of active listening because the trainer hears that the client is looking to lose

a little weight and get in better shape, and then confirms understanding by paraphrasing this back to the client in question form. Choices *A*, *B*, and *D* do not use active listening and may display lack of empathy, especially in the case of choice *D*, which comes across as somewhat harsh.

24. B: This is an example of supportive feedback, which is a means of encouraging the client, particularly during difficult parts of a workout. Evaluative feedback helps the client understand what parts of a particular movement he or she is mastering and to make improvements on incorrect movements or form during the learning process. Descriptive feedback is provided at the completion of a movement or workout in a concise fashion, providing a summary of what was observed and what can be improved or changed in subsequent efforts. Corrective feedback should be given to a client immediately, especially if something is unsafe.

25. A: This is an example of evaluative feedback, which is a means of encouraging the client during challenging parts of a workout. This type of feedback guides the client to make improvements with form or movements and fosters a greater understanding of what parts he or she is mastering in a given exercise or workout.

26. D: Obese. John's BMI is 30.1 kg/m^2 which puts him in the obese category (greater than 30 kg/m^2). The BMI categories are: Underweight = BMI of less than 18.5, Normal weight = 18.5 to 24.9, Overweight = 25 to 29.9, Obesity = BMI of 30 or greater.

27. D: Feedback should be timely and given as soon as possible after movement assessment while it is still fresh in the client's mind. Options *B* and *C* are incorrect because the trainer should give feedback more often than just after assessments or sporadically. Feedback provides motivation and when it is descriptive, corrective, or evaluative, it provides education and helps the client to improve. Option *A* is not necessarily wrong, but should just occur more than after every session, including after assessments as well as individual exercises within a given workout.

28. B: Programmatic barriers include not knowing how to structure a workout or what exercises to perform and in what way; previously attempting programs that were too hard, causing injury, frustration, or burnout; or programs that were too time-consuming, causing the client to feel like a failure. On the opposite end of the spectrum, programs that are not challenging enough can also cause boredom and lead to staleness, leading to program abandonment. By designing customized, appropriately challenging, and varied exercise programs, trainers can help keep clients engaged and improving towards their goals.

29. A: The Socio-Ecological Model addresses relationships and considers that behaviors, such as a client's motivation to exercise, are influenced by interpersonal relations in the surrounding environment, community, policy, and law. Using this model, trainers can improve program adherence by ensuring the client has a good social support system such as an exercise buddy and an environment conducive to exercise such as a gym in a convenient location or a recreational sports league close to work.

30. A: Goals that are not challenging enough have a tendency to cause the client's motivation to drop. Trainer should help clients set a mixture of both short-term and long-term goals. The risk of major relapses in healthy behaviors can be reduced by assuring clients that short lapses are inevitable and should not be considered failures, ensuring the social support system is positive and consistent, and making a list of possible causes of relapses and using the list to brainstorm solutions for when such issues arise.

31. A: There cannot really be too much intrinsic motivation, and the more intrinsic motivation clients have, the more likely they are to continue with their healthy behavior.

32. D: Establishing a points system to win prizes after completing sessions each week is an example of a good external reward system for Tina. Because she is new to exercising, extrinsic rewards (factors outside of the exercise itself that help to support the desire to be physically active), may be especially important because the exercise itself is more painful and, because of discomfort and lack of fitness, less rewarding in and of itself. Extrinsic rewards include things like a free T-shirt or iTunes gift card for workout music after completing a certain number of sessions. S.M.A.R.T. goals should be set as well, and reduced session fees may work. However, twenty sessions is a lot when a new client is struggling to get through each one. Neither of these choices is likely to be as good a motivating factor initially as the points system because they may feel intangible. Reminding her of the benefits of exercise and the risks of inactivity is an intrinsic reward and likely more motivating later on.

33. B: The Social Cognitive Theory states that behavioral change is influenced by the triad of interactions of the environment, personal factors, and behavior itself. Trainers can help clients develop self-regulatory strategies such as self-monitoring physical activity and setting personal goals and rewards, planning activity in advance, and having reasonable expectations. The trainer should help the client build self-efficacy.

34. B: Choice *B* affirms the connection between positive habits and negative habits in the formation of healthier habits, which is an integral part of habit stacking. New positive habits are attached, or stacked, to old negative habits, which leads to a healthier overall lifestyle for clients. Choices *A* and *D* are incorrect because habit stacking involves lifestyle choices, like eating more vegetables or drinking more water, rather than the design of fitness programs. Choice *C* is incorrect because habit stacking involves both preexisting negative behaviors and new, positive behaviors.

35. B: Choice *B* establishes the connection between behavior and brain function, which is central to synaptic pruning. Choice *A* is incorrect because synaptic pruning does not directly affect the regulation of nutrients. Choice *C* is incorrect because connections are maintained between parts of the brain responsible for both negative and positive behaviors. Choice *D* is incorrect because synaptic pruning does not directly influence protein structures.

36. C: Choice *C* articulates a proactive strategy for managing client expectations. Trust is the key to managing client expectations, and trainers who take the time to notify clients of interruptions go a long way to build trust with their clients. Choice *A* is incorrect because trainers should never prioritize one client's sessions over another client's sessions. Choice *B* is incorrect because trainers devise fitness plans that balance client ambitions with attainable goals. Choice *D* is incorrect because trainers should remain realistic about the capacity of service they are humanly equipped to provide.

Assessment

37. A: The five main components of health-related physical fitness are cardiovascular fitness, muscular strength, muscular endurance, flexibility, and body composition. Muscular power is related to exercise

performance and is a measure of strength to speed. It isn't one of the five components of fitness that directly relates to health.

38. C: Clients who are apparently healthy are not required to get medical clearance prior to starting an exercise program. These include children, adolescents, men less than forty-five years, and women less than fifty-five years who do not have CAD risk factors or symptoms, any known disease, and who did not answer "yes" to any questions on the PAR-Q. Choices *A* and *B* are not correct, and *D* provides too high of an age cutoff for "apparently healthy males."

39. D: Risk stratification is not included on the trainer-client agreement. In fact, the agreement may be discussed and signed prior to stratifying the client. The personal trainer and client are under contract law, so the trainer-client agreement is a written document signed by both parties describing the services, the involved parties, and the expectations of each, as well as a timeline of delivery, cost, and payment including aspects such as the cancellation policy and contract termination.

40. A: Waist circumference greater than 100 cm or a BMI ≥ 30 kg/m^2 indicates obesity and meets the criteria as a positive risk factor of CAD. Although either alone counts as a positive risk factor, the trainer should bear in mind that the waist circumference is probably a greater warning sign since it is more directly assessing abdominal obesity (shown to be detrimental to health), while BMI can be elevated in muscular individuals and is looking at total body density, not abdominal size.

41. C: Current use of lipid-lowering medications is a positive sign of CAD, even if cholesterol levels are normalized with medication usage. Other positive signs include the following:

- Family history of myocardial infarction
- Coronary revascularization
- Sudden death in a first-degree relative before age fifty-five in males or sixty-five in females
- Cigarette smoking, current or past six months
- Taking anti-hypertensive medications or systolic blood pressure ≥ 140 mmHg or diastolic pressure ≥ 90 mmHg confirmed by at least two separate measurements on different occasions
- Total cholesterol > 200 mg/dL, LDL > 130 mg/dL or low HDL < 40 mg/dL
- Fasting blood glucose: ≥ 100 mg/dL confirmed by at least two separate measurements on different occasions
- Waist circumference of > 100cm (39 inches) or BMI ≥ 30 kg/m^2
- A sedentary lifestyle

42. D: Intermittent claudication is an achy, cramping feeling typically of the lower legs that may come and go with exercise due to occlusion of blood vessels. Edema is tissue swelling due to an imbalance between fluids coming out of circulation in blood vessels into tissues or back into circulation from tissue. Dizziness upon standing is orthostatic hypotension and may cause syncope. Delayed onset muscle soreness (DOMS) is microscopic tissue damage that appears twenty-four hours after exercise.

43. C: The lumbar and cervical spine both have natural lordotic curves, but the lumbar region may display pronounced lordosis beyond 60 degrees, which is deemed abnormal. Particularly with obesity prevalent in today's society, lumbar lordosis is seen more frequently. The thoracic and sacral spines display kyphotic curves.

44. D: I, II, and IV. A client is low risk if he/she has one or fewer risk factors. The client should still be asymptomatic and less than the age of forty-five or fifty-five for men and women, respectively. Option III is no risk factors, but the client can have up to one. Thus, all of the other choices are incorrect.

45. A: Type I Diabetes results from little to no insulin production from the beta cells in the pancreas. It is an autoimmune disease and typically diagnosed in childhood. Type II Diabetes is not a result of inadequate production of insulin; typically, there is a sufficient amount in circulation, but the cells are not responsive to it.

46. D: Increasing chest discomfort is a relative, not absolute, indication to terminate an exercise test. With absolute indications such as the three choices (new chest pain, cyanosis, and client's request to stop), the test must stop even if the client wants to continue, is near the end, or has not reached test termination criteria. The test may continue with relative indications so long as the client feels decent and the monitoring physician approves continuation.

47. A: RPE, or rate of perceived exertion, is a subjective measure of intensity given by the client during exercise, typically a number from six to twenty on the Borg Scale, with six being no effort and twenty indicating maximal effort. An RPE of twelve to sixteen has been shown to yield improvements in cardiovascular fitness. Because Tom is on a beta-blocker, which typically alters heart rate, the heart rate becomes an unreliable measure of exertion. Choice *B*, an RPE of fifteen to eighteen, is a greater intensity than recommended for aerobic exercise. It may be conditioning the anaerobic systems more and not be sustainable for the duration of the endurance bout.

48. D: Guidelines suggest this order:

1. Skinfold
2. 1RM bench press
3. Push-up test
4. Step test
5. Sit-and-reach

The reason there are guidelines for the order of assessments is to ensure that one assessment does not affect another. Measurements of physical attributes should be first since they don't cause fatigue. Agility tests come next, there were none listed in this practice question's answer choices. Muscular strength tests should follow to optimize peak strength before prematurely fatiguing muscles through drawn out muscular endurance tests like the push-up test. In this case, the muscular test is the 1RM bench press. While there should be a rest period following this assessment, note that since it's just "One Rep Max", it won't be too tiring nor will it be aerobic. Next comes sprint tests (none here), and then local muscular endurance tests. Push-ups are a principal example of this. After muscular endurance tests, anaerobic tests and then aerobic capacity tests should be conducted. Step tests are one of the latter. Finally, once the muscles have been given sufficient warm-up to prevent injury, flexibility tests should be performed.

49. D: Reassessment is recommended typically every four to twelve weeks, depending on the frequency of sessions, goal difficulty, and client personality. Trainers should be mindful of reassessing each component of fitness (cardiovascular, muscular strength and endurance, flexibility, and body composition), noting which areas need renewed focus and compare results to baseline. Choice *A*, every two to three weeks, is likely too short of an interval to notice progress and may result in disappointing

the client and reducing motivation and satisfaction. Choices *B* and *C* are too long of a timeframe between assessments, which can also reduce motivation and thwart goal drive because it feels "too far away."

50. D: Tim is high risk because he has a known metabolic disease—the Type 1 Diabetes. The other risk factors do not even factor into his stratification because having the disease automatically makes him high risk.

51. B: Sarah has one risk factor—the smoking. Her BMI is normal. She has no known family medical history and has healthy blood pressure and blood work. She is also active.

52. C: Tina has the following four risk factors: age (58 is greater than 55 years old), obesity (her BMI at 30.9 is greater than 30 kg/m^2), low HDL (< 40 mg/dL), and physical inactivity. Smoking is not a risk factor since she quit more than six months ago. Her blood pressure and fasting glucose are normal. Although her mother died of an MI, this does not count as a risk factor at age sixty-six.

53. B: The sub-scapula site is a diagonal fold on line connecting inferior angle of scapula to a point 0.8 inches from the medial border. The other three sites listed are vertical folds.

54. B: When triglycerides are greater than 150 mg/dL, it is considered a risk factor or symptom of metabolic disease. The waist circumference at 85 cm is less than the 88 cm risk factor, and the HDL at 50 mg/dL is higher than the 40 mg/dL cutoff, which is a good thing and therefore not considered a risk factor. The fasting blood glucose is less than 100 mg/dL, so it is also normal.

55. A: Balance is the ability to control the center of mass within the base of support without falling. The wider the base of support and the lower the center of gravity, the easier it is to maintain balance. Center of gravity is the location of a theoretical point that represents the total weight of an object. Base of support is the part of an object that serves as the supporting surface, often thought of as feet in contact with the ground. The base of support also refers to the area between the feet as well, not just the physical structures of the body in contact with the supporting surface. Choice *C* is incorrect because a person cannot easily widen the center of gravity of the body. The center is a fixed point, so it can be moved, but it cannot be expanded. Choices *B* and *D* are incorrect because raising the center of mass would make it harder to balance.

Program Design

56. C: The needs analysis will help to determine the types of movements and physical requirements of a client's fitness goals or sport, how much time he or she has to train for the sport, and whether the client is a beginner or advanced client. Based on this information, appropriate exercises for developing the specific skills that the client needs (i.e., dynamic correspondence) and be selected and the appropriate progression can be planned based on how much time he or she can dedicate to training.

57. B: Dynamic correspondence involves choosing an appropriate exercise for a client based on his or her sport. For this question, it is important to note that the number of repetitions for plyometric exercises is related to the skill level of the client. Beginner clients should perform 80 to 100 repetitions while intermediate and master clients should perform 100 to 120 repetitions and 120 to 140 repetitions, respectively. Lower-body plyometric exercises are beneficial for clients who need to sprint, jump, and make other forceful lower-body movements. Upper-body plyometrics are important for sports that require throwing, catching, tackling, and blocking.

58. A: The two-for-two rule provides a method for gradually increasing a client's strength-training load. Using this method, the client should add two repetitions to the last set for two training sessions in a row. Then, the training load can be increased during the following session. In this question, the client should add two repetitions to the third set. Therefore, he or she will do eight repetitions instead of six. The client should continue this pattern for two training sessions in a row before increasing the load.

59. B: A bone mineral density level between 1 and 2.5 standard deviations below the young adult comparator group indicates that the woman has osteopenia. Osteoporosis is defined as a bone mineral density of 2.5 or more standard deviations below the normal range for young adults. Sarcopenia refers to the loss of muscle mass, causing decreases in strength and power.

60. B: The heart rate reserve increases and the resting heart rate decreases. Heart-rate reserve is defined as the difference between the maximal heart rate and the resting heart rate. Even though heart rate initially increases during exercise, resting heart rate decreases as a person adapts to aerobic activity. As resting heart rate decreases, the heart rate reserve will increase because the difference between maximal and resting heart rate will increase.

61. C: Longer resting periods improve cardiovascular conditioning. When a client needs to improve cardiovascular conditioning, he or she may decrease resting time to bolster aerobic endurance.

62. D: Periodization involves planning and organizing a client's entire training program (strength training, range of motion, conditioning, sports drills, etc.) and planning the training loads and volumes to generate physiological changes in a certain amount of time. The training macrocycle represents the developmental goals for the client over the entire training program. The breaks the macrocycle into two- to six-week segments to reach specific training goals. The preparatory phase is the client's offseason or preseason period.

63. A: Open kinetic chain exercises allow the loaded limbs to move freely while closed kinetic chain exercises limit this movement. Pull-ups and lunges are closed kinetic chain exercises because the client cannot freely move his or her hands or feet when they are planted on the ground. Hamstring curls and leg extensions allow the limbs to swing freely, so these are open kinetic chain exercises.

64. A: Training for muscular hypertrophy requires six to twelve repetitions. Completing more than twelve repetitions improves muscle endurance, while doing fewer than six repetitions improves strength as long as the resistance lifted poses the appropriate challenge at the given repetition level. Using three different exercises per muscle group can significantly increase muscle growth.

65. B: Muscle balance is crucial for any strength-training program because a lack of balance causes the body to have abnormal movement patterns and increases the risk of injury. Creating muscle balance means to improve strength ratios between opposing muscle groups. An example of muscle balance is a 3:4 strength ratio between hamstrings and quadriceps.

66. D: Multi-joint exercises stimulate muscles the most and allow for the greatest amount of loading during resistance training. Primary exercises are core exercises that are sport-specific and involve large muscle groups and multiple joints. Structural exercises are core exercises that load the spine. Assistance exercises engage small muscle groups and single joints.

67. C: Circuit training improves mental focus and requires a client to do a variety of exercises (from most intense to least intense) with little rest in between sets. This training program improves cardiorespiratory function and has a high metabolic cost, which leads to increased body-fat loss.

68. A: Exercises should be ordered from most to least technical, with power movements first, core exercises second, and single-joint exercises last. Olympic lifts are power movements and require extensive technique, whereas biceps curls require little technique and involve a single joint.

69. A: Serial drills are sport-specific and combine continuous and discrete drills. Continuous drills have no beginning or end, and they are helpful for improving running and jumping. Discrete drills help to develop movement patterns and improve a client's strength and power.

70. A: Training intensity must be decreased to improve speed. Increasing training volume and changing the duration of rest periods between sets will also promote physical adaptations in the client.

71. B: The unloading/deloading week uses lower training volumes and decreases intensity so that the client can recover and be prepared for future training sessions. This training week allows the client to continue improving neural patterns and promotes supercompensation.

72. D: Doing exercises on an unstable or uneven surface (e.g., doing bodyweight squats or push-ups on a BOSU) helps to improve neuromuscular control by stimulating and challenging the nervous system in new ways, which necessitates adaptation.

73. A: The complex-training model combines heavy resistance training with intense plyometrics to challenge the nervous and musculoskeletal systems. Only answer Choice *A* combines a heavy resistance exercise (80% to 90%) with intense plyometrics.

74. B: A marathon runner requires a great deal of cardiovascular endurance. Even though this runner's score was relatively low for 1RM bench press (40th percentile vs. 70th), it is still more important to increase the runner's cardiovascular endurance, given the demands of the sport, compared to upper body strength. The 70th percentile leaves a large margin for improvement. Even though VO_2 max does have a large genetic component, it is likely that this runner can significantly improve marathon times by targeted endurance training. The need for upper body strength is much less important in distance running, although muscular endurance is important.

75. D: The greater the intensity of training, the more recovery time the client needs before the next training session. Therefore, clients training at high intensity should have fewer training sessions per week than clients training low intensities.

76. C: Interval training involves working at higher levels of intensity compared with one's VO_2 max. Interval lengths and rest periods are very different. Aerobic clients use a 1:1 work/rest ratio during interval training.

77. B: The amortization phase is the transition between the eccentric and concentric phases. A muscle shortens in the concentric phase and lengthens in the eccentric phase. When a client begins a biceps curl, this is the concentric phase. When he/she lowers the weight, this is the eccentric phase.

78. A: Muscle spindles are essential to the stretch-reflex response because they are the primary proprioceptive structures in the muscle. Muscle spindles respond to eccentric muscle action.

79. D: The Karvonen method allows for the calculation of target heart rate by using resting heart rate.

Exercise Technique and Training Instruction

80. C: Because resistance machines are often used in the seated position and they only allow movement in one given plane, the core does not need to work to stabilize the body and they do not improve sports-specific skills as well as free weights. Benefits of resistance machines include the fact that they can be used more easily without a spotter, they can be particularly helpful for newer clients to learn proper form and control the motion within the desired plane of movement, and due to the support they provide, clients can often lift higher maximal weights and isolate specific muscles, improving absolute strength.

81. A: The Valsalva maneuver can be used in certain core exercises, with care, as a way to increase torso rigidity to aid in support of the vertebral column, which lessens compressive forces on the intervertebral discs and supports the normal and neutral lordotic lumbar spine. Blood pressure can increase with the Valsalva maneuver, but this is not a benefit, and in fact, can cause undesirable dizziness and disorientation.

82. A: Box jumps, depth jumps, and medicine ball throws are examples of plyometrics. Agility exercises include things such as ladder drills and cones; non-traditional modalities might include kettlebells, heavy ropes, and tires; and speed training involves sprint training and foot drills.

83. A: During agility exercises, weight should be concentrated on the forefoot to allow for quick movements and changes in direction.

84. D: Incorporating yoga training into a client regimen can be beneficial for improving core strength, flexibility, and mental focus and relaxation. Because it involves bodyweight only, it improves relative strength but not absolute strength.

85. D: Doing exercises on an unstable or uneven surface (e.g., doing bodyweight squats or push-ups on a BOSU) helps to improve neuromuscular control by stimulating and challenging the nervous system in new ways, which necessitates adaptation.

86. C: The most challenging part of a strength exercise is called the sticking point. In a bench press, this is where the direction of the bar changes from coming down toward the chest to being pushed back up.

87. B: For most strength exercises, the client should exhale through the mouth during the concentric phase through the sticking point and then inhale through the nose during the eccentric phase. Breathing should be slow and controlled.

88. D: Mirrors and video analysis can be used to provide visual feedback regarding form and technique to guide corrections. They do not correct form or technique in and of themselves, but are useful tools to help identify such issues and begin the process of correcting improper technique. For safety and to reduce liability, strength trainers should always focus on monitoring clients.

89. C: This athlete's symptoms and history are consistent with GAS. GAS occurs when the body is subjected to external loading. Firstly, the athlete will experience soreness, stiffness, and decreased performance (alarm phase). Secondly, his body will return to normal (resistance phase). Thirdly, his body will adapt and his muscle mass and strength will increase (supercompensation phase).

90. C: Depth of squats is often limited by Achilles tendon tightness. For clients who are limited in squat depth due to tight Achilles tendons, elevating the heels on a weight plate or other incline will help achieve a deeper squat, despite limited range of motion in the ankles.

91. D: Exercises in the seated and supine positions require five points of contact for optimal body support: the head is firmly situated on the bench or back pad, the shoulders and upper back are evenly placed firmly on the bench or back pad, the buttocks are positioned evenly on the bench or seat, and both feet are placed flat on the floor.

92. A: In a supinated grip, palms face upward toward the face and knuckles face the floor. In a pronated grip, knuckles are up and palms face the floor.

93. C: Negative resistance training is best described as lifting heavier weights on the lowering, eccentric portion and getting assistance from spotters during the lifting, concentric phase. It is a specific resistance training protocol based on the concept that most clients can handle heavier loads on the eccentric portions of exercises, but are not able to lift the load concentrically, so they need assistance. However, if they are only to use the load they can handle concentrically, they are never fully challenging the stronger eccentrically working muscles, so negative resistance training addresses this discrepancy. It is an advanced lifting technique.

94. B: Bodyweight training, such as pull-ups, push-ups, chin-ups, squat thrusts, lunges, yoga, jumping jacks, and planks, provides resistance in the form of bodyweight, so it improves relative strength and core strength, is low-cost, and improves body control. Because external weights are not used, it does not improve absolute strength.

95. A: The grip pattern where palms face the floor and the knuckles face the ceiling is called a pronated grip.

96. B: Golgi tendon organs are stimulated in PNF stretching and cause relaxation of the stretched muscle by its own contraction.

97. D: Activation of muscle spindles is decreased in PNF stretching, which capitalizes autogenic inhibition to send inhibitory signals from the Golgi tendon organs to the brain. These inhibitory signals override the excitatory impulses from the muscle spindles, which causes the muscle to gradually relax. Normally, stimulation of muscle spindles induces a contraction of the stretched muscle.

98. B: In order of decreasing percentage of total training volume, for a distance runner's program, cardiovascular/metabolic conditioning should be prioritized because this forms the foundation of the runner's fitness, followed by muscular endurance, which is also needed for endurance running. Plyometrics will help build some power, strength, and speed, and may help strengthen the anatomy to prevent injuries. Agility is least necessary as a focus for endurance runners, since they are mostly trying not to change speed or direction, and especially because the question is asking about percentage of volume and not frequency.

99. C: This question is tricky because it is asking about the frequency of various components of training, so the focus is not only on the specifics of tennis, but also on general guidelines for frequency of types of training in a program. Tennis requires strong cardiovascular fitness, so this should form the foundation of the training program. Since some amount of aerobic conditioning should occur on essentially all training days in a program, cardiovascular conditioning activities should be performed the most, both in volume and frequency. Speed and agility are incredibly important for successful tennis playing as well; it is here that planning safe programming in terms of frequency comes into play.

Speed training likely should take on a larger percentage of training volume (a greater number of total minutes dedicated to speed training during the week compared to agility), but speed training should be limited to just a few days per week to allow the body to fully recover from the demands and damage it causes. Agility is best completed in short, frequent bouts due to its high cognitive demand. Therefore, agility should occur more frequently than speed training. Plyometrics develop explosive power, which is important for tennis players, but should be limited to two days per week to prevent injury from overtraining and overstressing the anatomy.

100. C: During a heavy front-loaded squat, there should be 2 spotters—one positioned on either end of the bar—to help balance it and to remain in constant communication with each other and the lifter.

101. A: The hold-relax PNF protocol begins with a 10-second passive pre-stretch held at the point of mild discomfort. Then the partner applies a flexion force while the client holds and tries to resist the force, creating an isometric contraction for 6 seconds. After this, the client relaxes back into a passive stretch lasting 30 seconds. This is now a deeper stretch than the initial pre-stretch due to autogenic inhibition.

102. B: Static stretches should follow the workout, especially for excessively stiff clients or those with past injuries. It can improve the muscle tension and joint relationship over time. Static stretches performed prior to exercise can reduce explosive power and increase joint laxity when stiffness is required for energy conservation, placing a client at greater risk of injury.

103. B: While care and caution should be employed for all clients doing plyometrics, the football player poses the greatest risk of injury due to his weight. Because of the demand on the body, proper technique is imperative to avoid injury. Heavier clients (over 220 pounds) should also be monitored for any joint tenderness because the forces on their joints coupled with the weight of the body can place excessive stress on the tissues. Special care must be considered for previously injured clients, senior clients, prepubescents, and those with balance issues. Proper footwear and soft, rubberized flooring or grass should be used to reduce landing forces.

104. D: Muscle spindles detect rapid movement and initiate the stretch reflex. Golgi tendon organs are mechanoreceptors that control the flexibility and extensibility of the muscles and joints when they are stretched or during reactive forces or muscular contractions. Extrafusal fibers are the main skeletal muscle fibers in a muscle.

105. A: Static stretches should be held for about 30 seconds and performed for two to three sets for maximal efficacy They should follow a workout for clients with chronic tightness, and not precede it.

106. A: Spotters should use a solid, wide base of support and a neutral spine position. Spotters should use an athletic stance, with feet slightly wider than hip-width apart, knees flexed, arms and hands up and in the ready position and as close to the bar and client without touching them as possible. Bodyweight should be equally and soundly distributed on both feet, which should be firmly planted on the ground. Knees should not be locked but should maintain a degree of flexion, ready to support the weight and go into a squat if necessary to accept the weight of the bar. Locking the knees can be dangerous, since it places excessive stress on the knee ligaments and cartilage as well as the lower leg muscles and bones and the low back.

107. D: Choice *D* is correct because auditory cueing depends on clear verbal instructions that can help clients mentally visualize the instructions being given. Choice *A* is incorrect because visual cueing techniques demonstrate the proper way to complete an exercise. Choice *B* is incorrect because kinesthetic cueing techniques prompt clients to learn new exercises by doing them. Choice *C* is incorrect because, while most cueing techniques involve some elements of visual, kinesthetic, and auditory cueing, this cueing technique is not best described as a combination of all three techniques.

108. A: Choice *A* is correct because trainers reassess client progress throughout a fitness program to determine when to make progressions or regressions. Choice *B* is incorrect because trainers assign screening assessments before a fitness program begins to determine safe exercises for new clients. Choices *C* and *D* are incorrect because neither program assessments nor performance assessments refer to the types of assessments assigned by trainers to clients.

Professional Development and Responsibility

109. D: Teaching the client exercises to do during work travel assignments helps avoid relapses in healthy behaviors and is prudent for certified personal trainers to do to help clients develop self-efficacy and an exercise habit, despite the barrier of travel. Customized nutrition plans should be from registered dieticians or nutritionists; licensed massage therapists should provide therapeutic massage; and diagnosing meniscal tears is the role of a physician.

110. A: Recertification occurs every two years, and you need to have 2.0 CECs, remain CPR/AED certified, and pay the recertification fee.

111. A: Personal injury liability insurance protects against libel, slander, and invasion of privacy. Professional liability insurance protects against injuries caused by services or negligence. Commercial liability insurance covers individuals and the business against incidents and accidents that occurred at the facility and must be purchased by trainers who own their own studios.

112. B: One of the benefits of obtaining certification as an NASM personal trainer is that insurance companies recognize the certification and offer liability insurance, but this must be purchased and does not come automatically and inclusively with passing exam grades.

113. A: Health Insurance Portability and Accountability Act (HIPAA) defines individually identifiable health information such as demographics, prior and current health history, social security number, etc. FERPA is the Family Educational Rights and Privacy Act, and it relates mainly to protected information about education, particularly in school settings.

114. B: The law of supply and demand in the trainer's given geographical area largely dictates the price range for services. Trainers should research the fees that certified personal trainers in the area charge and aim to price their services accordingly, justifying potentially higher fees for experience, educational level, or provided services.

115. D: While modeling a healthy lifestyle is important, it does not reduce liability risk for trainers. Trainers should be mindful to adhere to NASM risk stratification and guidelines for clearance and medical supervision, rehearse emergency action plans, maintain CPR certification, abide by the NASM Scope of Practice for certified personal trainers and adhere to the Code of Ethics.

116. D: A client is low risk if they have one or fewer risk factors, but he or she should still be asymptomatic, and less than the age of forty-five or fifty-five for men and women, respectively. Condition III has no risk factors, but the client can have up to one, so all of the other choices are invalid.

117. C: Clients who are apparently healthy are not required to get medical clearance prior to starting an exercise program. This includes children, adolescents, men less than forty-five years, and women less than fifty-five years who do not have CAD risk factors or symptoms, known disease, and who did not answer "yes" to any questions on the PAR-Q. *A* and *B* are not correct, and *D* provides too high of an age cutoff for "apparently healthy males."

118. A: When a certified personal trainer fails to perform what is typically considered to be a standard practice of care, it may be deemed to be negligence.

119. C: Medicine balls should be checked weekly or so for cracks, which can cause sand to leak. Unless they are old or used a lot, medicine balls do not need to be checked prior to every use. More importantly, even if they do have sand leaks, they should not injure a client when they are starting to fall apart. Exercise bands routinely thin and can snap, and cables often fray, both of which can be very dangerous. Emergency stop buttons on cardio equipment should also be checked prior to usage.

120. B: Scanning and making digital copies of client files for the facility computer could breach privacy unless the files are password-protected.

Practice Test #2

Basic and Applied Sciences and Nutritional Concepts

1. Women tend to have what kind of body fat distribution?
   a. Gynoid
   b. Android
   c. Abdominal
   d. Visceral

2. Which of the following lists the correct kilocalories per gram of the macronutrients?
   a. Carbohydrate 4 kcal, protein 4 kcal, alcohol 9 kcal, fat 9 kcal
   b. Carbohydrate 4 kcal, protein 4 kcal, alcohol 7 kcal, fat 9 kcal
   c. Carbohydrate 4 kcal, protein 9 kcal, alcohol 7 kcal, fat 9 kcal
   d. Carbohydrate 4 kcal, protein 4 kcal, alcohol 4 kcal, fat 9 kcal

3. Which of the following is FALSE regarding the female athlete triad?
   a. It can put an athlete at greater risk for fracture.
   b. Although it's called the female athlete triad, males can also have it.
   c. Females with the triad typically have infertility issues.
   d. It can increase risk of musculoskeletal injuries.

4. According to USDA recommendations, which of the following is not true?
   a. Eat at least half of your grains as whole grains
   b. Focus on low-fat and fat-free dairy over full fat
   c. Consume a variety of whole food (unprocessed and unrefined) vegetables and fruits
   d. Limit seafood intake

5. Optimal hydration is ideal, but what is the minimum recommended replacement rate for fluid lost during exercise?
   a. 8 oz. for every pound lost
   b. One cup for every pound lost
   c. One pint for every pound lost
   d. One quart for every pound lost

6. Which is NOT a component of the female athlete triad?
   a. Amenorrhea
   b. Overtraining
   c. Loss of bone density
   d. Disordered eating

7. What is the maximum amount of water as measured by percent body weight that can be lost before significant decline in performance and health occur?
   a. 1 to 3%
   b. 3 to 5%
   c. 5 to 8%
   d. 8 to 10%

8. You have been training Sarah for two years. Initially she was 120 pounds at 5'4" and now she is 101 pounds. She often gets weak and dizzy during workouts, and you notice she does the elliptical on her own over two hours per day. She also has become more withdrawn and never partakes in any of the meet-and-greet snack buffets at the fitness center anymore. While you can't be sure, you suspect she may be battling which of the following?
   a. Type 1 diabetes
   b. Anorexia nervosa
   c. Bulimia nervosa
   d. Type 2 diabetes

9. Karen wants to lose 20 pounds, which would put her BMI at 23 kg/m^2. She wants your recommendation for how much of a calorie deficit she should aim for with healthy weight loss. What do you recommend for overall health improvement and weight loss?
   a. Eat 500 to 1000 fewer kcal per day
   b. Eat 1000 to 1500 fewer kcal per day
   c. Eat 250 to 500 fewer kcal per day and expend 250 to 500 more kcal per day
   d. Eat 500 to 1000 fewer kcal per day and expend 500 to 1000 more kcal per day

10. Which of the following terms means a stretch or tear to ligaments at a joint?
   a. Sprain
   b. Strain
   c. Fracture
   d. Dislocation

11. Which of the following is NOT an intrinsic risk factor for musculoskeletal injury?
   a. Training program too advanced
   b. Obesity
   c. Abnormal bony alignment
   d. Strength or flexibility imbalance

12. Spondylolisthesis may present as which of the following?
   a. Shoulder pain
   b. Neck pain
   c. Knee pain
   d. Low back pain

13. Recommended body fat levels for men age thirty-five and older is best described as which of the following ranges?
   a. 5 to 13%
   b. 3 to 5%
   c. 10 to 25%
   d. 20 to 25%

14. Essential fat for women is roughly which of the following ranges?
   a. 8 to 12%
   b. 3 to 5%
   c. 5 to 8%
   d. 15 to 20%

15. What is the role of acetylcholine in muscle contraction?
    a. To propagate the action potential across the neuromuscular junction
    b. To initiate the action potential so that voluntary muscle contraction can occur
    c. To bind to troponin, which alters the position of tropomyosin, causing the actin to become pulled towards the center of the sarcomere.
    d. To initiate relaxation by flooding back into the sarcoplasmic reticulum and preventing actin and myosin from interacting

16. What must occur in tandem with functional overreaching to prevent overtraining?
    a. Adequate stress to induce physiological adaptations
    b. A preload period
    c. A de-load period
    d. Adequate recovery between reps and sets

17. What is the order of structures through which inspired air travels en route to the lungs?
    a. Nasal cavities, trachea, bronchioles, bronchi, alveoli
    b. Nasal cavities, trachea, bronchi, bronchioles, alveoli
    c. Nasal cavities, bronchioles, bronchi, trachea, alveoli
    d. Nasal cavities, bronchi, trachea, bronchioles, alveoli

18. Which of the following describes two variables that have an inverse relationship?
    a. As one variable increases, the other increases exponentially
    b. As one variable increases, the other increases linearly
    c. As one variable increases, the other decreases
    d. As one variable increases, the other remains constant

Client Relations and Behavioral Coaching

19. Which of the following includes all of the appropriate methods of communication with clients?
    a. Email, phone, text messaging, in person
    b. Phone, in person
    c. Email, in person, phone
    d. In person, text messaging, phone

20. Which would be best for a kinesthetic learner?
    a. Reading about proper squatting technique
    b. Trying to squat back into a chair before a full body squat
    c. Watching video tutorials of squatting form
    d. Listening to you explain the major form tips for a perfect squat

21. Which of the following is most correct regarding eating disorders?
    a. Eating disorders are not attributed to genetics.
    b. Eating disorders can be resolved in a matter of months.
    c. Eating disorders align with a set of specific criteria.
    d. Eating disorders are usually attributed to stress.

22. An elevated heart rate and upset stomach are examples of which of the following?
    a. Trait anxiety
    b. State anxiety
    c. Cognitive anxiety
    d. Somatic anxiety

23. Generally speaking, what's the most significant source of a client's self-efficacy?
    a. The client's past performances
    b. The coach's feedback or support
    c. Vicarious experiences
    d. Physiological arousal and emotional/mood states

24. Which of the following is NOT true about withdrawal when considering substance abuse?
    a. It manifests as physiological and substance-specific cognitive symptoms
    b. Examples of symptoms can include paranoia, hallucinations, cold sweats, shivering, nausea, vomiting
    c. It happens when an individual stops abusing the substance, and when he or she attempts to reduce the amount taken.
    d. It results in needing greater amounts of the substance to achieve the desired effects.

25. Which of the following is NOT true regarding internal and external cuing?
    a. Most research has found that internal cues are more effective at improving motor learning and movement performance.
    b. With an external cue, an athlete focuses on how the movement or performing it will affect the outcome of the exercise or the environment at large.
    c. With an internal cue, an athlete focuses on the movements and feelings in their own limbs or body as the exercise or movement is being performed.
    d. An internal cue for an athlete doing a plank could be, "Pull your belly button toward your spine."

26. The operation of processing environmental, external, and internal cues that come to one's awareness is known as which of the following?
    a. Conscious thinking
    b. Attention
    c. Subconscious thinking
    d. Mindful engrossment

27. Which of the following is defined as the use of recreating successful events or endeavors within the client's mind?
    a. Mental arousal
    b. Mental imagery
    c. Mental stimulation
    d. Mental practice

28. Social acceptance, trophies, awards, and induction into a hall of fame are all examples of which of the following?
    a. Extrinsic motivation
    b. Self-motivation
    c. Intrinsic motivation
    d. Positive self-talk

29. Adaptation that occurs from stress placed on the body is the definition of which of the following?
    a. Specific adaptation syndrome
    b. Acute adaptation syndrome
    c. Exercise resistance syndrome
    d. General adaptation syndrome

30. Which of the following is NOT considered a form of feedback during instruction?
    a. Augmented feedback
    b. Segmented feedback
    c. Knowledge of results
    d. Knowledge of performance

31. Which of the following is defined as administering tasks, objects, or events that would likely decrease the occurrence of a negative operant?
    a. Negative punishment
    b. Positive punishment
    c. Negative reinforcement
    d. Positive reinforcement

32. During training, removal of an element of the workout that the client considers negative represents which of the following reinforcement techniques?
    a. Negative reinforcement
    b. Positive reinforcement
    c. Negative punishment
    d. Positive punishment

33. Which of the following accurately describes an operant?
    a. A behavior reinforced by a stimulus
    b. The avoidance of a specific behavior
    c. The motivation to avoid a punishment
    d. The motivation to earn a reward

34. Which of the following accurately describes the inverted-U theory?
    a. As the arousal levels rise, performance levels will increase proportionally
    b. Arousal levels increase performance up to an optimal level, but further increases are associated with reduced performance
    c. Arousal levels have no effect on performance and therefore should not be focused on throughout training sessions
    d. As arousal levels decrease, performance increases as the athlete becomes more comfortable and less anxious

35. Which of the following relates to the intensity and focus of one's effort?
    a. Motivation
    b. Motive to achieve success
    c. Motive to avoid failure
    d. Reinforcement

36. Which of the following is NOT associated with optimal arousal levels?
    a. Increased mental activation
    b. Increased performance anxiety
    c. Increased positive thoughts
    d. Increased control in decision-making tasks

Assessment

37. Which of the following lists of joint types is in the correct order for increasing amounts of permitted motion (least mobile to most mobile)?
    a. Hinge, condyloid, saddle
    b. Saddle, hinge, condyloid
    c. Saddle, condyloid, hinge
    d. Hinge, saddle, condyloid

38. Which of the following is the correct order of behavioral change stages according to the trans-theoretical model?
    a. Precontemplation, Contemplation, Preparation, Action, Maintenance
    b. Preparation, Precontemplation, Contemplation, Maintenance, Action
    c. Preparation, Contemplation, Precontemplation, Action, Maintenance
    d. Precontemplation, Preparation, Contemplation, Action, Maintenance

39. Which is the most likely stage in the trans-theoretical model for a client to say, "I exercised once last week, and I'll try to exercise twice this week"?
    a. Preparation
    b. Precontemplation
    c. Contemplation
    d. Action

40. Which of the following neurotransmitters helps strengthen the synaptic pathways involved in learning a behavior through reinforcement?
    a. Epinephrine
    b. Serotonin
    c. Norepinephrine
    d. Dopamine

41. Match the behavioral change model with the best descriptive choice.
    a. Social Cognitive Theory: addresses relationships; behaviors, such as a client's motivation to exercise, are shaped by interpersonal relations, the surrounding environment, community, policy, and law.
    b. Health Belief Model: the perceived seriousness of a potential health problem is the main predictors of behavioral change.
    c. Socio-Ecological Model: clients actively shape their lives and learn by thinking, feeling, reflecting, and observing themselves in a social context.
    d. Theory of Planned Behavior: the client's level of motivation for behavioral change is shaped by their attitudes and behaviors that will most like occur in the allotted timeframe

42. Ligaments connect what?
    a. Muscle to muscle
    b. Bone to bone
    c. Bone to muscle
    d. Muscle to tendon

43. Which of the following reflects the correct blood flow pathway (heart-valve-vessel)?
    a. Right atrium, left atrium, right ventricle, mitral valve, left ventricle, aorta
    b. Right atrium, mitral valve, right ventricle, systemic circulation, left atrium, left ventricle, aorta
    c. Right atrium, right ventricle, left atrium, tricuspid valve, left ventricle, aorta
    d. Right atrium, right ventricle, pulmonary circulation, left atrium, mitral valve, left ventricle, aorta

44. Which of the following terms means "movement away from the body's midline"?
    a. Abduction
    b. Adduction
    c. Pronation
    d. Supination

45. What muscle is the primary antagonist in knee flexion?
    a. Hamstrings
    b. Quadriceps
    c. Gastrocnemius
    d. Tibialis anterior

46. In what plane does shoulder flexion occur?
    a. Sagittal
    b. Frontal
    c. Transverse
    d. Coronal

47. What is the primary energy pathway for ATP production for an intense two-minute bout of activity?
    a. Aerobic metabolism
    b. Krebs cycle
    c. Glycolysis
    d. ATP-PC system

48. Which of the following is NOT an adaptation to chronic cardiovascular exercise?
    a. Increased heart chamber size
    b. Increased stroke volume
    c. Increased cardiac output
    d. Increased submaximal heart rate

49. Which of the following is true about delayed onset muscle soreness (DOMS)?
    a. It typically peaks twenty-four to seventy-two hours post-workout, especially after eccentric exercises.
    b. It typically peaks twenty-four to seventy-two hours post-workout, especially after concentric exercises.
    c. It typically peaks twelve to twenty-four hours post-workout, especially after eccentric exercises.
    d. It typically peaks twelve to twenty-four hours post-workout, especially after concentric exercises.

50. Pectoralis major is doing what type of contraction during a pushup?
    a. Isokinetic
    b. Isometric
    c. Isotonic
    d. Eccentric

51. Which of the following types of joints are correctly matched with the anatomic joint example given?

    I. Cartilaginous: pubic symphysis
    II. Saddle: thumb carpal-metacarpal
    III. Plane: sutures in skull
    IV. Pivot: radial head on ulna

    a. Choices I, II, and III
    b. Choices I, II, and IV
    c. Choices I, III, and IV
    d. All are correct

52. A client's confidence in their ability to make the behavioral change is known as what?
    a. Self-determination
    b. Self-esteem
    c. Self-efficacy
    d. Determination

53. Which of the following may indicate trainer-client incompatibility?
    a. The client has never exercised before, and the trainer is a competitive athlete.
    b. The client is male, and the trainer is female.
    c. The client prefers to text and email, but the trainer likes talking on the phone or in person.
    d. The client is available to train weekdays, but the trainer only has weekend availability.

54. The FITT-VP framework for developing a comprehensive fitness plan stands for which of the following?
    a. Flexibility, Intensity, Time, Type, Variety, Purpose
    b. Fervency, Integrity, Time, Type, Volume, Purpose
    c. Follow-up, Intensity, Time, Type, Validity, Progress
    d. Frequency, Intensity, Time, Type, Volume, Progression

55. Paul is a thirty-eight-year-old recreational runner training for a local 10k. He is running five days a week and feeling good, but he wants to train with you to prevent injury. He is 72 inches tall and weighs 225 pounds. He takes Lipitor and a multivitamin. His blood pressure is 112/70 mmHg. His total cholesterol is 210 mg/dL. His father and mother are both alive, but his uncle died at age fifty from a stroke. Paul does not smoke or drink. He has medical clearance from his physical last week to begin a strength-training program with you. Which of the following do you recommend for his cardiovascular assessment?
    a. Astrand-Rhyming cycle ergometer test
    b. 1.5 mile run test with physician present
    c. Rockport walk test
    d. Astrand-Rhyming cycle ergometer with physician present

Program Design

56. What does specificity refer to?
    a. The flow of a training program's specific sessions
    b. The specific goals of the client
    c. Exercises for muscle groups related to a client's specific goal
    d. A client's specific statistics (age, weight, etc.)

57. What does program progression refer to?
    a. A client's overall progress
    b. Modifications to ensure a client progresses
    c. A client's perception of progress
    d. Progression in a client's age

58. Which of the following is true regarding a client's medical history?
    a. It should not be considered
    b. It should be discussed thoroughly
    c. It does not indicate illness or injury
    d. It is not necessary for program planning

59. What does interval training refer to?
    a. Sessions performed indoors or outdoors
    b. Discontinuing workouts after the warm-up and cardiovascular component
    c. Maintaining steady speed throughout the workout
    d. Changing speed and intensity of workouts during a session

60. What does continuous training refer to?
    a. Performing the same workout for the entire duration of the session
    b. Engaging in the same workout every session throughout the training program
    c. Maintaining a steady speed throughout a cardiovascular exercise
    d. Continuing from one exercise to the next without rest

61. What does circuit training refer to?
    a. Engaging in indoor or outdoor activities only
    b. Allotting one specific exercise focus per session
    c. Using a combination of cardiovascular and strength training exercises
    d. Working all major muscle groups in one session

62. Which of the following is true regarding activities of daily living?
    a. They are not important for program design
    b. They should be performed outdoors
    c. They should be practiced in sessions
    d. They should be considered when designing a training plan for a client

63. For weight loss, recommendations include all EXCEPT?
    a. Frequent cardiovascular activity
    b. Increased caloric intake
    c. Higher number of resistance training sets
    d. Increased frequency of flexibility training

64. Regarding athletic performance enhancement, which of the following statements is true?
    a. Sports-specific activities should be included in training
    b. Only major muscle groups involved in the specific sport should be the focus
    c. Diet does not need to be considered
    d. Sessions do not require warm-up or cool-down periods

65. Which of the following statements is true about advanced resistance training exercises?
    a. They should only be recommended for weightlifters
    b. They should not be performed by seniors
    c. They require clients to have progressed to a certain level of fitness first
    d. They include swimming, cycling, and running

66. Which of the following statements is true about plyometric training?
    a. It uses machines primarily
    b. It includes box jumps and bounding drills
    c. It is contraindicated for pregnant women
    d. It should be used only in programs for advanced clients

67. Which of the following statements is true about pyramid training?
    a. It focuses on clients' skills in gymnastics
    b. It requires a client to be in the supine position throughout the training session
    c. It uses only leg muscles
    d. It includes high reps of low weight progressing to low reps of high weight

68. The six motor skills related to physical fitness include all of the following EXCEPT?
    a. Creativity
    b. Agility
    c. Power
    d. Balance

69. What is the bench press an example of?
    a. A cardiovascular exercise
    b. A chest exercise
    c. A range of motion exercise
    d. An advanced exercise contraindicated for healthy seniors

70. What is the plank exercise an example of?
    a. An exclusively outdoor exercise
    b. A swimming exercise
    c. An abdominal and core exercise
    d. An exercise not recommended for children and adolescents

71. When should pregnant women consider modifying the exercise?
    a. Before eating
    b. After eating
    c. After the first trimester
    d. Only in exercises focused on abdominals and legs

72. Which of the following statements is true about range of motion exercises?
    a. They are only necessary for seniors
    b. They should never be performed by cardiac patients
    c. They should be included in all training programs
    d. They should be performed twice weekly

73. Which of the following statements is true about cardiovascular exercises?
    a. They include swimming, running, and cycling
    b. They include stretching specific joints
    c. They are contraindicated for children and adolescents
    d. They should only be performed outdoors

74. Which of the following statements is true about strength training exercises?
    a. They can be performed with body weight or external resistance modalities
    b. They include swimming, running, and cycling
    c. They are contraindicated for pregnant women
    d. They should only include exercises using machines

75. Which of the following is true for healthy populations?
    a. They require medical clearance for exercise
    b. They do not require monitoring of exertion during exercise
    c. They do not require rest or hydration during sessions
    d. They should incorporate cardiovascular, resistance training, and flexibility in their programs

76. Trainers should follow which of the following guidelines for clients with chronic conditions?
    a. They should not engage in any cardiovascular activities
    b. They should avoid range of motion exercises
    c. They should follow a low-calorie diet
    d. They should incorporate low- to moderate-impact activities in their program

77. Which of the following is true for clients with arthritis and osteoporosis?
    a. They benefit from low-impact cardiovascular exercise
    b. They should adhere to major dietary restrictions
    c. They frequently miss training sessions
    d. They should not perform outdoor cardiovascular exercise

78. Which of the following guidelines is true regarding obese clients?
    a. They should not perform range of motion exercises
    b. They should not perform strength-training exercises for the legs
    c. They should avoid planking and abdominal crunches
    d. They should perform cardiovascular activity five to seven days per week

79. The proper flow of activities in a training session looks most like which of the following?
    a. Stretching, strength training, cool-down, cardiovascular
    b. Warm-up, training, cool-down, stretching
    c. Warm-up, stretching, cool-down, strength training
    d. Cardiovascular, stretching, warm-up, cool-down

Exercise Technique and Training Instruction

80. Which of the following is an appropriate cardio modality for a client who needs weightbearing, non-impact exercise?
    a. Treadmill
    b. Stationary bike
    c. Elliptical
    d. Stair stepper

81. What does the Valsalva maneuver entail?
    a. Exhaling fully and then increasing abdominal pressure by trying to inhale while holding the glottis closed
    b. Exhaling fully and then increasing abdominal pressure by trying to inhale while trying to open the glottis for deep belly breathing
    c. Inhaling using deep belly breathing and then increasing abdominal pressure by trying to exhale while holding the glottis closed
    d. Inhaling using deep belly breathing and then increasing abdominal pressure by trying to inhale while holding the glottis closed

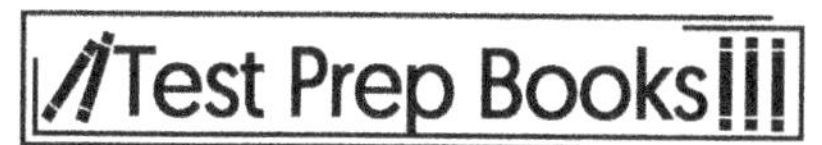

82. What improper technique must the strength and conditioning professional be cognizant of when observing clients doing agility drills to ensure that joints are not enduring unnatural and unhealthy stress?
    a. Failing to extend the hips, knees, and ankles upon acceleration
    b. Failing to flex the hips, knees, and ankles upon acceleration
    c. Failing to extend the hips, knees, and ankles upon deceleration
    d. Failing to flex the hips, knees, and ankles upon deceleration

83. All EXCEPT which of the following are true regarding adjustments for a stationary bike?
    a. The forefoot should stay in contact with the pedals of the bicycle throughout the pedal stroke
    b. At least five or ten degrees of knee flexion should occur at the bottom of the pedal stroke
    c. The handlebar height should ensure the athlete is in an upright position and the shoulders are prevented from rounding forward while pedaling
    d. Terminal knee extension should be avoided during the downward pedal stroke

84. What is the order of the four segments that explain each motion of the lower legs throughout the sprinting movement?
    a. Eccentric braking phase, concentric propulsive phase, recovery phase, ground preparation
    b. Ground preparation, concentric propulsive phase, eccentric braking phase, recovery phase
    c. Concentric propulsive phase, eccentric braking phase, recovery phase, ground preparation
    b. Ground preparation, concentric propulsive phase, recovery phase, eccentric braking phase

85. When using starting blocks for sprinting, which of the following best describes optimal hand position?
    a. Hands should be slightly less than shoulder-width apart with the fingers held together and thumbs under the shoulders.
    b. Hands should be slightly wider than shoulder-width apart with the fingers held together and thumbs under the shoulders.
    c. Hands should be slightly less than shoulder-width apart with the fingers spread apart and thumbs under the armpits.
    d. Hands should be slightly wider than shoulder-width apart with the fingers spread apart and thumbs under the armpits.

86. Free weight exercises have all of the following benefits over resistance machines EXCEPT which of the following?
    a. They may be completed without a spotter.
    b. They can improve core stability.
    c. They can provide a more sports-specific strength training method.
    d. Each exercise can be performed in a variety of ways, rather than strictly dictated in one certain way.

87. Which athlete would benefit most from agility work on most days of the week?
    a. A soccer midfielder
    b. A baseball pitcher
    c. A shot putter
    d. A swimmer

88. Which athlete would benefit most from plyometrics at least three days per week?
    a. A cross country runner
    b. A hockey player
    c. A figure skater
    d. A swimmer

89. All BUT which of the following are forms of PNF technique?
    a. Contract-relax
    b. Contract-relax with agonist contraction
    c. Hold-relax with agonist contraction
    d. Hold-relax

90. The number of required spotters is dependent on all EXCEPT which of the following?
    a. The load being lifted
    b. The number of strength coaches available
    c. The experience and skill of the athlete and spotters
    d. The physical strength of the spotters

91. When spotting over-the-face barbell exercises, the spotter should use what type of grip on the bar?
    a. Hook grip
    b. Pronated grip
    c. Alternated grip
    d. Supinated grip

92. What is the term used for the portion of the movement where the force of the external resistance will peak due to joint angles?
    a. Peak point
    b. Maximal force zone
    c. Full-intensity position
    d. Sticking point

93. Which of the following accurately describes the amortization phase during plyometric training?
    a. The eccentric, lowering action of the body before the concentric muscle action
    b. The concentric, upward movement of the body
    c. The counteraction of the body to increase the stretch reflex
    d. The phase between eccentric and concentric muscle action of the body

94. When adjusting a stationary bicycle to the needs of the client, what position should the knee be in at the full downward stroke of the pedal?
    a. The knee should be terminally extended
    b. The knee should be in flexion around 90 degrees
    c. The knee should be flexed 5–10 degrees
    d. The knee should be slightly extended

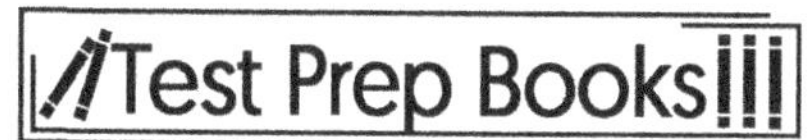

95. What can be done to ensure proper breathing patterns are maintained during anaerobic conditioning?
    a. Intensities can be increased
    b. Rest periods can be decreased
    c. Water can be given to the athlete
    d. Rest periods can be increased

96. All EXCEPT which of the following are benefits of static stretching?
    a. Increased range of motion
    b. Enhanced recovery
    c. General body warmup
    d. Useful as a corrective exercise

97. If the client is continuously showing signs of the knees caving in during hip, knee, and ankle free-weight exercises, which of the following would NOT be a good verbal command for the technical flaw that needs correcting?
    a. "Keep outside pressure on the way up."
    b. "Keep your hips engaged throughout the movement."
    c. "Keep your chest up during the entire movement."
    d. "Your knees should track over, but not beyond, the toes."

98. Which of the following is NOT a segment of lower-limb breakdown of sprinting mechanics?
    a. Eccentric braking period
    b. Concentric propulsive phase
    c. Ground preparation phase
    d. Acceleration phase

99. What is the placement of the hands relative to the body when utilizing proper arm action during running, walking, and jogging?
    a. During the upward movement, the hand should reach as high as the chest and during the downward movement, the hand should reach as low as the lateral hip
    b. During the upward movement, the hand should reach as high as eye level, and during the downward movement, the hand should reach as low as the naval
    c. During the upward movement, the hand should reach as high as the jaw, and during the downward movement, the hand should reach as far back as the glutes
    d. During the upward movement, the hand should reach as high as the chest, and during the downward movement, the hand should reach as low as the anterior hip

100. During the first couple strides of a sprint, how does the force displacement shift?
    a. From horizontal displacement to vertical displacement
    b. From vertical displacement to horizontal displacement
    c. From transverse displacement to vertical displacement
    d. From transverse displacement to horizontal displacement

101. Which is NOT a symptom of overtraining?
   a. Lowered resting heart rate
   b. Depression or moodiness
   c. Sleep disturbances
   d. Changes in appetite or body weight

102. Which of the following is NOT recommended for an athlete suffering from a heat-related illness?
   a. Move to the shade
   b. Drink fluids
   c. Remove excess clothing
   d. Continue the workout indoors

103. Which of the following is NOT an overuse injury?
   a. Shin splints
   b. Tennis elbow (lateral epicondylitis)
   c. Metatarsal stress fracture
   d. Groin strain

104. What happens to the performance of clients that become overtrained?
   a. It improves
   b. It declines
   c. It stays the same
   d. It improves slightly before declining

105. Which of the following is NOT a sign of a heat-related illness?
   a. Cramping
   b. Inability to speak clearly
   c. Lack of perspiration
   d. Reduced heart rate

106. To control the spread of germs in the facility, what should clients be taught and instructed to do?
   a. Supplement with Vitamin C and zinc
   b. Wear appropriately supportive sneakers
   c. Wipe down all used equipment after use with antibacterial agents
   d. Engage the emergency stop buttons on cardio equipment

107. Which of the following is the correct order of phases for designing a new fitness facility?
   a. Pre-design, design, construction, pre-operation
   b. Design, pre-construction, construction, pre-operation
   c. Pre-design, design, pre-construction, pre-operation
   d. Pre-planning, design, pre-construction, construction

108. Practices that trainers can implement to foster a safe training environment include all EXCEPT which of the following?
   a. Clearing loose equipment from the floor
   b. Encouraging teamwork and positive, supportive attitudes
   c. Mopping wooden floors and checking wooden platforms for cracks
   d. Keeping weight benches and lifting platforms as close together as possible

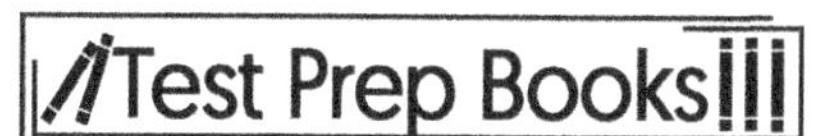

Professional Development and Responsibility

109. Which of the following is NOT within the scope of practice of a certified personal trainer?
   a. Stretching a client after a session
   b. Listening to a client's concerns about his stressful job
   c. Prescribing a home exercise program
   d. Making dietary recommendations for post-workout snacks

110. A pregnant client is found unconscious and not breathing. You send someone to call 911 and the scene is safe. How would you proceed with CPR/AED?
   a. Wait for EMS. You cannot give CPR or use an AED on a pregnant woman
   b. Begin CPR and rescue breathing but do not use an AED on a pregnant woman
   c. Begin CPR, rescue breathing, and normal adult AED intervention
   d. Give two rescue breaths and use AED as normal but do not do CPR chest compressions on a pregnant woman

111. Benefits of spotting a client during exercise include all of the following except?
   a. Ensuring the client is using correct form
   b. Demonstrating good spotting form so the client can help you
   c. Making sure the client and surrounding clients are safe
   d. Staying more actively engaged as the trainer

112. A ____________ business structure has separate legal entities with owners and shareholders. They are more time-consuming, costly, and harder to set up and terminate but there is less personal responsibility for liabilities and debts.
   a. Sole proprietorship
   b. Limited Liability Company (LLC)
   c. Corporation
   d. Partnership

113. Career development practices include all of the following EXCEPT?
   a. Earning CECs and attending conferences
   b. Wearing professional attire and appropriate footwear
   c. Reading current health and fitness research
   d. Giving talks and seminars at community events

114. A business plan should include:

      I. Vision, mission, values, goals
      II. Emergency action plan
      III. Job descriptions and staffing needs
      IV. Financial plan including revenue sources and start-up costs

   a. All of the above
   b. Choices I, II, and IV
   c. Choices I, III, and IV
   d. Choices I and IV

115. To control the spread of germs in the facility, clients should be taught and instructed to do which of the following?

a. Supplement with vitamin C and zinc
b. Wear appropriately supportive sneakers
c. Wipe down all equipment after use with antibacterial agents
d. Engage the emergency stop buttons on cardio equipment

116. To organize a budget in a professional and reproducible way, it is prudent for trainers to use which of the following?

a. Neatly organized paper and pen spreadsheets
b. Credit card sales only; don't accept cash or check
c. Digital software like QuickBooks or Microsoft Excel
d. An accountant

117. When can private, personal identifying information from a client's file be accessed without permission?

a. When a new trainer fills in
b. When the client is having a medical emergency
c. When the spouse needs to access information
d. When sending in taxes so the IRS can get a copy

118. How would you treat a minor open wound?

a. Employ universal precautions (such as latex gloves) and wash hands immediately after. Use soap and water to clean the wound, then leave open to air out.
b. Employ universal precautions (such as latex gloves) and wash hands immediately after. Use a germicide cream and cover with a sterile bandage.
c. Employ universal precautions (such as latex gloves) and wash hands immediately after. Use soap and water to clean the wound, then cover with germicide cream and a sterile bandage.
d. Employ universal precautions (such as latex gloves) and wash hands immediately after. Use a flat hand and fingers to apply pressure and control the bleeding in minor wounds and elevate it above the client's heart as long as no fracture is suspected.

119. Shakiness, weakness, abnormal sweating, mouth or finger tingling, visual disturbances, confusion, and seizures can be signs of what?

a. Hyperglycemia
b. Hypoglycemia
c. Overtraining
d. Sudden cardiac arrest

120. How often should emergency procedures should be reviewed and rehearsed?

a. Every month
b. Every week
c. Every three months
d. Twice per year

Answer Explanations #2

Basic and Applied Sciences and Nutritional Concepts

1. A: Due to being estrogen dominant, females tend to have a gynoid, or pear-shaped distribution of body fat (accumulated more on the hips and thighs). Testosterone in higher concentrations causes an android or apple-shaped fat distribution in men, concentrating more body fat on the abdomen as visceral fat.

2. B: The energy in kcal for the macronutrients are as follows: carbohydrate 4 kcal, protein 4 kcal, alcohol 7 kcal, and fat 9 kcal.

3. B: The female athlete triad is a condition that only females experience. One of the cornerstones is amenorrhea, or cessation of menstrual cycle, which can cause infertility issues. While men can have disordered eating, they do not have the triad effect of the amenorrhea and its subsequent hormonal influence on reducing bone density. The female athlete triad can increase the risk of fracture and musculoskeletal injury, due to the loss of bone mass and the negative energy balance, which compromises recovery and healing.

4. D: The USDA encourages seafood consumption a minimum of twice per week, as well as making at least half of all grains whole grains, focusing on low-fat and fat-free dairy over full fat, and consuming a variety of whole food vegetables and fruits.

5. C: Optimal hydration is ideal, which would mean equal intake for excretion, but a minimum of one pint should be consumed for every pound lost during exercise, and then more can be consumed after exercise is over.

6. B: Overtraining is not directly part of the female athlete triad, although it may feed into some types of disordered eating. Amenorrhea, disordered eating, and loss of bone density are the three components of the triad.

7. B: Before experiencing significant performance-reducing dehydration, studies show that the body can experience a loss of about 3 to 5% of total mass in water. Beyond 5%, dehydration is too severe, and the person can suffer dangerous health and performance loss.

8. B: Sarah may be suffering from anorexia nervosa, an eating or body image disorder consisting of starvation and inadequate intake. It can lead to dizziness, and her compulsive cardio workouts are consistent with a desire to burn calories. Sarah seems to be avoiding eating as well.

9. C: ACE recommends a daily calorie deficit of 500 to 1000 kcal for those looking to lose weight, so options *A* or *C* are the first to be considered. The recommendation is that this deficit is achieved through increasing physical activity to raise energy expenditure and simultaneously reduce caloric intake. This dual-pronged approach has been shown to improve total health in addition to helping reduce weight, because physical activity is independently associated with greater health, while adding activity preserves lean body mass during a caloric deficit.

10. A: A sprain is a stretch or tear to ligaments at a joint while strains are tears or stretches to tendons and muscles. Fractures are cracks or breaks in bones or cartilage and dislocations occur when joint articulations become incongruous.

11. A: Extrinsic risk factors are those that influence injury risk outside of the individual such as training programming errors. Intrinsic risk factors are directly related to the individual and are typically physical in nature, such as obesity, abnormal bony alignment, or strength of flexibility imbalances.

12. D: Spondylolisthesis is a fracture in the pars interarticularis of the spine and presents as low back pain. It is especially prevalent in adolescent athletes in sports requiring spinal extension such as gymnastics and weightlifting.

13. C: Recommended body fat levels for men age thirty-five and older is 10 to 25%.

14. A: Essential fat for women is roughly 8 to 12%. This amount is needed to protect vital organs and maintain minimal levels of health and body function. Essential fat is higher in women than men.

15. A: Acetylcholine is a neurotransmitter that is released in the axon terminal after the action potential has been sent down the axon terminal. Acetylcholine then travels across the neuromuscular junction and binds to the sarcolemma. In this way, acetylcholine creates a "bridge" to propagate the action potential into the muscle cell. Depolarization initiates an action potential, so Choice *B* is incorrect. Choices *C* and *D* are functions of calcium.

16. C: Functional overreaching involves increasing stress on the body until no further stress can be placed on it without an adequate period of recovery called the de-load period. Overtraining can occur when the training load reaches a peak and is not followed by a period of de-load because stress becomes too great and detrimental consequences can occur to the athlete. Choice *D* is incorrect because the de-load period is more of a macrocycle (days or weeks) factor versus the acute recovery between sets of reps.

17. B: Inspired air first enters the naval cavities, which humidify, purify, and warm the air. The air then moves to the trachea, which is the first-generation passage. The trachea splits into the left and right main bronchi. The bronchi bring the inspired air into the lungs, where it undergoes separation into advanced generations known as bronchioles. Bronchioles branch into the alveoli, which are the last generation and the location where the gases are exchanged during respiration.

18. C: When the independent and dependent variable display an inverse relationship, as one variable increases, the other decreases. This can also be described as a negative correlation. Choice *A* describes an exponential relationship, Choice *B* describes a positive correlation. Choice *D* describes variables that are not correlated.

Client Relations and Behavioral Coaching

19. A: Depending on the individual client's comfort, preferences, and the content of what needs to be discussed, trainers can rely on a variety of communication methods such as email, phone, text messaging, and face-to-face conversations.

20. B: Kinesthetic learners learn best through movement, physical involvement, and experience. Trainers working with kinesthetic learners should demonstrate an exercise and then have the client try a

simplified version of the movement such as completing an unweighted repetition of the exercise or moving through a partial range of motion. Before trying the full resistance or movement, these intermediate steps can demonstrate understanding while reducing injury risk. Auditory learners grasp information best through listening, so Choice *D* would be best for them. Visual learners learn through watching an observation, so Choice *C* would be best for these learners. Intellectual or cognitive learners would do well with reading about proper squat technique.

21. C: This option is correct, since the other statements about eating disorders are not accurate. An eating disorder is a diagnosed mental illness with a specific set of eating patterns and behaviors as described in the *Diagnostic and Statistical Manual of Mental Disorders* (DSM) published by the American Psychiatric Association. Eating disorders are attributed to genetics, cannot be resolved in a matter of months, and are not attributed to stress.

22. D: An elevated heart rate and upset stomach are physical manifestations of anxiety, which are considered somatic anxiety. Trait anxiety, Choice *A,* is considered to be part of one's personality, predisposing a client to perceive many situations as being threatening when in fact, no physical or psychological danger exists. State anxiety, Choice *B,* is a continually changing component of mood that is the subjective perception of tension and apprehension associated with increased arousal of the autonomic and endocrine systems. Cognitive anxiety, Choice *C,* is the thought process responsible for the perception of anxiety as negative.

23. A: Self-efficacy refers to the client's perception of their ability to perform a situation-specific task successfully. The most significant source of self-efficacy for most clients is their past performance experiences. The other choices listed are sources of self-efficacy, but they tend to be less impactful.

24. D: Choice *D* describes building tolerance to a drug. The other choices listed are indeed true about withdrawal from a substance.

25. A: While both types of cues have their place and some degree of merit, most research has found that external cues—not internal cues—are more effective at improving motor learning and movement performance. The other answer choices are true.

26. B: Attention is the operation of processing environmental, external, and internal cues that enter one's awareness throughout training and competition. It is important for clients to ensure that their attention and level of focus is based on task-relevant stimuli and keep their attention off of task-irrelevant stimuli.

27. B: Mental imagery involves recreating successful events within the mind of the client. This recreation can entail every sensory aspect of the event, such as what might be seen, heard, smelled, and felt. By recreating a successful endeavor, the client will increase the desire to experience such events again. The mental image does not need to be limited to competition; it may include a successful practice, or rehearsal, in preparation to the event.

28. A: When observing motivation, successful clients demonstrate both intrinsic and extrinsic motivation. Extrinsic motivation involves the desire for external rewards from successful outcomes of training and competition. Examples include social acceptance, trophies, awards, induction into a hall of fame, and praise. Intrinsic motivation involves the internal desire to be successful, the client's attitude/desire, and the internal satisfaction gleaned from participation. It is important to note that cleints are usually not solely motivated by extrinsic or intrinsic factors, but from a combination of both.

29. D: Adaptation can occur from any stressor that is placed on the human body, a phenomenon called general adaptation syndrome (GAS). When stress is placed upon the body over time, the body will begin to react accordingly and try to build resistance or tolerance to that stress. In the case of exercise as the stressor, the body adapts by increasing neural recruitment of muscle fibers, increases muscle fiber size and density, increasing mitochondrial density, etc., depending on the specific training program.

30. B: Segmented feedback is not considered a form of feedback during instruction. Throughout training, especially during learning periods, feedback can have a major impact in eliciting the desired movement patterns. Feedback involves providing the client with information about their movements patterns or performance of an exercise. This information can then be used to correct any faults in technique or execution. Augmented feedback, knowledge of results, and knowledge of performance are all forms of feedback commonly used.

31. B: Positive punishment and negative punishment are considered reinforcement techniques. When administering punishment reinforcement techniques, the professional aims to decrease the occurrence of a given undesirable operant; therefore, decreasing the occurrence of the operant can increase the success of the client. Positive punishment relates to administering tasks, objects, or events that would likely decrease the occurrence of the negative operant, such as adding extra reps.

32. A: Negative reinforcement involves the removal of a certain element that the client views negatively. An example of using this technique is if an client completes the workout with a great attitude, then he or she wouldn't have to perform the resisted runs at the end. By removing the negative element (difficult resisted runs), the probability of the operant occurring again might increase.

33. A: An *operant* is a specific outcome that is targeted through stimulus conditioning, though it is not initially the result of a specific stimulus; instead, at first, it is a behavior that occurs spontaneously. It is through the different reinforcing or deterring techniques (or consequences from the operant) that the operant becomes the targeted outcome of a stimulus. Four different reinforcement techniques can be used to reinforce the operant and increase the probability of its occurrence. These techniques are positive reinforcement, negative reinforcement, positive punishment, and negative punishment.

34. B: Although higher arousal levels are associated with higher performance outcomes, heightened arousal states are finite and can become detrimental if the arousal level becomes too high. The inverted-U theory describes this phenomenon. It states that arousal levels up to a certain level increase performance, but further increases in arousal are associated with reduced performance.

35. A: The intensity and focus of one's effort is a product of motivation. Motivation for competition and training, as well as a desire to be successful, can have major implications to the outcomes of training. Successful clients usually possess a combination of both intrinsic and extrinsic motivation.

36. B: Optimal arousal levels are very important in attaining success. Being able to achieve optimal arousal levels can have a major impact on the outcome and performance. When optimal arousal levels are achieved, increases can be seen in mental activation, positive self-thoughts, and decision-making tasks. Although performance anxiety can be associated with arousal levels, this problem is often observed when the arousal levels rise too high, so they are no longer "optimal."

Assessment

37. A: All three joint types given are synovial joints, allowing for a fair amount of movement (compared with fibrous and cartilaginous joints). Of the three given, hinge joints, such as the elbow, permit the least motion because they are uniaxial and permit movement in only one plane. Saddle joints and condyloid joints both have reciprocating surfaces that mate with one another and allow a variety of motions in numerous planes, but saddle joints, such as the thumb carpal-metacarpal joint, allow more motion than condyloid joints. In saddle joints, two concave surfaces articulate, and in a condyloid joint, such as the wrist, a concave surface articulates with a convex surface, allowing motion in mainly two planes.

38. A: The trans-theoretical model describes the client's process of getting ready to start exercise and consists of five stages: precontemplation, contemplation, preparation, action, and maintenance. In precontemplation, the client is not intending to take action toward changing physical activity and is not considering becoming physically active. During contemplation, the client intends to increase physical activity within the next six months. By the preparation stage, the client has developed a plan of action toward behavior change and will be making changes in the immediate future (next thirty days) and/or is inconsistently engaging in some amount of physical activity, but not at least thirty minutes of moderate-intensity activity for five or more days per week. In the action stage, the client is engaging in at least thirty minutes of moderate-intensity activity for five or more days per week but has done so for less than six months. Lastly, in maintenance, the client has been actively maintaining the changes made during the action stage; the new behaviors have been established for six months or more, and the client is now working to prevent relapse.

39. A: The preparation stage is the correct response because the client is inconsistently engaging in some amount of physical activity (in this case, once or twice per week) and not at least the recommended thirty minutes of moderate-intensity activity for five or more days per week. Note that in the contemplation stage, the client likely has not begun any sort of activity, not even once or twice a week, but is making plans to do so in the coming six months. In the action stage, the client would be regularly engaging in the activity and therefore would be doing it more often than the "once or twice a week" client in the example.

40. D: Dopamine helps strengthens the synaptic pathways involved in learning a behavior through reinforcement of the behavior. Several diseases are caused by disturbances of dopamine or its pathways. Parkinson's disease can result from too little dopamine activity, while Schizophrenia may be due to an excess of dopamine. Serotonin is the only other one of the choices that is a neurotransmitter, and involved in happiness/mood. Epinephrine and norepinephrine are hormones involved in the fight or flight response with stress.

41. B: The Health Belief Model is one in which the perceived seriousness of a potential health problem is the main predictor of behavioral change. The other models are not correctly matched with their meanings or are inaccurate. With the Theory of Planned Behavior, the client's level of motivation for behavioral change is shaped by their attitudes, subjective norms, and perceived control; behaviors in a timeframe are not part of this model. Social Cognitive Theory posits that clients actively shape their lives and learn by thinking, feeling, reflecting, and observing themselves in a social context. In the Socio-Ecological Model, behaviors, such as a client's motivation to exercise, are shaped by interpersonal relations, the surrounding environment, community, policy, and law.

42. B: Ligaments connect bone to bone. Tendons connect muscle to bone. Both are made of dense, fibrous connective tissue (primary Type 1 collagen) to give strength. However, tendons are more organized, especially in the long axis direction like muscle fibers themselves, and they have more collagen. This arrangement makes more sense because muscles have specific orientations of their fibers, so they contract in somewhat predictable directions. Ligaments are less organized and have more of a woven pattern because bone connections are not as organized as bundles of muscle fibers, so ligaments must have strength in multiple directions to protect against injury.

43. D: Blood returning to the heart from the body enters the right atrium and then moves through the tricuspid valve into the right ventricle. After filling, the right ventricle contracts, and the tricuspid valve closes, pushing blood through the pulmonary semilunar valve into the pulmonary arteries for pulmonary circulation, after which it enters the left atrium. Contraction of the left atrium moves blood through the bicuspid valve into the left ventricle (the largest heart chamber). When the bicuspid valve closes and the left ventricle contracts, blood is forced into the aortic valve through the aorta and on to systemic circulation.

44. A: Abduction is movement away from the body's midline (out to the side). Side-lying leg raises is a common exercise used to strengthen the gluteus medius and is an example of abduction. Adduction is the opposite—movement towards the body's centerline. Pronation is rotating up or inward, while supination is rotating down or outward. These latter two terms often describe movement of the forearm or ankle.

45. B: Antagonists are muscles that oppose the action of the agonist—the primary muscle causing a motion. Hamstrings are the primary knee flexors—the agonists—and the quadriceps fire in opposition. The gastrocnemius does cross the knee joint, so it is a knee flexor, although secondary to the hamstrings. The tibialis anterior is on the shin and is involved in dorsiflexion.

46. A: Shoulder flexion occurs in the sagittal plane (as does most flexion from anatomical position). Shoulder flexion is bringing the arm forward up towards overhead. The sagittal plane is viewing the body from the side, dividing the body into right and left sections. Abduction and adduction occur in the frontal plane and in rotation, such as trunk twists, and typically occur in the transverse plane.

47. C: Glycolysis is one of the anaerobic (without oxygen) metabolic pathways for producing ATP. It generates ATP from carbohydrate (glucose) metabolism that is used for two to three minutes of high intensity activity. The ATP-PC system is the other anaerobic pathway. It uses ATP stored in muscles; however, there is very little, so it is sufficient only for about ten-second high intensity bouts of activity at a time. The aerobic pathway involves the Krebs cycle. ATP is generated through the breakdown of carbohydrates and fats and, to a lesser degree, proteins. It supplies energy during long-duration endurance activities and is used when the other energy systems are depleted or insufficient, but this takes a relatively long time and would be inefficient for short bursts of energy.

48. D: Increased submaximal heart rate is not a chronic adaptation to cardiovascular exercise; in fact, heart rate decreases at a given submaximal workload due to improvements in cardiorespiratory economy. Heart chamber size increases, as does preload (the amount of blood that fills a chamber before it contracts to eject it), resulting in a higher stroke volume per heartbeat. This means that more blood, oxygen, and nutrients get moved per pump of the heart. Blood volume and hemoglobin content of the blood also increases.

49. A: DOMS typically peaks at twenty-four to seventy-two hours after exercise session completion, but may begin to develop twelve to twenty-four hours post-exercise. It is most likely to occur after high-repetition eccentric exercises, such as downhill running, as a result of microscopic damage to muscle fibers (a side effect of the repair process).

50. C: In isotonic contractions, the muscle exerts constant tension such as in a pushup or squat. Isometric contractions, like planks, are ones in which there is no change in muscle length. The body is static, and muscles are contracting to stabilize and hold the body stable against gravity. Isokinetic contractions are ones that move through the range of motion at a constant speed, but they are rarely used in practice due to the limited manufactured isokinetic equipment (some Cybex machines are isokinetic as are dynamometers). Eccentric are lengthening contractions, such as the lowering phase of a biceps curl.

51. B: Choices *I*, *II*, and *IV* are correct. Here are examples of correct matches:

- Fibrous: sutures in skull
- Plane: intercarpal
- Saddle: thumb
- Hinge: elbow
- Condyloid: wrist
- Pivot: radial head on ulna
- Cartilaginous: pubic symphysis

52. C: Self-efficacy is a client's confidence in their ability to make a behavioral change. Self-determination is the desire to participate in an activity for one's own satisfaction, not for impressing others. Self-esteem is satisfaction in one's own worth or value, and determination is a quality that a client possesses that keeps him or her pursuing a goal or challenge, despite the work involved.

53. D: If the client and trainer are not available at the same day or time to train, they are incompatible, at least until one or both schedules change. The fact that they are different sexes should have no bearing on compatibility, so Choice *B* is wrong. Choice *C* is not inherently an absolute incompatibility, especially because it states that both prefer one method (but does not indicate they cannot modify this). Choice *A* is not an issue as many clients will be less-trained or less-competitive than their trainers.

54. D: FITT-VP stands for Frequency, Intensity, Time, Type, Volume, Progression

55. B: This question requires the application of several concepts, including stratifying risk, knowing when you need a physician present during testing, and the best test selection for the goals of the patient. Paul has two risk factors for CAD: his BMI is 30.5 kg/m^2 (obese because > 30 kg/m^2), and he takes Lipitor, which is a lipid-lowering medication. Two risk factors put him in the moderate risk stratification, where physician supervision is recommended during maximal testing and not necessary for submaximal testing. Astrand-Rhyming is a submaximal cycle ergometer test. It would be an okay choice for Paul, but because he is a runner, he is likely to have a suboptimal performance on this modality since he will experience local muscle fatigue (quadriceps). As moderate risk, Choice *D* can be ruled out because he does not need a physician present. Choice *C*, the Rockport Walk Test, is a low-level test that predicts VO_2 max. It is not a very good choice for Paul because his fitness is going to be significantly higher than this test, and he likely wants a more accurate idea of his aerobic capacity. The best choice is the 1.5 mile run test, which will play to his strengths and give a great assessment of his VO_2 max, but should be physician-supervised given his risk classification. There is nothing inherently wrong with needing a physician around during testing, and the trainer should think about the goals of the client instead of the easiest option available.

Program Design

56. C: Specificity in exercise training program refers to focusing exercises on improving the strength and power of muscle groups and movements unique to a specific sport or client's goals. For example, a competitive 50 m butterfly swimmer would heavily train the upper back and shoulders, isolating the rhomboids, deltoids, latissimus dorsi, levator scapulae, and multifidus.

57. B: As a client's fitness level improves, trainers employ program progression techniques, which keep the client adequately challenged so that improvement occurs. Trainers must reassess clients at regular intervals so that they can evaluate and modify the stimulus given in the training program. Modifications to the frequency, intensity, duration, and mode of exercise must occur consistently in order to avoid plateaus in training and ensure that the client remains challenged, and continues to improve in all areas of physical fitness.

58. B: Before engaging in an exercise-training program and in order to design and implement an effective and safe program, trainers must be familiar with the client's medical history. A trainer can best determine what exercises will be of maximum benefit and minimal risk of aggravating previous or current conditions by knowing all previous and current illnesses and injuries that the client has experienced.

59. D: Interval training involves workloads completed at a high level of exertion for brief periods interspersed with intermittent periods of rest, changing the speed and intensity of the workout. By challenging the cardiovascular and muscular systems to their maximum potential, providing only short rest periods, and then returning to high intensity efforts, interval training conditions the cardiovascular system, increases endurance, and maximizes metabolic functioning for improved weight loss.

60. D: Continuous training involves maintaining a steady speed and intensity of cardiovascular exercise. This type of training improves muscular endurance and metabolic functioning because the cardiovascular system is challenged for an extended period of time at a continuous effort.

61. C: Circuit training implements periods of cardiovascular exercise with intermittent strength training exercises. By challenging the cardiovascular system and muscular strength, circuit training also improves overall cardiovascular and muscular endurance, metabolic pathways, and muscular strength.

62. D: A Client's ADLs, or activities of daily living, should be considered when designing an effective and individualized exercise training program. If a client sits or stands for extended periods of time, performs repetitive motions throughout the day, uses upper or lower body muscle groups more than others, or has difficulty with movements in the early or late hours of the day, trainers may need to design specific exercises tailored to improve the client's quality of life. Such exercises may focus on cardiorespiratory fitness, strength, and/or flexibility.

63. B: For clients desiring weight loss, cardiovascular activity performed five to seven days per week is essential. Resistance training and flexibility exercises should also be components of the overall program along with a reduced-calorie diet.

64. A: Clients with goals of improving athletic performance require an exercise-training program that implements the principles of specificity and program progression. It should focus on the incorporation of exercises specific to the physical requirements of the intended sport.

65. C: Advanced resistance training methods can be useful for clients who have progressed through an exercise-training program and are ready for an additional challenge. Such advanced methods, such as kettlebells and supersets, improve fitness level and can help a client achieve their fitness goals, while providing variety and preventing boredom and plateaus.

66. B: Plyometric training requires the client to perform fast repetitions of speed- and power-focused exercises often with jumping and explosive movements such as box jumps and bounding drills.

67. D: Pyramid training involves high repetitions of exercises using a low weight, then progresses to fewer repetitions with a higher weight. These exercises can be performed in a variety of positions and can focus on a specific muscle group or all the major muscle groups.

68. A: Trainers should try to implement exercises to improve the client's efficiency and proper form. These supporting exercises should focus on the six motor skills related to physical fitness: agility, balance, coordination, reaction time, speed, and power.

69. B: The bench press is an example of a chest exercise. Back and chest muscles such as the pectoralis major and minor are targeted with exercises such as the bench press, dips, pull-ups, push-ups, and lat pull-downs.

70. C: The plank exercise is an example of an abdominal and core exercise. Abdominal muscles respond to core-focused exercises such as crunches, leg raises, and plank exercises. While planks can improve the strength and endurance of all major muscle groups used in maintaining proper posture during the plank, the core is mainly targeted in this isometric hold.

71. C: Pregnant women should consider modifying exercise after the first trimester. Pregnant clients with no contraindications are encouraged to continue to moderately exercise on a daily basis if they have done so before their pregnancy. Each trimester should be considered in order to make proper adjustments, such as discouraging supine exercises after the first trimester.

72. C: Range of motion exercises should be included in all training programs. Flexibility enables the body to perform movements in their full range of motion. Muscular strength and endurance play an integral role in optimal physical fitness by supporting the bone structure of the skeletal system and allowing for voluntary movements. Strength training helps maintain crucial muscle mass that can deteriorate with age and sedentary lifestyles.

73. A: Cardiovascular endurance refers to the ability of the cardiovascular system to efficiently pump blood throughout the body, delivering blood and essential oxygen to the muscles, tissues, and organs. Regular cardiovascular exercises such as swimming, running, and cycling strengthen this system and improves the functioning of all components (i.e. heart, blood vessels, arteries, etc.).

74. A: Strength training exercises improve muscular strength and endurance, and can be performed with body weight alone or a variety of external resistance modalities. Muscular strength and endurance play an integral part in physical fitness by supporting the skeletal system and allowing for voluntary movements; exercise programs can greatly improve the strength and endurance of muscles, helping to maintain crucial muscle mass that can deteriorate with age and inactivity.

75. D: Healthy populations such as adults, seniors, children, adolescents, and pregnant women should incorporate cardiovascular, resistance training, and flexibility in their programs. This balanced approach to fitness ensures the entire body is addressed and no imbalances are created.

76. D: Clients with chronic conditions should incorporate low- to moderate-impact activities in their exercise program. Clients with a chronic disease will require medical clearance to engage in exercise, to ensure the safety and efficacy of the prescribed program.

77. A: Clients with arthritis and osteoporosis should engage in low-impact cardiovascular exercise for twenty to sixty minutes three to five days per week, gradually increasing the intensity and duration as the client's fitness and ability improve. Adequate rest should be taken if the client experiences any pain or discomfort before engaging in exercise again.

78. D: Obese clients should perform cardiovascular exercise five to seven days per week. The exercise should be performed at a moderate intensity for forty-five to sixty minutes. These exercises should be low-impact, such as swimming or walking, and should gradually include a wider variety of activities as the client's fitness improves. Risk of injury is greater in those with excessive body weight.

79. B: Warm-up, training, cool-down, stretching. A brief warm-up period of five to ten minutes allows a client to increase their cardiovascular activity and engage their muscles, helping to safely perform more rigorous activities efficiently during the workout. The main training stimulus comprises the bulk of the workout and follows the workout. It should include a variety of five to ten exercises involving the cardiovascular and musculoskeletal systems. Following the training stimulus stage, a cool-down at low-intensity permits the heart rate to return to normal, the metabolic byproducts of anaerobic respiration get shuttled to the liver, and the venous blood in the extremities returns to systemic circulation. Stretching the major muscle groups, as well as any specific muscles targeted in the workout, should end the training session, preventing lactic-acid buildup and discomfort.

Exercise Technique and Training Instruction

80. C: The elliptical machine provides a non-impact form of exercise while still being a weightbearing modality because the user is standing upright against gravity. The treadmill and the stair stepper, Choices *A* and *D,* are not non-impact exercise, so they are incorrect. The stationary bike, Choice *B,* is not a weightbearing modality, so it is incorrect.

81. C: The Valsalva maneuver can help provide stability. It involves inhaling using deep belly breathing and then increasing abdominal pressure by trying to exhale while holding the glottis closed. This built-up abdominal pressure helps the athlete maintain a neutral spine, which increases the stability and safety of the movement or exercise.

82. D: Personal trainers should ensure that as the client is moving through agility drills, he or she is properly flexing the hips, knees, and ankles upon deceleration to help attenuate forces. A common mistake is to change direction with a stiff, extended leg. This can be very unsafe, as it places high forces on the joints of the body.

83. A: The midfoot, rather than the forefoot, should be in contact with the pedals for optimal biomechanics and force production. The other adjustments listed coincide with the recommendations for stationary bikes.

84. A: The sprinting movement includes four main segments or phases for the lower legs. The first segment is the eccentric braking period of the lead leg. In this phase, the lead leg is extended, the ankle is pointed toward the knee, and the knee is slightly flexed so that it does not lock out terminally. The concentric propulsive phase begins once the transfer is made through the foot. During this segment, the lead leg applies a vertical force to the ground to propel the body forward, and the lead leg is pulled under the body until it releases from the ground. As the athlete propels forward, the lead leg becomes the trailing leg as it reaches the next segment, which is the recovery phase. During the recovery phase, the ankle starts dorsiflexing and the knee starts flexing as it recovers and prepares for another ground contact. The last segment is ground preparation. As the trailing leg starts to prepare to become the lead leg, the knee flexes to the same position that it acquired during the eccentric braking segment.

85. B: When using starting blocks for sprinting, the athlete should place their hands just behind the starting line slightly wider than shoulder-width apart with the fingers held together. The thumb should bridge out to the side and should be directly under the shoulders, ready to support bodyweight.

86. A: Exercises with free weights should use a minimum of one or two spotters when an athlete moves the bar over the head or face, has it on the front of the shoulders, or has it on the back during the execution. Resistance machines frequently do not need a spotter because they have safety features designed into them, but for certain maximal lifts, a spotter is recommended. Free weight training can improve core stability and can provide a more sports-specific strength training method. Each exercise can be performed in a variety of ways, rather than strictly dictated in one specific way.

87. A: Soccer requires a great deal of agility, so these athletes benefit from agility work on most days in each training cycle. Because agility technique takes a high degree of focus and cognition, it is best to complete it in high-frequency, short-duration sessions in a training program. This is usually accomplished by short agility drill sessions most days of the week.

88. B: Hockey players need to have significant explosive power, strength, and speed, so they benefit greatly from plyometrics, which develop explosive power. Three days per week is about the maximum frequency that is recommended for plyometrics, given their intensity and the demand they place on the anatomic structures of the body and physiologic systems. Beyond this, there is increased risk of injury, even in experienced athletes. Most athletes can benefit from some plyometric training, but such a frequency is not needed for the endurance athletes listed.

89. B: There are three forms of PNF stretching: hold-relax, contract-relax, and hold-relax with agonist contraction, which all begin with 10-seconds of passive pre-stretch held at the point of mild discomfort. In the hold-relax, after the pre-stretch, the partner applies a flexion force while the athlete holds and tries to resist the force, creating an isometric contraction for 6 seconds, then the athlete relaxes back into a passive stretch lasting 30 seconds, which is now a deeper stretch than the initial pre-stretch due to autogenic inhibition. The hold-relax with the agonist contraction uses the idea of reciprocal inhibition whereby the contraction of the agonist muscle causes relaxation of the antagonist. Therefore, after the regular hold-relax protocol, the second passive stretch is replaced with an active stretch to further increase stretch.

90. B: The required number of spotters is determined by the load being lifted, the experience and skill of the athlete and spotters, and the physical strength of the spotters. The spotters must be strong enough to handle the load that the athlete is lifting with little notice and sometimes in less than ideal angles and positions, so it is crucial that spotters are honest with themselves and the lifter about their abilities. It is safer to err on the side of caution and use multiple spotters when necessary, as long as they can be accommodated spatially around the lift without being overly cumbersome.

91. C: When spotting over-the-face barbell exercises, the spotter should use the alternated grip pattern, usually narrower than the athlete's grip. In this position, one hand is supinated and one is pronated.

92. D: During every exercise, there is a portion of the movement where the force will peak. This portion of the movement is termed the sticking point, and the athlete should learn to exhale during this time. Having a basic understanding of when the sticking point is during each exercise will allow the trainer to accurately cue the athlete through each exercise. Often, faulty movement patterns will occur during the sticking point because this point involves the most force on the athlete's body, so fatigue and compensatory mechanisms are common.

93. D: During plyometric training, after the energy is loaded into the muscle and tendons, there will be a brief period when the body changes direction and the muscle action shifts from eccentric to concentric work. This period is termed the amortization portion of the exercise. Although this could be considered an isometric portion of the exercise, the common terminology in plyometric training is amortization. Once the brief amortization period occurs, the muscles will start concentrically contracting.

94. C: Slight flexion of the knee (around 5–10 degrees) will prevent terminal knee extension and keep the knees in a healthy joint angle range. Although terminal knee extension can sometimes be a safe position during strength training, it is not considered to be safe in a conditioning training session where repetitive fatigue will occur. It is important to adjust the seat according to the athlete's anthropometry.

95. D: The only way to ensure proper breathing mechanics are employed during high-intensity anaerobic conditioning activities is to increase the length or frequency of rest periods when the athlete begins to fatigue. When fatigue occurs, the shoulders will begin to round forward, placing the athlete in a position where the aerobic system will be compromised. Understanding appropriate work-to-rest ratios for the goals of the training session is important when programming anaerobic conditioning activities.

96. C: Although a general warmup is important to perform before any stretching activity, it is not a benefit of static stretching. The main benefits of static stretching include increasing the range of motion of the joints, enhancing recovery, and serving as part of a corrective or rehabilitation program when done properly.

97. C: Knees caving in during hip, knee, and ankle free-weight exercises is a common mistake observed in many training sessions. Having the ability to correct this common flaw is important in ensuring a safe and effective training environment. Although the chest should be high during the entire execution of the movement, this verbal cue would not have any benefit for the stated flaw. By cueing the athlete to maintain outward pressure and ensure proper knee tracking, the hips will stay engaged and the athlete will correct the mistake of having the knees cave in during the movement.

98. D: The segments that comprise lower-limb sprinting mechanics include the eccentric braking period, the concentric propulsive phase, the recovery phase, and the ground preparation phase. Although the acceleration phase is a segment of sprinting mechanics, it is not a phase of the lower-limb mechanics.

99. A: Proper arm action is important during walking, jogging, and running exercises. As the right leg is coming forward, the left arm should be coming forward, and as the left leg is coming forward, the right arm should be coming forward. Natural movement at the shoulder joint is needed when utilizing these types of exercises. Throughout arm action, the elbow should stay flexed around 90 degrees and the hands should be in a relaxed position. The hands should come as high as the chest or sternum during the upward motion and back down to the lateral hip in the downward motion. By maintaining the full range of motion at the shoulder joint, the efficiency of the movement will increase.

100. A: When starting, the athlete should either be in an upright position, in a downward position in a three- or four-point stance, or in a downward position set in starting blocks. When the athlete is in any of the downward positions, the lead leg should be flexed to around 90 degrees and the trailing leg should be flexed to around 130 degrees. When starting, the athlete should focus on applying maximum force through the ground with both feet to propel their body forward horizontally. Within the first couple of strides, the athlete will transfer the force from horizontal displacement to gradual vertical displacement.

101. A: Overtraining is a condition that occurs when an individual trains with too much frequency and/or intensity, causing fatigue, greater injury risk, sleep issues, changes in appetite or body weight, lack of motivation, depression or moodiness, and performance decline. Signs of overtraining also include elevated resting heart rate, soreness that does not resolve within a day or two after exercise (as is normal with resistance training), and increased susceptibility to illness.

102. D: To resolve heat-related illness, athletes should drink plenty of fluids, remove excess layers of clothing, and move to the shade. Once symptoms have set in, it is too late to continue the workout inside. Exercise will need to stop. To prevent heat-illness in the first place, the workout can take place inside.

103. D: Groin strains are typically an acute injury. Overuse injuries such as stress fractures, shin splints, and tendonitis can occur when the workload is too high and insufficient rest and recovery leads to tissue damage.

104. B: During times of overtraining, performance will decrease. The human body can no longer adapt to the increasing stress of the training sessions and begins to gradually decline in performance. The central nervous system will become affected, and many other signs and symptoms will begin to show.

105. D: Being able to evaluate clients while performing exercises in extreme temperatures is a responsibility of the trainer. Signs and symptoms of heat-related illnesses include goose bumps, lack of perspiration, cramps, inability to speak clearly, difficulty in standing or walking, dizziness, and nausea. Reduced heart rate is not associated with a heat-related illness, but instead is a symptom of a cold-related illness.

106. C: To control the spread of germs in the facility, clients should be taught and instructed to wipe down all used equipment after use with antibacterial agents. The other options are practices that clients should be taught as well, but do not help prevent the spread of germs.

107. A: The order of phases for designing a new fitness facility are: pre-design, design, construction, pre-operation.

108. D: Practices that trainers can implement to foster a safe training environment include clearing loose equipment from the floor, mopping wooden floors, and checking wooden platforms for cracks. Emotional safety is enhanced through encouraging teamwork and positive, supportive attitudes. Weight benches and platforms should not be as close as possible; they require a minimum of 36 inches of clearance for walking around them safely, keeping distance between athletes lifting weights, spotting, and preventing injuring a nearby client.

Professional Development and Responsibility

109. C: This was a tricky question. While providing home exercise programs is a common task for personal trainers, trainers must be careful not to "prescribe" anything, even workouts, because prescribing indicates medical or curative expertise, and that falls outside of the personal trainer's scope of practice. Trainers may create and provide home exercise programs. The other options are all valid too.

110. C: Certified personal trainers are required to act in cases of emergency and maintain CPR and AED certifications. A pregnant client receives CPR and AED the same as all other adult victims. In fact, it's even more important because two lives are on the line!

111. B: Spotting clients while lifting weights and assisting clients with all types of equipment and exercises helps monitor their form and provides an effort to reduce injury risk and maximize training benefit. It helps prevent weights from dropping and rolling, which can distract and injure others in the vicinity. It is not for the trainer's personal workout benefit.

112. C: Unlike in sole proprietorships and partnerships, in corporations there are separate legal entities with owners and shareholders. They are more time-consuming, costly, and harder to set up and terminate but hold a higher level of professionalism, have an easier time receiving loans, and risk less personal responsibility for liabilities and debts. The business pays taxes on profits, and individual owners also must pay taxes on their dividends from the payment from their shares.

113. B: Wearing professional attire and appropriate footwear for fitness show the trainer's professionalism and readiness to work, but they are not career development practices. Career development practices are methods of furthering education and business skills or ways to improve a trainer's level of expertise. This can be done in a variety of ways including earning CECs and attending conferences, staying abreast of current health and fitness research, and giving talks and seminars at community events.

114. C: A business plan typically does not include an emergency action plan. That is a separate but very crucial document. Business plans should include the vision, mission, values, and goals of the company. It also should include a full detail of the business legal structure and all job descriptions with expected salaries and required experience. It also should include policies of the business such as those centered on cancellations or late arrivals, and a thorough financial plan that contains startup costs for things such as equipment, location, and supplies, as well as expected revenue sources (what services are offered), prices, payment methods, funding, and sometimes financial projections for a certain number of years.

115. C: To control the spread of germs in the facility, clients should be taught and instructed to wipe down all equipment after use with antibacterial agents. The other options are things that clients should be taught as well, but do not help prevent the spread of germs.

116. C: To organize a budget in a professional and reproducible way, it is prudent for trainers to use digital software like QuickBooks or Microsoft Excel. Keeping digitized spreadsheets of profits and expenses is an organized way to manage budget, preferable over handwritten accounting due to its professionalism, reproducibility, and ease of sending to an accountant or business advisor for tax purposes or audits.

117. B: A client's file with all health, demographics, prior workouts, and emergency contact information should be with the trainer during testing and training sessions with that client. Should an emergency arise, trainers and staff need to have quick and easy access to pertinent information. Trainers need to obtain written and signed permission for other distribution of the file.

118. C: Universal precautions (such as latex gloves), washing the wound with soap and water, then covering it with germicide cream and a sterile bandage is the basic treatment for all minor wounds. Trainers assisting clients with minor wounds should always wash their hands immediately after treatment, even with the use of latex gloves. To control the bleeding in major wounds, use a flat hand and fingers to apply pressure, then elevate the affected body part above the client's heart as long as no fracture is suspected. Trainers should call EMS and place pressure over the brachial or femoral artery if bleeding is not slowing for upper or lower extremity injuries, respectively.

119. B: Signs of hypoglycemia include shakiness, weakness, abnormal sweating, mouth or finger tingling, visual disturbances, confusion, and seizures. If such symptoms occur, the trainer should stop exercise immediately and use a glucometer to test blood sugar, if possible. If blood sugar is low, trainers should administer glucose in the form of food or drink.

120. C: To ensure understanding and preparedness, emergency procedures should be reviewed and rehearsed by involved staff at least quarterly (every three months).

NASM Practice Test #3

To keep the size of this book manageable, save paper, and provide a digital test-taking experience, the 3rd practice test can be found online. Scan the QR code or go to this link to access it:

testprepbooks.com/bonus/nasm

The first time you access the tests, you will need to register as a "new user" and verify your email address.

If you have any issues, please email support@testprepbooks.com.

Dear NASM Test Taker,

We would like to start by thanking you for purchasing this study guide for your NASM exam. We hope that we exceeded your expectations.

Our goal in creating this study guide was to cover all of the topics that you will see on the test. We also strove to make our practice questions as similar as possible to what you will encounter on test day. With that being said, if you found something that you feel was not up to your standards, please send us an email and let us know.

We would also like to let you know about other books in our catalog that may interest you.

ACSM

This can be found on Amazon: amazon.com/dp/1637754477

ACE

amazon.com/dp/1628457740

CSCS

amazon.com/dp/163775535X

We have study guides in a wide variety of fields. If the one you are looking for isn't listed above, then try searching for it on Amazon or send us an email.

Thanks Again and Happy Testing!
Product Development Team
info@studyguideteam.com

FREE Test Taking Tips Video/DVD Offer

To better serve you, we created videos covering test taking tips that we want to give you for FREE. **These videos cover world-class tips that will help you succeed on your test.**

We just ask that you send us feedback about this product. Please let us know what you thought about it—whether good, bad, or indifferent.

To get your **FREE videos**, you can use the QR code below or email freevideos@studyguideteam.com with "Free Videos" in the subject line and the following information in the body of the email:

a. The title of your product

b. Your product rating on a scale of 1-5, with 5 being the highest

c. Your feedback about the product

If you have any questions or concerns, please don't hesitate to contact us at info@studyguideteam.com.

Thank you!

Made in the USA
Las Vegas, NV
12 November 2024

11633730R00155